Crisis, Movement, Strategy

# Historical Materialism
# Book Series

VOLUME 163

The titles published in this series are listed at *brill.com/hm*

# Crisis, Movement, Strategy

*The Greek Experience*

*Edited by*

Panagiotis Sotiris

BRILL

LEIDEN | BOSTON

Library of Congress Cataloging-in-Publication Data

Names: Sotiris, Panagiotis, editor.
Title: Crisis, movement, strategy : the Greek experience / edited by Panagiotis
     Sotiris.
Description: Leiden ; Boston : Brill, [2018] | Series: Historical materialism book
     series, ISSN 1570-1522 ; volume 163 | Includes bibliographical references and
     index.
Identifiers: LCCN 2018027513 (print) | LCCN 2018029155 (ebook) |
     ISBN 9789004280892 (e-book) | ISBN 9789004291348 (hardback : alk. paper)
Subjects: LCSH: Greece–Economic conditions–2009- | Greece–Economic policy–
     2009- | Debts, Public–Greece–History–21st century. | Financial crises–
     Greece–History–21st century. | Recessions–Greece–History–21st century.
Classification: LCC HC295 (ebook) | LCC HC295 .C75 2018 (print) |
     DDC 330.9495–dc23
LC record available at https://lccn.loc.gov/2018027513

Typeface for the Latin, Greek, and Cyrillic scripts: "Brill". See and download: brill.com/brill-typeface.

ISSN 1570-1522
ISBN 978-90-04-29134-8 (hardback)
ISBN 978-90-04-28089-2 (e-book)

# Contents

List of Figures and Tables    VII
Notes on Contributors    IX

Introduction    1
  *Panagiotis Sotiris*

1    The Greek Crisis: Causes and Alternative Strategies    13
  *Stavros Mavroudeas*

2    Imperialist Exploitation and Crisis of the Greek Economy: a
     Study    40
  *George Economakis, Maria Markaki, George Androulakis and
  Alexios Anastasiadis*

3    The Class Dimension of the Greek Public Debt Crisis    67
  *Ioannis Zisimopoulos and George Economakis*

4    Consolidation of Authoritarian Rule in the EU: the Parallel Processes
     of the Troika's Emergence and the Economic Governance
     Reforms    87
  *Yiorgos Vassalos*

5    Labour under Attack during the Period of Crisis and Austerity    119
  *Giannis Kouzis*

6    *'First Comes Indignation, Then Rebellion, Then We Shall See'*: Political
     Crisis, Popular Perception of Politics and Transformation of
     Consciousness amid the Rebellious Cycle of 2010–11 in Greece    131
  *Eirini Gaitanou*

7    Reshaping Political Cultures: the 'Squares Movement' and Its
     Impact    155
  *Angelos Kontogiannis-Mandros*

8    Political Crisis, Crisis of Hegemony and the Rise of Golden Dawn    177
  *Despina Paraskeva-Veloudogianni*

9     The Crisis and the Strategy of the Greek Ruling Class    203
         *Spyros Sakellaropoulos*

10    From Resistance to Transitional Programme: the Strange Rise of the
      Radical Left in Greece    229
         *Christos Laskos and Euclid Tsakalotos*

11    In Search of the Modern Prince: a Critical Absence Reconfirmed
      through the Greek Experience    244
         *Alexandros Chrysis*

12    From Resistance to Hegemony: the Struggle against Austerity and the
      Need for a New Historical Bloc    267
         *Panagiotis Sotiris*

      Index    299

# List of Figures and Tables

## Figures

1.1 Competing explanations of the Greek crisis   17

1.2 Basic alternative scenarios and their variations   30

2.1 Terms of trade of the Greek economy, total and intra EU trade, 1960–2013   57

2.2 Imports and exports of goods and net exports of goods as a percentage (%) of GDP, Greece, 1990–2013   58

2.3 Intra EU-27 trade as a percentage (%) of total trade, EU-27 and Greece, 1999–2013   59

3.1 General government consolidated gross debt as % of GDP in Greece, EU-27 and Eurozone-17 (2000–13)   73

3.2 Real GDP growth rate in Greece, EU-27 and Eurozone-17, 2000–13   73

3.3 Total general government expenditures in Greece and EU-27 as % of GDP, 2000–13   76

3.4 Public employment in Greece and OECD-21 countries as % of labour force (2001, 2011)   77

3.5 Total general government revenues in Greece and EU-27 as % of GDP, 2000–13   77

3.6 Taxes on labour and capital as % of the total taxation in Greece and the EU-27, 2000–11   78

3.7 Indirect taxes in Greece, EU-27 and Eurozone-17 as % of total taxation, 2000–11   79

3.8 Changes in the middle classes' employment (self-employed without employees), 2008–14   83

## Tables

2.1 Technological level of imports and exports of goods, Eurozone-18 countries, selected years   52

2.2 Exports structure of Greece (%), 2013   53

2.3 Income elasticities of demand for imports by technological level, total economy, Greece, 1990–2013   54

2.4 Income elasticities of demand for imported goods, Greece   55

2.5 Share of exports and imports of goods of Greece to Eurozone-18 and EU-27 (%), all sectors and selected sectors, selected years, 1990–2013   60

2.6 Ratio of Greek exports to imports of goods, for all trade partners, Eurozone-18 and EU-27 countries, all sectors, selected years, 1990–2013   61

2.7   Main trade partners of Greece, 1990 and 2013    62
3.1   Income taxes of legal entities and individuals as % of total income taxation
      (financial years 2006–11)    79
3.2   Certified – collected VAT of financial years 2006–11    82
10.1  400 initiatives in 60 Greek cities, in around 70 areas of Athens    236

# Notes on Contributors

*Alexios Anastasiadis*
studied at the Economics Department of the University of Piraeus (B.A. Economics) and Erasmus University of Rotterdam (M.Sc. in Econometrics). He is currently a Ph.D. student in the Department of Business Administration at the University of Patras. His research interests mainly focus on the roots of the recent economic crisis in the US economy.

*George Androulakis*
was awarded his B.Sc. and M.Sc. degrees from the Department of Mathematics, University of Patras, Greece, where he also received his Ph.D. in Unconstrained Optimisation Methods. He is an Associate Professor at the Department of Business Administration; he also teaches on the postgraduate course in Mathematics for Decision Making, University of Patras. His interests are focused on non-linear unconstrained optimisation, neural networks training, optimal Runge-Kutta methods, systems of non-algebraic and/or transcendental functions, and quantitative methods.

*Alexandros Chrysis*
studied law and political science at the Universities of Athens and Leicester. He is Professor at Panteion University of Social and Political Sciences (Department of Sociology). He teaches History of Ideas and Philosophy of History. He has written a number of books and articles on the Enlightenment and Marxism.

*George Economakis*
is Associate Professor of Political Economy at the Department of Business Administration of the University of Patras. He studied at the Economics Department of the University of Athens (B.A. Economics, 1984) and Panteion University (M.Sc. in Regional Development, 1988, and Ph.D. in Political Economy, 1998). He has published in many academic journals and has co-authored several books.

*Eirini Gaitanou*
holds a Ph.D. from King's College London (Department of European and International Studies), having presented a thesis entitled 'Forms and characteristics of the social movement in Greece in the context of the economic and political crisis', focusing on the forms of political participation and the transformation of actors' consciousness in relation to this participation and experience. She

has been active in the social movements in Greece for over a decade and has participated in both practical and theoretical debates during this time.

### Angelos Kontogiannis-Mandros

received his Ph.D. from the Department of European and International Studies at King's College London. He holds a B.A. in Political Science (University of Athens), an M.Sc. in Political Behaviour (University of Essex) and an M.Sc. in Social and Cultural Psychology (London School of Economics). He has also worked on various posts in the polling industry.

### Giannis Kouzis

is a Professor in the Department of Social Policy at Panteion University, Athens. He received his Ph.D. from Paris x University. Since 1991 he has been in charge of labour relations research at the Institute of the Greek Trade Union Confederation (INE-GSEE).

### Christos Laskos

teaches in Greek secondary education. He has a Ph.D. in the Sociology of Education. With Euclid Tsakalotos he co-wrote *Crucible of Resistance: Greece, the Eurozone and the World Economic Crisis* (London: Pluto, 2013).

### Maria Markaki

received her Diploma in Mechanical Engineering and her Ph.D. in Applied Economics from the National Technical University of Athens. She is a post-doctoral researcher at the Panteion University of Athens. She has participated in several research programmes and has over 50 publications in journals, book collections and conference proceedings.

### Stavros Mavroudeas

is Professor of Political Economy at the University of Macedonia. He received his Ph.D. from Birkbeck College, University of London (1990). He has published articles in many academic journals and has authored several books in English and in Greek. He is a founding member of the Greek Association of Political Economy and has subsequently served in its governing council.

### Despina Paraskeva-Veloudogianni

has an M.A. in political theory from the Department of Politics, University of Athens. She is currently a Ph.D. candidate at the University of Athens. She has written a book on Golden Dawn, *The Enemy, the Blood and the Punisher: Analyzing Thirteen Speeches of Golden Dawn's 'Leader'* (Athens: Nisos, 2015 [in Greek]).

*Spyros Sakellaropoulos*
received his Ph.D. from the University of Paris VIII. He is an Associate Professor in the Department of Social Policy at Panteion University, Athens. He has published in several academic journals and is the author of several books.

*Panagiotis Sotiris*
received his Ph.D. from Panteion University Athens. He has taught Social and Political Theory and Philosophy at the University of Crete, Panteion University, the University of the Aegean, the University of Athens and the Hellenic Open University.

*Euclid Tsakalotos*
is a Professor at the University of Athens. He has previously taught at Athens University of Economics and Business. He has a Ph.D. from Oxford University. He has been a member of the Greek Parliament since 2012, he was Alternate Minister for International Economic Relations in the first SYRIZA-ANEL government and has been Minister of Finance since July 2015.

*Yiorgos Vassalos*
is a political scientist based in Brussels and Strasbourg specialising in interest representation in the EU. He was a researcher for the Corporate Europe Observatory for six years. He is currently working on his Ph.D. on the working relations of EU agents with financial lobbyists on drafting EU financial regulation in the University of Strasbourg. He has written on EU economic governance and austerity policies in Greece. He is also active in anti-austerity movements.

*Ioannis Zisimopoulos*
studied at the Economics Department of the University of Patras (B.A. Economics, 2004), Department of Business Administration of the University of Patras (M.B.A., 2008). He is a Ph.D. candidate in Industrial Relations and Political Economy at the Department of Business Administration of the University of Patras. His work has been published in proceedings of international conferences and academic journals.

# Introduction

*Panagiotis Sotiris*

Towards the end of 2009 the newly elected government of Giorgos Papandreou started facing what seemed like an acute debt crisis. Debt to GDP ratio had reached 120% and it seemed impossible to avoid some form of bail-out programme for the Greek economy on the part of the European Union. As the then finance minister stressed in February 2010, Greece was like the 'Titanic' going straight towards an iceberg. The increased awareness that there was a sovereign debt crisis looming in Greece led to greatly increased premiums on Greek debt, leading to the possibility of a default. The Greek government had already contacted the IMF seeking its assistance. At that time, the IMF had already discussed the possibility of an internal devaluation process for countries in single currency areas,[1] where the only way to restore competitiveness is by a reduction in nominal wages (since the single currency excludes most forms of real wages reduction such as inflation, etc.).

In the end, this negotiation led to a combined bail-out programme by the infamous Troika (namely the EU, the IMF, and the ECB). Although the IMF had initially insisted on the need for a debt restructuring programme, which is part of its standard procedure in such cases, the EU representatives refused, fearing that this might lead to immediate losses for European and in particular French and German banks that were holding large quantities of Greek debt. This initial bail-out programme and the loan agreement that was its materialisation was accompanied by the first Memorandum of Understanding, a set of commitments undertaken by the Greek government, which included a combination of harsh austerity measures and budgetary targets along with an extensive set of neoliberal structural reforms.[2] From that moment on, the word 'Memorandum' became associated with a particular combination of austerity and reduced sovereignty.

What followed was a unique sequence of social and political developments that combined an economic recession without precedent, the imposition of forms of economic supervision and limited sovereignty that had never before been used to such an extent in a member state of the European Union, a series of social struggles and protests that made Greece synonymous with mass

---

1  See Blanchard 2007.
2  European Commission 2010.

strikes, occupations and violent street clashes, and a deep political crisis that brought tectonic changes to the political landscape, in the end catapulting a relatively small radical left party to power.[3] After five years of austerity and neo-liberal reforms, the events of the summer of 2015, when SYRIZA attempted to counter the Troika's blackmail by resorting to a referendum that overwhelmingly rejected austerity, only to be followed by a painful acceptance of a Third Memorandum, showed that we are yet to exit this period of social disaster in a manner that would be more positive for those social strata that have paid the price for the Memorandums, namely the vast majority of the subaltern classes.

The extent and depth of the political and social transformations cannot be explained simply by reference to the extremely negative consequences of the social crisis. The catalytic factor was a sequence of struggle and protestation without precedent. In a certain way, this can account for the differences in social and political dynamics between Greece and other EU countries that faced aggressive austerity packages. This had to do with not only the repertoire of protest that was used (mass strikes, occupation of public spaces, mass street clashes, movements of civil disobedience, solidarity networks), but also the many ways that these movements enabled the formation of alternative collective identities of struggle, thus facilitating the shifts in relations of political representation.

At the same time, the meteoric electoral rise of SYRIZA – that challenged the 2012 elections and won the 2015 election – for the first time since the 1970s brought forward the possibility that the non-social-democratic Left could achieve governmental power. This meant that questions of strategy became important not just in abstract but also in very concrete and immediate terms. At the same time, this also brought forward the question of the programme and of what demands can reverse austerity and at the same time initiate a process of potentially socialist transformation.

The results of the political crisis also included the electoral rise of the neo-fascist Golden Dawn, which rose from a relatively marginal presence to parliamentary representation, despite its openly neo-Nazi rhetoric and its cult of violence that led to the murder of Pavlos Fyssas in 2013.[4]

At the heart of all these debates there is the question of Europe. The Greek crisis and the social and political violence of the EU-imposed austerity packages opened up the question of Greece's relation to the European Integration

---

3   Kouvelakis 2011; Lapavitsas et al. 2012; Sakellaropoulos and Sotiris 2014.
4   Psarras 2014a.

Process and in particular its participation in the Eurozone, hence the many debates on the question of whether the solution requires a rupture with the European Union.

The present volume attempts to discuss some of these questions, combining analysis of the economics of the Greek crisis, the policies of the European Union, the theoretical questions that relate these developments to the broader global capitalist crisis, and the new forms of social protest movements that emerged.

∴

The first contribution by Stravros Mavroudeas offers a survey of the different theoretical approaches to the Greek crisis, especially in relation to the question of Greece's participation in the Eurozone. It surveys the competing explanations of the Greek crisis and the alternative strategies (associated with these explanations) proposed in order to surpass this crisis. The competing explanations are categorised in three main groups (Mainstream, Radical, and Marxist). Mavroudeas argues that the Marxist explanations can better grasp the deep structural character of the Greek crisis and he offers a criticism of recent radical positions that have focused upon financialisation. Regarding the strategy of the IMF-EU-ECB Economic Adjustment Programmes (EAPs) and the strategy of renegotiation of the EAPs towards a less pro-cyclical and less austere policy mix, Mavroudeas stresses that the first version is an overambitious bourgeois strategy that endangers the politico-economic stability of the system, whereas the second version is an incoherent and unreliable strategy because it depends upon the partial success of the first version. Regarding those strategies that call for a rupture with the European Integration process, Mavroudeas distinguishes between a strategy of restructuring outside the European Monetary Union (EMU) but within the European Union (EU), and a strategy of restructuring through complete disengagement from the EU. He argues that the first version is a middle-of-the-road approach that disregards the deeply structural character of the Greek crisis. In contrast, the second version offers a coherent alternative strategy answering the problem of the crisis from the perspective of the working class.

In their contribution, George Economakis, Maria Markaki, George Androulakis and Alexios Anastasiadis suggest that within the European Union and the Economic Monetary Union, Greek capitalism follows an 'extraverted' development model which implies a low international 'structural' competitiveness. This model of development leads to systematic transfers of value to the imperialist countries (expressed as persistent trade deficits), forming the foundations of the current Greek economic crisis in the conjuncture of global economic crisis. They attribute the deeper problems of Greek capitalism to its development model, and not to the high public debt or the rising organic composition of capital. This is a process of value extraction, i.e. imperialist exploitation, in the sphere of circulation, based upon inter-sectoral competition and terms of trade. The dissimilarity of trade-production structure between the Greek economy and the hard core of its commercial competitors in the Eurozone is the crucial parameter of this process. This is expressed in the deterioration of the Greek terms of trade. The production-trade structural dissimilarity between Greece and the other Eurozone countries takes the form of an important imbalance between the structure of supply (products of low technology, low composition of capital and low income elasticity of demand) and the composition of demand (products of high technology, composition of capital and income elasticity of demand). This, in a certain sense, is more important than simply the problems induced by the single currency. Therefore, Greece is facing unfavourable terms of trade within the hard core of its EU competitors (i.e. the EMU). In conditions of deep depression, Greek capitalism appears to be seeking an 'escape' from the unfavourable terms of trade within the EU-EMU. This 'escape' politically indicates that the national currency and the exit of Greece from EU are necessary conditions for the disengagement of the Greek economy from the 'unevenness' within the EU-EMU. However, in order to overcome the 'extraversion', radical productive reorganisation in a socialist direction is also required.

Ioannis Zisimopoulos and George Economakis, in their contribution, attempt to deal with the class dimension of the Greek debt crisis. They oppose the commonly held view that attributes the huge public debt to the oversized public sector, and instead attempt to confront the public debt crisis through the restriction of public spending and the increase in revenues derived mainly from the salaried classes. For the two writers, the real problem of Greek public debt lies in low public revenues. Focusing on the composition of tax revenues and studying their evolution, the chapter ascertains the deep class dimension of the taxation system and the formation through tax evasion of a class alliance between the bourgeoisie and the middle classes. This brings forward the deep class dimension of the taxation system in Greece. Moreover, Zisimopoulos and Economakis deal with the question of the restructuring of the public sector in the period of the Memorandums. Based upon this particular theoretical approach, they turn to the question of public debt in Greece, in order to demonstrate that the main problem had to do with reduced public revenues. In light of this approach, the perennial problem of tax evasion in Greece emerges not as an expression of the dysfunctional character of Greek society, but rather as the form of social alliance between the bourgeois and the middle classes, in the background of a deeply class-oriented tax system. However, the two writers stress that in a conjuncture of economic depression, the proletarianisation of parts of the middle classes jeopardises the class alliance of the bourgeoisie with the middle classes.

Yiorgos Vassalos in his own contribution deals with the many ways in which the European Union and its move towards forms of European economic governance is at the heart of the problems faced by European societies today, in particular countries that are under Troika supervision, such as Greece. For Vassalos, the implications of the Troika and economic governance reforms on the quality of democracy, the welfare state, and the social situation are huge. Human rights have been blatantly violated by the conditions the Troika imposed on governments subjected to the bail-outs. The economic governance agenda pushes for attacks on established social rights in core EU countries, such as national-level collective bargaining or protection against unjust dismissal. This double path of reform in the EU (Troika/ESM mechanisms and economic governance) leads to important changes in the nature of the EU, as a unique transnational political construction. Vassalos analyses the mechanism of the Memorandums of Understanding and how European Institutions and the IMF have imposed on European countries policies that express the most aggressive demands of the corporate elites, suggesting that instead of the 'shared sovereignty' to which European treaties refer, we are rather dealing with a form of neo-colonialism. All Memoranda include measures that reduce pay in both the private and the public sectors, facilitate lay-offs of public sector employees, reduce the bargaining power of labour, and call for increases in retirement age along with cuts in pensions and public spending. He then proceeds to explain how these mechanisms go hand-in-hand with changes in European economic governance that impose budgetary discipline and neoliberal reforms under pressure from European business groups. Vassalos thinks that the European Union is becoming a dystopia for the vast majority of its citizens, eliminating social rights and gains and severely undermining democracy. The third part of Vassalos's contribution deals with political reactions to the European Union. He analyses the positions of the Far-right concerning European Integration in order to show that in reality this kind of far-right euroscepticism is not in opposition to the core of the dominant capitalist logic. Regarding left-wing parties such as SYRIZA and Podemos, Vassalos stresses the contradiction between their acceptance of European Institutions and their denunciation of austerity. He insists that the only way for countries to avoid austerity and social devastation and to stop the rise of the Far-right is to have a policy of ruptures with the European Union and of disobedience of its Treaties.

Giannis Kouzis's contribution deals with the devastating changes the period of the Memoranda brought to labour relations and labour law. For Kouzis we are dealing with the deregulation of an entire labour relations paradigm, a process that was already underway since the 1990s but that took even more aggressive forms in the Memoranda period. In fact, labour deregulation was one the main *political* strategies inscribed in the Memoranda, by means of a process of deregulation in both the public and the private sectors, which included dismantling of the collective bargaining system, facilitation of mass lay-offs, extensive wage reduction and increased unemployment, along with a general worsening of workplace conditions and labour relations in the public sector that also made the situation even worse in the private sector and led to the expansion of flexible forms of employment. Thus, Greece became a testing ground for European labour market deregulation and aggressive neoliberal reforms.

Eirini Gaitanou's contribution attempts to analyse the particular social and political dynamics of the protests and contestation cycle of 2010–11. For Gaitanou the current crisis in Greece is not restrained to the economic sphere but pervades all aspects of the political sphere, revealing a deep crisis of political representation and legitimisation of the State and its institutions. In Gramscian terms, we can even talk of a crisis of hegemony. This process has had an extensive impact on the lives of people, but it has also led to the eruption of massive social movements. The period after the beginning of the imposition of the Memoranda policies in 2010, and up to early 2012, was a period of mass social mobilisation, constituting what Gaitanou calls *a rebellious cycle*. Gaitanou offers an overview of the extent of the transformations of Greek society and of the dynamics of the movements. Moreover, she studies the crisis of existing forms of political representation, as well as the emergence of alternative forms of political participation and how people's conscience was transformed, especially in relation to their conceptualisation of the political. Gaitanou stresses the development of new relations of people with politics and the changes in their relationship with various forms of political representation (existing and/or new ones). She stresses the new characteristics of the movements, and in particular the new forms of grassroots coordination and democracy. In theoretical terms, Gaitanou studies the constitutive terms of subjectivity and class consciousness within specific conditions, based on a Marxist philosophy of praxis approach that attempts to see how social praxis itself transforms the very field of possibilities for emancipation. Finally, the main conclusions from fieldwork research via in-depth interviews is presented, concerning people's perception of politics and the transformation of their consciousness in relation to participation in the movements. What comes out

of her empirical fieldwork contains elements of both transformation and radicalisation, but also of a difficulty in forming, through this personal experience,
a specific alternative form of political self-constitution. This is seen to result in
part from the strategic weakness of the Left, especially in its failure to elabor-
atean alternative positive engagement and a convincing strategy and vision of
both social organisation and political function.

Angelos Kontogiannis-Mandros's contribution deals in particular with the
dynamics of the Squares Movement, namely the movement that occupied
squares all over Greece in May–July 2011, forming one of the most important
experiences of the cycle of protest and contention in 2010–12. Kontogiannis-
Mandros begins by analysing the evolution of the Greek political system in
the period from 1996 to 2010, the period usually defined as the era of modernisation. For Kontogiannis-Mandros, modernisation is in fact a hegemonic
project combining neoliberalism and europeanism that was also based upon
the political convergence of the two parties that formed the poles of Greek
bipartisanism, PASOK and New Democracy. However, there were economic
contradictions, political deficiencies, and social resistances that undermined
this hegemonic project. The period of the crisis led to a protest cycle without
precedent. In 2011 there were 445 strikes and work stoppages throughout the
country, including six 24-hour and two 48-hour general strikes. However, the
focus of Kontogiannis-Mandros's analysis is the squares movement, which was
not just massive – with around 25% of the population participating, in one
way or another, in the movement – but also a process outside of party politics and the traditional mobilisations of the Left. It was a movement that was
highly innovative in its forms of organising, which included self-organisation
of everyday life, mass assemblies, thematic assemblies and public talks. It was
the dynamic and new confidence brought by the squares movement that led to
the escalation of social conflict of October 2011 and the deepening of the political crisis, which took the form of an organic crisis that led to the fall of the
Papandreou government and the formation of the Papademos government. In
the 2012 elections SYRIZA managed to become the main austerity force, mainly
by insisting that the goal should be a government of the Left. For Kondogiannis-
Mandros, despite the weaknesses and inconsistencies of its proposal, the mere
articulation of the strategy of the 'government of the Left' offered it a definite lead in the anti-memorandum camp. Regarding the legacy of the squares
movement Kondogiannis-Mandros stresses its novelties: occupation of public
space as a basic form of protest; the assembly as a form of grassroots democracy
exemplified in the wave of popular assemblies in the period that followed; the
multiplication of solidarity initiatives. However, gradually the anticipation in
the 2012–15 period of a SYRIZA government led to a decline in the dynamic of
self-organisation.

One of the most striking manifestations of the political crisis has been the emergence of the neo-fascist Golden Dawn party, which rapidly rose from a marginal position to parliamentary representation. This is the subject of Despina Paraskeva-Veloudogianni's contribution. Paraskeva-Veloudogianni attempts to place the rise of Golden Dawn in the context of social and political crisis in Greece and in particular the shifts in relations of political representation. She also stresses the importance of the authoritarian turn in Greek politics after 2011, which facilitated the appeal of the neo-fascist discourse of Golden Dawn. In particular, she stresses the fact that despite the impressive magnitude and intensity of social protest and contestation in Greece, the authoritarian post-democratic refusal to change even minor aspects of austerity led to frustration in large parts of the population. In this context, Golden Dawn offered its own version of a nation in danger and in a 'state of emergency', taking advantage of both the authoritarian and anti-immigrant turn of the systemic Right and the association of all systemic parties with social devastation, and projecting its own version of solidarity 'for Greeks only' and far-right 'anti-systemic' discourse. Paraskeva-Veloudogianni puts the judicial procedure against the leadership of Golden Dawn, after the murder of Pavlos Fyssas in September 2013, into the perspective of both the pressure from the anti-fascist movement and the threat that the electoral rise of Golden Dawn posed to the Samaras government. However, she notes that the arrests and the judicial processes did not manage to seriously reduce the appeal of Golden Dawn and she warns that the continuation, under the government of a left-wing party, of the imposition of a condition of reduced popular sovereignty and austerity will continue to fuel the rise of reactionary and neo-fascist ideologies. The potential answer to this continues to be the radical dynamic expressed in moments such as the 5 July 2015 referendum.

Spyros Sakellaropoulos's contribution deals with the formation of bourgeois strategy in Greece, putting it into historical perspective. He begins with the *Megali Idea* (Grand Idea) strategy of the nineteenth century, whose irredentism placed territorial expansion above economic development, up until the Asia Minor disaster of 1922, which put an end to territorial expansion and led to a switch of emphasis to economic development. The arrival of refugees from Asia Minor after the exchange of populations with Turkey increased the available labour force and enhanced economic development. However, in the 1930s there was an intense political crisis as a result of not only the economic crisis but also the intensification of internal class-related contradictions and the emergence of the Communist Party as a significant force. The result of the political crisis was the Metaxas dictatorship in 1936. The emergence of the Communist-led Resistance during the German Occupation led to the Greek Civil War and the defeat of the Left that laid the ground for the post-WWII development of Greek capitalism, which in the 1950s and especially the 1960s registered high growth rates. After the 1967–74 military dictatorship, the restoration of democratic institutions and the legalisation of the Communist Left coincided with the effort to integrate Greece into the EEC. Moreover, in the 1990s and 2000s we had a combination of the process of integration into the European Union – and the pressures it put upon Greek economy and society – and of processes of capitalist restructuring. The bourgeois strategy that emerged comprised low labour costs, flexible social relations, the revival of the construction sector in view of the large public works especially around the Olympics period, continuing importance of the more cosmopolitan shipping industry, reliance on EU funding, and the increased role of private banking capital. This strategy was met with relative success, because growth was combined with a lack of competitiveness and increased indebtedness. The reaction was a radical change in strategy for the Greek bourgeoisie. This included a change in social alliances with a rupture of the alliance between the bourgeoisie and the traditional petty bourgeois strata and even with non-monopoly bourgeois strata. In turn, this was accompanied by a new configuration of the state apparatus in the Memoranda period and increased authoritarianism. There were also changes in the balance of forces between different sections of the bourgeoisie, with energy, water supply, and petroleum goods industries becoming more important, in addition to changes in the export patterns of the Greek economy and a turn towards new export markets. In a certain way, there is a trade-off between the imposition of a condition of limited sovereignty, which is close to a hybrid form of protectorate, and the enhancement of capitalist profitability.

Christos Laskos and Euclid Tsakalotos in their contribution attempt to describe the strategy of SYRIZA before the January 2015 elections (their essay was written before the election). They attempt to describe how SYRIZA managed to articulate a hegemonic project for Greece and to become the major anti-austerity political force in Greece, especially after it called for a government of the Left in the 2012 elections. The fact that the dominant parties opted to support aggressive neoliberal policies was an abandonment of large parts of society and this created a political space for SYRIZA to emerge as the leading force of the anti-austerity struggle. Laskos and Tsakalotos argue that the rise of SYRIZA was based upon its participation in all the major social struggles in the 2000s up to and including December 2008. In particular, they stress how SYRIZA, based upon this experience, participated in all the major forms of protest, from the mass strikes to the movement of the squares and the initiatives of solidarity. They stress the importance of solidarity initiatives, which constituted a direct intervention to address urgent social needs, proved that the Left

could be more effective, broadened the appeal of the Left, and had an immediate ideological impact. On this basis, the two writers insist that before the
January 2015 election SYRIZA had indeed a transition programme and its effort
to move social movements and initiatives onto the terrain of the State combined, Laskos and Tsakalotos argue, a Gramscian conception of the 'integral
State' with a Poulantzian conception of the transformation of the State.

Alexandros Chrysis in his own contribution suggests that, from an anticapit-
alist point of view, there are two ways of dealing with the mass demonstrations
and protests which took place in Greece during the last years of the economic,
socio-political and cultural crisis. The first is the one offered by post-Marxist
thinkers such as Negri, Žižek and Badiou. The other is a potentially Marxist and
Gramsci-inspired conception of revolutionary politics. Regarding Negri's interventions, Chrysis considers Negri's theoretical attempt to combine the internationalist content of contemporary social movements with radical political-
institutional forms as problematic, especially since Negri bases his propositions
on a certain conceptualisation of the irreversibility of European Integration.
Regarding Žižek, Chrysis is particularly critical of the former's reference to a
new salaried bourgeoisie in Greece, especially since this is based on a mis-
reading of the social structure of Greece. Regarding Badiou's positions on the
Greek crisis and movement, Chrysis insists that the Greek experience does not
correspond to the historical type of riot, especially since after the moment of
mass protests in 2010–12 a period of relative stability followed. For Chrysis, post-
Marxist positions cannot account for this relative stabilisation of the relation of
forces in the conjuncture, since they do not tackle the 'organisation question',
namely the question of the political party, since they all, in one way or another,
reject the very necessity of a party of proletarian hegemony. Chrysis opposes
what he defines as a Gramscian conception of the Party to Negri and Hardt's
emphasis on horizontal forms of organisation and to Badiou's call for a new
'revolutionary political discipline'. In contrast, what is missing in the current
conjuncture, especially in Greece, is this kind of process of creating a collective
political and ideological organisational form that could be an actual political
vanguard. For Chrysis, all the main political forms of the Greek Left fail to be
this kind of New Prince: SYRIZA remains a reformist electoral front, the Communist Party (KKE) promotes a sectarian form of neo-Stalinism, and ANTARSYA
remains a loose and divided coalition. Consequently, the challenge of building
exactly this kind of organisational form remains.

My own contribution attempts to deal with the questions of radical left
strategy in a period of crisis. Austerity has been the battle cry of capitalist elites
in recent years as a response to the difficulties regarding the emergence of a
new regime of accumulation that would guarantee a steady capitalist growth

after the structural crisis of 2007–8. The Eurozone has been at the epicentre of the attempt to impose austerity and violent neoliberal reforms leading to Greece being used, in a certain sense, as a testing ground for such policies. The result has been a political crisis that in certain moments took an almost insurrectionary dynamic, leading to tectonic shifts in relations of political representation. It was this combination between social and political crises of a sequence of struggles without precedent that led to the electoral earthquake of February 2015 and the formation of the first SYRIZA-led government. However, lacking the kind of 'organic relation' to the subaltern classes that marks the emergence of an 'historical bloc', and without a programme of ruptures with the embedded neoliberalism of the Eurozone and the EU treaties, SYRIZA sought an impossible compromise with Greece's creditors, and despite the massive rejection of austerity in the 5 July 2015 referendum, the government was ultimately forced to capitulate and agree to a third Memorandum. This development, along with other developments, such as the faltering of the dynamics of the important movements globally, poses the question of strategy. The position of this essay is that this requires rethinking in terms of a potential historical bloc, which is a strategic, not an analytical, concept. Such a strategy for a new historical bloc entails the following: a rethinking of the notion of popular sovereignty; a radical and transformative approach to political power and a new conception of dual power that could incorporate the collective knowledge and ingenuity emerging in the movements and the new forms for popular counter-power; the rethinking of the transitional programme as alternative narrative; and the rethinking of political fronts and organisations as collective laboratories of programmes and new forms of mass political intellectuality.

∴

Apart from the contributors, many people have, directly or indirectly, helped bring this volume to fruition. Sebastian Budgen embraced this project from the beginning. Stathis Kouvelakis, Giorgos Kalampokas, George Nikolaidis, Despina Koutsoumba, and David McNally have offered points of inspiration, criticism, and suggestions that are reflected in many of the contributions in this volume. We really want to thank them.

∴

However, the most important inspiration for this volume has been the struggles and collective hopes and aspirations of the people in Greece. Without the unique display of courage, determination, and resistance that we saw in many moments in the course of recent years, without this feeling that in critical moments mass popular movements can indeed change the course of history and open up alternatives, this volume and the attempt to deal with questions of strategy would not have been possible. In one way or another, the lives of all the contributors were changed by this experience. We have all been deeply marked by this sequence of struggle and hope and by the fact that for some time Greece was indeed a laboratory of struggle and hope. We hope that this volume makes the best use of the Greek experience in the debates regarding left strategy today. The future indeed lasts a long time, and there are many pages of it yet to be written.

## References

Blanchard, Olivier 2007, 'Adjustment within the Euro. The Difficult Case of Portugal', *Portuguese Economic Review*, 6: 1–21.

European Commission 2010, *The Economic Adjustment Programme for Greece*, EURO-PEAN ECONOMY Occasional Papers no. 61, available at: http://ec.europa.eu/economy_finance/publications/occasional_paper/2010/pdf/ocp61_en.pdf

Kouvelakis, Stathis 2011d, 'The Greek Cauldron', *New Left Review*, 72: 17–32.

Lapavitsas, Costas, A. Kaltenbrunner, G. Labrinidis, D. Lindo, J. Meadway, J. Michell, J.P. Painceira, E. Pires, J. Powell, A. Stenfors, N. Teles, and L. Vatikiotis. 2012, *Crisis in the Eurozone*, London: Verso.

Psarras, Dimitris 2014, *The Rise of the Neo-Nazi Party 'Golden Dawn' in Greece: Neo-Nazi Mobilization in the Wake of the Crisis*, Brussels: Rosa Luxemburg Stiftung.

Sakellaropoulos, Spyros and Panagiotis Sotiris 2014, 'Postcards from the Future: The Greek Debt Crisis, the Struggle against the EU-IMF Austerity Package and the Open Questions for Left Strategy', *Constellations*, 21, 2: 262–73.

# CHAPTER 1

# The Greek Crisis: Causes and Alternative Strategies

*Stavros Mavroudeas*

## Introduction

The Greek crisis is a major incident of the wider EU crisis. Despite the rather small size of the Greek economy, its connections and the timing of its crisis have asymmetrically big repercussions not only on the EU but also on the world economy. This chapter evaluates the competing explanations of the Greek crisis and the alternative strategies – roughly associated with these explanations – proposed in order to surpass this crisis. This evaluation is conducted from the 'partisan' perspective of Marxism. The structure of the chapter is the following.

The first part reviews the analytical and empirical arguments of the competing explanations. These are categorised into three main groups: Mainstream, Radical, and Marxist. It is argued that the Marxist explanations (associated with the Tendency of the Rate of Profit to Fall (TRPF)) have analytical and empirical superiority against their rivals. In particular, they can better grasp the deep structural character of the Greek crisis.

The second part presents the basic alternative economic strategies. These are categorised into two main groups, which are also subdivided into two versions each. The first strategy aims to surpass the crisis within the auspices of the EU and the EMU (European Monetary Union). It basically follows the fundamental Greek and European bourgeois prerogatives. It is subdivided into two versions: (1) a strategy of more or less faithful implementation of the IMF-EU-ECB Economic Adjustment Programmes (EAPs), and (2) a strategy of renegotiation of the EAPs towards a less pro-cyclical and less austere policy mix. It is argued that the first version is an overambitious bourgeois strategy that flirts with endangering the political and social stability of the system. The second version is a non-autonomous strategy in the sense that it depends upon the (at least) partial success of the first version. This makes it an incoherent and unreliable strategy.

The second strategy questions either part or the whole of Greek capitalism's strategic choice of participating in the European integration. It is also subdivided into two versions: (1) a strategy of leaving the EMU but remaining within the EU, and (2) a strategy of complete disengagement from the EU (i.e.

© KONINKLIJKE BRILL NV, LEIDEN, 2018 | DOI:10.1163/9789004280892_003

leaving the political structures, the common market and the EMU). It is argued that the first version is a middle-of-the-road approach that does not offer a coherent alternative to the bourgeois strategies since it disregards the deeply structural character of the Greek crisis. Finally, it is argued that the second version offers a coherent alternative strategy answering the problem of the crisis from the perspective of the working class.

## 1      Competing Explanations of the Greek Crisis

Since the eruption of the Greek crisis, several analytical streams have competed in order to explain its causes and to suggest relevant solutions. Rather unsurprisingly, the different explanations of the Greek crisis offered fall within the main camps of economic analysis today. That is, they belong to Mainstream economics, Radical Political Economy, or Marxist Political Economy.

Mainstream economics is the dominant tradition in economics. It stems from the neoclassical economics that dethroned Political Economy in the beginning of the twentieth century, subsequently becoming the economic orthodoxy. It is essentially a supply-side, value-free and micro-based economics that considers economic crisis an abnormality created by chance events and not caused by systemic problems. After the Keynesian challenge of the interwar and postwar years (that proposed a demand-side analysis and a possibility crisis theory), Mainstream economics morphed into Hicks's post-Keynesian neoclassical synthesis (which merged neoclassical methods and Keynesian macroeconomics). With the neoliberal onslaught of the 1980s (as expressed by Monetarism initially and New Classicals thereafter), Mainstream economics became even more conservative. The bulk of Keynesians (as exemplified by the New Keynesians) followed suit by adopting most of the neoconservative agenda. This realignment led to the New Consensus Macroeconomics, which is a merger of neoliberal economics with New Keynesianism. New Consensus Macroeconomics constitutes the current economic orthodoxy and dominates all the influential centres of economic policy making.

Mainstream economics does not need a crisis theory. Neoclassicism argues that capitalism is a perfect system that, under normal circumstances and agents' behaviour, will not face crises. Disequilibria can occur only when some agent acts irresponsibly by violating perfect competition and inscribing rigidities in the system. Consequently, an economic crisis does not have deep structural causes; rather it is the chance outcome of some abnormal intervention. New Keynesianism, on the other hand, dropped Keynesianism's possibility theory of crisis and also maintained that crises stem from policy errors. The

Mainstream perspective can recognise weak structural causes as the mid-term consolidation of abnormal destabilising behaviours and institutions. Concomitantly, Mainstream economics (a) failed utterly to foresee the 2007–8 global capitalist crisis, and (b) ex post diagnosed it as simply a financial crisis caused by the irresponsible exorbitant leverage caused by the financial sector's 'golden boys' and a lack of prudent supervision. Thus, they focus solely on the financial sector and totally disregard the 'real economy'.

Radical Political Economy differs from both Classical and Marxist Political Economy as well as from traditional Keynesianism. It consists of several approaches that usually blend elements of Classical and Marxist Political Economy with post-Keynesianism and Institutionalism. It discards the Labour Theory of Value (LTV) and uses Keynesian macroeconomics for its analysis. This current acknowledges the structurally crisis-prone nature of capitalism but does not recognise one fundamental systemic mechanism as a cause of crisis.[1] Rather, it argues that each specific crisis can have a different cause. This means that when it comes to the specific analysis of a crisis, Radical Political Economy opts for a middle-range, historically specific cause of the crisis, rather than a systemic cause. This perspective may facilitate adaptability to historical circumstances, but it also weakens its explanatory power and very often leads to agnosticism.[2] The eclectic character of Radical Political Economy leads it to very wide and rather contradictory variations. For example, pure post-Keynesian analyses recognise as the fundamental cause of crisis the Keynesian lack of adequate demand. On the other hand, many other Radical currents emphasise mid-term institutional factors. In general, Radical approaches attribute both the global 2007–8 crisis and the Greek crisis to some intermediate factor (usually neoliberalism and the EMU correspondingly), but not to the basic systemic contradictions of the capitalist system.

Marxist Political Economy has a more developed crisis theory than any other economic tradition. For Marxism, economic crisis is not an accidental anomaly on the surface of capitalism's modus operandi, but an expression of the inherent contradictions of the capitalist mode of production. Marxist analysis focuses on both capitalism's fundamental contradiction (the capital-labour conflict) and secondary contradiction (intra-capitalist competition)

---

1 For example, within Marxist theory there are several currents that recognise a different mechanism as the fundamental systemic cause of economic crises in general. The three historical currents are: (1) falling profitability, (2) underconsumption, and (3) capitalism's inherently anarchic character.

2 For a critique, see Mavroudeas 2012a, ch. 3, p. 8.

and studies them through the special toolbox of LTV.[3] It accurately conceives
of capitalism as a system normally passing from periods of boom to periods
of bust. Henceforth, crises are not accidental anomalies but normal instances.
There is a vibrant debate within Marxism regarding the fundamental crisis
mechanism. A number of theories have been proposed: underconsumptionism, capitalism's anarchic nature, and TRPF. This chapter follows the falling
profitability perspective as the more coherent and realistic crisis theory. However, there is a fundamental difference between Marxist economic analysis and
crisis theory and that of not only Mainstream economics but also Radical Political Economy. For Marxism the profit motive (and the profit rate) is the main
variable of the capitalist system. Consequently, a crisis (whatever its causal
mechanism) is related to a fall in profitability. This is the major difference
between Marxist macroeconomic models and Radical ones (e.g. Kaleckian
models). Following on from these theses, for Marxism, every major economic
crisis is necessarily geared in the fundamental relations of the capitalist mode
of production and particularly in the dominant sphere of the total circuit of
capital (the sphere of production). This argument does not exclude cases of
crises caused by problems in the sphere of circulation or distribution, but it
considers them as an exception. In particular, crises caused by instabilities in
the financial system do exist but they must be related – even ex post – to the
sphere of production. Moreover, such crises cannot be either major or protracted.

A concise picture of the competing explanations of the Greek crisis is presented in Figure 1.1.

### Mainstream Explanations

There are three versions of Mainstream explanations.[4]

The first and older one considers the Greek crisis as a special 'Greek disease' because Greece is a special type of economy which is prone to fiscal
profligacy. It was expressed in reports by the governing EU and ECB bodies
and also from the Bank of Greece.[5] It identified the Greek 'disease' with two
major deficiencies of the Greek economy: (1) large and persistent fiscal deficits
financed through borrowing (which created large external debts), and (2) fal-

---

3  LTV argues that production is the primary sphere of economic activity and human labour
   is the sole factor creating wealth. In a market-based system (e.g. capitalism) the system of
   prices (the system through which commodities are exchanged) is determined by the system
   of labour values (the quantities of labour required in order to produce these commodities).

4  For an extensive presentation, see Mavroudeas and Paitaridis 2015a.

5  EC 2010.

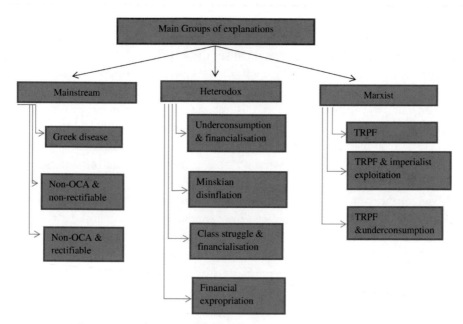

FIGURE 1.1  *Competing explanations of the Greek crisis*

ling competitiveness. More specifically, it maintains that the Greek economy is characterised by low productivity, high relative wages and a big public sector. High wages are the product of the big public sector which is clientelist, has low productivity and a falling ability to collect taxes (due to clientelism fomenting tax evasion). Consequently, fiscal deficits are accumulated. These are financed through loans causing a widening external debt (expressed in a deteriorating current account). Cheap borrowing was possible because since the entrance to the EMU, Greece benefited from low interest rates. Moreover, Greece forfeited statistical data and thus violated the provisions of the Maastricht Treaty. With the advent of the 2007–8 crisis, international financial markets started scrutinising fiscal deficits and external debts. Consequently, the unsustainability of the Greek debt was discovered and the crisis erupted. Thus, the deep fiscal cuts of the first Economic Adjustment Programme (EAP) for Greece were justified. In order to justify the expansion of austerity measures to the private sector, the problem of competitiveness was surfaced. It was argued that not only the public but also the private sector is characterised by low productivity, high wages and rigid labour market regulation culminating in a falling competitiveness. Consequently, the current account worsened not only because of public borrowing but also because of diminishing exports and increasing imports. High wages fuelled consumption, which was directed towards imports, since domestically produced goods were uncompetitive. The analytical foundation of the 'Greek disease' version is the *Twin Deficits Hypothesis* (TDH), which contends that when an economy is characterised by both fiscal and current account deficits, it is the former that causes the latter.

The second explanation – having mainly Anglo-Saxon origins (either neo-liberal[6] or New Keynesian[7]) – argues that whatever national 'disease' exists, it is aggravated by the fact that the EMU is not an Optimal Currency Area (OCA).[8] Therefore, it is prone to asymmetric shocks that exacerbate national 'diseases'. This version argues that the EMU cannot be rectified and its collapse is on the agenda. It also usually agrees with the TDH diagnosis of the national causes of the crisis.

The third version is a 'middle-of-the-road' blend. It considers the Greek crisis as a combination of national policy errors (high fiscal deficits and debt) with problems created by the EMU's incomplete architecture. Moreover, it argues that these problems can be solved with the deepening of the EU's economic and political unification. This explanation is expressed mainly by European analysts who are in favour of European unification but have ideological (basically Keynesian) and/or practical reservations regarding the actual process of European integration.[9] Then this argument about the EMU's incompleteness is linked to the deteriorating current account imbalances that subvert its function. More specifically, the existence of a North-South dichotomy within the EMU – with euro-centre economies having current account surpluses and euro-periphery economies suffering from current account deficits – is recognised as a source of malignancies that threaten its existence.

The analytical and empirical foundations of the mainstream explanations are extremely shaky. All of them ultimately attribute the internal causes of the Greek to TDH.[10] Consequently, they identify the Greek crisis as simply a debt crisis. Then wages are posited as the factor triggering both the fiscal and the current account deficits. It is argued that Greek (nominal) unit labour costs increased faster than those of the other European countries leading to worsening fiscal and current account deficits.

---

6    E.g. Feldstein 2010.

7    E.g. Krugman 2012.

8    The OCA theory (Mundell 1961) argues that a currency union of different economies has to fulfil several crucial requirements (e.g. high factors mobility, structural economic convergence, a fiscal equilibration mechanism). Most analyses of the EMU agree that these requirements are missing.

9    E.g. De Grauwe 2010.

10   Only some variants of the third explanation differ by stressing the EMU's trade disequilibria as an independent factor causing the Greek problem.

First, TDH's applicability for Greece is disputed. For example, Nikiforos, Carvalho and Schoder argue that while TDH is confirmed for the pre-accession to the EMU period (1960–80), it is rejected for the post-accession period (1981–2007).[11] For the latter period the opposite is confirmed: trade (and thus current account) deficit has caused increasing budget deficit.

Second, the argument that the increasing Greek *nominal unit labour costs* caused the falling competitiveness is unsustainable. Competitiveness depends on not only cost factors (like wages) but mainly structural factors (sectoral structure of the economy, composition of exports, etc.). Moreover, the Kaldor paradox shows that competitiveness is seldom associated with high wages. Also, contrary to Mainstream assertions, Greek wage increases have been constantly lagging behind productivity increases. Thus, the Greek *real unit labour costs* (i.e. the wage share in the product) have been falling continuously for a considerable period.

But the Mainstream explanations of the Greek crisis also have wider problems. They inordinately consider the Greek crisis as independent of the 2007–8 global crisis, whereas the links between them have become obvious. Additionally, they fail to appreciate the fundamental structural dimensions of the Greek problem and instead relegate it to the realm of policy errors and/or weak structural origins. The first explanation considers the Greek case as a national specificity created by bad policies. The second and third explanations recognise a rather weak structural cause. It concerns mainly the sphere of circulation (i.e. how the common currency is related to diverse national economies) and has little to do with the sphere of production per se. Concomitantly, Greek and the Eurozone crises are attributed solely to the EMU's architecture. However, nowadays even the Mainstream views recognise implicitly the structural dimension of the Greek crisis. Much of the emphasis of the 2nd EAP for Greece is on structural reforms that aim to change the foundations of the Greek economy.

### Radical Explanations

Radical explanations of the Greek crisis are dominated by the 'financialisation' thesis.[12] There are some other versions. Stathakis argues that the Greek crisis is a mainly fiscal crisis caused by Greek capital's notorious tax evasion and cronyism.[13] Indeed Greek capital almost always had these properties. But

11   Nikiforos, Carvalho and Schoder 2014.
12   For a detailed critique of the 'financialisation' explanations, see Mavroudeas (2015a, 2015b).
13   Stathakis 2010.

it is simplistic to attribute the crisis to them. If it were so, the crisis should have erupted long before. Laskos and Tsakalotos add to Stathakis's point the arguments about the EMU's trade imbalances and the increasing inequality (that is supposed to cause some covert form of underconsumptionism).[14] Neither of them is a sufficient explanation of the crisis. Particularly, the underconsumptionist explanation does not fit the empirical data as the period preceding the onset of the crisis was characterised by a spectacular growth in consumption.

The partial nature and the weaknesses of these other Radical explanations facilitated the popularity of the 'financialisation' thesis. The latter argues *erroneously* that in modern capitalism, finance (i.e. the operation of money capital) assumes an increasing primacy in relation to other capitalist activities. With regard to Marxism this thesis goes back to Rudolf Hilferding.[15] However, Hilferding did not dispute the classical Marxist relationship between surplus value and interest.[16] In contrast, 'financialisation' argues that interest ceases to be a part of surplus value and that it acquires an independent existence. Concomitantly, money capital not only dominates 'productive' capital but it is also autonomised from it. Particularly, marxisant 'financialisation' theories (e.g. Lapavitsas's *financial expropriation*)[17] argue that finance directly exploits workers by lending to them at usurious rates. In toto, 'financialisation' describes a new stage of capitalism or even a 'new capitalism' that is neither realistic nor analytically coherent.[18] This 'new capitalism' is characterised by (a) a financial system based on the stock exchange (and not traditional banking), and (b) a permanent and high indebtedness of private households. The first channel 'financialises' capital's activity. The second channel empowers finance to directly exploit workers (and others) and not to depend upon 'productive' capital's extraction of surplus value. Additionally, regarding the 2007–8 crisis, 'financialisation' argues that it is not a crisis à la Marx (i.e. rooted in the sphere of production), but a financial crisis (a crisis of financialised capitalism). In this they essentially agree with Mainstream theories.

Three Radical 'financialisation' explanations of the Greek crisis have been proposed.

---

14    Laskos and Tsakalotos 2011.

15    Hilferding 1981.

16    Surplus value is extracted by 'productive' capital at the sphere of production and then it is redistributed between profits (accruing to 'productive' capital), interest (accruing to 'non-productive' finance capital), and commercial profits (accruing to 'non-productive' commercial capital).

17    Lapavitsas 2008.

18    On this see Mavroudeas 2015b.

The version by Lapavitsas et al. agrees with the Mainstream explanations that the Greek crisis is basically a debt crisis (i.e. caused by unsustainable twin deficits).[19] However, they consider these as symptoms of a 'wider malaise' having its roots in (a) financialised capitalism, and (b) the EMU. Financialisation caused the 2007–8 crisis (through leverage that created unsustainable bubbles), which is not a crisis à la Marx (that is, profitability played no role in it), but simply a financial crisis. The world crisis affected the EMU's fragile foundations (because it is not an OCA). Particularly, it aggravated its trade imbalances that stem from its neo-mercantilist character (the fact that it is a monetary union that favours the euro-core versus the euro-periphery). This neo-mercantilism is explained as an inverted image of the Mainstream argument about falling competitiveness caused by Greek relative wage increases. Lapavitsas et al. implicitly accept that competitiveness depends solely on wages. They argue that the euro-core (and especially Germany) was more competent in pressurising wages and thus acquired a permanent competitive advantage against the euro-periphery. This is the Mainstream argument in reverse: the cause of the problem is the over-prudent North and not the light-hearted South.

Thus, the Eurozone was polarised in a North with trade surpluses and a South with debts. This imbalance was equilibrated for a period by the North loaning to the South (in order for the latter to buy its products). The eruption of the 2007–8 crisis disrupted this structure as international financial markets questioned the creditworthiness of the South's sovereign debts and the Eurozone's crisis began. Lapavitsas's policy proposal was Grexit because the EMU is unrectifiable.

Lapavitsas's explanation does not pay any attention to the production sphere (e.g. the production structure of the Greek and the other EMU economies) and to the profit rate (the critical variable of Marxist analysis). Consequently, he does not recognise any process of imperialist exploitation between the North and the South (in the Marxist and not the neo-mercantilist sense). Moreover, he accepts uncritically the Mainstream arguments about relatively high wages being the cause of Greece's deteriorating competitiveness (for example, he accepts uncritically the high nominal unit labour costs argument).

Also, his 'financialisation' argument does not fit the Greek data.[20] First, Greek capitalism was always a bank-based system rather than a 'financialised' one. Second, private household debt is a new and rather limited phenomenon

---

19    Lapavitsas et al. 2010.

20    On this, see Mavroudeas 2015b.

in Greece compared to the Western experience. It was traditionally low, it started increasing rapidly after the introduction of the euro and it collapsed with the advent of the crisis. In toto, neither the entrepreneurial nor the household aspect of 'financialisation' is valid in the Greek case. Therefore, 'financialisation' cannot be discovered in Greece and has to be imported from outside. It is the global crisis that brings 'financialisation' in Greece through public (and not private) external debt.

Lapavitsas's policy suggestions are also problematic. If the Greek crisis is simply a debt crisis, then it may be solved not by exiting the EMU but by reforming it towards a full OCA (i.e. by unifying it fiscally and politically). If the crisis is something more profound and has to do with the sphere of production, then exiting the EMU and remaining within the Common Market will not suffice. A full exit from the EU is required.

The second 'financialisation' explanation is offered by Milios and Sotiropoulos.[21] Contrary to Lapavitsas, they argue that it was not falling competitiveness that caused high indebtedness, but the other way around. The EMU, by bundling together countries with very different rates of growth and profitability, leads to increased borrowing by the euro-periphery because its higher profit rates (and relative lack of capital) attract funds from the euro-core. The euro boosted this trend because it allowed euro-periphery countries to borrow at low interest rates. Foreign loans boosted the euro-periphery's domestic demand, therefore giving rise to increasing inflation and the deterioration of competitiveness. Milios and Sotiropoulos essentially reject the North-South divide as an expression of the problematic Dependency theory. For them foreign loans were not a trick to rob Greece, but a perfectly natural phenomenon that helped boost growth. On this point they agree with the Mainstream arguments in Greece that the EU helped Greece's development. Indeed, the pre-crisis Mainstream argument was that current account deficits were good imbalances because euro-periphery countries with relatively low levels of real GDP per capita were catching up with richer north European economies. Greater growth opportunities and expectations of faster productivity growth justified elevated levels of fixed investment relative to the pool of domestic savings, hence the need for a current account deficit. Thus, Milios and Sotiropoulos implicitly accept the Mainstream convergence thesis.[22] This argument flies in

---

21    Milios and Sotiropoulos 2010.

22    Mainstream economics maintains that capitalism is inscribed with a convergence tendency as, by assumption, less developed countries have higher growth rates than more developed ones. Thus, sooner or later the former will catchup with the latter. In reality

the face of reality. Greece's sustained current account deficit did not finance investment in productive assets but was used to buy the euro-core's imported goods. Thus, instead of being developed, Greece's productive structure was actually eroded. As a corollary, instead of converging with the EU, Greece actually – after a period of convergence – started to diverge.

Moreover, Milios and Sotiropoulos's analysis replicates the 'strong Greece' story presented before the crisis by the Mainstream academic and official circles. Then 'financialisation' enters: modern capitalism is financialised and leads to extreme leveraging and financial bubbles. The 2007–8 crisis (which they too understand as a mere financial one) derailed the hitherto malevolent euro-periphery's current account deficits. In order to sustain them, fiscal deficits were augmented and this led to the euro-periphery's collapse.

For Milios and Sotiropoulos, the EMU played only a peripheral role. Although they accept that the EMU is not an OCA and it is a neoliberal project, they do not envisage a Grexit, but the EU's progressive restructuring.

The third 'financialisation' explanation is proposed by Argitis and follows Minsky's theory.[23] He argues that Greek capitalism is characterised by (a) weak and obsolete technological structure, (b) structurally weak competitiveness causing chronic and significant current account deficits, and (c) strong and extensive cronyism between private businesses and the state. The 'strong state' (together with its central bank) managed the inflation–disinflation process (by using the fiscal deficits more as a redistributive tool than as an anti-cyclical one) in order to bolster capitalist profitability.

Problems started arising with Greece's accession to the EMU as its traditional economic structure was dismantled without being replaced with another, equally functional one. After entering the EMU, the 'strong state' remained but lost its central bank (as the latter followed the ECB's policies). Consequently, debt management became dysfunctional and the financialisation of the economy (that is, the increase in leverage) became necessary. This increased the inherent instability of the capitalist economy (as Minsky's Financial Instability Hypothesis suggests). Then the 2007–8 crisis (which, for Minskians, was caused by the neoliberal liberalisation) derailed the already unstable Greek capitalism. The 'strong state' without a strong central bank could not manage and control the debt inflation–disinflation process. Hence, the Greek crisis erupted.

---

this convergence thesis is not verified. Instead, as Marxism argues, uneven development is an organic characteristic of capitalism.

23    Argitis 2012.

In general, Minskian theory is rightfully criticised as (a) phenomenological, and (b) focusing excessively on the financial system and neglecting the real economy. It has also been criticised for having a very narrow and poor understanding of the role of fiscal and monetary policy and an unwarranted emphasis on monopolies.

Regarding the Greek crisis, the Minskian explanation has additional problems. The more significant one is that the Greek crisis was not caused by excessive private debt. On the contrary, the latter is small when compared to that of the more developed Western economies. Thus, it cannot be convincingly argued that the Greek problem was borne from the inflation–disinflation circle of private debt. It is for this reason that Argitis leaves aside the typical mechanism of the Financial Instability Hypothesis and sticks more to Minsky's previous work on the significance of the political and institutional framework for securing the stabilisation of the financial system.[24] His central argument is that the disintegration of the 'strong state – strong central bank' pair led to the inability of functionally managing the inflation–disinflation process. However, this argument is disputable because:

(a)   It unwarrantedly assumes that the policy of the Bank of Greece was always accommodative during the post-dictatorship period.
(b)   It equally unjustifiably implies that, after the accession to the EMU and the relinquishing to it of the monetary and exchange rate policy, the government and the Bank of Greece lost any ability to exert discreet policies.

Finally, if Argitis's explanation is correct, then the obvious policy suggestion is Grexit. But this is something that he rejects.

Concluding, Radical 'financialisation' explanations of the Greek crisis have serious analytical and empirical deficiencies. The former derive from the superficiality of the 'financialisation' thesis and its inability to study the production sphere of the economy. The latter stem from the fact that both channels of 'financialisation' are insignificant in the Greek case. Consequently, they fail to appreciate the deep structural character of the Greek crisis (the fact that it is caused by capitalism's deep systemic contradictions) and attribute it to weak structural factors (especially the EMU). These deficiencies are expressed in their policy proposals which revolve around the EMU: either exiting the EMU or rectifying it. Thus, they fail to see that Greece's problems are not caused

---

24    Argitis 2012.

solely by the EMU, but began long before with its incorporation into the European common market. Exiting or rectifying the EMU will not solve these fundamental problems.

### Marxist Explanations

Marxist explanations follow a different analytical path from both the Mainstream and Radical ones. They focus upon deep systemic and structural crisis mechanisms. Thus, they pay particular attention to (a) 'real accumulation' (more accurately to the sphere of production) and its characteristics (technological and sectoral structure, organic composition of capital (OCC), etc.), and (b) profitability. Moreover, they employ the LTV as their analytical toolbox. These features differentiate Marxist explanations from marxisant Radical explanations. The Marxist perspective argues that the Greek crisis is part of the 2007–8 global economic crisis. Both are displays of deep structural crisis mechanisms of the capitalist system (and particularly the TRPF). These structural crisis tendencies were aggravated by the subordinate position of Greek capitalism within the European imperialist bloc. Consequently, they propose a strong structural explanation of the Greek crisis. Regarding their policy suggestions, all Marxist explanations agree that what is required is a long-term transitional programme aiming at the creation of a socialist economy. They also agree that the crucial intermediate anchor of such a programme is Greece's disengagement from the EU (and not simply from the EMU). This would liberate the ability to create a self-centred economy serving the people's interests and able to democratically plan the long-term structural transformations required in order to restructure the Greek productive system.

Three Marxist explanations have been proposed. Maniatis and Passas attribute the Greek crisis to a long-term TRPF that was expressed in the 1973 crisis and the inability of subsequent capitalist restructurings to sufficiently and sturdily rectify this fall.[25] Focusing on the movement of the profit rate, they delineate three major postwar periods of capital accumulation. The first one (1958 till the mid-1970s) was the 'golden age' of Greek capitalism: high profit rates (despite a slightly falling trend) caused high rates of capital accumulation and output growth, significant increases in productivity growth and increases in the real wage for productive workers and workers in general, even with a rising rate of surplus value. It was followed by the stagflation crisis period (1973–4 till 1985). OCC's significant increase during the 'golden age' combined with the fall in the rate of surplus value and the profit share as a result of successful labour

---

25   Maniatis and Passas 2015.

struggles after the fall of the military dictatorship, produced a sharp fall in profitability negatively affecting investment, output growth, productivity, real wage
growth and employment. Then came the period of neoliberalism (after 1986)
characterised by a dramatic increase in labour exploitation. However, the resultant recovery in profitability was not coupled with a sufficient devalorisation
of capital and a significant decrease in unproductive labour because of their
political infeasibility at that time. The insufficient recovery of profitability resulted in a low rate of investment, output growth and slow productivity growth.
Even the anaemic output growth of the period, especially after 1995 (when the
initial boost of neoliberal arrangements and institutions had lost steam and
profitability during the neoliberal period had peaked) was achieved through
the indirect impact of the financial bubbles created mostly by the expansive
monetary policy of that period. However, this euphoria became increasingly
divorced from 'real accumulation', leading to the burst bubbles in 2009 and the
eruption of the crisis, lagging two years from what had happened in the major
capitalist economies. Fundamentally, the crisis resurfaced due to the low profitability of capital, a result of capital overaccumulation caused by the rising
OCC.

Economakis, Androulakis and Markaki distinguish four basic phases.[26] The
first phase (1960–73) represents the 'golden era' of Greek capitalism when the
profit rate increased significantly, peaking in 1973 (as OCC was low for this
period). Wages increased but with a significant lag behind labour productivity, leading to a decreasing labour share. The 1973 crisis ended the postwar
'golden age' of Greek capitalism. During the next phase (1974–85), profitability declined as labour struggles intensified after the fall of the dictatorship. Also
the OCC increased, contributing to the falling profitability trend. The decline in
profitability of this period ended in 1985, when neoliberal restrictive policies
were inaugurated. The 1986–2006 phase of neoliberalism was characterised
by a weak recovery of profitability that stayed well below the levels achieved
during the 'golden age' of Greek capitalism. There was also a non-significant
decrease in the OCC because there was insufficient destruction of capital during the crisis. The last phase is that of the crisis (2007–12). During that phase
there is a rapid fall in profitability leading to the lowest levels for the entire
1960–2012 period. This is accompanied by a dramatic increase in the OCC. The
main conclusion of Economakis, Androulakis and Markaki is that the Greek
crisis is essentially a competitiveness crisis. Additionally, they argue that the
deep depression that followed the troika austerity policies has led to a sharp

---

26    Economakis, Androulakis and Markaki 2015.

decline in profitability, mainly because of the resultant fall in demand. This underconsumption, however, is only the form of appearance of Greek capitalism's deeper problems as its previous development model became unsustainable.

Mavroudeas and Paitaridis have proposed a third Marxist explanation that also recognises the TRPF as the fundamental cause of both the 1973 and the 2007–8 crises.[27] This explanation – similarly to the first Marxist explanation and dissimilarly to the second – employs the distinction between productive and unproductive labour and measures its variables accordingly (i.e. for the productive sector and not for the whole economy). Another important feature of this explanation is the importance placed upon the 'external' dimension. It is argued that Greece's is a middle-range capitalism with limited imperialist abilities that strives to exploit other areas and at the same time falls prey to the exploitation from its more developed western partners.

Three major postwar periods are discerned. During the 'golden age' (1960–73) Greek capitalism exhibited a remarkable profitability leading to a strong growth rate and also increased competitiveness; all of them leading to the ascendance within the international division of labour. However, the Greek postwar 'golden era' differed substantially from the western one, inasmuch as it did not include a developed welfare state and was based on the suppression of wages. Moreover, it had a significant imperialist component as Greek capitals expanded remarkably their activities, particularly in the Mediterranean area and in the Middle East. As in the more developed western capitalisms, the 1973 global crisis put an end to Greek capitalism's 'golden era'. The 1973 crisis in Greece was an overaccumulation crisis caused by the TRPF. It was triggered by the slowdown of the rate of surplus value and the rapid increase in the OCC. Moreover, the 1973 crisis coincided with the fall of the dictatorship, which further limited the ability of capital to exploit labour. In order to defuse the post-dictatorship radicalism, Greek capital resorted to progressive income redistribution policies. Greek capitalism's evolution was de-coupled from the West: it adopted Keynesian income redistribution policies later than the West and at a time when the latter turned to neoliberalism. At the same time, Greek capital made the strategic choice to participate in the European integration process in order to upgrade itself from a middle-range imperialism to a partner in one of the major global imperialist blocs. This contemporary 'Big Idea' of Greek capitalism was fraught with risks from its very beginning. Especially, it led to a declining competitiveness that caused a deteriorating

---

27    Mavroudeas and Paitaridis 2015b.

current account deficit. However, these Keynesian policies failed to bolster the profit rate because they applied the successful postwar western recipes in totally different socio-economic conditions. Postwar growth-boosting Keynesian policies were successful because the war had devalorised the previously overaccumulated capitals. This was not the case with the 1973 crisis as capitals remained critically overaccumulated in the aftermath of the crisis. Therefore, as soon as the post-dictatorship popular radicalism was checked, Greek capital abandoned progressive Keynesian policies and turned to capitalist restructuring policies, inaugurating thus its second postwar era (1985–2007).

This period was marked by capitalist restructuring waves, which strived to reverse the falling profitability and the overaccumulation of capital. Their policies revitalised the counteracting forces to the TRPF by (a) increasing the rate of surplus value, (b) reducing the value of labour power, (c) reducing the value of constant capital, (d) reducing turnover time, (e) increasing foreign trade, and (f) reaping imperialist extra-profits from abroad. These restructurings were only partially successful. There was a recovery of the profit rate but this never reached the level achieved in the beginning of its fall. Moreover, capital was insufficiently devalorised as Greek capitalism shied away from the deep and painful devalorisation required. Thus the fundamental problems remained and the 'financialisation' tricks and the 'artificial growth' only postponed and at the same time augmented them.

The 2007–8 crisis abruptly ended this euphoria. The 'artificial boom' collapsed and the underlying profitability crisis resurfaced. The 'financialisation' deus ex machina postponed the crisis but, at the same time, exacerbated the problem of overaccumulation. As soon as productive capital's profitability started to deteriorate, crisis re-emerged in all its glory. 'Financialisation' gave only a temporary respite to the crisis of profitability but at a very high cost. It increased significantly the portion of surplus value extracted by productive capital but accruing to money capital. This further aggravated the falling profitability of productive capital and set the whole house on fire. Additionally, imperialist extra-profits collapsed as the Balkan economies entered recession and competition with other stronger imperialisms was aggravated. In addition, the global financial collapse ended cheap credit. Thus, Greek capitalism abruptly fell into crisis.

This crisis is characterised as a dual crisis of overaccumulation (caused by the TRPF) and imperialist exploitation (that traumatised Greek capital's profitability and productive structure). This dual crisis took the form of the twin deficits (fiscal and current account deficit). The fiscal deficit was augmented because the state rushed to subsidise the private sector. The current account deficit was already worsening because of the falling competitiveness of Greek capital vis-à-vis its western competitors. Then the one reciprocally worsened the other. That is, contrary to the Mainstream twin deficits hypothesis, both deficits are expressions of the falling profitability of Greek capitalism.

## 2      Alternative Economic Strategies

This section delineates the basic alternative scenarios and their variations for exiting the Greek crisis. Two are the main tenets behind this scheme. The first is that the Greek crisis is a structural one and the twin deficits (fiscal and current account) are not the cause but the result. This choice was explained in the previous sections. The second tenet is that the structural characteristics of the Greek crisis depend crucially upon the relationship of Greece with the EU. This choice stems from the following reasons. First, the Greek crisis is part of the EU crisis. It came about, to a great extent, because of Greece's accession to the EU. Additionally, once the crisis erupted, its course was crucially charted by policies dictated by the EU. Second, the accession to the European integration project was and remains a strategic choice for the Greek bourgeoisie (for its own interests) whereas popular interests were at variance from this from the outset. This divergence increased since the eruption of the crisis and the imposition of the EAPs. Consequently, the relation to the EU has a profound secular impact upon the future course of the Greek economy. In a nutshell, it is posited that the Greek economy requires a radical structural overhauling (solving also its debt problem) and its relation to the EU critically shapes the form of this restructuring.

Two basic scenarios are discerned. The first scenario suggests the restructuring of the Greek economy according to the prerogatives and the constraints of European integration. The second scenario proposes the restructuring of the Greek economy outside the framework of the EU. Moreover, the first scenario is subdivided into two versions. The first version is the pro-cyclical austerity policy of the Greek EAPs formulated by the troika (the EU, the ECB, and the IMF). This version proposes negotiation of the EAPs that keeps the bail-out loans and aspects of the fiscal consolidation and structural restructuring, but adds some anti-cyclical elements together with a pause in the austerity policies (through some form of neo-Keynesian policy mixes). The second basic scenario is also subdivided into two versions. The first version suggests exiting from only the EMU. The second version deems as necessary the complete disengagement from both the EMU and the EU.

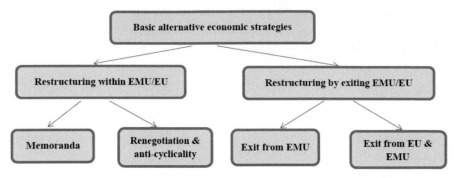

FIGURE 1.2  *Basic alternative scenarios and their variations*

### *Restructuring within the EMU/EU*
#### The EAPs' Strategy

The Greek EAPs constitute the Mainstream strategy of solving the crisis that has been imposed upon Greece by the unequal alliance between the EU's dominant countries and the Greek bourgeoisie (in the sense that the former have the upper hand and the latter concedes, fearing the worse and despite losing ground). It follows the Mainstream conceptions of the crisis as a 'Greek disease' leading to a debt crisis on the basis of the TDH. Their guiding principle is that Greek capitalism's restructuring should take place within the EU's framework. This implies that the Greek economy will become even more a part of EU value chains and follow the EU's transnational prerogatives rather than adopt a self-centred path. Given the small size and the inferior productivity and technical expertise of the Greek economy, this choice necessarily dictates that Greece will remain – and even be demoted further to – a middle- to low-class appendage of these trans-European value chains producing low value-added goods on the basis of low wages and cheap assets. In a nutshell, given the course of the intra-imperialist struggles between the EU and the other major global capitalist blocs, Greece is destined to be part of the group of European poor and dependent 'special economic zones'.[28] This group of countries has limited economic sovereignty and plays a peripheral role to the EU's core economies.

The EAPs' central aim is to solve the debt crisis and at the same time restructure the Greek economy. Solving the debt crisis is necessary since Greek debt is unviable. But this cannot be done – or even if accomplished, it will not last – with the current productive structure. Moreover, the course of the global recession dictates the restructuring of the EU's 'architecture' and the creation of

---

28      Mavroudeas 2012b.

these European 'special economic zones'. This very ambitious task in itself is complicated further by the persistence of the global recession and the concomitant aggravation of intra-imperialist clashes.

The Greek EAPs are modified versions of the IMF's Structural Adjustment Programmes (SAPs) formulated in the 1980s under the auspices of the Washington Consensus (that is, the fusion of neoliberal and conservative Keynesian views regarding the world economy). These are pro-cyclical programmes[29] in the sense that their measures (austerity, etc.) consciously deepen the crisis, believing that in this way it will 'bottom' sooner and the rebound will also be very strong (V-shaped recovery). This view rejects the postwar Keynesian orthodoxy that dictated first anti-cyclical measures to alleviate the crisis and afterwards structural changes to avoid future crises. Essentially, neoconservative pro-cyclical views mimic, in a distorted way, Marxism's argument that capitalism can surpass an overaccumulation crisis only by drastic capital devalorisation (i.e. through destruction and reconstitution).

SAPs' prescription for ailing and debt-ridden economies is the following:

(1)  Fiscal consolidation (to reduce fiscal deficit);
(2)  Labour Market deregulation (to improve competitiveness);
(3)  Restructuring the economy from public-sector based to private-sector driven (through privatisations);
(4)  Currency devaluation (to improve competitiveness);
(5)  Opening up of the economy (to attract foreign capital);
(6)  Debt restructuring (to alleviate the debt burden).

Their purported aim is to create an open, competitive economy relying on export-growth and foreign direct investment. The implicit objective is to subjugate it to western multinational enterprises.

The Greek EAPs follow this prescription with significant modifications because this is the first time such a large programme has been implemented in a developed capitalist economy and an EMU member. Because of the immediate failure of the 1st EAP, the Greek EAPs are four-year programmes (contrary to IMF's three-year tradition). There is no devaluation (because of the EMU) and thus a greater burden is placed upon 'internal devaluation' (i.e. austerity on wages). There was only a belated and insufficient debt restructuring (with the 2nd EAP) because the EU's dominant countries rejected it for political and economic reasons. Additionally, the Greek programme is front-loaded (contrary

---

29    Weisbrot et al. 2009.

to the IMF's advice) because the EU wanted to solve the problem soon and avoid contagion to the rest of the Eurozone. For all these reasons, the Greek programme is a very problematic one. This has been verified by its systematic failure to reach its milestones[30] and its obvious inability to achieve its final target (a 120% debt to GDP ratio by 2020).

In Mainstream debates this systematic failure has been attributed to the underestimation of the fiscal multiplier.[31] In other words, the structural changes (i.e. making the private sector the locomotive of the economy and the shrinkage of the public sector) had a bigger recessionary effect on the economy than originally envisaged. What is usually brushed under the carpet in these debates is the fact that the purported substitution of public activities by private ones did not happen, for a very good reason. In a crisis (and in the midst of a global economic downturn), where structural changes with an uncertain outcome are implemented, no private capital (with the possible exception of adventurers and cronies) invests.

However, the fundamental problem of the EAPs' strategy is much broader. Both its immediate and its structural measures disrupt Greek capitalism's entire postwar architecture and have profound political and economic consequences. First, they violently change capital's internal structure, which affects corporate groups, the sectoral structure, the import-export balance, etc. This means that powerful economic groups of the past are at risk while new ones are trying to emerge. As this process is very painful and takes time, it makes intra-capitalist rivalries and conflicts extremely brutal. Furthermore, foreign capital expands at the expense of domestic capital. Second, small and medium enterprises (SMEs) – a traditionally strong branch – are shrinking rapidly as the concentration and centralisation of capital proceeds very intensively. This pushes the small bourgeoisie – which historically was massive compared to Western standards – towards proletarianisation and undermines one of capital's fundamental class alliances. Moreover, it destabilises crucial economic processes that are not adequately replenished by other ones. Third, the living standards of the great majority of the population have to be reduced from that of a euro-periphery country to that of a Balkan or even a Third World economy. Only with such a rapid devaluation of the value of labour power and a corresponding increase in labour's exploitation can profitability recover. Fourth, it is

---

30    For example, for the period from May 2010 to May 2013, GDP forecasts have been revised
      downwards eight times. Similarly, the forecasts for the required fiscal austerity measures
      have changed from 25 bn. initially to 66 bn.
31    Blanchard and Leigh 2013.

only in this way (i.e. through a large depreciation of capital and a simultaneous increase in its profitability), that Greek capitalism can emerge from its
crisis and resume the process of capital accumulation (i.e. economic growth).
But this requires a deeper and more prolonged recession than the one envisaged, as the private sector is reluctant to take the risk of restructuring and the
public sector is weakened. In addition, the restart of economic growth does
not mean the end of austerity but the opposite. In order to sustain the capital profitability, austerity should be continued and deepened. Otherwise the
recovery of capitalist accumulation will stop again and recession will return.
Finally, even when the process of capitalist accumulation restarts, this will happen with Greek capitalism downgraded and weakened within the international
capitalist system.

Summarising, the heavy-handedness of the project violently disrupts crucial
economic and social balances. This transposes the crisis from its primarily economic ground to the social and political field, and can lead at any time (even
in a phase where normal economic growth might seem restored) to uncon-
trollable socio-political turbulence. Nevertheless, the Greek and the EU ruling
classes know there is no alternative. The Keynesian proposal of anti-cyclical
policy and mild austerity – because even Keynesian scenarios accept some kind
of austerity – cannot resolve the crisis. The conservative New Keynesian policy
of stimulating demand – which is the only one discussed in official and social-
democratic circles – does not envisage any kind of pro-labour income redistribution but mainly anti-recessionary measures which limit capital's devalorisation. These policies may smoothen the course of the crisis (at least in the beginning), but instead of solving the problem of overaccumulation, they exacerbate
it. Thus, ultimately, they extend and deepen the crisis instead of solving it.

### Renegotiation and Anti-cyclicality

Juxtaposed to the EAPs' strategy, an alternative strategy within framework of
European integration is being proposed from official Greek circles (like the
soon betrayed New Democracy's 2012 electoral programme and SYRIZA's 2015
one) and also several international circles. It follows, implicitly or explicitly,
the conservative Keynesian logic outlined before and suffers from the same
deficiencies. It stems from either the 3rd Mainstream explanation or some
of the Radical explanations. Essentially, it accepts EAPs' bigger role, but asks
for a partial renegotiation of this with the aim of blending it with elements
of anti-cyclicality (implying reduced austerity). This leads to smoothening the
programme's heavy-handedness and extending its schedule.

SYRIZA's 2015 governmental programmatic declarations exemplify this view.
First, they asked for an extension of the loan repayment schedule, reducing

cash-flow problems. This might involve a debt roll-over, a 'development clause' (linking loan repayment to growth), and an interest rate reduction (although these are already low). Second, they envisage some discreet measures assuaging the burden placed on labour (some labour market reregulation, measures combating unemployment, increasing minimum wages and poorer pensions) and a limited increase in the Public Investment Programme (PIP). Third, a European investment plan (seldom called 'Marshall plan') is asked to regenerate economic activity. Practically, the two last clauses suggest the introduction of some counter-cyclical policies. Unsurprisingly, following from the weak structural Mainstream and Radical explanations that lay behind it, this strategy does not propose a blueprint for the restructuring of the Greek economy. Therefore, and by limiting its framework within European integration, it is not a self-centred development strategy and necessarily succumbs to the EU's dominant prerogatives that lead to the 'China-isation' of the euro-periphery.

The compromise proposed by this strategy is unattainable and, for this reason, the latter is unrealistic. The logic of pro-cyclical restructuring is completely opposed to that of anti-cyclical restructuring and cannot coexist peacefully. The anti-cyclical restructuring requires much more time and has ambiguous results. In contrast, the pro-cyclical restructuring reflects the very underlying logic of the capitalist system. The case of anti-cyclical expansion and restructuring has been tested in Greece after the 1973 crisis with disappointing results – from the perspective of the system. The main reason for the failure was that a capitalist crisis of overaccumulation cannot be dealt with by a further strengthening of capital accumulation even if accompanied by austerity policies against labour. Only with a sufficient devalorisation of the overaccumulated capitals can capitalism resume a relatively sustainable accumulation. The example of the postwar 'golden age' – both in the West and in Greece – is typical. Expansionary macroeconomic policies have managed to trigger a relatively long period of high growth because the destruction of capital during the war (and the corresponding discipline and intensification of labour) preexisted. The only case, in current circumstances, in which such a policy mix can take place is if the EAPs' pro-cyclical programme has succeeded. Then there might be room for a respite by adopting some anti-cyclical measures in order to let off some socio-political steam. So long as the prospects of the Greek crisis remain ambivalent, the possibility for such a policy mix is minimal.

For all these reasons and not because of some purported ideological blindness, the EU's dominant centres vehemently reject this strategy for the time being.

### *Restructuring by Exiting the EMU/EU*
#### Exit from the EMU

This alternative – that proposes exiting from the EMU while remaining in the EU – stems from some of the Radical explanations of the Greek crisis. It is subdivided into a variant that supports a confrontational exit from the EMU and another that supports a consensual exit. The first is proposed in confrontation with the EU as 'blackmail' to achieve better treatment within the EU. The second is proposed as a compromise with the EU.

The rationale behind this proposal is the following. It is argued that by leaving the EMU, Greece will re-acquire the tools of monetary and exchange rate policy. Then through a competitive devaluation it will improve the competitiveness of internationally tradable Greek products. This will improve the trade balance and ultimately the external current account balance. Also, because of the increase in the price of imported products, this process will lead to a certain productive restructuring, as there will be import-substitution. Its first part (i.e. improving competitiveness through devaluation) is itself extremely vulnerable. To achieve a significant and sustainable increase in competitiveness, currency devaluation is not enough as, by itself, the latter has only short-lived effects. A significant improvement in competitiveness requires profound changes in the production structure of the economy that require considerable time. For example, the existing structure of exports makes this extremely problematic as the main part of these exports (e.g. oil derivatives) depends on imports of intermediate goods. At this point the answer is provided by the second part of this strategy (i.e. import substitution). But here a crucial dilemma arises. If this process is left to private initiative, it is extremely slow and uncertain as to its depth and intensity. If promoted through state intervention, it requires economic planning and very strong and discreet industrial policy that is prohibited within the European Common Market.

The main weakness of this strategy is that it ignores the deep structural problems of the Greek economy and tries to come to terms with them indirectly through the monetary channel. The consensual version of the necessary restructuring impinges upon the EU's institutional prohibitions. The confrontational variant leads necessarily to the total exit from both the EMU and the EU. But this corollary is either ignored or evaded by the proponents of this variant. Consequently, this strategy is incomplete and unrealistic.

#### Exit from the EU and the EMU

This alternative strategy is the complete opposite to the EAPs' strategy. It stems from the Marxist explanations that recognise the deep structural character of the Greek crisis. It derives from the recognition that Greek capitalism's crisis has been shaped radically and aggravated further by its participation in the European imperialist integration in general – not only in the EMU. More specifically, Greece's structural problems began with its accession to the European Common Market. Its accession to the EMU simply aggravated some of their aspects. This is more explicitly pronounced by Mavroudeas and Paitaridis,[32] who show that Greek capitalism suffers from imperialist exploitation (i.e. expropriation of value) by its more developed EU partners. This imperialist exploitation is based on unequal exchange in trade (based on the difference of OCCs, i.e. different productive and technological structures) as expressed in Greece's worsening terms of trade. It is further compounded by the incorporation of the Greek economy as part of EU-wide value chains (i.e. supra-national production chains). Given – among other things – the small size, the geographical position and morphology and, particularly, the mid- to low technological and productive expertise of the Greek economy, it necessarily ended as a lower part of these value chains. Additionally, this led to:

(a)   Greece's extensive (but not complete) deindustrialisation (as either the finished manufactures or their intermediate inputs are to a great extent imported);
(b)   the degradation of Greece's primary sector (caused to a great extent by the Common Agricultural Policy);
(c)   the creation of an hypertrophic services sector (because of tourism and the flight of Greek capitals to the covertly protected non-internationally tradable sectors).

The EMU augmented these structural problems both internally (e.g. by worsening income distribution and facilitating imports) and externally (e.g. as the euro's high exchange rate hit extra-EU competitiveness). Consequently, Greece's incorporation into the European imperialist integration led to the worsening of its position in the international division of labour and the rapid deterioration of the living and working conditions of workers and the middle classes.

This strategy argues that in the context of the European imperialist integration, there is no positive outlook for the working people in Greece. Therefore, it proposes the total exit from the EU and the adoption of a self-centred development model for the Greek economy geared towards working people's interests. This is a progressive developmentalist strategy aiming to restructure Greece's economy (and especially its productive structure) in an internally consistent

---

32    Mavroudeas and Paitaridis 2015b.

manner (i.e. creating strong national inter-sectoral forward and backward link-ages) and by favouring labour's interests (against those of capital). It is organised along short-term and long-term axes. The short-term axes are:

(1) Default on the external debt. Apart from the moral and political justifications, this option has to do with the fact that, objectively, the Greek external debt is unviable.
(2) Imposition of capital controls in order to prevent capitals' flight abroad and secure the banking sector.
(3) Nationalisation of the banking system, as it has been already rescued – within the EAPs' provisions – by public money but without acquiring ownership and management. Additionally, this option is necessary in order to use it to finance development.
(4) Tax reform reversing the tax repressiveness of previous systems (benefiting the wealthier strata) and creating a progressive tax system (i.e. increasing the tax burden for the wealthier and alleviating it for the poorer). This must be coupled with the elimination of capitals' notorious tax evasion.
(5) Exit from the EMU, introduction of a new currency and a managed exchange rate policy. This can combine a controlled devaluation (to boost short- and mid-term competitiveness) in combination with a system of price controls (to avoid any undue inflationary increases in particular types of mass consumption goods). The exchange rate policy can also draw on a series of other tools (e.g. a system of multiple exchange rates, barter trade, currency swaps, etc.).
(6) Exit from the EU (that is, the Common Market and the political framework) in order to allow for the implementation of this programme.

The main long-term and simultaneously crucial element of this strategy is the creation of an economic reconstruction plan. This would be based on the public sector and implemented through public investment. It should be constructed via broad democratic procedures, cover the whole economy, and have – at least in its major parts – a directive and not an indicative character. Moreover, the reconstruction of key areas and sectors of the economy – particularly those of strategic importance – should be under public control and/or ownership.

The fundamental merits of this alternative strategy are that (a) it is based on an accurate diagnosis of the structural problems of the Greek economy, and (b) it proposes a radical pro-labour solution rather than intermediate and questionable compromises. Of course, its implementation requires radical political and social changes in Greek society.

## Conclusions

This chapter has argued that the Greek crisis is a deeply structural one. It derives from long-term structural deficiencies and is exacerbated by Greece's incorporation in the EU. Marxist explanations are better at grasping this fact than their Mainstream and Radical counterparts. Their superiority stems, to a great extent, from their analytical focus on real accumulation and long-term processes.

The alternative strategies for surpassing the Greek crisis reflect, *grosso modo*, the different streams of explanations. It is argued that the EAPs' strategy represents the basic Mainstream perspective. It is an analytically weak and politically risky project but, at the same time, it is the only way for capital. Its direct adversary is the strategy of reconstructing the Greek economy outside the EU and on the basis of labour's interest. This chapter argues that it is the latter strategy that can offer a way forward for the Left and the labour movement. On the contrary, middle-of-the-road strategies – like mixing the EAPs with anti-cyclical elements, or leaving the EMU but remaining within the EU – are deemed unrealistic and unstable.

## References

Argitis, George 2012, *Bankruptcy and Economic Crisis: Failure and Breakdown of the Greek Model of Capitalism*, [in Greek] Athens: Alexandreia.

Blanchard, Olivier and Daniel Leigh 2013, *Growth Forecast Errors and Fiscal Multipliers*, IMF Working Paper.

De Grauwe, Paul 2010, 'The Greek Crisis and the Future of the Eurozone', *EuroIntelligence*, March.

Economakis, George, George Androulakis and Maria Markaki 2015, 'Profitability and Crisis in the Greek Economy (1960–2012): An Investigation', in *Greek Capitalism in Crisis: Marxist Analyses*, edited by Stavros Mavroudeas, London: Routledge.

European Commission 2010, *The Economic Adjustment Programme for Greece*, EUROPEAN ECONOMY Occasional Papers no. 61, available at: http://ec.europa.eu/economy_finance/publications/occasional_paper/2010/pdf/ocp61_en.pdf

Feldstein, Martin 2010, 'The Euro's Fundamental Flaws: The Single Currency was Bound to Fail', *International Economy*, Spring: 11–12.

Hilferding, Rudolf 1981 [1910], *Finance Capital*, London: Routledge.

Krugman, Paul 2012, 'The Revenge of the Optimum Currency Area', *New York Times*, 24 June.

Lapavitsas Costas 2008, 'Financialised Capitalism: Direct Exploitation and Periodic Bubbles', SOAS.

Lapavitsas Costas, Annina Kaltenbrunner, Duncan Lindo, Joe Michell, Jesus Painceira, E. Pires, Jeff Powell, Alexis Stenfors and Nuno Teles 2010, 'Eurozone in Crisis: Beggar Thyself and Thy Neighbour', *Research on Money and Finance*, Occasional Report.

Laskos, Christos and Euclid Tsakalotos 2011, *No Turning Back: Capitalist Crises, Social Needs, Socialism*, [in Greek], Athens: KaPsiMi editions.

Maniatis, Thanassis and Costas Passas 2015, 'The Law of the Falling Rate of Profit in the Post-War Greek Economy', in *Greek Capitalism in Crisis: Marxist Analyses*, edited by Stavros Mavroudeas, London: Routledge.

Mavroudeas, Stavros 2012a, *The Limits of Regulation: A Critical Analysis of Capitalist Development*, Cheltenham: Edward Elgar.

Mavroudeas, Stavros 2012b, 'The Crisis of the European Union and the Failure of Its "Salvation Plans"', *Spectrezine*, available at: http://www.spectrezine.org/crisis-european-union-and-failure-its-%E2%80%98salvation-plans%E2%80%99

Mavroudeas, Stavros (ed.), 2015a, *Greek Capitalism in Crisis: Marxist Analyses*, London: Routledge.

Mavroudeas, Stavros 2015b, 'Financialisation and the Greek case', in *Greek capitalism in crisis: Marxist Analyses*, edited by Stavros Mavroudeas, London: Routledge.

Mavroudeas, Stavros and Dimitris Paitaridis 2015a, 'Mainstream Accounts of the Greek Crisis: More Heat than Light?', in *Greek Capitalism in Crisis: Marxist Analyses*, edited by Stavros Mavroudeas, London: Routledge.

Mavroudeas, Stavros and Dimitris Paitaridis 2015b, 'The Greek Crisis: A Dual Crisis of Overaccumulation and Imperialist Exploitation', in *Greek Capitalism in Crisis: Marxist Analyses*, edited by Stavros Mavroudeas, London: Routledge.

Milios, John and Dimitris Sotiropoulos 2010, 'Crisis of Greece or crisis of the euro? A view from the European "periphery"', *Journal of Balkan and Near Eastern Studies*, 12, 3: 223–240.

Mundell, Robert 1961, 'A Theory of Optimum Currency Areas', *The American Economic Review*, 51, 4: 657–65.

Nikiforos, Michalis, Laura Carvalho and Christian Schoder 2014, 'Twin Deficits in Greece: In Search of Causality', *IMK Working Paper* no. 143, December.

Stathakis, George 2010, 'The Fiscal Crisis of the Greek Economy', Paper presented in 1st conference of the International Initiative for Promoting Political Economy and the Greek Scientific Association of Political Economy, 10–12 September, University of Crete.

Weisbrot, Mark, Rebecca Ray, Jose Cordero and Juan Montesino 2009, 'IMF-Supported Macroeconomic Policies and the World Recession: A Look at Forty-One Borrowing Countries', Washington, D.C.: CERP.

# CHAPTER 2

# Imperialist Exploitation and Crisis of the Greek Economy: a Study

*George Economakis, Maria Markaki, George Androulakis and Alexios Anastasiadis*

## Introduction

The United States' economic crisis appeared at the epicentre of the recent global economic crisis. It has been previously evidenced[1] that during the neo-liberal era the profit rate of the US non-financial corporate business sector recovered, without however reaching its mid-1940s and mid-1960s historical levels.[2] In close relation to the re-regulations, which took place during the neo-liberal era, a feeble profit rate recovery paved the way for the boom of the financial sector. From this point of view, the recent US economic crisis can be interpreted as a possible result of a 'plethora' of profit-seeking capital in the financial sector,[3] rather than a crisis of 'financialisation'.[4] However, US economic crisis fuelled a global credit risk reassessment and within these circumstances the Greek economic crisis emerged.[5] In this respect and considering the high Greek public debt,[6] it is not surprising that the majority of the Greek Marxist Left initially considered the Greek economic crisis – and bankruptcy – as a mere 'public debt crisis'. However, if the high public debt were the main cause

---

1 Economakis, Anastasiadis and Markaki 2010.
2 Economakis et al. 2010, pp. 479 ff.
3 Economakis et al. 2010, p. 486.
4 For a critique of the 'financialisation thesis' as the interpretation of the recent economic crisis, see Mavroudeas 2015, pp. 84–9.
5 The global economic crisis turned part of private debt into public debt, which led to a crisis of insolvency, due to the soaring of interest rates. Thus, the global crisis appeared as a public debt crisis (Milios 2011; see also Economakis, Androulakis and Markaki 2015, p. 130; see also in this volume Zisimopoulos and Economakis).
6 The Greek public debt as a percentage of Gross Domestic Product (GDP) is much higher than the Eurozone public debt (see Economakis, Androulakis and Markaki 2015, p. 130). The consolidated debt of the general government, as a percentage of GDP, had reached 110% of GDP in 2005 (Bank of Greece 2013, p. 41, Table 22). For a further analysis of Greek public debt, see in this volume Zisimopoulos and Economakis.

of an economic crisis and bankruptcy, then other economies would have been bankrupt before Greece, e.g. the Japanese, whose gross public debt as a percentage of GDP reached 248% in 2015.[7]

From a completely different perspective, other Marxists examine the Greek economic crisis primarily in the context of the 'law' of the falling rate of profit. According to this point of view, 'inadequate profitability remains the fundamental cause of crisis ... and this holds true for the case of the Greek economy as well'.[8] Thus, the crisis of the Greek economy should be examined through the prism of 'the Marxian law of the tendency of the rate of profit to fall'.[9] Yet, as it has been previously evidenced,[10] during the period 2007–12 the rising of the intensity of net capital stock (or the net capital stock per employee, which resembles the Marxian technical composition of capital), which impacts negatively on profitability, was mainly due not to the net capital stock increase, but to the employment reduction, under the impact of a very important reduction in the capacity utilisation ratio. Consequently, in the given technological level, intensity of net capital stock rise implies underemployment of capital, due to the reduction of capacity utilisation ratio, i.e. to the activation of the underconsumptionist aspect of the crisis.

However, in the conjuncture of global economic crisis, underconsumption is only a visible aspect of deeper problems of Greek capitalism, i.e. of the model of its development in the 2000s.

After entering the Eurozone, and before the global economic crisis, the Greek economy displayed a high growth rate, as expressed by the GDP's average growth rate. Between 2000 and 2007 the net domestic product increased in constant prices (2005) by 31.41%.[11] However, this period of 'over-growth' was also a period of high current account deficit,[12] which created a need for

---

7    OECD. Stat Extracts. In Japan's example we can, however, point out other important macroeconomic variables (such as household net saving rates, current account balance, etc.), which make the public debt only a part of the economic problem and not the actual problem (see Economakis, Androulakis and Markaki 2015, p. 131).

8    Maniatis and Passas 2015, p. 107.

9    Ibid.

10    Economakis, Androulakis and Markaki 2015, p. 147.

11    OECD. Stat Extracts, own calculations; see also Economakis, Markaki and Androulakis 2014.

12    The current account balance is steadily negative and deteriorating from the mid-1990s until 2008, when the single EU market was introduced (in 1993) and the drachma was revaluated in real terms (in order to join the European single currency). These developments removed the Greek economy's ability to use measures of trade protectionism or exchange rate policy as a means of addressing the competition of foreign goods – the latter even before Greece's entry into the Eurozone. The current account deficit reduction

increasing external borrowing.[13] More specifically, after entering the Eurozone, the Greek economy based its development on the growth of productive sectors which were not exposed to international competition (non-tradable goods and services). Furthermore, this was even more pronounced compared to the EU-27 as a whole. Therefore, the model of economic growth of Greece during the 2000s was not based upon improvementof its international competitive position and it did not lead to increased competitiveness.[14] The rising incomes in the sectors of non-tradable commodities augmented the demand of tradable ones from abroad, reproducing high deficits in the balance of goods and services.[15] The significant reduction in the cost of domestic borrowing in the 2000s led to the reproduction of this model of development[16] based on 'over-consumerism' and manifested primarily as 'high propensity to consume imported goods'.[17] This 'over-consumerism' of imported goods is related to the 'intensely consumerist type of the Greek economy',[18] and hence to the low level of domestic savings.[19] The coverage of the current account deficit had to be financed with equal net capital inflows. In 2000–8, the financing of the current account deficit relied on international capital market funding, mainly through the issuance of bonds and Treasury bills[20] that eventually created debt. So, the financing of the current account deficit did not rely on FDI that would create development instead of debt.[21] Economic growth with a high current account deficit reached its limit in 2007 when the onset of global economic

---

after 2008 reflects, among other things, the reduction of the trade deficit because of the depression and the consequent reduction in import payments and the increase in exports, which is attributed to the improvement in cost competitiveness (i.e. labour costs reduction) (see Economakis, Androulakis and Markaki 2015, pp. 131–2; see also below).

13   The gross external debt (of private and public sector) is powered by current account deficit. The Greek economy exhibits a serious deterioration of the gross external debt. The gross external debt from 138.25% of the GDP in 2007 (Bank of Greece 2013, p. 38, Table 19) is expected to reach 229.48% of the GDP in 2013 (Bank of Greece 2014, p. 89, Table v.16).

14   Economakis, Androulakis and Markaki 2015, p. 134; see also Economakis, Markaki and Anastasiadis 2015; Economakis et al. 2014.

15   Economakis, Androulakis and Markaki 2015, p. 134; see also Economakis, Markaki and Anastasiadis 2015; Economakis et al. 2014.

16   Economakis, Androulakis and Markaki 2015, p. 135; see also Economakis et al. 2014.

17   Bank of Greece 2011, p. 8.

18   Fotopoulos 2010, p. 51.

19   Economakis, Androulakis and Markaki 2015, p. 131; see also Economakis et al. 2014.

20   Bank of Greece 2012, p. 96.

21   Bank of Greece 2012, p. 93; see also Lapavitsas et al. 2010, pp. 9, 11–13; Economakis, Androulakis and Markaki 2015, p. 133; Economakis et al. 2014.

crisis blocked this model of development. In the conjuncture of the global economic crisis, as the financial sphere entered a process of reassessment of credit
risks, the transfer of 'savings' from the European 'centre' to the European 'periphery' stopped.[22] The ensuing implementation of the austerity measures of the
Memoranda, which followed the recourse of Greece to the financial support
mechanism of the Troika (European Commission, European Central Bank and
International Monetary Fund) in 2010, blocked capitalist reproduction, displaying an underconsumption crisis, deep depression and a rapid decrease in
profitability.[23] Thus, the Greek economy emerged as the main 'weak link' of the
EU-EMU 'imperialist chain'.

According to this study the deeper problems of Greek capitalism are attributed to its development model, and not to the high public debt or the rising
organic composition of capital. Greek capitalism follows an 'extraverted' model
of development within the frame of the EU-EMU, which implies low international competitiveness. It is this model of development that leads to systematic
transfers of value to the imperialist countries (expressed as persistent trade
deficits) forming the foundations of the current Greek economic crisis in the
conjuncture of the global economic crisis.[24] This is a process of value extraction, i.e. imperialist exploitation in the sphere of circulation, which expresses
the 'unevenness' of development with the EU-EMU. The crucial parameter
of this process is the dissimilarity of trade-production structure between the
Greek economy and the hard core of its commercial competitors (Eurozone),
which is expressed in the deterioration of the Greece terms of trade.

In the following analysis, we will investigate the aspects of the 'extraversion'
of Greek capitalism. We will initially address the theoretical frame of this study
in the following section.

1          **Theoretical Framework**

*Value Extraction in the Sphere of Circulation*[25]
Analysing the factors that counteract the manifestation of the 'law' of the
tendential fall in the profit rate, Marx writes on foreign trade:

---

22    See Milios 2011.

23    Economakis, Androulakis and Markaki 2015, pp. 135, 147–8.

24    From this point of view the contemporary Greek debt crisis and bankruptcy are attributed
      not only to the public debt, but also to the fact that the latter is emerging in the view of
      development 'unevenness' within the EU-EMU.

25    For a detailed analysis, see Economakis et al. 2014.

> Capital invested in foreign trade can yield a higher rate of profit [...] because it competes with commodities produced by other countries with less developed production facilities, so that the more advanced country sells its goods above their value, even though still more cheaply than its competitors. In so far as the labour of the more advanced country is here a labour of a higher specific weight, the profit rate rises, since labour that is not paid as qualitatively higher is nevertheless sold as such. The same relationship may hold towards the country to which goods are exported and from which goods are imported: i.e. such a country gives more objectified labour in kind than it receives, even though it still receives the goods in question more cheaply than it could produce them itself. In the same way, a manufacturer who makes use of a new discovery before this has become general sells more cheaply than his competitors and yet still sells above the individual value of his commodity, valorising the specifically higher productivity of the labour he employs as surplus labour. He thus realizes a surplus profit.[26]

Thus, 'the unevenness ... in world economy'[27] is one of the factors counteracting the manifestation of the Marxian 'law' of the tendential fall in the profit rate due to the rising organic composition of capital observed in more advanced countries.

This is a process of value (surplus value) extraction, i.e. imperialist exploitation in the sphere of circulation, as a consequence of uneven development in the 'imperialist chain'. Through value appropriation the more advanced (imperialist) countries 'shed' their crisis trends to the less advanced. Correspondingly, the less advanced countries experience potential crisis trends that break out as persistent trade deficits.

Therefore, '[t]he imperialist centre grows at the expense of the dominated bloc through the appropriation of value inherent in the system of international prices'.[28] Value appropriation by the imperialist countries, *ceteris paribus*, is realised through international *intra-sectoral* competition and *the terms of trade changing*, against the less advanced countries, in international *inter-sectoral* competition. In the following analysis, the value appropriation is examined

---

26    Marx 1991, pp. 344–5.
27    Lenin 2010, p. 118.
28    Carchedi 2001, p. 114. In this analysis, international prices are not production prices (see below).

without the 'binding' assumption of an internationally uniform profit rate and international production prices.[29]

### International Intra-sectoral Competition[30]

The various productive sectors are faced as direct competitors per like product at the international level. Thus, the international intra-sectoral competition of national capitals resembles the intra-sectoral competition at the national level. The international conditions of production, not the national ones, determine the value of commodities of a sphere (or sector) of production in the world market. Consequently, as a rule, the international sectoral value of a commodity is different from its national sectoral value. At the international level, the international market value is to be viewed as the average value of the commodities produced internationally in a particular sphere. Within the frame of international intra-sectoral competition, demand and supply must balance out in order for this international market value to emerge. This international market value constitutes the international 'market price'. Thus, what international intra-sectoral competition brings about is the establishment of a uniform international market value and market price out of the national values of commodities.

Assuming that at the international level there are no measures of trade protectionism (such as tariffs on imported goods and/or import quotas or export subsidies) and no distinct national currencies (i.e. a customs and monetary union exists), then the most productive national sectoral capitals of higher organic composition selling at the uniform international market price would be able to realise a surplus profit. Considering total national capitals (of a country), the (relatively) more advanced country could then realise a surplus profit

---

29    According to Busch (1987, pp. 59–60), the 'law of international equalization of profit rates' has as its starting point not the exports of capitals, but the international competition of unevenly developed capitals in commodity exports. The extent of international capital inflows-outflows and the international movement of labour do not create the conditions for the development of an international inter-sectoral competition; thus the conditions of an international uniform profit rate and of international production prices are not met. However, the international trade of unevenly developed capitals creates a 'slight tendency' of equation of international differences in national profit rates. Because of this tendency, the lower national average profit rates of the more advanced countries compared to the less advanced increase, and respectively the national average profit rates of the less advanced countries are negatively affected.

30    The analysis that follows is based on 'the theory of the modification of the law of value in the world market'. In connection with this, see among other works Busch 1983, 1987, 1992; Milios 2000; Economakis et al. 2014.

in the world market. Thus, the international intra-sectoral competition will result in the increase of the profit rates of the more advanced countries and respectively in the reduction of the profit rates of the less advanced countries. In this process, the trend of destruction of less productive national capitals will result in capital 'centralisation'.[31] This will eventually lead to the international dominance of the most productive capitals and to the trade deficits in less advanced countries. It should be emphasised that as this capital destruction occurs, a trend towards *dissimilar* production-trade structures between more and less advanced countries emerges. For the less advanced countries, these structural dissimilarities will be expressed as deteriorating terms of trade (see below).

Obviously, measures of protectionism (tariffs, etc. or national currency devaluation) could limit this process of destruction – provided that import prices are raised and export prices diminish.

### International Inter-sectoral Competition and Terms of Trade

The more advanced countries mostly produce and export commodities of higher organic composition of capital, higher technological level[32] and higher income elasticity of demand compared to those produced by the less advanced.[33] Thus, the more advanced countries compared to the less advanced fundamentally differ in the structure of production-trade. This *structural dissimilarity* is reflected in the different 'relative income elasticities' of demand (i.e. income elasticities of demand for an economy's exports against those for its imports)[34] and is expressed as 'disequilibrium between the structure of supply and the composition of demand'[35] for the less advanced countries.

The different 'relative income elasticities' of demand between more and less advanced countries suggest that as the income increases, the demand for the products from the more advanced countries is higher than that for the products from the less advanced (as a consequence of the so-called 'Engel's law'). This results, *ceteris paribus*, in faster growing prices of the products produced by the more advanced countries, i.e. the terms of trade change against the less advanced countries. Simultaneously, the price elasticity of demand for

---

31    Marx 1990, p. 777.

32    'Technological innovations reduce variable capital and increase constant capital (i.e. increase the OCC [organic composition of capital]) per unit of capital invested' (Carchedi 2001, p. 94).

33    Krugman 1989; Economakis, Markaki and Anastasiadis 2015; Economakis et al. 2014.

34    Krugman 1989.

35    Furtado 1964, p. 170.

the imports of the less advanced countries is low. As a result, the economic growth is accompanied by increasing import payments, i.e. trade deficits for the less advanced countries.[36]

In value terms, the faster increase in the prices of the products of the more advanced countries compared to those of the less advanced expresses a trend of rising *international market prices* of the first over their *international sectoral values* and correspondingly a trend of reduction of *international market prices* of the latter under their *international sectoral values*. It is a *trend* of international inter-sectoral *non-equivalent exchange*, in which the less advanced country 'gives more objectified labour in kind than it receives', per unit of invested capital. Thus, value is transferred from the less advanced countries (and capitals of lower organic composition) to the more advanced countries (and capitals of higher organic composition). This value extraction induces a trade deficit for the less advanced countries and trade surplus for the more advanced.

In conditions of dissimilarity in the structure of production-trade between the more and less advanced countries, any trade protectionist measures or national currency devaluation does not offer any protection for the less advanced countries. On the contrary, national currency devaluation will deteriorate the terms of trade of the less advanced countries.[37] As Carchedi suggests, national currency devaluation means that the exporters of more advanced countries 'appropriate more international value in its money form for each unit exported (disregarding ... whether exports are discouraged or not)'.[38]

### 'Extraverted' versus 'Autocentric' Economy[39]

The international competitiveness of a national economy refers to its ability 'to realise central economic policy goals, especially growth in income and employment, without running into balance-of-payments difficulties'.[40] The international competitiveness is not mainly dependent on 'price' or 'cost' factors that determine the 'price' or 'cost' competitiveness but on 'structural' factors – such as technological opportunities, technical infrastructure and production capacities. These factors constitute the productive structure and the related 'externalities' and determine the 'structural' competitiveness of a national economy.[41]

---

36    Economakis, Markaki and Anastasiadis 2015; Economakis et al. 2014.

37    Economakis et al. 2014.

38    Carchedi 2001, pp. 100–1.

39    The analysis is based on Economakis, Markaki and Anastasiadis 2015; see also Economakis et al. 2014.

40    Fagerberg 1988, p. 355.

41    Ilzkovitz, Dierx, Galgau, and Leib n.d., p. 2; Nurbel 2007, p. 65.

'*Kaldor's paradox*' confirms the validity of the distinction between 'price' or 'cost' and 'structural' competitiveness. According to 'Kaldor's paradox' there is

> a lack of empirical relationship between the growth in unit labour costs and output growth ... Kaldor found, for the postwar period, that those countries that had experienced the greatest decline in their price competitiveness (i.e., highest increase in unit labour costs) also had the greatest increase in their market share.[42]

The relative income elasticities of demand are systematically connected to the growth rates of a national economy and trade deficits.[43] On the other hand, the relative income elasticities of demand represent the 'structural' factors that determine the 'structural' competitiveness (and thus the international competitiveness), explaining 'Kaldor's paradox'[44] and expressing the terms of trade of a national economy.

The higher income elasticity of demand that characterises the exports of more advanced countries toward those of the less advanced reflects the greater diversification of the domestic production of the former toward the production of the latter.[45] Greater diversification of the productive structure of a national economy means a more complete, articulated and interdependent economic structure, i.e. greater domestic sectoral productive linkages. The latter strengthen 'the positive impact of economic growth on overall productivity'.[46] Thus, greater domestic sectoral productive linkages are related to the spillover effects, 'in terms of technology transfer and absorption'.[47]

Accordingly, the higher the income elasticity of export demand, the more diversified the production structure of a national economy, the greater the domestic sectoral productive linkages, and consequently, the higher its international competitiveness.[48]

The industries that depend primarily on their inter-industry transactions are those in manufacturing.[49] The development of manufacturing industry would

---

42    Felipe and Kumar 2011, pp. 3–4.
43    See also Thirlwall 1979; Krugman, 1989.
44    Fagerberg 1996.
45    Krugman 1989.
46    Peres 2006, p. 68.
47    Rios-Morales and O'Donovan 2006, pp. 55–6.
48    See Cimoli, Primi and Pugno 2006, p. 92; European Commission 2009, p. 75.
49    On the contrary, services are more independent from other sectors, in comparison to the manufacturing sector (Pilat and Wölfl 2005, pp. 3, 36).

generate domestic productive linkages, spillover effects, capital accumulation and technological externalities. Manufacturing industry is the 'driver of innovation and technological change',[50] given that it represents the main bulk of business expenditure on R&D.[51]

Therefore, there is *a structural interrelation* between the degree of diversification of the productive structure of a national economy, the strength of its domestic sectoral productive linkages, the level of its industrial and technological development (and the resultant externalities) and its international trade profile – as it is depicted by the relative income elasticities of demand which express the terms of trade.

Amin argues that an 'autocentric' economy has strong domestic productive linkages and weak external productive linkages, while an 'extraverted' economy is quite the opposite.[52]

Given the above, we understand that compared with an 'autocentric' economy an 'extraverted' economy is characterised by: relatively weak domestic sectoral productive linkages, and simultaneously by: strong specialisation; relatively low level of industrial and technological development; 'unfavourable' relative income elasticities of demand, and accordingly relatively low international competitiveness – which is expressed through unfavourable terms of trade and trade deficits. Thus the dissimilarity in production-trade structure between more and less advanced economies is depicted in the distinction between 'extraverted' and 'autocentric' economies.

From the above it is inferred that the international competitiveness of a national economy is mainly dependent on the 'structural characteristics' that compose the distinction between 'extraverted' (less advanced) and 'autocentric' (more advanced) economies. In accordance with 'Kaldor's paradox', 'extraversion' explains that the low international competitiveness of a national economy is attributed not to low 'price' or 'cost' competitiveness, but to low 'structural' competitiveness.

Therefore, a relatively 'extraverted' national economy is the field of realisation of surplus profit for the more advanced national economies in the context of international intra-sectoral competition – especially in the absence of any form of protectionism. At the same time, a relatively 'extraverted' economy is a subject of value extraction in the frame of international inter-sectoral competition through terms of trade changing – regardless of whether or not any form

---

50    Cimoli et al. 2006, p. 88.

51    Pilat, Cimper, Olsen and Webb 2006, p. 26.

52    Amin 1976, pp. 237–8.

of protectionism exists. In the absence of protectionism, the reproduction of 'extraversion' will enhance the increase in the relative weight of the second process of value extraction – due to the destruction of national capitals producing like products to those of more advanced, through international intra-sectoral competition.

## 2       The 'Extraversion' of the Greek Economy: Empirical Evidence

In the official neoliberal argumentation, the low economic competitiveness of the Greek economy is explained by the rigid labour market which leads to wage increases and losses in 'price' competitiveness.[53]

However, the Greek economy is an economy of low wages within the EU-15 frame. During the period 2000–10, i.e. before the imposition of Memoranda, the Greek average annual wages (in 2010 USD PPPs and 2010 constant prices) remained the lowest in the EU-15, with the exception of Portugal.[54] Labour costs decreased further due to the Memoranda's austerity measures of 'internal devaluation'. Moreover, considering 'Kaldor's paradox', while 'Greece belongs to a group of countries with low labour costs per unit of output ... the more competitive countries ... are those with higher labour costs and vice versa'.[55] Therefore, the neoliberal argument, which links the low competitiveness of the Greek economy with employees' increased requirements, is rejected by the evidence. The low competitiveness of the Greek economy is attributed to low 'structural' competitiveness.[56]

### Trade Structure and the Technological Level
The neoliberal argumentation, however, recognises that '[t]he widening of the trade deficit ... reflects ... *the inability of domestic supply to meet domestic and foreign demand in terms of both composition and growth*'.[57] In fact, this 'inability' is an expression of the production-trade structure dissimilarity between Greece and its international trade competitors (mainly EU countries), stated otherwise as the 'disequilibrium between the structure of supply and the composition of demand' (see above).[58]

---

53    Bank of Greece 2010, p. 28.
54    OECD. Stat Extracts; see also Economakis, Markaki and Anastasiadis 2015.
55    Ioakeimoglou 2011, pp. 50–3.
56    Economakis, Markaki and Anastasiadis 2015; Economakis et al. 2014.
57    Bank of Greece 2009, p. 121.
58    Economakis et al. 2014.

For a comparison, Table 2.1 shows the external trade data of goods[59] of Greece and other Eurozone-18 countries. Among Eurozone-18 countries, Greece occupies one of the lowest positions, in the percentage share of HT and Medium-High Technology exports to total exports for all selected years. For instance, in 2013 Greece was in the penultimate position, with Portugal being last, in the percentage share of High Technology exports to total exports. In addition, among Eurozone-18 countries Greece occupied one of the lowest positions in the percentage share of High Technology and Medium-High Technology exports to total exports; only Latvia for 2000–10 and Luxemburg for 2010 displayed lower percentages. This is clear evidence of the production-trade structure dissimilarity between Greece and the other Eurozone-18 countries.

For the year 2013 this dissimilarity is also apparent in Table 2.1, seeing the ratio of the percentage share of High Technology and Medium-High Technology exports to total exports (shown by A) to the percentage share of High Technology and Medium-High Technology imports to total imports (shown by B). Greece displays the minimum ratio among the Eurozone-18 countries, which underlines the significant mismatch between the Greek structure of production-export and import demand, for High Technology and Medium-High Technology products.

In 2013, as shown in Table 2.2, the main export sectors of goods in the Greek economy were: 'Coke and Refined Petroleum Products' (Medium-High Technology), 'Food, beverages and tobacco' (Low Technology), 'Chemical and pharmaceutical products' (Medium-High Technology and High Technology), 'Basic Metals' (Medium-Low Technology), 'Agriculture, hunting, forestry and fishing' (Low Technology) and 'Textiles, wearing apparel, leather and related products' (Low Technology).[60] Therefore, Greek exports are mainly dominated by sectors of the low and medium technological levels.[61]

---

59   We restrict our analysis to the external trade of goods, due to the lack of sectoral and trade partners' data on services' exports that makes the analysis of the structure and orientation of the latter not feasible. On the other hand, the focus on external trade of goods is consistent with the limited importance of services in sectoral domestic productive linkages (see above).

60   For a sectoral classification which responds to the technological level, see OECD 2005; Di Mauro, Forster and Lima 2010, p. 40, Table 10.

61   The structure of Eurozone-18 exports is significantly different. The main export sectors for 2012 were: 'Transport equipment' (Medium-High Technology), 'Machinery and equipment n.e.c.' (Medium-High Technology), 'Chemical and pharmaceutical products' (Medium-High Technology and High Technology), 'Computer, electronic and optical products' (High Technology) and 'Food, beverages and tobacco' (Low Technology) (see OECD. Stat Extracts).

TABLE 2.1    *Technological level of imports and exports of goods, Eurozone-18 countries, selected years*

| | Rate of HT exports to total exports (%) | | | | | Rate of HT and MHT exports to total exports (%) | | | | | Rate of HT and MHT imports to total imports (%) | (A)/(B)* |
|---|---|---|---|---|---|---|---|---|---|---|---|---|
| | | | | | | (A) | | | | | (B) | |
| | 1995 | 2000 | 2005 | 2010 | 2013 | 1995 | 2000 | 2005 | 2010 | 2013 | 2013 | 2013 |
| Austria | 9.46 | 14.30 | 13.31 | 13.31 | n.a. | 46.97 | 53.08 | 55.12 | 55.35 | n.a. | 54.43 | 1.02 |
| Belgium | 9.26 | 13.43 | 18.91 | 17.12 | 14.85 | 52.38 | 55.80 | 61.01 | 60.42 | 58.43 | 59.90 | 0.98 |
| Estonia | 10.95 | 31.20 | 21.02 | 10.80 | 15.01 | 32.55 | 48.58 | 44.31 | 39.12 | 44.14 | 49.73 | 0.89 |
| Finland | 15.00 | 27.33 | 25.43 | 11.71 | n.a. | 40.23 | 51.08 | 53.53 | 45.10 | n.a. | 57.45 | 0.79 |
| France | 18.98 | 25.09 | 23.08 | 26.06 | 26.99 | 59.81 | 65.06 | 64.47 | 65.15 | 64.47 | 58.21 | 1.11 |
| Germany | 15.06 | 19.99 | 19.82 | 17.80 | 17.78 | 68.31 | 71.33 | 70.85 | 70.16 | 70.83 | 60.02 | 1.18 |
| Greece | 4.30 | 9.58 | 13.09 | 13.15 | 7.32 | 16.54 | 23.78 | 29.99 | 31.27 | 19.19 | 42.66 | 0.45 |
| Ireland | 40.67 | 49.95 | 52.22 | 41.76 | 37.91 | 62.09 | 81.09 | 84.19 | 85.37 | 83.35 | 58.89 | 1.42 |
| Italy | 9.78 | 11.78 | 10.68 | 9.16 | n.a. | 48.40 | 50.41 | 50.18 | 50.06 | n.a. | 55.35 | 0.90 |
| Latvia | 4.93 | 4.59 | 5.42 | 10.81 | 11.53 | 25.76 | 13.70 | 19.50 | 27.54 | 27.21 | 37.36 | 0.73 |
| Luxemburg | n.a. | 13.84 | 10.18 | 8.49 | 7.46 | n.a. | 35.59 | 35.52 | 30.98 | 31.90 | 48.59 | 0.66 |
| Netherlands | 21.31 | 32.60 | 31.51 | 25.25 | n.a. | 52.15 | 59.94 | 60.85 | 59.14 | n.a. | 61.50 | 0.96 |
| Portugal | 8.11 | 10.30 | 11.22 | 7.09 | 6.12 | 33.95 | 41.86 | 40.59 | 37.55 | 35.34 | 50.64 | 0.70 |
| Slovakia | n.a. | 5.19 | 11.56 | 21.45 | 19.77 | n.a. | 49.92 | 53.19 | 62.98 | 65.40 | 63.91 | 1.02 |
| Slovenia | 9.28 | 10.45 | 10.96 | 13.55 | 15.44 | 45.79 | 50.85 | 56.56 | 61.53 | 60.44 | 49.62 | 1.22 |
| Spain | 8.63 | 10.14 | 11.24 | 10.56 | 9.97 | 56.08 | 57.05 | 56.25 | 54.00 | 52.92 | 56.48 | 0.94 |
| Cyprus | 9.99 | 8.54 | 41.92 | 33.33 | 42.91 | 24.13 | 26.96 | 60.71 | 54.35 | 62.18 | 29.92 | 2.08 |
| Malta | 64.78 | 68.73 | 55.25 | 42.44 | n.a. | 72.31 | 75.45 | 71.33 | 55.11 | n.a. | 43.21 | 1.28 |

Note: HT: High Technology, MHT: Medium-High Technology

n.a.: not available

* For Austria, Finland, Italy, Netherlands and Malta, (A)/(B) is estimated for the year 2012 due to data availability

SOURCE: OECD. STAT EXTRACTS, OWN CALCULATIONS

TABLE 2.2    *Exports structure of Greece (%), 2013*

| 1  | Agriculture, hunting, forestry and fishing | 7.7  |
|----|--------------------------------------------|------|
| 2  | Mining and quarrying                       | 1.5  |
| 3  | Food, beverages and tobacco                | 11.9 |
| 4  | Textiles, wearing apparel, leather etc.    | 4.5  |
| 5  | Wood and products of wood and cork,        | 0.2  |
| 6  | Paper and printing                         | 0.7  |
| 7  | Coke and refined petroleum products        | 38.7 |
| 8  | Chemical and pharmaceutical products       | 8.8  |
| 9  | Rubber and plastics products               | 2.1  |
| 10 | Other non-metallic mineral products        | 1.6  |
| 11 | Basic metals                               | 7.8  |
| 12 | Fabricated metal products                  | 1.8  |
| 13 | Computer, electronic and optical products  | 2.1  |
| 14 | Electrical equipment                       | 2.5  |
| 15 | Machinery and equipment n.e.c.             | 1.9  |
| 16 | Transport equipment                        | 1.6  |
| 17 | Furniture; Other manufacturing             | 1.0  |
| 18 | Electricity and gas                        | 0.6  |
| 19 | Other activities                           | 0.4  |
| 20 | Total Waste                                | 0.7  |
| 21 | Confidential and unallocated               | 1.9  |

SOURCE: OECD. STAT EXTRACTS, OWN CALCULATIONS

Given the above, and on the basis of our theoretical assumptions, we come to the conclusion that the Greek economy, in comparison with the other Eurozone economies, mainly produces and exports products of lower organic composition of capital[62] and of lower income elasticity of demand.[63]

---

62    An indication for this claim is given in Economakis et al. 2014. Specifically, it is argued that the technical composition of capital (expressed as the average ratio of net capital stock per employee for the total economy, from the period 1960–2013) of the Greek economy is lower than that of the largest industrial countries of the Eurozone and the EU (Germany, France, Italy), and similarly or smaller sized countries (like Belgium and Ireland) and also, comparing with Southern European countries, lower than that of Spain and higher than that of Portugal (for the latter the available data are for the period 1977–2013).

63    See also Bank of Greece 2003, p. 32; Athanasoglou 2010, p. 175; Gibson 2010, p. 344; Economakis et al. 2014.

TABLE 2.3    *Income elasticities of demand for imports by technological*
            *level, total economy, Greece, 1990–2013*

| | |
|---|---|
| Total Imports | 1.501 |
| Imports from High Technological Sectors | 2.454 |
| Imports from ICT* Sectors | 1.982 |
| Imports from Medium-High Technological Sectors | 0.900 |
| Imports from Medium-Low Technological Sectors | 1.757 |
| Imports from Low Technological Sectors | 1.982 |

* Information and Communication Technology (OECD 2005)

SOURCE: OECD. STAT EXTRACTS, OWN CALCULATIONS

In other words, the production-trade structure dissimilarity between Greece and the other Eurozone countries documents an important imbalance between the structure of supply (products of low: technology, composition of capital and income elasticity of demand) and the composition of demand (products of high: technology, composition of capital and income elasticity of demand). Therefore, Greece is facing unfavourable terms of trade within the hard core of its EU competitors (i.e. the EMU).

The fact that the economic growth during the 2000s resulted mostly from the production of non-tradable goods and services – i.e. from sectors not exposed to the international competition – is another expression of production-trade dissimilarity between Greece and the other Eurozone countries, which results in the dominance of imported goods in the domestic market.

### Income and Price Elasticities of Demand for Imports

Table 2.3 depicts the income elasticities of demand for imports of the Greek economy for the whole period 1990–2013, arranged by technological level.

Income elasticity of demand is expressed by the slope of the line (i.e. the $\beta$) of the equation:

$$\ln M = \ln a + \beta \cdot \ln Y$$

where M: import demand for goods and Y: net national income.

All data are expressed in million dollars and current prices (Source: OECD. Stat Extracts).

Table 2.3 indicates that income elasticities of demand for imports are: i) higher for the imports of High Technological level; ii) positives for all technological levels; and iii) greater than 1 for all technological levels, with the

TABLE 2.4   *Income elasticities of demand for imported goods, Greece*

| 1990–2002 | 1991–2003 | 1992–2004 | 1993–2005 | 1994–2006 | 1995–2007 | 1996–2008 | 1997–2009 | 1998–2010 | 1999–2011 | 2000–12 | 2001–13 |
|---|---|---|---|---|---|---|---|---|---|---|---|
| 0.070 | 0.499 | 0.905 | 1.239 | 1.515 | 1.713 | 2.080 | 2.282 | 2.451 | 2.590 | 2.220 | 1.507 |

SOURCE: OECD. STAT EXTRACTS, OWN CALCULATIONS

exception of the Medium-High technological level.[64] The above means that, with the exception of the Medium-High technological level, a one-unit increase in net national income results in a more than one increase in the demand for imported goods. It is clear that during this period the development of the Greek economy was accompanied by serious value transfers across the entire range of imported goods.

In order to see the evolution of income elasticities of demand for total imports during 1990–2013, we estimated the value of e (the $\beta$ of equation lnM = lna + $\beta \cdot$ lnY) for periods of k years. Statistical tests showed that all results are significant when k=13 years. The values of e for k=13, are presented in Table 2.4.

As can be observed in Table 2.4, there is a continuous increase in income elasticities of demand for imports of the Greek economy inhibited only slightly in the last period, which incorporates the period of deep depression. In particular, after 1993 the income elasticities of demand for imports overcame the unit. Consequently, the Greek economy is augmenting by being exposed in value transfers abroad during the last two decades, i.e. especially after the abolishment of any kind of (trade or exchange rate) protective policy.

Given that Greek exports are characterised by low income elasticity of demand, the increasing income elasticities of demand for imports suggest deteriorating 'unfavourable' relative income elasticities of demand, thus leading to deteriorating terms of trade. The terms of trade deterioration express the low 'structural' competitiveness of the Greek economy.

Simultaneously, the high income elasticity of demand for imported (industrial in general) goods is combined with low price elasticity of demand for

---

64    It must be noted that in intermediate and capital goods imports, the higher income elasticity of demand is in Medium-Low and Low Technology imports. This finding indicates that the domestic production tends to develop towards the production of low technology and income elasticity of demand products (under the assumption that the technological level of a sector's intermediate and capital goods inputs is reflected in its final output) (Economakis et al. 2014).

these goods.[65] As a result, the high growth rates of the Greek economy were accompanied by increased imports payments and growing external debt. It is a process of value extraction, i.e. imperialist exploitation, in the sphere of circulation.[66]

Considering production-trade dissimilarity between Greece and the other Eurozone countries, it could be inferred that the Greek economy has been subjected to value extraction mainly on the base of international inter-sectoral competition.

### Strong Specialisation, Low Industrial Development, Weak Inter-sectoral Linkages and 'Extraversion'

The 'unfavourable' income elasticities of demand of the Greek economy for imports and exports are accompanied by exports that are not sufficiently differentiated.[67] This reflects the strong specialisation profile of the Greek economy, compared with the other EU national economies. Greece is a small country and it is among the top five countries of EU exhibiting 'a strong specialisation profile' – the others being Malta, Bulgaria, Romania and Latvia.[68]

This 'profile' is accompanied by a relatively low level of industrial development: in 2013 the share of manufacturing (without Energy and Constructions) in the total gross value added of the Greek economy was 9.67%, while for the EU-27 countries this amounted to 15.12%, and for Eurozone-18 countries 15.75%.[69]

Furthermore, examination of inter-sectoral linkages of the Greek economy within the EU[70] has shown that the Greek economy displays relatively weak inter-sectoral linkages, compared with other EU economies.[71]

Consequently, the Greek economy is an 'extraverted' economy of the EU, since it displays all the 'structural characteristics' of 'extraversion': namely, relatively weak domestic sectoral productive linkages; strong specialisation; relatively low level of industrial and technological development; 'unfavourable' rel-

---

65    See Bank of Greece 2000, p. 209.

66    Economakis et al. 2014.

67    Athanasoglou, Georgiou and Bakinezou 2010, p. 179.

68    European Commission 2009, p. 61; see also Economakis, Markaki and Anastasiadis 2015; Economakis et al. 2014.

69    Eurostat Database.

70    Strong productive inter-sectoral linkages of a national economy can be expressed, in the input-output analysis framework, by relatively high backward linkages or backward multipliers, and vice versa (Economakis, Markaki and Anastasiadis 2015).

71    Economakis, Markaki and Anastasiadis 2015; Economakis et al. 2014.

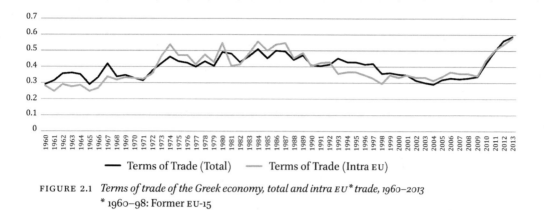

FIGURE 2.1    *Terms of trade of the Greek economy, total and intra EU\* trade, 1960–2013*
                   \* 1960–98: Former EU-15
                   SOURCE: AMECO

ative income elasticities of demand; relatively low international competitiveness – which is expressed by unfavourable terms of trade and trade deficits,[72] until the recent crisis. Thus, the revealed dissimilarity of trade-production structure between the Greek economy and the other Eurozone-18 economies is a manifestation of the Greek economy's 'extraversion' within the EU. We will focus on Greek terms of trade in the following analysis.

## 3    Terms of Trade and Trade Dynamics of the Greek Economy

Figure 2.1 shows the terms of trade of the Greek economy both globally and intra EU as a ratio of exports of goods (in fob prices) to imports of goods (in cif prices). The two ratios follow similar trends, expressing the trade binding of Greece in the context of intra EU trade. The terms of trade of the Greek economy – which indicate a continuously negative trade balance (ratio less than the unit) – had been improving, with some fluctuations, until the mid-1980s. Since then, and especially during the 1990s, i.e. after the abolishment of any kind of (trade or exchange rate) protective policy (see above), they exhibit a continuous deterioration, up to 2008. After then (that is, during crisis), the reduction in import expenditures and the amelioration of export performance have led to their improvement (see Figure 2.2). Nonetheless, the trade balance remains negative.

---

72    Thus, 'over-consumerism' is an expression of 'extraversion'. In this connection, see Fotopoulos 2010, pp. 50–4; Economakis et al. 2014.

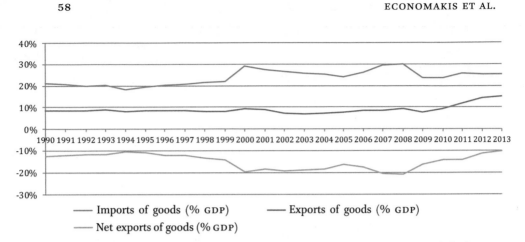

FIGURE 2.2 *Imports and exports of goods and net exports of goods as a percentage (%) of GDP,*
*Greece, 1990–2013*
SOURCE: OECD. STAT EXTRACTS

It has been noted that the reduction in imports expenditure is attributed to
the depression, while the amelioration of export performance is attributed to
the labour costs reduction.

As to the latter, it has been shown[73] that the export performance of the Greek
economy during 1960–2012 was primarily linked not to the production of high
composition of capital, but to low labour cost products. This is consistent with
the finding that the Greek economy, and its export structure, is dominated by
sectors mainly producing commodities of low income elasticity of demand.
These sectors are of low technology and low and medium-low skilled labour.
The latter is related to lower labour compensations. From this point of view
the low 'structural' competitiveness and the poor export performance of the
Greek economy confirms 'Kaldor's paradox'.

Concerning imports, this development could be attributed to the depression, since income reduction causes demand reduction for products of higher
income elasticity of demand; see in Table 2.4 the reduction in income elasticity
of demand for imports in the last period, and in Figure 2.1 the improvement
in the terms of trade after 2008. It is notable that the reduction in imports is
accompanied by a considerable reduction in EU-27 imports to Greece, as seen
in Figure 2.3.

Figure 2.3 shows the intra EU-27 trade and its importance for EU-27 and
Greece. We should note that until the mid-2000s the Greek intra EU-27 imports

---

73    Economakis, Androulakis and Markaki 2015, pp. 146, 150.

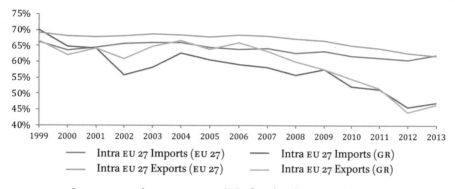

FIGURE 2.3   *Intra EU-27 trade as a percentage (%) of total trade, EU-27 and Greece, 1999–2013*
SOURCE: EUROSTAT DATABASE

and exports follow the average trend of the EU-27 countries (although at a lower percentage than that of the EU-27 average). Although the EU-27 still remains the main field of competition for the Greek economy, after the mid-2000s there is a trend of *partial de-Europeanisation* of Greek external trade, which intensified from 2009 onwards. It is a clear trend of detachment of the Greek economy from intra EU trade, both in exports and imports of goods.[74]

Let us look more systematically at aspects of this differentiation in the Greek external trade.

### The De-Europeanisation Trend

We will first examine the evolution of the share of exports and imports of Greece to Eurozone-18 and EU-27 countries, for the total of exports and imports as well as for the exports and imports of the main Greek export sectors[75] during 1990–2013.

From Table 2.5's data, the following can be inferred:

a.   There was a significant decrease in the share of Greek exports to the Eurozone-18 and EU-27 countries during the examined period, with the exceptions of sector's 8 exports – expressed by the negative LSGR for the total of Greek exports and, with the above exception, for all the examined sectors. This decrease suggests a deterioration of the country's compet-

---

74   See also Economakis et al. 2014.

75   These sectors are: (1) 'Agriculture, hunting, forestry and fishing', (3) 'Food, beverages and tobacco', (4) 'Textiles, wearing apparel, leather and related products', (7) 'Coke and refined petroleum products', (8) 'Chemical and pharmaceutical products', and (11) 'Basic metals'.

TABLE 2.5    *Share of exports and imports of goods of Greece to Eurozone-18 and EU-27 (%), all sectors and selected sectors, selected years, 1990–2013*

| Sector | | Exports | | | | | Imports | | | | |
|---|---|---|---|---|---|---|---|---|---|---|---|
| | | 1990 | 2000 | 2010 | 2013 | LSGR* 1990– 2013 | 1990 | 2000 | 2010 | 2013 | LSGR* 1990– 2013 |
| All sectors | Eurozone-18 | 61.41 | 61.41 | 42.94 | 29.89 | −2.50 | 60.24 | 49.16 | 41.91 | 36.16 | −1.91 |
| | EU-27 | 73.20 | 73.20 | 62.61 | 43.76 | −1.55 | 69.76 | 60.79 | 51.28 | 46.20 | −1.70 |
| 1 | Eurozone-18 | 64.27 | 64.27 | 44.91 | 43.98 | −1.27 | 36.36 | 52.29 | 42.39 | 31.48 | −0.82 |
| | EU-27 | 73.00 | 73.00 | 62.28 | 62.50 | −0.70 | 41.90 | 62.84 | 62.48 | 57.21 | 0.57 |
| 3 | Eurozone-18 | 60.50 | 60.50 | 47.82 | 50.97 | −0.89 | 73.17 | 70.93 | 67.84 | 65.42 | −0.47 |
| | EU-27 | 77.58 | 77.58 | 70.76 | 71.73 | −0.27 | 86.70 | 86.90 | 84.02 | 84.42 | −0.31 |
| 4 | Eurozone-18 | 71.43 | 71.43 | 45.10 | 43.62 | −2.78 | 77.41 | 56.33 | 53.40 | 50.62 | −1.78 |
| | EU-27 | 84.68 | 84.68 | 69.39 | 66.66 | −1.32 | 82.65 | 69.14 | 64.47 | 65.12 | −1.29 |
| 7 | Eurozone-18 | 39.84 | 39.84 | 20.91 | 10.12 | −3.94 | 26.10 | 23.38 | 13.38 | 24.28 | −1.86 |
| | EU-27 | 44.06 | 44.06 | 37.77 | 13.02 | −3.43 | 39.03 | 29.64 | 15.49 | 30.14 | −2.10 |
| 8 | Eurozone-18 | 38.91 | 25.47 | 37.49 | 33.60 | 0.46 | 57.74 | 56.22 | 53.95 | 56.47 | 0.19 |
| | EU-27 | 63.86 | 63.27 | 73.61 | 70.25 | 0.90 | 82.62 | 82.44 | 79.19 | 80.56 | −0.08 |
| 11 | Eurozone-18 | 68.69 | 52.92 | 46.35 | 41.69 | −1.74 | 52.30 | 34.94 | 32.31 | 30.78 | −2.52 |
| | EU-27 | 76.60 | 66.97 | 69.07 | 65.29 | −0.20 | 65.60 | 52.58 | 44.72 | 43.65 | −2.39 |

* LSGR: 'The least-squares growth rate … is estimated by fitting a linear regression trend-line to the logarithmic annual values of the variable in the relevant period. [...] The calculated growth rate is an average rate that is representative of the available observations over the entire period' (The World Bank 2003, p. 249).

SOURCE: OECD. STAT EXTRACTS, OWN CALCULATIONS

itive position in relation to the Eurozone-18 and EU-27 countries. Consequently, the rising Greek exports, during crisis, were accompanied by a reorientation towards countries outside the EU and Eurozone.

b.    LSGR is smaller for the Eurozone-18 compared with EU-27 countries for the total of exports and the main exporting sectors of the Greek economy. Consequently, there was a greater decline in exports to the Eurozone-18 against the EU-27 countries.

c.    With the exception of a small increase in the share of imports from the EU-27 for sector 1 and in the share of imports from the Eurozone-18 for sector 8, LSGR is negative for the total of Greek imports and for all the examined sectors. Consequently, the diminishing Greek imports, during

TABLE 2.6    *Ratio of Greek exports to imports of goods, for all trade partners, Eurozone-18 and EU-27 countries, all sectors, selected years, 1990–2013*

|  | 1990 | 2000 | 2010 | 2013 | LSGR 1990–2013 |
|---|---|---|---|---|---|
| All countries | 0.41 | 0.37 | 0.34 | 0.59 | 0.01 |
| Eurozone-18 | 0.42 | 0.31 | 0.35 | 0.49 | −0.59 |
| EU-27 | 0.43 | 0.36 | 0.42 | 0.56 | 0.16 |

SOURCE: OECD. STAT EXTRACTS, OWN CALCULATIONS

crisis, were accompanied by a reorientation towards countries outside the EU and Eurozone.

d.   With the exception of sectors 7 and 8, LSGR is smaller for the Eurozone-18 countries in comparison with EU-27 countries for the total of Greek imports and for all the examined sectors. This indicates that there was a greater restriction of imports from the Eurozone-18 countries than from the EU-27 countries.

e.   Given that there was a greater decline in Greek exports to the Eurozone-18 against EU-27 countries and a greater restriction of imports to Greece from the Eurozone-18 than from the EU-27 countries, it could be concluded that there was a greater detachment of Greek external trade from the Eurozone than from the EU.

In order to further examine the trends of the Greek external trade, in Table 2.6 the evolution of the ratio of Greek exports to imports for all trade partners, Eurozone-18 and EU-27 countries for all sectors during 1990–2013 is depicted.
From Table 2.6's data, it is evident that:

a.   LSGR is positive for all countries and EU-27, but it is negative for Eurozone-18. This finding confirms the conclusion of the greater detachment of the Greek external trade from the Eurozone than from the EU.

b.   LSGR for EU-27 countries is bigger than LSGR for all countries. This finding expresses the continuing binding of the Greek external trade in the context of intra EU-27 trade.

c.   The ratio of Greek exports to imports is less than the unit in all cases and in all years, which means that the Greek trade balance is continuously negative. Nevertheless, compared with the beginning of the period (1990), in 2013 there was an amelioration of the ratio. This amelioration turns the

TABLE 2.7    *Main trade partners of Greece, 1990 and 2013*

| Exports | | Imports | |
|---|---|---|---|
| 1990 | 2013 | 1990 | 2013 |
| Germany (22.20%) | Turkey (11.74%) | Germany (20.80%) | Russian Federation (14.37%) |
| Italy (17.06%) | Italy (8.93%) | Italy (15.40%) | Germany (9.55%) |
| France (9.61%) | Germany (6.47%) | France (8.09%) | Italy (7.65%) |
| UK (7.28%) | Bulgaria (5.11%) | Netherlands (6.73%) | China (4.77%) |
| USA (5.60%) | Cyprus (4.17%) | Japan (5.92%) | France (4.66%) |
| Netherlands (3.45%) | UK (3.55%) | UK (5.26%) | Netherlands (4.61%) |
| Cyprus (2.51%) | USA (3.42%) | Belgium (3.74%) | Bulgaria (3.03%) |
| Belgium (2.03%) | FYROM (2.73%) | USA (3.68%) | Spain (2.91%) |
| Sweden (1.61%) | France (2.35%) | Spain (2.02%) | Belgium (2.80%) |
| Spain (1.47%) | Romania (2.20%) | Switzerland (1.80%) | UK (2.44%) |

SOURCE: OECD. STAT EXTRACTS, OWN CALCULATIONS

order of Greece's main trade partner between 1990 and 2013: from EU-27 → Eurozone-18 → All countries to All countries → EU-27 → Eurozone-18. This finding depicts the trend of partial de-Europeanisation of Greek external trade.

This trend is clearly evident from the data of Table 2.7.

Between 1990 and 2013, major EU countries (like Germany, Italy, France, UK, Netherlands, Belgium) were downgraded as main export partners of Greece, while countries of lower development level and/or countries outside the EU or the Eurozone (like Turkey, Bulgaria, Cyprus, FYROM) were upgraded.

Additionally, the same period, major EU countries (like Germany, Italy, France, Netherlands, UK and Belgium) were downgraded as main import partners of Greece, while countries of lower development level and/or countries outside the EU or the Eurozone (like Russian Federation, China and Bulgaria) were upgraded.

## Conclusion

From the analysis, we conclude that the Greek economy is an 'extraverted' economy of the EU and that this is why it emerged as the main 'weak link' of the

EU-EMU 'imperialist chain' in the conjuncture of the global economic crisis. It is this 'extraversion' that led to systematic transfers of value to the imperialist countries – expressed as trade deficits – that formed the foundations of the current crisis: activation of potential crisis trends owing to imperialist exploitation in the conjuncture of global economic crisis.

The manifestation of the Greek economy's extraversion and the crucial parameter of these value transfers is the dissimilarity of production-trade structure between the Greek economy and the hard core of its trade competitors (Eurozone), which is expressed in the deterioration of Greek terms of trade up to 2008. The latter means that the Greek economy has been subjected to value extraction mainly on the basis of international inter-sectoral competition.

In the conjuncture of economic crisis, through the reduction in intra EU imports and the increase in extra EU exports (to countries of a lower development level), Greek capitalism appears to be seeking an 'escape' from the unfavourable terms of trade within the EU-EMU. The terms of trade improvement after 2008 probably also reflect this partial reorientation.

Politically, this 'escape' indicates that the national currency and the exit of Greece from the EU are necessary conditions for the disengagement of the Greek economy from the 'unevenness' within the EU-EMU. However, in order to overcome the 'extraversion', radical productive reorganisation is also required. The latter presupposes the overthrow of capitalist power, since this power historically created the 'extraverted' model of Greek capitalist development.

### References

Amin, Samir 1976, *Unequal Development: An Essay on the Social Formations of Peripheral Capitalism*, Hassocks, Sussex: The Harvester Press.

Athanasoglou, Panagiotis P., Evagelia Georgiou and Konstantina Bakinezou 2010, 'Export performance of the Greek economy: the impact of competitiveness and of trade composition', in *Current Account Balance of Greece: causes of unbalances and proposals of policy*, edited by Georgios Oikonomou, Isaac Sabethai and Georgios Simigiannis [in Greek], Athens: Bank of Greece.

Athanasoglou, Panagiotis. P. 2010, 'Imports: the role of trade structure and domestic supply', in *Current Account Balance of Greece: causes of unbalances and proposals of policy*, edited by Georgios Oikonomou, Isaac Sabethai and Georgios Simigiannis [in Greek], Athens: Bank of Greece.

Bank of Greece 2000, *Annual Report 1999*, Athens: Bank of Greece

Bank of Greece 2003, *Annual Report 2002*, Athens: Bank of Greece.

Bank of Greece 2009, *Annual Report 2008*, Athens: Bank of Greece.

Bank of Greece 2010, *Annual Report 2009*, Athens: Bank of Greece.

Bank of Greece 2011, *Summary of Annual Report 2010*, Athens: Bank of Greece.

Bank of Greece 2012, *Annual Report 2011*, Athens: Bank of Greece.

Bank of Greece 2013, *Summary of Annual Report 2012*, Athens: Bank of Greece.

Busch, Klaus 1983, 'The discussion in F.R. of Germany about the global market', [in Greek], *Theseis*, 5: 93–108.

Busch, Klaus 1987 [1978], *The Crisis of European Community*, [in Greek], Athens: Erato.

Busch, Klaus 1992 [1991], *Europe since 1992: economic, ecological and social perspectives of the single market*, [in Greek], Athens: Kritiki.

Carchedi, Guglielmo 2001, *For Another Europe: A Class Analysis of European Integration*, London: Verso.

Cimoli, Mario, Annalisa Primi and Maurizio Pugno 2006, 'A low-growth model: Informality as a structural constraint', *Economic Commission for Latin America and the Caribbean / ECLAC, CEPAL Review*, 88: 85–102.

di Mauro, Filippo, Katrin Forster and Ana Lima 2010, 'The global downturn and its impact on euro area exports and competitiveness', *ECB Occasional Paper Series*, 119.

Economakis, George, Alexis Anastasiadis and Maria Markaki 2010, 'US Economic Performance from 1929 to 2008 in Terms of the Marxian Theory of Crises, with Some Notes on the Recent Financial Crisis', *Critique*, 38, 3: 465–87.

Economakis, George, Maria Markaki and George Androulakis 2014, 'Extraversion and crisis of the Greek economy: a study', *Bulletin of Political Economy*, 8, 2: 175–204.

Economakis, George, George Androulakis and Maria Markaki 2015, 'Profitability and Crisis in the Greek Economy (1960–2012): An Investigation', in *Greek Capitalism in Crisis: Marxist Analyses*, edited by Stavros Mavroudeas, London: Routledge.

Economakis, George, Maria Markaki and Alexios Anastasiadis 2015, 'Structural Analysis of the Greek Economy', *Review of Radical Political Economics*, 47, 3: 424–45.

European Commission 2009, *EU industrial structure 2009: Performance and competitiveness*, Luxembourg: European Communities.

Fagerberg, Jan 1988, 'International Competitiveness', *The Economic Journal*, 98: 355–74.

Fagerberg, Jan 1996, 'Technology and Competitiveness', *Oxford Review of Economic Policy*, 12, 3: 39–51.

Felipe, Jesus and Utsav Kumar 2011, 'Unit Labor Costs in the Eurozone: The Competitiveness Debate Again', *Levy Economics Institute of Bard College, Working Paper*, 651, available at: http://www.levyinstitute.org/pubs/wp_651.pdf

Fotopoulos, Takis 2010, *Greece as a protectorate of the super-national elite: The Need for Direct Exit from the EU and for A Self-Reliant Economy*, [in Greek], Athens: Gordios.

Furtado, Celso 1964, *Development and Underdevelopment*, Berkley: University of California Press.

Gibson, Heather D. 2010, 'Sectoral growth of the Greek economy for the period 1995–

2003' in *Current Account Balance of Greece: causes of unbalances and proposals of policy*, edited by Georgios Oikonomou, Isaac Sabethai and Georgios Simigiannis, [in Greek], Athens: Bank of Greece.

Ilzkovitz, Fabienne, Adriaan Dierx, Olivia Galgau, and Karolina Leib n.d., *Trade performance and Structural competitiveness. Developments in the Euro Area: are member states equipped to meet the globalization challenges of the 21st century?*, available at: http://research.stlouisfed.org/conferences/integration/Galgau-paper.pdf

Ioakeimoglou, Ilias 2011, *Labour Cost, Profit Margins and Competitiveness in Greece 1995–2009*, [in Greek], Athens: INE GSEE/ADEDY.

Krugman, Paul 1989, 'Differences in income elasticities and trends in real exchange rates', *European Economic Review*, 33: 1031–54.

Lapavitsas, Costas & A. Kaltenbrunner, G. Lambrinidis, D. Lindo, J. Meadway, J. Michell, J.P. Painceira, E. Pires, J. Powell, A. Stenfors, N. Teles 2010, *The Eurozone between Austerity and Default*, RMF occasional report.

Lenin, Vladimir Ilyich 2010 [1917], *Imperialism: The Highest Stage of Capitalism*, London: Penguin.

Maniatis, Thanassis and Costas Passas 2015, 'The Law of the Falling Rate of Profit in the Post-War Greek Economy', in *Greek Capitalism in Crisis: Marxist Analyses*, edited by Stavros Mavroudeas, London: Routledge.

Marx, Karl 1990 [1867], *Capital*, Vol. 1, London: Penguin Classics.

Marx, Karl 1991 [1894], *Capital*, Vol. 3, London: Penguin Classics.

Mavroudeas, Stavros 2015, 'Financialisation and the Greek case', in *Greek capitalism in crisis: Marxist Analyses*, edited by Stavros Mavroudeas, London: Routledge.

Milios, John 2000, *The Greek Social Formation*, [in Greek], Athens: Kritiki.

Milios, John 2011, 'The Greek Crisis as a Version of the Global Economic Crisis and EMU Crisis', Paper presented at the International Conference, *Public Debt and Austerity Policies in Europe: The Response of the European Left*, [in Greek], Organization: The European Left Party, Coalition of the Left and Nicos Poulantzas Institute, available at: http://youpayyourcrisis.blogspot.com/2011/03/blog-post_7459.html#more

Nurbel, Alain 2007, 'The Global Competitiveness Of The Nation: A Conceptual Discussion', *Journal of Business & Economics Research*, 5, 10: 63–72.

OECD 2005, *Directorate for Science, Technology and Industry: Stan Indicators. 1980–2003*, Paris: OECD, available at: http://www.oecd.org/dataoecd/3/33/40230754.pdf

Peres, Wilson 2006, 'The slow comeback of industrial policies in Latin America and the Caribbean', *Economic Commission for Latin America and the Caribbean / ECLAC, CEPAL Review*, 88: 67–83.

Pilat, Dirk, Agnès Cimper, Karsten B. Olsen and Colin Webb 2006, 'The Changing Nature of Manufacturing in OECD Economies', *OECD STI Working Paper*, 9, Paris, available at: OECD: http://dx.doi.org/10.1787/308452426871

Pilat, Dirk and Anita Wölfl 2005, 'Measuring the interaction between manufacturing

and services', *OECD STI Working Paper* 5, Paris: OECD, available at: http://dx.doi.org/
10.1787/882376471514

Rios-Morales, Ruth and David O'Donovan 2006, 'Can the Latin American and Caribbean countries emulate the Irish model of FDI attraction?', *Economic Commission
for Latin America and the Caribbean / ECLAC, CEPAL Review*, 88: 49–66.

The World Bank 2003, *World Development Report 2003: Sustainable Development in a
Dynamic World – Transforming Institutions, Growth, and Quality of Life*, Washington,
D.C.: The World Bank and Oxford University Press.

Thirlwall, Antony P. 1979, 'The Balance of Payments Constraint as an Explanation
of International Growth Rate Differences', *Banca Nazionale del Lavoro Quarterly
Review*, 32, 128: 45–53.

## Online Sources

AMECO: http://ec.europa.eu/economy_finance/ameco/user/serie/SelectSerie.cfm
Eurostat Database: http://epp.eurostat.ec.europa.eu/portal/page/portal/statistics/
search_database
OECD. Stat Extracts: http://stats.oecd.org/

# CHAPTER 3

# The Class Dimension of the Greek Public Debt Crisis

*Ioannis Zisimopoulos and George Economakis*

## Introduction

The global economic crisis turned part of the private debt into public debt, which has led to a crisis of insolvency, due to soaring interest rates. Thus, the global crisis appears to be a public debt crisis, which, for the first time after World War II, has affected the advanced capitalist social formations to a great extent.[1] The gross public debt in the advanced economies continued to grow as a percentage of the Gross Domestic Product (GDP), exceeding 100% for the first time in 2011. In the European Union (EU) and the Eurozone, the gross public debt has increased considerably in recent years. However, the Greek public debt as a percentage of GDP is much higher than the EU and the Eurozone public debt, and has seriously deteriorated in the last few years.[2] At the same time, the Greek economy faces a high and growing gross external debt (of both the private and the public sectors).[3]

Before the recent debt crisis and deep depression that followed, financing deficits relied mainly on raising funds from the international financial market, particularly through bond issuing and Treasury bills that created debt. Since 2009, the debt crisis has emerged in Greece as the country has been excluded from the international capital markets and the spreads on Greek government bonds have been high.[4]

Greek governments and international organisations have attributed the huge public debt to the oversized public sector, which has systematically created fiscal deficits. Thus, Greek governments (2010–14) in collaboration with the troika of the European Commission (EC), the European Central Bank (ECB) and the International Monetary Fund (IMF), have attempted to confront the public debt crisis through the restriction of public spending and the increase in revenues mainly derived from the salaried classes. This economic policy (that

---

1 Milios 2011; Economakis, Androulakis and Markaki 2015, p. 130.
2 Economakis, Androulakis and Markaki 2015, p. 130; see also above.
3 Economakis, Androulakis and Markaki 2015, p. 133; see also in this volume Economakis et al.
4 Economakis, Androulakis and Markaki 2015, p. 133; see also in this volume Economakis et al.

© KONINKLIJKE BRILL NV, LEIDEN, 2018 | DOI:10.1163/9789004280892_005

had been imposed regardless of the economic and social consequences)[5] was one of the main goals of the imposed adjustment programmes (Memoranda).

In this chapter, the argument concerning the effects of the size of the public sector on the increase in Greek public debt is disputed. The size of the Greek public sector is examined, comparing the total general government expenditures and revenues as a percentage of GDP with those of the EU-27 countries. The analysis shows that the real problem of Greek fiscal deficits lies in low public revenues. The total general government revenues in Greece as a percentage of GDP before the public debt crisis were well below the EU-27 total general government revenues.

Focusing on the composition of tax revenues (i.e. revenues deriving from taxes on capital and labour, as well as indirect taxation that mainly burdens the salaried classes) and studying their evolution, this chapter ascertains the deep class dimension of the taxation system in Greece. Moreover, investigation of tax evasion leads to the conclusion that it was the basic means for the construction and maintenance of the class alliance between the bourgeoisie and the middle classes.

The chapter is structured as follows: In the first section, a review of the literature concerning the definition of the public sector is undertaken and the methodologies used to measure the size of the public sector are presented. In the second section, a brief consideration of the public sector restructuring during the previous decades in accordance with the principles of the so-called 'New Public Management' is given. In the third section, the public debt crisis in Greece and the nature of state intervention are briefly examined. The fourth section includes an examination of the general government expenditures and revenues, focusing on the investigation of the taxation system, and its class dimension, and of tax evasion as a class alliance between the bourgeoisie and the middle classes. The chapter ends with some concluding remarks.

## 1        Definition of the Public Sector

The term public sector has often been (incorrectly) used as a synonym of the government.[6] A generally accepted definition of the public sector is difficult

---

5   The implementation of the Memoranda's austerity measures blocked capitalist reproduction displaying underconsumption crisis (Economakis, Androulakis and Markaki 2015, p. 147), which was accompanied by a sharp rise in unemployment, from 12.6 % in 2010 to 27.3 % in 2013 (AMECO).

6   Pathirane and Blades 1982, p. 261.

due to the variation of its parts among countries and the restructuring measures – such as new management practices, partly privatisation – that have
'blurred the boundaries' between the private and public sectors.[7]

Even though there are differences in the public sector structure between different countries, it is possible to define it through its main sub-sectors. The
definition given by the Commission of the European Communities, the IMF,
the Organisation for Economic Co-operation and Development, the United
Nations and the World Bank, refers to the public sector as the sector that is
composed by the general government and the public corporations.[8] Alternat-
ively, the public sector is defined as the sector that consists of the sub-sectors
of the general government and the public sub-sectors of the non-financial and
financial corporations.[9]

According to Andersen et al. the European public sector (or public sector
labour markets) contains five sub-sectors which are divided on the basis of
their socio-economic activity: (1) central administration including state administration, the legal system, the police, the armed forces, the diplomatic corps,
etc.; (2) regional and local administration; (3) public services including education, healthcare, social security etc.; (4) public utilities including public transport, postal services, telecoms, water supplies, etc.; and (5) industry/finance
including industry, banking, etc.[10]

### Notes on the Measurement of the Size of the Public Sector
In the literature, a variety of measures have been recommended for the determination of the size of the public sector, such as: value added, compensation of
employees, public employment as a part of the total employment, capital formation, saving and net lending figures. However, few studies have used these
measures in order to make transnational comparisons[11] about the size of the
public sector.[12]

---

7    Olsen 1996, p. 11.
8    Commission of the European Communities et al. 2009, p. 435.
9    Commission of the European Communities et al. 1993, p. 537.
10   Andersen et al. 1997, p. 38.
11   According to Beaumont (1992, p. 8), '[t]hose relatively few studies which have used a
     variety of measures have indicated that judgments about the size of the public sector
     in an individual country that are highly sensitive to the definition and measures used.
     For example, it has been suggested that the USA has a medium-sized public sector when
     measured by government consumption expenditure or government employment, but a
     much smaller one if the measure used is total public sector final demand or total public
     sector employment'.
12   Pathirane and Blades 1982, p. 264; Beaumont 1992, p. 8.

The indicator that is frequently used for the measurement of the public sector is the ratio of government expenditures to the total output of the economy, i.e. the GDP. This ratio can adequately express the trends of the size and development of the public sector.[13]

According to the Commission of the European Communities et al. the general government expenditures can be divided into two categories: (1) expenditures for collective services that include the general public services, defence, public order and safety, economic affairs, environmental protection, housing and community amenities; and (2) expenditures for individual services that include health, recreation, culture and religion, education and finally social protection.[14] In its definition of the general government expenditures, the OECD clarifies that 'publicly owned units producing (all or mostly) market goods and services are not in the government sector but are instead recorded as public corporations'.[15]

There are two kinds of problems concerning the measurement and transnational comparability of the general government expenditures. The first problem concerns the differentiations of the scope of general government, as in many countries hospitals, for example, are recorded as belonging to the government sector and in other countries as being public corporations.[16] The second kind of problem concerns the recording or not of public corporations in general government expenditures. According to the official definition in the ESA (European System of Accounts) 95, public corporations are not recorded in general government as long as they are market producers.[17] However, '[b]y convention, the general government sector includes all public corporations that are not able to cover at least 50% of their costs by sales and are therefore considered non-market producers'.[18]

## 2      The Restructuring of the Public Sector: General Context

The patterns of the public employment have been challenged not only in the current crisis but also during the past three decades. The argument that is often used by the governments in order to challenge the existing patterns of public

---

13      Beeton 1987, pp. 297–8; Mahler 1992, p. 311; Masters et al. 2008, p. 309.

14      European Communities et al. 2009, pp. 190–1.

15      OECD 2011a, p. 60.

16      OECD 2011b, p. 66.

17      See ESA 95, paragraph 2.69.

18      Eurostat 2009, p. 42.

employment is that 'the growth of public expenditure is unsustainable, and that the size and scope of the public sector requires reappraisal'.[19]

In the 1980s, in many developing countries the cuts in public expenditure had been imposed by the IMF adjustment programmes.[20] The preconditions set by the IMF for the granting of the loans were 'fiscal stability, through measures such as the increase of tax exemptions for businesses, strengthening the banking system, privatizations, the opening of the trade and the effectiveness of public administration in the direction of liberal restructuring'.[21] In Europe, in the 1990s, the pressures for the restriction of public expenditures were reinforced due to the requirements that were set by the Maastricht Treaty and the criteria for entrance in the European Monetary Union.[22]

The questioning of public employment held in the context of the wider questioning of the supposed 'non-rational' functioning of the welfare state and the alleged rationalisation through the so-called New Public Management (NPM). The development of new models of public administration, which adopt business/market operating criteria for the state functions, provides the theoretical documentation for the neoliberal deregulation of the welfare state.[23] Through the NPM the state emerged mainly as an 'imitator' of private sector practices in industrial relations, while at the same time it is considered a 'model employer' or 'innovator', that sets the best practices as an example for the private sector.[24] The latter means that state practices reinforce the deregulation of labour relations in the private sector (see also below).

The restructuring reforms of the public sector in the 1990s aimed at a reduction of the public expenditures in accordance with the NPM. In this frame '[t]he claim for a "limited governance" was presented both as imperative and ideologically neutral, in view of an alleged and undeniable reality of inflated state competences and public spending'.[25] The restructuring reforms had two main dimensions that directly affected industrial relations in the public sec-

---

19    Bach 1999, p. 3.
20    According to Beaumont (1992, p. 23) 'a survey of seventy-eight adjustment programmes in developing countries supported by IMF resources in 1980–3 reported that almost 90 per cent involved proposed public expenditures reductions, with fully two-thirds of these involving some form of public sector wage restraint'. See also Markantonatou 2011, pp. 60–1.
21    Markantonatou 2011, p. 60.
22    Andersen et al. 1997, p. 39; Hyman 2008, p. 265.
23    Markantonatou 2011, pp. 54–6.
24    Hyman 2008; Leat 2007; Bach and Winchester 2003.
25    Markantonatou 2011, p. 56.

tor: (1) the market orientation; and (2) the adoption of new forms of management. The first included the introduction of market-type mechanisms through privatisations, tendering and through the introduction of 'internal markets'[26] in the public sector. The second included: (1) organisational changes, and especially the adoption of employment flexibility; (2) the management of financial resources; and (3) the creation of various forms of responsiveness.[27]

## 3       Public Debt Crisis in Greece and the Nature of State Intervention: Introductory Remarks

As seen in Figure 3.1, the Greek public debt as a percentage of GDP is much higher than the average EU-27 and the Eurozone-17 public debt during 2000–13.

The Greek public debt reached or exceeded 100% of GDP during the examined period. It has constantly deteriorated after 2002,[28] while in 2009 it displayed a sudden increase. The latter is attributed to the incorporation of the accumulated debt of public enterprises in the public debt due to the inclusion of public enterprises in general government expenditures. This revealed the true extent of the financial derailment of the country up until 2009.[29] However, it should be noted that the increase in the public debt in 2009 as a percentage

---

26    According to Lacey '[an internal market can be described by] its characteristics:
      –  It is "internal", meaning that the activities carried out in the market remain in the public sector.
      –  Within the overall budget envelope for the activity in question, resources are no longer allocated to providers by bureaucratic decision, but by user choice. For example, in the case of education, money should follow the pupils; in health, money should follow the patients.
      –  The provision of services is split from their financing.
      –  Resources are earmarked by activity and by market (for example, education vouchers cannot be encashed and thus have no value outside the school system).
      –  Prices in the internal market are not normally determined by supply and demand but by bureaucratic diktat or negotiated between purchaser and provider within a heavily regulated framework' (Lacey 1997, p. 142).
27    Andersen et al. 1997, pp. 42–3; Morgan et al. 2000, p. 79; Markantonatou 2011, pp. 54–60.
28    The significant reduction in the cost of borrowing in the 2000s as the result of the single monetary policy can be found on the basis of this development (see Economakis, Androulakis and Markaki 2015, p. 135).
29    Ministry of Finance 2011, p. 29. Obviously, Greek public corporations were considered as 'non-market producers'; see the previous discussion on the definition of the public sector.

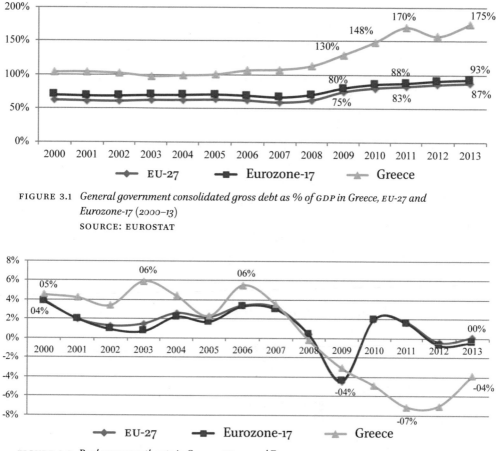

FIGURE 3.1  *General government consolidated gross debt as % of GDP in Greece, EU-27 and*
*Eurozone-17 (2000–13)*
SOURCE: EUROSTAT

FIGURE 3.2  *Real GDP growth rate in Greece, EU-27 and Eurozone-17, 2000–13*
SOURCE: EUROSTAT

of GDP is due less to the reclassification of public enterprises, and more to the
depression, i.e. the reduction in GDP[30] (see Figure 3.2).

As noted, Greek governments and international organisations attribute the
huge public debt (and thus the public debt crisis) to the oversized public sector,
which systematically created fiscal deficits. Thus, the two Memoranda, which
followed Greece's recourse to the financial support mechanism of the EC-ECB-
IMF in 2010, imposed the reduction in the public debt through the reduction
in public expenditures and the downsizing of the public sector itself.

_____

30    Lapatsioras and Sotiropoulos 2011, pp. 111–12.

It must be noted, however, that beyond the reduction in public expenditures, but in accordance with this reduction, the attempt to restructure the public sector in Greece took place before the Memoranda and independently of them. For instance, the Law 2889/2001 for the reformation of the national health system and the Law 4009/2011 for the reformation of higher education, reflect the adoption of the new forms of management in the Greek public sector (i.e. both market criteria for the function of the public sector and new forms of administration have been adopted).

According to Markantonatou, the principles of NPM 'are present' in the Memoranda 'tending to serve as the theoretical foundation' of imposed reforms[31] (see the state as an 'imitator' of private sector practices in industrial relations). However, given that, as noted, the state acts not only as an 'imitator' of private sector practices but also as a 'model employer', the reforms related to public employment and civil servants' compensations function as a prerequisite for the imposition of neoliberal deregulation measures of labour relations in the private sector.[32]

### The Interventions in the Greek Public Sector after the Memoranda: a Codification

The fiscal adjustment is the basic aim of the adjustment programmes imposed by the Greek state and the troika. The Memoranda and the laws that followed them have embedded this aim.

The main interventions in the public sector concerning public employment and wages are as follows:

- The commitment to the privatisation of state owned enterprises (public utilities) (Law 3986/2011; Law 4046/2012) has been undertaken. Such development will affect decisively the power of trade unions in the state owned enterprises.
- The rule '1 new recruitment for every 5 retirements' until 2015 has been legislated (Law 3833/2010; Law 3845/2010; Law 3899/2010; Law 4024/2011; Law 4046/2012). Moreover, the reduction by 10% per year until 2015 (50% for 2011) of recruitments under fixed-term contracts in public utilities and in the public sector in general has been legislated (Law 3899/2010; Law 3986/2011; Law 4093/2012). Moreover, recruitments under permanent employment or under open-ended contracts in local authorities and in public organisations

---

31    Markantonatou 2011, p. 72.
32    See Kouzis (2010a, p. 16; 2010b, p. 209; 2011, pp. 7–8).

governed by private law (for employees who have completed primary or secondary education), have been suspended until 2016 (Law 4093/2012). These settings combined with the labour reserve are expected to lead to a drastic reduction in public employment.

- The labour reserve has been introduced (Law 3986/2011). This measure constituted a warning for redundancies (Law 4024/2011; Law 4093/2012), aiming at a decrease of 150,000 employees in total employment in the public sector up to 2015 (Law 4046/2012). At the same time the organic posts of employees who have been under the scheme of pre-retirement availability (Law 4024/2011) or transferred to other organisations (Law 4093/2012) have been abolished. The abolition of permanent employment in public utilities (Law 4046/2012) is also a warning for future redundancies and for further shrinking of the public sector of the economy.
- The retirement age in the public sector has been increased, leading many civil servants to voluntary retirement (Law 3863/2010). According to Law 4093/2012 the general minimum retirement age increased to 67 years.
- All types of remuneration (bonuses, etc.) of civil servants and military personnel have been reduced by 8%; the remuneration (bonuses, etc.) of employees in public utilities, co-operatives, etc. has been reduced by 3% (Law 3845/2010).
- The reduction in public servants' salaries (Law 4024/2011) has extended to employees in public utilities (Law 4093/2012).
- Christmas, Easter and holiday benefits were reduced by Law 3845/2010 and were totally abolished by Law 4093/2012. Moreover, there is a commitment to a further reduction in wage costs in the public sector, if necessary (Law 4046/2012). The wage bill for public utilities fell, in 2009–10, by 15% (Ministry of Finance).
- The salaries were frozen for the years 2010–11 (Law 3871/2010; Law 3899/2010).
- Part-time employment both in the private (Law 3846/2010; Law 3899/2010) and in the public sector (Law 3986/2011) has been promoted.
- The working time of employees in the public sector has increased from 37.5 to 40 hours per week (Law 3979/2011).
- In accordance with the new institutional and legal framework, the terms of collective agreements or arbitration decisions that provided wage increases for the employees of the public utilities were cancelled (Law 3833/2010; Law 3871/2010; Law 3899/2010) leading to the abolition of their binding character.

In the following analysis, questions concerning the size of the Greek public sector and the taxation system are investigated.

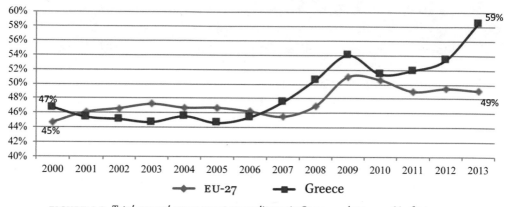

FIGURE 3.3  *Total general government expenditures in Greece and EU-27 as % of GDP, 2000–13*
SOURCE: EUROSTAT

## 4        The Size and the Revenues

### General Government Revenues and Expenditures

The reforms, imposed by the Greek state and the troika, were based on the supposed oversize of the Greek public sector, as it is expressed through public expenditures. The latter are considered the main cause of the fiscal deficits and debt.

However, considering the ratio of government expenditures to GDP as the indicator of the public sector's size, from Figure 3.3 it is obvious that, during 2000–10 (i.e. before the Memoranda), the size of the Greek public sector followed the average size of the public sector of the EU-27 countries. The sharp increase in the total general government expenditures since 2010 has been attributed, as noted, to the inclusion of public enterprises in 2009 in general government expenditures. However, the increase in the total general government expenditures as a percentage of GDP after 2010 was mainly the result of the depression, i.e. of the biggest decrease in GDP (see also Figure 3.2) compared to the decrease in total general government expenditures in absolute terms.[33]

Moreover, as seen in Figure 3.4, both the employment in the general government and the total public employment in Greece as a percentage of the labour force were lower than those of 21 OECD countries in 2001. In 2011, the

---

33    It must be also noted that while 'the primary expenditures are significantly lower than the European average ... (the interest expenses on the debt were higher than in other Eurozone countries and the EU)' (Lapatsioras et al. 2011, p. 139).

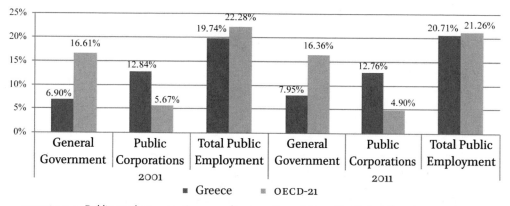

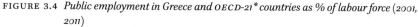

FIGURE 3.4 *Public employment in Greece and OECD-21\* countries as % of labour force (2001, 2011)*
*\* The calculations are based on available data for 21 member countries of OECD; no (complete) data is available for Australia, Austria, Belgium, Chile, Hungary, Iceland, Israel, Italy, Japan, Korea, Portugal, Turkey, and the United States.*
SOURCE: OECD (2013, P. 103), OWN CALCULATIONS

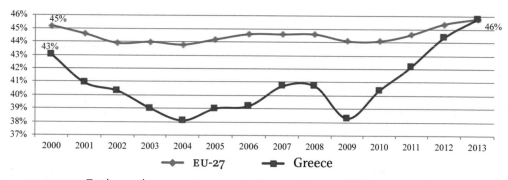

FIGURE 3.5 *Total general government revenues in Greece and EU-27 as % of GDP, 2000–13*
SOURCE: EUROSTAT

total public employment in Greece as a percentage of the labour force only slightly exceeded the OECD-21 average total public employment.

As can be seen from Figure 3.5, the real problem of the fiscal deficits lies in government revenues. The total general government revenues in Greece as a percentage of GDP before the public debt crisis were well below the EU-27 total general government revenues.

### Taxes on Labour and Capital in Greece and the EU-27

In Figure 3.6 it is shown that, during the 2000s, despite the deteriorating public debt, taxes on capital decreased as a percentage of GDP, becoming slightly higher than taxes on capital of the EU-27. On the contrary, during the same

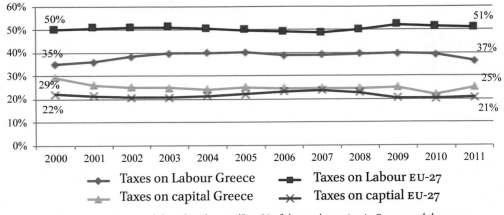

FIGURE 3.6  *Taxes on labour\* and capital\* as % of the total taxation in Greece and the EU-27,*
*2000–11*
\* For the definitions of taxes on labour and capital, see Eurostat 2013, pp. 273–7
SOURCE: EUROSTAT (2013, PP. 218, 226)

period, the taxes on labour as a percentage of GDP increased. It must be noted
that although taxes on labour were considerably below those in the EU-27, the
tax burden on labour increased substantially, if we consider that the inversely
progressive indirect taxes[34] are an important and growing part of the total
taxes.

In Figure 3.7 we can see that indirect taxes as a percentage of the total taxation in Greece are well above the average of the EU-27 and the Eurozone
indirect taxes.[35]

### Income Taxation in Greece

As can be seen from the data depicted in Table 3.1, income taxes burdened
mostly wage earners and pensioners. From 2006–11, the tax burden (on income) increased for wage earners and pensioners by 6.83 percentage points,
while the tax burden on the income of other individuals (entrepreneurs, self-
employed, etc.) increased by 1.44 percentage points, and the business profit tax
(for legal entities) decreased by 8.27 percentage points.

---

34    The regular Value Added Tax (VAT) increased from 19% to 21% according to the Law
      3833/2010 and from 21% to 23% according to the Law 3845/2010.

35    Therefore, respectively, direct taxation in Greece is much lower than in the EU-27 and the
      Eurozone (see also Lapatsioras et al. 2011, pp. 135–6).

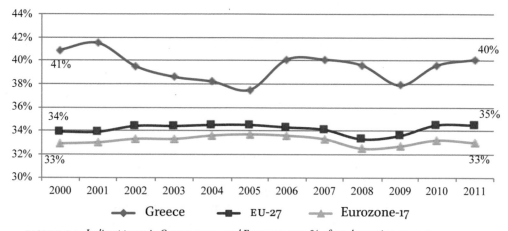

FIGURE 3.7  *Indirect taxes in Greece, EU-27 and Eurozone-17 as % of total taxation, 2000–11*
SOURCE: EUROSTAT (2013, P. 178)

TABLE 3.1  *Income taxes of legal entities and individuals as % of total income taxation*
(*financial years 2006–11*)

| Financial year | Taxes of legal entities* | Taxes of individuals | | Total |
|---|---|---|---|---|
| | | Wage earners/ pensioners | Other individuals** | |
| 2006 | 37.74 | 48.26 | 14.00 | 100 |
| 2007 | 36.33 | 50.09 | 13.58 | 100 |
| 2008 | 35.01 | 47.95 | 17.05 | 100 |
| 2009 | 30.79 | 52.59 | 16.62 | 100 |
| 2010 | 28.67 | 55.54 | 15.79 | 100 |
| 2011 | 29.47 | 55.09 | 15.44 | 100 |

* They are referred to taxes on income (profits) of SA, Limited Companies, General Partnership Companies, Limited Partnership Companies and Joint Ventures (Vasardani 2011, p. 18).

** Include taxes on income of non-wage earners and non-retiree: sole traders, self-employed, farmers/ranchers, traders, industrialists, rentiers.

Note: For definitions of the various categories of income tax, see the General Secretariat for Information Systems 2011.

SOURCE: GENERAL SECRETARIAT FOR INFORMATION SYSTEMS (2007, P. 4; 2008, P. 2; 2009, P. 4; 2010, P. 4; 2011, P. 4; 2012, P. 5)

We must point out that the rate of corporation tax (on undistributed profits) fell from 40% in 1994 (Law 2238/1994) to 35% in 2004 (Law 3296/2004) and 22% in 2012 (Law 3842/2010), with the potential to decrease to a level of 20% by 2014.

### Tax Evasion as a Class Alliance between the Bourgeois and Middle Classes

From the above analysis it could be inferred that low tax revenues in Greece were accompanied by a deep class-oriented taxation system. However, low tax revenues were also related to an extended tax evasion, which is often presented as a 'national problem'. Tax evasion is finally 'loaded' to employees, who are subject to an unbearable tax burden, especially during the debt crisis.

Two important consequences of tax evasion[36] are: (1) the restriction of the redistributive function of progressive taxation mainly at the expense of wage earners and pensioners; and (2) the increase in the borrowing needs of the state, as a result of revenue leakage that could finance government expenditures.[37]

Important clues of legal entities' tax evasion are presented by Vasardani:

> Regarding the legal persons, from 221,363 firms that submitted a tax return in 2009, 97,037 (or 44%) of them reported zero profits, while the vast majority (209,311 enterprises or 95%) reported taxable profits under 120,000 Euro. The total reported income in the financial year 2009, which amounted to 16.7 billion, was 14% lower compared to the previous year, and led to lower participation of legal entities in the distribution of tax burdens. The average taxable profit amounted to 75,485 Euros for each firm, while last year the average taxable profits had reached 90,895 Euros. It must be noted that, although profits of Greek firms showed a downward trend during the period 2006–9, they remained significantly higher as a percentage of GDP compared to other countries in the Eurozone, such as Austria, Belgium, Germany, France and Holland.[38]

---

36   According to Vasardani (2011, p. 15), 'the concept of tax evasion could be described as the illegal act of deliberate concealment of taxable income and other tax elements during the declaration and calculation of tax due, and the non-payment of tax due to the relevant government authorities'.

37   Vasardani 2011, p. 15; see also Lapatsioras et al. 2011, pp. 136–7.

38   Vasardani 2011, pp. 20–1.

On the other hand, as Matsaganis and Flevotomou pointed out, income tax evasion (as reflected in reported income) was virtually non-existent on the part of wage earners[39] for the period 2004–5, since they declared a smaller income by 0.6% in relation to the real one, while in the case of pensioners tax evasion was zero. Moreover, the declared income from farmers and self-employed was smaller than their real income by 52.9% and 24.4% respectively. The total income tax evasion in 2004–5 reached about 10%, which corresponds to 26.1% reduced tax revenues.[40]

Artavanis et al. pointed out that tax evasion originating from self-employment was 28 billion in 2009, representing 31% of the budget deficit.[41]

An indication of latent tax evasion of the middle classes is the fact that in 2009 83% of the non-wage earners/non-pensioners (sole traders, freelancers, farmers, etc.) declared an income which was below the non-taxable limit of 10,500 Euro while 47% declared zero income. In contrast, only 53% of wage earners/pensioners declared an income which was below the non-taxable limit of 10,000 Euro and only 0.2% declared zero income.[42]

The tax evasion problem has also worsened due to unreported work, which hides taxable income – based on (large and small) employers' terrorism against employees. Unreported work was estimated at 25% in 2010.[43]

Simultaneously, as is shown in Table 3.2, indirect taxation seems to be not only a strong aggravating factor for employees and pensioners – because of its inverse progressive nature – but also a factor of revenue shortfalls, since it is associated with serious divergences between the tax revenues that are certified by authorities and the tax revenues that are finally collected by them (VAT).

Thus, while wage earners and pensioners – from whom revenues from indirect taxation basically derive – were burdened during the period 2006–11 with an average of 5.2 billion Euro, only 6.48% (i.e. about 340 million Euro) of these taxes were collected and included in public revenues.

So it was not just the 'large capital' that evaded taxes; it was also a broader social coalition, which included the middle classes.[44] It was about an open

---

39      The case of income concealment by employees is assigned to the agreement between employers and employees, aiming to the reduction of labour costs (Matsaganis and Flevotomou 2010, pp. 22–3).

40      Matsaganis and Flevotomou 2010, pp. 19–20; see also Vasardani 2011, p. 18.

41      Artavanis et al. 2012, pp. 4, 29.

42      Vasardani 2011, p. 20.

43      Vasardani 2011, p. 17.

44      For the determination of middle-class sub-collectivities, not as parts of the same class but as different classes, see Milios and Economakis 2011.

TABLE 3.2    *Certified – collected VAT of financial years 2006–11*

| Financial year | Certified VAT (euros) | Collected VAT (euros) | Collected VAT as % of certified VAT |
|---|---|---|---|
| 2006 | 3,269,256,716.18 | 251,874,916.44 | 7.70 |
| 2007 | 3,846,473,371.79 | 269,670,734.21 | 7.01 |
| 2008 | 4,364,100,937.12 | 319,477,113.93 | 7.32 |
| 2009 | 8,146,596,306.20 | 617,298,530.40 | 7.58 |
| 2010 | 5,410,163,737.35 | 244,428,847.85 | 4.52 |
| 2011 | 6,413,316,681.73 | 302,694,469.85 | 4.72 |
| Average | 5,241,651,291.56 | 334,240,768.71 | 6.48 |

* VAT = VAT certified for the first time + VAT of previous years + Tax settlement of previous years' VAT + Tax settlement of previous six years' VAT + Fines

SOURCE: GENERAL SECRETARIAT FOR INFORMATION SYSTEMS (2007, PP. 177–87; 2008, PP. 177–87; 2009, PP. 177–87; 2010, PP. 177–87; 2011, PP. 186–96*; 2012, PP. 218–29)

class alliance of the bourgeoisie, through the state, with the non-salaried social classes (middle classes) against salaried social classes.

However, the proletarianisation of parts of the middle classes in depression conditions, as reflected in the reduction in self-employed without employees (see Figure 3.8), jeopardises the class alliance of the bourgeoisie with the middle classes in this conjuncture.

## Conclusion

The global crisis was expressed in Greece as a public debt crisis. Greek governments and international organisations have attributed the huge public debt to the oversized public sector and have attempted to confront the public debt crisis through the restriction of public spending, in accordance with the NPM's principles, and the increase in revenues mainly deriving from the salaried classes. This economic policy was one of the main purposes of the imposed adjustment programmes (Memoranda). Nevertheless, the real problem of the public debt lies not in government expenditures, which as a percentage of GDP during 2000–10 (i.e. before the Memoranda) followed the average of the EU-27 countries, but in the low total general government revenues, which, as a percentage of GDP, were well below the EU-27 total general government revenues before the public debt crisis.

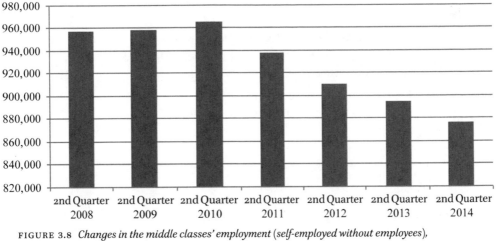

FIGURE 3.8  *Changes in the middle classes' employment (self-employed without employees), 2008–14*
SOURCE: EL.STAT

Low tax revenues in Greece were accompanied by, on the one hand, a deep class-oriented taxation system, and, on the other, an extended tax evasion which expressed an open class alliance of the bourgeoisie, through the state, with the non-salaried social classes (middle classes) against salaried social classes. However, the proletarianisation of parts of the middle classes amid depression conditions places the class alliance of the bourgeoisie with the middle classes into jeopardy.

### References

Andersen, Soren Kaj, Jesper Due and Jorgen Steen Madsen 1997, 'Multi-track approach to public-sector restructuring in Europe: impact on employment relations; role of the trade unions', *Transfer: European Review of Labour and Research*, 3, 1: 34–61.

Artavanis, Nikolaos T., Adair Morse and Margarita Tsoutsoura 2012, 'Tax evasion across industries: soft credit evidence from Greece', *Chicago Booth Paper No. 12–25*. Fama-Miller Center for Research in Finance – The University of Chicago, Booth School of Business, available at: http://papers.ssrn.com/sol3/papers.cfm?abstract_id=2109500

Bach, Stephen 1999, 'Changing public service employment relations', in *Employment Relations in Europe: Transformation, modernization or inertia?*, edited by Stephen Bach, Lorenzo Bordogna, Giuseppe Della Rocca and David Winchester, London: Routledge.

Bach, Stephen and David Winchester 2003, 'Industrial Relations in the Public Sector', in

*Industrial Relations: Theory and Practice*, edited by Paul Edwards, Oxford: Blackwell Publishing.

Bank of Greece 2012, *Summary of the Annual Report 2011*, Athens: Bank of Greece.

Beaumont, Phil B. 1992, *Public Sector Industrial Relations*, London: Routledge.

Beeton, Danny J. 1987, 'On the size of the public sector', *Applied Economics*, 19, 7: 927–36.

Bordogna, Lorenzo and Gian Primo Cella 1999, 'Admission, exclusion, correction: the changing role of the state in industrial relations', *Transfer: European Review of Labour and Research*, 5, 14: 14–33.

Commission of the European Communities – Eurostat, International Monetary Fund, Organisation for Economic Co-operation and Development, United Nations and World Bank 1993, *System of National Accounts 1993*, available at: http://unstats.un .org/unsd/nationalaccount/docs/1993sna.pdf

Commission of the European Communities – Eurostat, International Monetary Fund, Organisation for Economic Co-operation and Development, United Nations and World Bank 2009, *System of National Accounts 2008*, available at: http://unstats.un .org/unsd/nationalaccount/docs/SNA2008.pdf

Economakis, George, George Androulakis and Maria Markaki 2015, 'Profitability and crisis in the Greek economy (1960–2012): an investigation', in *Greek capitalism in crisis: Marxist Analyses*, edited by Stavros Mavroudeas, London: Routledge.

EL.STAT (Hellenic Statistical Authority). Labour Force Surveys for the years 2008–2013, available at: http://www.statistics.gr/statistics/-/publication/SJO01/-

ESA (European System of Accounts) 95, available at: http://eur-lex.europa.eu/legal -content/EN/TXT/PDF/?uri=OJ:L:1996:310:FULL&from=EL

Eurostat 2009, *European Economic Statistics*, Luxembourg: Office for Official Publications of the European Communities.

Eurostat 2013, *Taxation trends in the European Union: Data for the EU Member States, Iceland and Norway*, Luxemburg: Publications Office of the European Union.

General Secretariat for Information Systems 2007, *Statistical Bulletin of Tax Data 2006* [in Greek], Athens: Ministry of Economy and Finance, available at: http://www.gsis .gr/gsis/export/sites/default/gsis_site/PublicIssue/documents_Statistics/ statdeltio2006.pdf

General Secretariat for Information Systems 2008, *Statistical Bulletin of Tax Data 2007* [in Greek], Athens: Ministry of Economy and Finance, available at: http://www.gsis .gr/gsis/export/sites/default/gsis_site/PublicIssue/documents_Statistics /statdeltio2007.pdf

General Secretariat for Information Systems 2009, *Statistical Bulletin of Tax Data 2008* [in Greek], Athens: Ministry of Finance, available at: http://www.gsis.gr/gsis/export/ sites/default/gsis_site/PublicIssue/documents_Statistics/statdeltio2008.pdf

General Secretariat for Information Systems 2010, *Statistical Bulletin of Tax Data 2009*

[in Greek], Athens: Ministry of Finance, available at: http://www.gsis.gr/gsis/export/
sites/default/gsis_site/PublicIssue/documents_Statistics/statdeltio2009.pdf

General Secretariat for Information Systems 2011, *Statistical Bulletin of Tax Data 2010*
[in Greek], Athens: Ministry of Finance, available at: http://www.gsis.gr/gsis/export/
sites/default/gsis_site/PublicIssue/documents_Statistics/statdeltio2010v4.pdf

General Secretariat for Information Systems 2012, *Statistical Bulletin of Tax Data 2011*
[in Greek], Athens: Ministry of Finance, available at: http://www.gsis.gr/gsis/export/
sites/default/gsis_site/PublicIssue/documents_Statistics/statdeltio2011.pdf.

Hyman, Richard 2008, 'The State in Industrial Relations', in *The SAGE Handbook of
Industrial Relations*, edited by Paul Blyton, Nicolas Bacon, Jack Fiorito and Edmund
Heery, London: SAGE Publications.

International Monetary Fund 2012, "Greece: Request for Extended Arrangement Under
the Extended Fund Facility – Staff Report; Staff Supplement; Press Release on the
Executive Board Discussion; and Statement by the Executive Director for Greece",
*IMF Country Report No. 12/57, March 2012*, available at: http://www.imf.org/external/
pubs/ft/scr/2012/cr1257.pdf

Kouzis, Yiannis 2010a, 'Memorandum and employee relations' [in Greek], *Utopia*, 92:
15–19.

Kouzis, Yiannis 2010b, 'The evolution of the neoliberal deregulation of labour and crisis
as an excuse', in the collective volume, *The map of the crisis, the end of illusion* [in
Greek], Athens: Topos.

Kouzis, Yiannis 2011, 'Labour in the vortex of economic crisis: ten points' [in Greek],
*Utopia*, 97: 7–12.

Lacey, Robert 1997, 'Internal markets in the public sector: the case of the British National Health Service', *Public Administration and Development*, 17, 1: 141–59.

Lapatsioras, Spyros, John Milios and Dimitris P. Sotiropoulos 2011, 'Journey into defeat:
Policies facing the crisis or policies exploiting the crisis? Thoughts for a left strategy'
[in Greek], *Theseis*, 116: 117–144.

Lapatsioras, Spyros and Dimitris P. Sotiropoulos 2011, 'The arithmetic of public debt ...
not just for beginners' [in Greek], *Theseis*, 116: 89–115.

Leat, Mike 2007, *Exploring Employee Relations*, Oxford: Butterworth-Heinemann.

Milios, John 2011, 'The Greek crisis as a version of the global economic crisis and EMU
crisis'. Paper presented at the International Conference *Public debt and austerity
policies in Europe: The response of the European Left* [in Greek]. Organization: The
European Left Party, Coalition of the Left and Nicos Poulantzas Institute, available
at: http://youpayyourcrisis.blogspot.com/2011/03/blog-post_7459.html#more

Milios, John and George Economakis 2011, 'The Middle Classes, Class Places, and Class
Positions: A Critical Approach to Nicos Poulantzas's Theory', *Rethinking Marxism*,
23, 2: 226–45.

Mahler, Vincent A. 1992. 'Measuring public sector size in the advanced market economy
countries: The problem of deflators', *Social Indicators Research*, 27: 311–25.

Markantonatou, Maria V. 2011, 'State and new public management' [in Greek], *Theseis*, 116: 53–76.

Masters, Marick F., Ray Gibney, Iryna Shevchuk and Tom Zagenczyk 2008, 'The State as Employer', in *The SAGE Handbook of Industrial Relations*, edited by Paul Blyton, Nicolas Bacon, Jack Fiorito and Edmund Heery, London: SAGE Publications.

Matsaganis, Manos and Maria Flevotomou 2010, 'Distributional Implications of Tax Evasion in Greece', *GreeSE Paper No 31*, Hellenic Observatory Papers on Greece and Southeast Europe, LSE, available at: http://eprints.lse.ac.uk/26074/1/GreeSE_No_31.pdf.

Ministry of Finance 2011, *Introductory Report – State Budget 2011* [in Greek], available at: http://www.minfin.gr/documents/20182/225124/proypol2011_eis_ektesh.pdf/03a6948e-d6f9-4903-8696-1ec4cc8c99d0

Morgan, Philip, Nigel Allington and Edmund Heery 2000, 'Employment insecurity in the public services', in *The Insecure Workforce*, edited by Edmund Heery and John Salmon, New York: Routledge.

OECD 2011a, *National Accounts at a Glance 2010*, Paris: OECD Publishing.

OECD 2011b, *National Accounts at a Glance 2011*, Paris: OECD Publishing.

OECD 2013, *Government at a Glance 2013*, Paris: OECD Publishing.

Olsen, Torunn (ed.) 1996, 'Industrial Relations Systems in the Public Sector in Europe', Norway: Fafo Institute for Applied Social Science/EPSC: http://www.fafo.no/media/com_netsukii/195.pdf

Pathirane, Leila and Derek W. Blades 1982, 'Defining and Measuring the Public Sector: Some International Comparisons', *Review of Income and Wealth*, 28, 3: 261–89.

Vasardani, Melina 2011, 'Tax evasion in Greece: a general review', *Economic Bulletin*, 35: 15–25 [in Greek], Athens: Bank of Greece, available at: http://www.bankofgreece.gr/BogEkdoseis/oikodelt201106.pdf

### Online Sources

AMECO: http://ec.europa.eu/economy_finance/ameco/user/serie/SelectSerie.cfm

Eurostat: http://epp.eurostat.ec.europa.eu/portal/page/portal/statistics/search_database

Greek Ministry of Finance: http://www.minfin.gr

# Consolidation of Authoritarian Rule in the EU: the Parallel Processes of the Troika's Emergence and the Economic Governance Reforms

*Yiorgos Vassalos*

Right after the eruption of the financial crisis in Europe in 2008, Hungary (the EU economy most dependent on borrowing from abroad) became the first EU member state ever to be bailed-out by the International Monetary Fund (IMF). This was done in tandem with the European Union. It was the first time that Article 143 of the Treaty on the Functioning of the EU (TFEU)[1] was used to provide financial assistance to a member state with its own currency facing difficulties in relation to its balance of payments.[2] The only similar episode previously occurred in 1992, when the Bundesbank had to intervene to support the British pound, Italian lira and French franc, according to the rules of the European Exchange Rate Mechanism.[3] Hungary was also the first case ever of a Memorandum of Understanding with strict economic policy conditionality agreed between a member state and the EU in return for financial assistance.[4]

By 2010, the relative freeze of the interbank market had transformed the financial crisis into a sovereign debt crisis hitting the Eurozone, presented up to then as the 'economic hard core of the EU' and a 'safe haven' by the official propaganda. The first epicentre of the Eurozone debt crisis was Greece.

With the country being unable to deal with rising interest rates, the first ad hoc mechanism to bail-out a Eurozone country was urgently put in place, in April 2010. A much bigger sum than the 20 billion lent to Hungary was needed and a 'balance of payments assistance' fund – whose capital would be insufficient for such an intervention anyway – was clearly prohibited by the Treaties from being used in Eurozone countries.

---

1  Treaty for the European Union, Article 143.
2  Hodson 2011, p. 103.
3  *New York Times*, 21 January 1993.
4  Memorandum of Understanding between the European Community and the Republic of Hungary, p. 192.

© KONINKLIJKE BRILL NV, LEIDEN, 2018 | DOI:10.1163/9789004280892_006

Within the framework of this ad hoc mechanism, the IMF, the European Commission and the European Central Bank (ECB) were to dictate economic policy in detail, as a condition for loans from other Eurozone countries and the IMF aiming at avoiding Greece's default to private banks. This was the official birth of the Troika. The mechanism urgently put in place was in sharp conflict with the 'no bail-out clause' included in Article 125 of the TFEU.[5] This was the prelude to a series of very shaky legal constructions that marked the post-crisis reform of the EU. In late 2010, EU governments decided to quietly pass an amendment to the Lisbon Treaty (entered in force in 2009 after four years of stalemate) to allow financial assistance to Eurozone countries in order to 'safeguard the stability of the euro area' (Article 136).[6]

The same year (2010), the EU also made a modification to the Stability Pact introducing the 'European Semester' – a schedule of regular screening of the economic policies of all EU member states in Brussels, mainly by the Commission. This was the beginning of a big reform process followed by the Pact for the Euro (2011), two legislative packages on economic governance (the 'six-pack' and the 'two-pack') and a new 'Treaty on Stability, Coordination and Governance in the EMU' (TSCG) including the Fiscal compact. With these reforms the EU radically increased its clout on issues such as the level of salaries, pension systems, and even health and education budgets: a country in 'excessive deficit' now has to follow the Commission's recommendations in these areas, otherwise it risks fines or the freezing of its cohesion funds in a much more direct way than before.[7] These changes violated Article 153 of the TFEU, which

---

5   Article 125 TFEU: 'The Union shall not be liable for or assume the commitments of central governments, regional, local or other public authorities, other bodies governed by public law, or public undertakings of any Member State, without prejudice to mutual financial guarantees for the joint execution of a specific project. A Member State shall not be liable for or assume the commitments of central governments, regional, local or other public authorities, other bodies governed by public law, or public undertakings of another Member State, without prejudice to mutual financial guarantees for the joint execution of a specific project'.

6   'On 16 December 2010, the Belgian Government submitted, in accordance with Article 48(6), first subparagraph, of the TEU, a proposal for revising Article 136 of the TFEU by adding a paragraph under which the Member States whose currency is the euro may establish a stability mechanism to be activated if indispensable to safeguard the stability of the euro area as a whole and stating that the granting of any required financial assistance under the mechanism will be made subject to strict conditionality' (EU Summit conclusions December 2010).

7   When approving the 2014–20 multiannual budget, the EU introduced a provision to 'ensure that Cohesion Policy is better linked to wider EU economic governance: Programmes will have to be consistent with National Reform Programmes and should address the relevant reforms identified through country-specific recommendations in the European Semester. If neces-

stressed explicitly that EU action in social policy is only complementary to the one of member states and 'shall not affect the right of Member States to define the fundamental principles of their social security systems ..., shall not prevent any Member State from maintaining or introducing more stringent protective measures [for labour]', and shall not interfere at all with 'pay, the right of association, the right to strike'.

In 2012, based on the modification of Article 136 made in 2010, the European Stability Mechanism treaty was approved. It legalised Eurozone bail-outs[8] and the intervention of the Troika in member states that could not pay their debt. Up to 2013, four Eurozone countries had experienced the Troika mechanism (in addition to Spain, which had a partial version of it). The permanent surveillance mechanisms that were put in place in the meantime via the economic governance reforms aim at making sure that economically weaker countries will remain under tight tutelage even when they manage to come out of the Troika regime and return to borrowing from the financial markets. They also establish a framework of much stricter surveillance of all EU economies and they almost outlaw wealth redistribution towards labour by means of salaries in all EU member states through the thresholds adopted for the macro-economic indicator on unit labour cost.[9]

In 2013, the Banking Union legislation came to systematise the use of different methods aimed to avoid the collapse and/or nationalisation-socialisation of systemic banks. First, it is examined whether the bank in danger can be taken over by a bigger one. If this is not possible, shareholders and depositors will suffer a haircut. And if this is not enough, the bank will be recapitalised from the ESM. The government of the country where the bank is based will have to pay the final cost of the bail-out back to the ESM under the surveillance of the Troika. Richer countries like Germany will continue to provide liquidity to cover some of the cost for bailing-out banks in poorer countries (as already happened in all the Troika countries), but this will come in exchange for Ger-

---

sary, the Commission can ask Member States – under the so-called "macro-economic conditionality" clause – to modify programmes to support key structural reforms. As a last resort, it can suspend funds if economic recommendations are repeatedly and seriously breached' (European Commission 2013b).

8  The ESM as well as the TSCG later on are in very shaky legal ground: they are not EU Treaties or part of the EU law and they do not include all EU member states, but they are subject to the jurisdiction of the Court of Justice of the EU (CJEU) (Treaty establishing the European Stability Mechanism 2012).

9  According to the excessive imbalance procedure, a fine can be imposed when specific thresholds are violated. More details available at: http://ec.europa.eu/economy_finance/economic _governance/macroeconomic_imbalance_procedure/mip_framework/index_en.htm.

many and France having the main say (as guaranteed by voting rights according to the capital of each country within the ESM) over how to deal with failing banks, including the organising of transnational mergers.

In December 2012, EU leaders proposed a kind of 'Contractual Arrangements' in order to centralise even more economic governance in Brussels. Those agreements should be signed between the Commission and all governments on the basic elements of their economic and budgetary policy. Thus, the pursuit of these economic policies would be immune to political changes following elections. This measure, besides the ones already adopted, would enhance the ability of the Brussels-based bureaucratic institutions – mainly the Commission and the Council of the finance ministers (Eurogroup/ECOFIN) – to dictate policies in a way more similar to the Troika mechanism than to the pre-crisis practices.

In a document of June 2015, EU leaders also proposed: (1) a euro area Treasury (where votes could be allocated as in a stock company) centralising decisions on revenue and expenditure policy; (2) a Euro area system of Competitiveness Authorities to monitor labour costs; (3) strengthening the macro-economic corrective arm and reform implementation with early (Troika-like) intervention; (4) reinforcing the Eurogroup and its president; (5) a Treaty change to include the TSCG, the Euro+Pact, the Banking Union's Single Resolution Fund and the ESM into the body of the TFEU.[10]

In a quite perverted way, Contractual Arrangements were presented in EU Summit conclusions as something that would increase the 'ownership' of the programmes by the different countries and their 'democratic legitimacy and accountability'. The spirit of Contractual Arrangements was kept in the Commission's legislative proposal for turning the ESM into the European Monetary Fund presented in December 2017.[11] It will increase EU intervention in national budgets, already occurring under the 'two-pack'. Intervention of the EU over how national budgets – and therefore taxpayers' money – are spent is a direct attack on the core concept of bourgeois/parliamentary democracy. The EU recognises as much when it says that 'budgets are at the heart of Member States' parliamentary democracies'. It also recognises that it aims at radically weakening national parliaments: 'the provisions for democratic legitimacy and accountability should ensure that the common interest of the union is duly taken into account; yet national parliaments are not in the best position to take it into account fully'.[12]

---

10    Juncker et al. 2015, p. 18.
11    European Commission 2017.
12    19–20 December 2013, 'EU Summit Conclusions', available at: http://www.consilium .europa.eu/uedocs/cms_Data/docs/pressdata/en/ec/140245.pdf.

What is proposed in order to give such economic decisions an air of 'democratic legitimacy' is not their binding approval by both the European and the national parliament(s) concerned, but an undefined 'commensurate involvement' of the former and an even vaguer 'appropriate involvement of ... national parliaments in the proposed reform arrangements of a contractual nature and more broadly in the context of the European Semester' defined by each national government. The only concrete thing the EU is invoking in its effort of giving a fig-leaf of democratic scrutiny in all these reforms is the organisation of debates in the parliaments concluded by non-binding opinions.[13] The June 2015 EU leaders document makes crystal clear that their ambition up to 2025 is to give a purely consultative role to the European and National parliaments in economic governance issues. But making decisions and not debating the decisions of other entities is what makes parliaments sovereign. And a sovereign parliament is the defining feature of the bourgeois/parliamentary democratic polity. These ideas approved by EU summits or put forward by the five EU presidents are clearly moving outside the framework of bourgeois democracy and towards a type of transnational bourgeois authoritarianism.

The implications of the Troika/economic governance reforms for the quality of democracy, the welfare state, and the social situation are huge. The Charter of Fundamental Rights of the European Union has been blatantly violated by the explicit conditions of the Troika to governments attached to the bail-outs. The economic governance agenda pushes for attacks on established social rights in core EU countries such as national level collective bargaining or protection against unjustified dismissal. This double path of reform in the EU (Troika/ESM mechanisms and economic governance) brings a decisive qualitative change in the nature of the EU, as a unique transnational political construction.

A social upheaval without precedent has challenged the core content of these policies, first in the European South but increasingly in recent years in north-western Europe too (mass strikes and demonstrations in France, Belgium and the UK, for example). The political expression of these movements has been a complicated and contradictory matter. Political forces representing the classical EU consensus (conservatives/Christian democrats, social democrats and liberals) have been losing substantial forces all over the EU and even collapsing in some countries. A rising far-right opposition to the mainstream EU project does not put in question its key impetus against workers' rights and the welfare state. It fully agrees with these policy objectives but is against the 'pooling of sovereignty' in order to achieve them. It challenges the *transnational*

---

13    Van Rompuy et al. 2012.

but not the *autocratic* aspect of the reforms. If we focus on the programmes of far-right parties, we will see they basically preach for more intergovernmental co-operation between sovereign autocratic states that would repress labour by putting aside some 'liberal values' and through a much stricter policy vis-à-vis immigrant workers.

Left-wing political opposition to the dominant EU project rose mainly in Greece and Spain and to a lesser extent in Portugal, Ireland and Slovenia.[14] Up to 2015 at least, radical left forces in these countries have invested politically in the ability to push for a progressive reform of the EU. But social movements' demands – for more democracy, more commons, less unemployment and precariousness, jobs with rights and a better life – are increasingly in contradiction with the political, legal, and institutional construction of the EU. Greece's impressive capitulation in summer 2015 violently demonstrated as much. This poses the question of what strategy is to be followed vis-à-vis the EU by political and social forces that aim at breaking with neoliberalism.

1        The Troika's Rule over the European Periphery

Eight out of 28 member states of the EU with around 100 of its 500 million inhabitants have been subject to Memoranda of Understanding (MoU) by Troika-like mechanisms regrouping the European Commission, the IMF and the ECB when it comes to the five Eurozone counties (Greece, Portugal, Ireland, Spain and Cyprus) or the Commission, the IMF and the World Bank when it comes to member states outside the Monetary Union (Hungary, Romania and Latvia before its entry into the Eurozone).[15]

The European Commission and specifically its Directorate General on Economic and Financial Affairs (DG ECFIN) has been the institution doing most of the work of monitoring the day-to-day implementation of the Memoranda. It has set up special groups per country called 'the Task force' in the case of Greece or 'Support groups' in the case of Portugal, Cyprus, and others in order to 'provide technical assistance and to recommend legislative, regulatory, administrative and if necessary (re)programming measures'.[16]

---

14    The post-referendum stance of the Labour Party under Jeremy Corbyn in the UK can also be seen as a political reinforcement of left-wing opposition to the dominant EU project.

15    European Commission, 'Financial assistance in EU Member States', available at: http://ec .europa.eu/economy_finance/assistance_eu_ms/index_en.htm.

16    European Commission, 'Financial assistance to Greece', available at: http://ec.europa.eu/ info/business-economy-euro/economic-and-fiscal-policy-coordination/ eu-financial-assistance_en.

In practice, these groups are deployed in key national ministries and are charged with approving or disapproving everything coming out of them. Greek ministries often struggled with translating orders of the Troika and announcing them as public measures. Even laws voted for in parliament had to be revised after emails of disapproval were sent by the Task Force.[17]

The Memoranda were concluded with specific governments often under the threat of the ECB cutting off liquidity to domestic banks (as happened in the case of Ireland[18] or even in order to push for some anti-labour reforms in Italy),[19] but they engage future governments as well as future generations until the debt contracted has been paid back. More than once, the EU establishment put all its political weight into demanding the signatures of opposition party leaders in support of the programmes and even – in the case of Greece – in organising the dismissal of the elected Papandreou government to replace it with a three-party coalition including the racist far-right, in late 2011.[20] For imposing the third MoU on Greece in Summer 2015, the ECB actually did cut off liquidity until the Greek Parliament approves it. Seven of the eight governments that asked for EU financial assistance through a Memorandum (MoU), collapsed two to sixteen months later.[21] Future governments continued the programmes without essentially 'renegotiating' and 'modifying' them as promised to their voters.

The raison d'être of the Troika is to dictate austerity and market liberalisation measures without any consideration for their social consequences, and

---

17    Ravanos 2014.
18    Whelan 2012.
19    Jones 2011.
20    Spiegel 2014.
21    The Hungarian social-democratic party MSZP signed the first MoU in November 2008 and lost the elections to Orbán in April 2010. Latvian Prime Minister Ivars Godmanis asked for EU financial assistance in December 2008 and collapsed in February 2009. The Romanian government signed its first MoU in May 2009 and the first political party of the country (the PSD) stepped out of the government in December of the same year. Greece asked for help in April 2010 and Papandreou resigned in November 2011. Ireland signed the MoU in November 2011 and anticipated elections were called for February 2011 after which the Fianna Fáil–Green Party coalition was replaced in government by a Fine Gael–Labour coalition. Portuguese Prime Minister Socrates signed a MoU in May 2011 after he had announced his resignation in March 2011. He lost the June 2011 elections to Pedro Passos Coelho. Cypriot left-wing President Christofias asked for help in June 2012 and he lost the Presidential elections in February 2013. Spain signed a MoU only after Mariano Rajoy was elected in November 2011, but Zapatero had already started implementing radical anti-labour measures since May 2011.

impose them independently of election results and electoral programmes. This goes clearly against Article 1 of the Charter of the United Nations (1945) safeguarding 'the self-determination of peoples'.[22]

The severity and depth of the Troika's intervention goes far beyond the concept of 'shared sovereignty' promoted by the official or semi-official ideologues of the European Union for more than two decades. The dictates of the Troika might coincide with the wildest dreams of the top corporate elite in each country or even be developed jointly with it, but they certainly come to externally overthrow the social and political status quo and push things much further away from what the body politic,[23] the political society and civil society in each country could accept.

Institutions representing those who provide credits for the bail-outs (namely the Commission and the ECB representing the Eurozone governments and then the IMF) are the sovereigns par excellence in determining the content of the programmes.[24] Countries under bail-outs do not come to take any part of the sovereignty of creditor countries. It is clearly a one-way relationship in which the indebted country is sharing its sovereignty with its creditors, and not vice versa. Needless to say, there is a hierarchy among the creditor governments as well, and the ones contributing bigger chunks of capital have more of a say.

This situation is closer to a new, intra-European type of neo-colonialism than 'shared sovereignty'. The existence of a local corporate elite profiting from the Troika's intervention, while the majority of the population is severely hit, is another similarity with neo-colonialism. The dominant political discourse spread the sentiment of collective guilt among citizens, from Ireland to Greece: 'they all together contributed in provoking the economic crisis, by living beyond their means, enjoying too high wages and an excessively generous welfare state'. Therefore, collective punishment through the cuts was justified. Feelings of inferiority have also been cultivated in order to justify the EU tutelage. Here's an indicative incident; ahead of the 3rd German-Greek Assembly (DGV) of municipalities, Hans-Joachim Fuchtel, Representative of the Federal Chancellor for Greece, claimed that '3,000 Greek municipal workers do the

---

22  Charter of the United Nations, available at: http://www.un.org/en/documents/charter/chapter1.shtml.

23  'When any number of men have so consented to make one community or government, they are thereby presently incorporated, and make one body politic, wherein the majority have a right to act and conclude the rest' (Locke 1690).

24  'Sovereign is the one who decides on the state of exception', wrote the Nazi law theorist Carl Schmitt (Schmitt 1988 [1922]).

work of 1,000 of their German counterparts'.[25] There were many similar pejorative statements about Greek public servants and citizens in general, by Greek politicians too. Bailed-out nations had been 'mischievous' and the EU – led by Germany – had to discipline them.

Four types of measures can be found in nearly all the Memoranda: (1) Massive lay-offs and salary cuts in the public sectors. Due to the importance of public sectors to all economies, salary reductions were planned to have a severe downward impact on the private sector too; (2) Reduction in the public sector through massive privatisations and worsening of the state of health and education; (3) Making lay-offs easier and reducing the collective bargaining power of organised labour; (4) Increase in retirement age and reduction in employers' contribution to pension funds.

These measures interfered with national budgets and with wage-setting mechanisms and the regulation of social relations. In Greece, the Troika imposed the reduction in the private sector nominal minimum wage by 22% and the dismantling of national-level collective bargaining since it was reduced from a binding to a merely consultative-to-the-government exercise. National-level collective bargaining was abolished during the years of the Troika in Romania too.

After the passage of the Troika, organising a legal strike in Romania and Hungary is almost impossible. In Romania, a strike can take place only after an explicit refusal of the employer to negotiate and then a long compulsory procedure of conciliation under the ministry of Labour.[26] This means workers should wait for about a month after a conflict arises to be able to strike.[27] Strikes in all kinds of sectors – transportation, health, public sanitation and social assistance, telecommunications, public radio and TV, gas, heat, power and water – are only allowed if at least one third of normal activity is ensured. Many strikes occurred in Hungary during the MoU period (2008–10). Right after it, when Orbán came to power he passed a law according to which strikes are only lawful if employers and trade unions agree in advance on the minimum level of services to be provided! All nine strike initiatives that came before the Labour court in the first six months after the new law came into force have been pre-emptively banned. The higher court also ruled that strikes against government measures could not be deemed lawful.[28]

---

25    Kathimerini 2012.
26    Ticlea and Ticlea 2011, p. 194.
27    Damo 2012.
28    Eurofound 2012.

As a result of the application of the MoUs, all countries concerned experienced shorter or longer term recession periods, as well as a sharp decrease in real wages and a boom of unemployment especially among the youth, whose most specialised cohort emigrated en masse. Officially, the priority of MoUs was to deal with debt. But in all countries where they were applied, the debt actually increased. The debt has only been the pretext for anti-labour policies.

This invasive involvement of the EU on sensitive issues of national democracies provoked political radicalisation, first of the nationalist (and at the same time pro-EU) Right in Hungary, the first country to conclude a Memorandum. After the 2010 elections, while negotiating a second bail-out with the EU and the IMF, Orbán decided to take some measures he knew his creditors would not like: he nationalised some pension funds' assets, he forced banks to swallow losses on foreign-currency mortgages, and he limited the independence of the Hungarian central bank. He said Hungary could stand on its own feet without a MoU. Indeed, the EU and the IMF ceased talks in response to his measures. Government bonds were then downgraded to 'junk' by credit rating agencies and Hungary returned to recession in 2012, but all in all it did not do any worse than the countries the EU bailed-out from 2010 and on.

The EU continued to supervise the Hungarian economy as it does with all bailed-out countries through the post-programme surveillance (PPS) provided in the two-pack for Economic Governance until 75% of the EU debt is repaid (Article 14).[29] Through the European Semester recommendations, the EU continued to push for anti-labour and anti-welfare measures. In January 2012, the European Commission launched legal action against Hungary on limiting the independence of the central bank, the judiciary and the personal data protection agency.[30] The Commission proved it is a very selective 'guardian of the Treaties' by not simultaneously moving against Hungary's clear violations of social rights included in the EU Charter of Fundamental Rights (CFR). These infringements, though, have also occurred as a result of the Commission's own pressure through the MoU.[31]

---

29    Council Regulation (EU) No. 472/2013.

30    European Commission 2012.

31    No EU law or Treaty protects the independence of the judiciary in member states, but the Commission found an indirect way to go against the decision of the Hungarian government to curtail it. This demonstrates that the Commission can act when it has the political will to do so. With the Lisbon Treaty 'the Charter [CFR] became legally binding on the EU institutions and on national governments, just like the EU Treaties themselves'. 'Members of the College of Commissioners swore a solemn declaration to uphold the Charter as well

After modifying Hungarian law to comply with EU law regarding the central bank and the judiciary, Orbán declared that he wants Hungary to exit liberal democracy and build an illiberal state, which he sometimes defines as 'Christian democracy', and at the same time remain within the European Union. He does not see any contradiction between the two. EU institutions' reaction to the expression of these grave ambitions by Orbán has been close to non-existent. He and his political party Fidesz are the perfect illustration of how conservative, pro-capitalist political forces can agree on the anti-labour aspect of the dominant EU policy, but disagree on how much national sovereignty to share and whether (or how openly) some civic liberties should be demolished.

Under the new economic governance rules, Hungary became the first country to see its cohesion funds blocked for not complying with the Commission's recommendations. Hungary finally implemented them and the freeze was lifted on time before the first disbursement.[32]

## 2 Permanent Reforms in the EU Architecture

As the case of Hungary demonstrates, the bail-out and economic governance structures are completely complementary. 2011 was the first year in which the European Semester was applied: all national governments submitted their economic programmes to the Commission and the latter proposed recommendations rubberstamped by the Council of finance ministers. The six-pack on economic governance had not yet come into force, so imposing semi-automatic fines to countries under 'excessive deficit' or 'macro-economic imbalance' procedures that did not follow these recommendations was not possible for 2011.

In March 2011, EU leaders adopted the political and socio-economic manifesto that included their guiding principles for the economic governance reform: this was the Euro-plus Pact. They put forward four priorities: (1) integrate the prohibition of 'excessive deficits' into national constitutions or framework laws (debt brake); (2) keep wages low by (a) abolishing indexation where it exists, (b) 'decentralising' collective bargaining, (c) making sure wages evolve 'in line with productivity' and 'competitiveness' and therefore monitor unit labour costs in order not to let them increase, (d) ensuring public sector wages 'support the competitiveness effort in the private sector (bearing in mind their

---

as the Treaties in May 2010'. Nevertheless, the Commission considers it can take action against CFR violations only when EU law is violated too (European Commission 2013a).

32    European Council 2012.

important signalling effect)'; (3) increase the retirement age; (4) shift from direct taxes on revenue to indirect taxes on consumption (or from taxing the rich to taxing the poor).[33]

The Euro Pact plus was just a 'gentlemen's agreement'. First, the six-pack and the two-pack and then the Treaty on Economic Governance (TSCG) came to give the EU the necessary teeth to implement the directions included in it.

Beyond making penalties to countries violating deficit limits much more automatic,[34] the six-pack introduced an important novelty: the surveillance and sanction of 'macro-economic imbalances'. This was a brand new battle-axe in the weaponry of the EU against 'labour cost' in Europe. Surveillance was to be done on the basis of a scoreboard of 11 indicators.[35] The most interesting one is the nominal labour unit cost in relation to real GDP. This should not increase by more than 9% for Eurozone countries and more than 12% for non-Eurozone countries in three consecutive years. What is effectively banned through this rule is redistribution of GDP from capital to labour through wages. Although fines for 'excessive wages' have not yet been imposed, this 'alert mechanism' has been successfully used to push Belgium and Finland into freezing their wages or Luxembourg into postponing salary indexation.

The first priority of the Euro-plus Pact, to introduce the 'debt brake' in national constitutions or framework laws, was implemented with the Treaty on Stability, Coordination and Governance in the EMU (TSCG). According to this Treaty, the Court of Justice of the EU can impose fines equal to 0.1% of the gross domestic product to the signatory member states that have not integrated the 'debt brake'. The TSCG also introduced a new 0.5% 'structural deficit'[36] limit on top of the regular 3% deficit limit. Access to the funds of the European Stability Mechanism (ESM) is conditional upon adherence to the TSCG.[37]

The two-pack concluded in 2013 instituted a detailed control of all the Eurozone member states' draft budgets at EU level. By 15 October of each year, Euro-

---

33    Euro Plus Pact 2011.

34    Automaticity was ensured with the adoption of the reversed qualified majority, which means that the Commission's proposals for sanctions can only be rejected with two thirds of the votes of member states in the Council against them.

35    European Commission 2013c.

36    Structural deficit = Total deficit minus Cyclical deficit, minus One-off measures. It is highly improbable that two statistical services in the world agree on the calculation of one-off measures, for instance.

37    The Treaty on Stability, Coordination and Governance in the EMU (TSGC), 2 March 2012.

zone countries must submit their draft budgets for the following year to the Commission. By 30 November, the Commission will give an opinion on each draft budget. If it detects non-compliance with obligations under the Stability Pact, it will ask the Member State concerned to submit a revised plan. If the country does not follow these instructions, this is used as evidence to decide whether or not to launch an excessive deficit procedure that can lead to fines.[38]

All the above points (national budgets' surveillance, putting a ceiling on labour costs and radically increasing the economic policy powers of the Commission) have been among the wildest dreams of European transnational corporations that have expressed them through their lobby groups since 2002.[39] BusinessEurope, the umbrella organisation representing corporate employers' federations across the EU, has given a lot of input into the milestones of the economic governance reform (the six-pack,[40] the Euro-plus pact[41] and the TSCG[42]) and has seen its main demands reflected in the adopted legislation. The first two years of the European Semester process (2011 and 2012) have been like a fast-track implementation of BusinessEurope's wishes per country as they were expressed in its annual 'reform barometer'.[43]

National governments representing the neoliberal consensus, under the impulse of transnational corporations that often provide funds to the parties making up these governments, have given away essential powers to bureaucratic institutions, such as the European Commission, which are not subject to any electoral scrutiny. The new exercise of nominating as President of the Commission the candidate of the first political group (which was the EPP in 2014 with less than 30% of the votes in the European elections) is, of course, a caricature of democracy.[44] This way, neoliberal political forces (including the social democrats) shield their policies from democratic control and electoral changes. Taking advantage of the fact that they were in government at the time, they carved their policies in stone, so that it would be 'illegal' according to EU law to change them.

But there is not only a weakening of parliaments and formal representative democracy. There is also a clear hierarchy established between the nation

---

38    European Commission 2013d.

39    European Round Table of Industrialists (ERT) 2002.

40    Corporate Europe Observatory 2011b.

41    Corporate Europe Observatory 2011a.

42    Corporate Europe Observatory 2012.

43    Corporate Europe Observatory 2013.

44    There is also no obligation for member states to name as president the head of the first political group, but merely to 'take elections results into account'.

states that make up the Eurozone. The GDP of each country, which determines its contribution to the European Stability Mechanism, the ECB, and the Single Resolution Mechanism of the Banking Union, is the most decisive criterion in the construction of this hierarchy. Germany and France hold together 46% of the voting rights, while six countries out of the 17 of the Eurozone hold 85% of them. It is within this formal balance of powers that the conditions of the bail-outs of countries and banks or other endeavours to save banks (mergers, bail-ins, etc.) will be decided in the future. One of the declared objectives of the Banking Union is 'breaking the link between banks and sovereigns', which means that the bulk of banking activities in the Eurozone can be concentrated in the biggest of the too-big-to-fail private banks of the core EU countries and that no democratic control whatsoever needs to be applied to the financial sector. Countries have to urgently implement a series of measures when their deficits run above 3%, often due to fluctuations in the global financial markets. They are asked to take these measures in order to restore 'markets' confidence'. States must adapt to the needs of the markets without having many tools to tame those markets. According to the EU mantra, all that states can do to financial institutions is save them from bankruptcy and pretend they regulate them but never socialise them. The break between banks and states promoted by the Banking Union cannot be complete, since in the end only states can guarantee the existence of banks (even if they abstain from controlling them). The ESM/Banking Union reforms come to reorganise the relation between banks and states by giving the richest Eurozone states (and banks) the formal driving seat and putting the peripheral ones in a formally subordinate position.

Towards the end of 2014, the Commission made a first review of economic governance reforms, recognising that there are problems with the transparency of policy making and their impact on growth, (social) imbalances (read: inequalities) and convergence between poorer and richer member states (there is in fact growing divergence).[45] Nevertheless, the final conclusion was still positive; since deficits have declined, the reforms are on the right track and should continue. The June 2015 five presidents' manifesto states that the new way that the objective of 'convergence' is understood is not 'a way to equalise incomes between member states', but rather concerns 'similarly resilient national economic structures'.[46]

---

45    European Commission 2014a.
46    Juncker et al. 2015.

3      **The Meaning of the above Measures and Reforms in Terms of
       Fundamental Rights and the Nature of the EU**

Both the 2014 Commission's review of economic governance policies and statements by the vice-President of the Commission, Frans Timmermans, referring
to how the MoUs have been drafted,[47] indirectly recognise that there has been
no proactive assessment of the social impact of these policies whatsoever. The
European Parliament 'regrets the fact that the programmes in question were
designed without sufficient means to assess their consequences'. The parliament highlighted housing exclusion that resulted from the programmes as
a violation of the EU's Charter of Fundamental Rights and called on the EU
Agency for Fundamental Rights 'to assess thoroughly the impact of the measures on human rights'.[48]

Responding to parliamentary questions on this issue, competent European
Commissioners have altered between two types of response: the first is that
since MoUs are not legislative texts but bilateral international agreements
between a country and its creditors, the Charter of Fundamental Rights 'is not
applicable' (Moscovici, Katainen);[49] the second is that the 'The Plan developed
by the Troika in strict accordance with the Greek Government is based on the
Treaties ... but I would not go so far as to say that the Troika ... have violated
fundamental rights by imposing and agreeing on a reform package' (Timmermans).[50]

In 2014, Commissioners said that 'to this day, no violation of EC law has been
found as resulting from the implementation of measures under a programme'.
But the Parliament's resolution above shows they were not in a position to have
the slightest idea about it since no official, proactive or retrospective, assessment or inquiry on this issue has ever been undertaken for the MoUs implemented between 2010 and 2015.[51] Citizens of EU member states do not have
the right to go to the Court of Justice of the EU (CJEU) unless a Troika measure 'directly and adversely affects them as individuals'. The fact that collective

---

47    Frans Timmermans responded to a question from the Syriza MEP Kostas Chrysogonos as
      follows: '[I]t will be necessary, in future measures to be taken by the European Union, to
      have a thorough analysis about the social impact of measures taken in structural reform
      programmes' (Open Conference of Presidents of the European Parliament 2014).
48    European Parliament 2014a.
49    European Parliament 2014b.
50    The Treaties include the Charter of Fundamental Rights.
51    The first time such an assessment occured was in the third MoU signed with Greece in
      August 2015 (European Commission 2015).

appeals have to represent the totality of the persons concerned excludes any possibility of appeal by trade unions and other citizens' groups.[52] Greek and Portuguese unions actually tried to challenge the MoUs, but the CJEU refused to admit their cases.

Below we will see three examples of clear violations of social rights included in the EU Charter of Fundamental Rights that occurred in Greece and have never been subject to enquiries by an EU body. It is certain that similar violations have occurred in the seven other EU member states that have implemented Memoranda. The official pursuit of 'collective bargaining flexibilisation' undertaken under the various economic governance procedures suggests a tendency to violate this right in other member states, too.

1. Article 30 of the Charter of Fundamental Rights (CFR) provides that 'every worker has the right to protection against unjustified dismissal'.[53] In May 2010, as a condition of the MoU attached to the first Eurozone loan, the Troika said the government should 'amend employment protection legislation to extend the probationary period for new jobs to one year'[54] during which workers could be fired without any warning or reasoning. This loan condition was transposed into national law in December 2010. This being a generic provision applicable across sectors and professions, it exposed a big part of the workforce to unjustified lay-off. The only authority that examined the measure is the European Committee of Social Rights (ECSR) of the Council of Europe (47 member states) which judged that article 4.4 of the European Social Charter – which is actually the basis of inspiration for Article 30 of the CFR and 'recognise[s] the right of all workers to a reasonable period of notice for termination of employment' – has been violated.[55] Contrary to the Troika, which may suspend a loan, the ECSR does not have any clout to impose its decision. As a result, the law in question remains in place.

2. Article 31 of the CFR provides that 'every worker has the right' to 'fair and just working conditions' which 'respect his ... dignity'. In February 2012, the EU and the IMF extended a second loan to Greece on the condition of a 22 % reduction in the minimum salary in the private sector. This brought

---

52    As we mentioned in footnote 26, the CFR became in theory 'binding' with the Lisbon Treaty, but the Commission still refuses to act against violations unless secondary EU law is simultaneously violated.

53    Charter of Fundemental Rights of the European Union 2000.

54    European Commission 2010.

55    European Social Charter 1961.

the salary of young people to 440 Euros net. This was below the official poverty line. One year later, the ECSR ruled that this violated the right to a fair remuneration sufficient for a decent standard of living of young workers provided in the European Social Charter. It is clear that a legal salary beyond the poverty line is not fair and does not respect the dignity of young workers; therefore it violated the CFR as well. But no EU body or court has ever examined the conformity of this measure with the EU's own Charter.

3.  Article 28 of the CFR guarantees 'the right [of workers] to negotiate and conclude collective agreements at the appropriate levels [in accordance with national laws and practices] and ... to take collective action to defend their interests, including strike action'. Contrary to the spirit of the Greek Constitution which guarantees free collective agreements, the Troika dismantled them in three steps: In 2010, it imposed the primacy of agreements per enterprise vis-à-vis agreements per sector. In February 2012, it imposed that 'collective agreements which have expired will remain in force for a period of maximum 3 months. If a new agreement is not reached, after this period, remuneration will revert to the base wage ... until replaced by those in a new collective agreement or in new or amended individual contracts'. Thus, it has taken away any legal motive for employers to conclude collective agreements. In November 2012, the national-level collective negotiations defining this base wage (the national minimum salary) were downgraded from a compulsory to a consultative mandate for the government. The government can now define the minimum wage by decree. Just before the Samaras government collapsed at the end of 2014, the Troika was pushing it to change the legislation on how strikes are decided. In January 2018, Troika put deciding strikes with the absolute majority of a union's membership as a prerequisite for the disbursement of the loan's next tranche and the SYRIZA government got it voted in Parliament. Article 153 of the TFEU explicitly requires the EU not to interfere at all with 'pay, the right of association, the right to strike'. All the above measures imposed by the Troika violate both the CFR and the TFEU, but citizens and trade unions do not have an effective right to stand before the CJEU against these violations.

On the three cases above, we can quite safely say that the EU/Troika blackmailed successive Greek governments – using the loans as a stick – into violating the CFR. The EU has also provided full political coverage to the Greek government's civil mobilisation of four strikes in the period 2012–14 (Athens metro, maritime transports, secondary education and national electricity company)

in blatant violation of the Greek constitution and the CFR. Against these violations, only member states could go to the CJEU against the Commission, or the
Commission against member states, but they all lack the political will to do so.

This direct involvement of EU institutions and especially the Commission
(which is supposed to be the 'guardian of the Treaties') in violating the Treaties
is a very important development marking a qualitative change in the nature of
the EU.

Since its beginnings, the European Union tended to build its legitimacy
on being a 'community of democratic values', the 'guarantor of democracy in
Europe', as well as 'a global champion of human rights'. In the years following the outbreak of the crisis, its leadership has clearly omitted preserving the
image of a satisfactory human rights record in its effort to rescue its financialised economic model. The special envoy of the UN in Greece,[56] the International Federation of Human Rights,[57] the European Trade Union Confederation[58] and more, all testify to a clear responsibility of the EU in violating human
rights within its own borders.

We can observe a clear shift in the discourse of the Heads of EU institutions
as well as of political proponents of the EU in countries in which EU popularity
has started to rapidly decrease directly or indirectly; from positive profiling of
the EU as a guarantor of rights and the prospect for a better life, it has turned
into scaremongering that while the EU might be a competitive and tough environment to be in, it is still better than the 'horrors' that could come about if a
country dares to deal with the economic crisis outside the EU framework. Supporting the EU is no longer fuelled by hope, but by fear of the unknown.

Human rights protection is clearly no longer a priority for the EU. At the
end of 2014, the CJEU rejected the accession of the EU in the European Convention for Human Rights (ECHR) and it called to renegotiate the accession

---

56    Lumina 2013.

57    'Austerity measures adopted in response to the economic crisis have adversely impacted
      human rights, such as the rights to work and health, and curtailed fundamental freedoms
      in Greece. [The report exposes] policies that have ignored the adverse impact they were
      bound to have on society and points to the responsibilities that national and international
      institutions, particularly the EU and its member states, bear for such violations. The report
      reaches conclusions that are valid far beyond the Greek case, and indeed apply to all coun-
      tries that have been undergoing economic assistance in response to a severe economic
      recession' (FIDH 2014).

58    'Instead of acting as the guardian of the Treaty, the European Commission has not only
      allowed the IMF and the ECB to breach these principles, but has actually actively assisted
      in these breaches against major principles of the European Social Acquis' (ETUC 2015).

conditions. What the CJEU demands undercuts a central principle found in all human rights treaties: the competence of each state to decide what safeguards it puts in place to protect human rights. The CJEU wants the ECHR to recognise (a) 'the principle that the primacy of EU law prevents Member States from having higher human rights standards, where EU law has fully harmonised the matters concerned', and (b) the right for the CJEU to have the first and last word on the interpretation of EU law. This will mean that no effective external control of the failings of the EU and (within the scope of EU law) its Member States as regards human rights would be possible within the ECHR. According to the academic Steve Peers, 'far from enhancing the protection of human rights within the EU legal order, the EU's accession to the ECHR, on the terms which the CJEU insists upon, would significantly diminish it, for the EU would be compelled to ensure that it insulates itself against many human rights claims that might be brought against it'.[59]

There is a clear intention of the leadership of the EU to decouple the concept of the Rule of Law from respecting human rights and regress in terms of the democratic content given to this concept.[60] While non-democratic EU institutions can take more and more important decisions affecting citizens' lives and at the same time remain in a grey legal zone that renders them immune to citizens' political or legal actions, transnational companies ('corporate citizens') are given a more formal role in EU decision-making through the EU 'better regulation agenda'.[61] The impact of every piece of EU legislation to the competitiveness of corporations needs to be evaluated in impact assessments and any negative effects avoided. Competitiveness is the number one priority of the EU, carved in stone in the Treaties. And the way the EU leadership interprets this is by prioritising the global competitiveness of European corporations above all other concerns. This legitimises big business having the first and last word in all legislation and policies prepared at EU level and implemented in the 28 member states.

The European Union is transformed more and more into a dystopia for the vast majority of its citizens. Social rights established in the aftermath of the Second World War that have formed the backbone of modern democracies are put into the collimator. They concern the basic instruments of the socioeconomic majority (the low and medium salary earners) to exist politically, so that they can have a say over their fate. Formal democracy and civic rights are

---

59      Peers 2014.

60      European Commission 2014b.

61      Tansey 2014.

also under serious threat since grey zones are multiplying where citizens no longer have power and where democratic sovereignty is not 'pooled' but simply lost. The EU, on the other hand, is daily transformed into a 'corporate EUtopia'[62] where economic elites can impose on the rest of society more or less whatever they want.

Democracy is not something eternal and unchanged in time. It has been brought about and acquired its modern form through the movement of the masses from the eighteenth century and on. Basic elements of democracy – such as the universal suffrage and the welfare state – are achievements of the working-class movement. The evolution of democracy cannot be decoupled from social progress. Democracy either spreads into new fields – such as the economic one – and becomes more and more inclusive, or it shrinks and eventually disappears to go back to openly oligarchic forms.[63]

## 4        Far-Right and the EU: Opposition or Approximation?

Far-right political forces such as the French Front National (FN) are often portrayed as the political opposites and the absolute enemies of the EU project. Nonetheless, they share some policy objectives such as radically weakening the power of trade unions. In the programme of the FN we can read about 'the big reform of trade unions' it advocates, which would 'remove the "monopoly of representation" installed after the Liberation' (the 'irrefutable representation' has already been abolished but here the FN states its commitment to curtailing the role of the historical French trade union organisations) and 'would change the modalities for the election of employees' representatives'. It also says that the reformed unions it envisages 'would be less inclined to resort to strikes and demonstrations and more favourable to constructive concentration'.[64] These measures are very similar to what the Troika imposed, for instance, on Greece and has already helped to establish in Hungary and Romania: rendering strikes practically illegal.

---

62     Corporate Europe Observatory 2011c.

63     Official ideologues of the EU – such as the ECB's Benoît Cœuré – think that since contracts can be enforced and intellectual property rights assured in a certain area, then a 'political union' is already there. That is for sure not a sufficient condition for this political union to be a democratic one, but this does not seem to be too much of a concern for the EU leadership (Cœuré 2012).

64     Front National 2012, p. 67.

Moreover, the FN's approach on how to deal with finance is not radically different from what has been happening within the EU since 2008: 'In case of extreme necessity and risk for retail deposits, partial and temporary nationalization of investment banks in difficulty should be applied'.[65] The FN never defends a permanent nationalisation of banks, not even the creation of an important nationalised banking pole. The FN does not oppose the freedom of circulation of capital either.[66]

In the official positions of the FN, the EU is an originally good project of co-operation between 'neighbouring civilisations' and countries with comparable levels of socio-economic development, which has deviated from its original course. The FN does not propose the unilateral exit of France from the EU, but a renegotiation of the Treaties to radically change the framework in order to make it 'respect national sovereignties and identities. The restoration of French national sovereignty should be expected at the end of this [renegotiating] process'.[67]

Even exiting the Euro, which is aggressively promoted in the FN's political discourse, is much more moderately included in the party's programme where a consensual coordinated return to national currencies is defended after an agreement of the Eurozone's big core countries (France, Italy and Germany).[68] It is interesting that the FN refers to the concerns expressed by the patriarch of neoliberalism Milton Friedman regarding the architecture of the Euro in order to justify its position.

Similar positions are defended by most extreme-right forces in Europe (with the notable exceptions of Wilders's party in the Netherlands and Farage's party in the UK), such as the FPÖ, which says Austria should come out of the EU only if Turkey adheres to it and that the Eurozone should be divided in a hard north Euro and a soft south Euro, or Lega Nord which proposed the abandonment of the Euro by Italy, but supports the direct election of the President of the European Commission, more powers for the European Parliament, acceleration of the four unions (political, economic, banking and fiscal), Eurobonds and project bonds, the European Central Bank as lender of last resort and more as ways to reform the EU.[69] Vlaams Belang is verbally violent towards the EU – calling it an 'Islamosocialist' agenda (!), but what it is actually proposing is to

65    Front National 2012, p. 69.
66    Front National 2012, p. 49.
67    Front National 2012, pp. 48–9.
68    Front National n.d.
69    Lega Nord 2013.

'transform the EU into an intergovernmental co-operation' and 'change it into a multilateral treaty community'.[70]

The most extreme neo-Nazis within the EU, the members of the Golden Dawn in Greece, publicly expressed themselves in favour of the country remaining in the Eurozone during the critical 2012 elections and again during the edge of the summer 2015 negotiations. It should not go unnoticed that mass mobilisations in Ukraine – of which neo-fascists managed to become the avant-garde – started by protesting against the old government's decision not to ratify the association agreement with the EU. In return, the EU has provided full political support to subsequent governments in which neo-fascists played an indispensable role.

Proponents of the Colonels' regime in Greece (such as Makis Voridis) or of collaborationism with the Nazis in Belgium (such as Theo Francken) became ministers in governments having as their basic mission to implement the EU's socio-economic diktats.

The level of formal acceptance or disapproval of the EU varies within the European extreme and fascist right, but in general the latter supports its anti-union and anti-labour agenda and it pushes it to function in a more intergovernmental way. It also pushes to relax protection of religious and other sensitive minorities and to neglect civic rights of categories judged to come under 'delinquency'. These objectives are being well promoted in practice by the grey zones created through the ever greater intrusion of the EU into national competences having to do with the European arrest warrant, border control and other forms of police co-operation. This agenda fragments society, facilitates cheap provision of labour and prevents people from acting together on the basis of their common socio-economic interests. In any case, this is not as antithetical to the extreme right's agenda as is often presented.

Similarly, far-right parties did not campaign against the economic governance reforms and austerity as such, although they made bold statements on the failure of the EU to deal with the crisis.

## 5       The Left Opposition and Its Challenges

Left-of-social-democracy forces saw a sharp increase in Greece and Spain in the aftermath and as a result of mass popular mobilisations. Reversing all measures of labour market deregulation and welfare destruction imposed during the

---

70     Vlaams Belang 2013.

crisis has been their main slogan. Challenging the legitimacy of the debt has also been a central point in the political fermentations that led to their rein-forcement. These forces also deplore the erosion of democracy and promise to revitalise it by valorising grassroots experiences. They have a strong antiracist and internationalist stance and rights of all kinds (human rights, social rights, minorities, etc.) are prominent in their discourse. In a nutshell, their discourse stands clearly against the oligarchic tendencies of both the traditional parties of the EU-consensus and the extreme right, both of which demonstrate a pro-found mistrust of genuinely democratic processes and constantly look for an enlightened aristocracy to lead, basing its legitimacy on either its 'technocratic excellence' or its 'patriotic credentials'.

Syriza (before its capitulation) and Unidos Podemos are our main reference points here. Content-wise they clearly want to move in the opposite direction from everything that the neoliberal consensus has been doing in Europe in the last twenty years and even more so from 2008 onward. But in terms of explain-ing how this U-turn could come about, they remain at the level of wishes.

Before capitulation Syriza said that 'our Europe is on the antipodes of today's Europe; our Europe is the one of the Enlightenment and the radical critique of it, the one of revolutions, the welfare state, democracy, and mass social move-ments from below. The strategic aim of Syriza is the socialism of the 21st century in Greece and in Europe'. It reproaches 'Neoliberal forces for destabilising and undermining the European edifice' – as if it could be argued that the neolib-eral consensus was not the driving force behind the way Maastricht's EU was built – that basically needs to be saved. It affirms that 'Greece's perspective is interwoven with Europe's perspective'.

Syriza says 'Europe has to be re-founded in the direction of democracy, social justice and socialism'.[71] Podemos demands 'the abolition of the Lisbon Treaty ... and all Treaties that constructed the Neoliberal and antidemocratic Europe' and 'the opening of a process that will lead to the re-foundation of the EU insti-tutions through a Constitutional Assembly'.[72]

Syriza and Podemos demand a different Common Agricultural Policy prior-itising local and ecological production against the interests of big agribusiness, as well as a humane EU immigration policy.[73] They want to place the ECB under

---

71   Syriza 2013.

72   Podemos 2014.

73   In sharp contrast to this discourse, the second Syriza government has been at the forefront of implementing the 2016 EU-Turkey deal that jeopardises the UN's 1951 Refugee Conven-tion.

democratic control and establish it as a lender of last resort. The European Left Party – federating 20 left-wing parties – wants to give the 'European Parliament ... full powers and jurisdiction'. 'The European Commission must transfer its powers to the European and national parliaments and its role must be limited to its executive duties', it says.[74] Podemos talks about the 'democratisation of all the institutions including ... the EU administration and the appointment and control of the executive bodies of the EU'.

According to these left-wing parties, all these radical changes are to happen through the regular EU institutional process. However, such changes require Treaty modifications, and Treaties can only change by unanimity or in any case by a crushing majority of the national governments (as happened in the case of the TSCG). The biggest capitalist crisis since the 1930s (or maybe of all time) did not seem to have opened serious chances for the Left to take power in more than a handful of countries, and conditions favourable to this perspective do not appear simultaneously everywhere. Far-right parties headed the 2014 European elections in three countries (the UK, France and Denmark), while the Left came first only in Greece.

While approaching power, the programmes of Syriza and Podemos saw a retreat from citizen-led debt audits that would decide defaulting on its illegitimate part to a 'European convention on public debt' modelled after the 1953 London debt conference that reduced Germany's debt by half. When Syriza entered government, even this was hardly put on the agenda, being instantly dismissed by Juncker, who ironised that the Eurogroup was a permanent convention on debt. A debt truth committee was created by the Greek Parliament and published conclusions in favour of declaring a big part of the debt illegitimate that were never adopted by the Greek government.

We cannot help noticing the following contradiction: far-right parties are more in line with the content of EU policies, but in their discourse they are much more aggressive towards the EU than radical left parties. They feel much more comfortable suggesting unilateral gestures even when they do not necessarily mean them. If we look at their programmes carefully, both sides tend to promote their agenda through negotiated Treaty changes.

They both target the powers of the transnational and unaccountable bureaucracy of the Commission. The far-right would like to replace it with purely intergovernmental co-operation, and the radical left with the European Parliament and/or other elected and representative bodies. The far-right challenges the Commission because it is transnational, and the radical left because it is unac-

---

74   European Left 2013.

countable. The shift envisaged by the far-right is basically much less profound than the one promoted by the radical left. A formal hierarchy between the nation states making up the Union has been increasingly put in place as a reaction to the crisis – one that could lead to the creation of intergovernmental bodies surpassing or even replacing the powers of the Commission, while keeping the essential content of its policies promoting the interests of European economic elites within the EU and in the world. The problem with the left project of bringing the EU under democratic control is that the European Parliament is far from an optimal democratic body and its adherence to elementary democratic principles is questionable. It may be elected on the basis of universal suffrage but on the basis of 28 different electoral systems and – more importantly – of 28 distinct public spheres and debates. Calling for a European Constitutional Assembly would presuppose the existence of a European people. It is difficult to imagine the modalities of its election and even more socio-economic conditions that would create a simultaneous political momentum for a Constitutional Assembly all over Europe. Crises prompt institution building – as the post-crisis reform of the EU illustrates very well – but any new institutions which are not based on a genuine grassroots mobilisation and wide popular participation are curtailing existing democracy rather than taking it to a higher level.

Time is rather on the side of the far-right project, since the concept of democracy is increasingly ridiculed by the EU elites, social despair increases and the trust in collective solutions erodes further, because of the very material dismantling of social fabrics. In a situation of urgency, only urgent solutions have a chance to cut through and reverse the tide.

There was some timid consideration of unilateral movement within the radical Left too. The final document of the 4th European Left congress in 2013 reads: 'When the question of power becomes a practical reality, this includes consideration of the non-application of austerity policies, refusal to adhere to the European treaties and intergovernmental agreements such as the Fiscal Compact and renunciation of them, based on democracy and popular sovereignty'. Unfortunately, the power experience of Syriza by summer 2015 did not result in the refusal of adherence to the EU's socio-economic prerogatives, but in complete capitulation to them.

## Conclusion

The EU edifice has gone through a radical overhaul since the outbreak of the economic crisis. The legality of the reforms undertaken is shaky to say the least. The balance between the EU and national competences expressed in the Treaties has been violated in a 'great leap forward' to exit the crisis while preserving the profits of European transnational corporations, both financial and non-financial ones. Increasing the exploitation of working people and merchandising more areas of human activity are the basic recipes followed. Mass violation of fundamental rights – on whose recognition and protection the EU has based its legitimacy – occurred as a result of the EU's direct intervention in the socio-economic governance of member states.

These profound mutations beg the question as to whether they can be undone within the EU framework. Economic governance (six-pack, two-pack, cohesion funds' reform) and banking union legislation was adopted with two thirds of the member states' votes in the Council. It takes the vast majority of governments to change them. In practice, big countries that process the bulk of the votes can veto any attempt at change. The ESM and TSCG treaties have been adopted unanimously by the Eurozone governments and would need unanimity to be modified. The countries of the internal EU periphery that suffer the most from the policies these laws impose do not have the institutional power to change them. Even if one of the big countries sides with some of them, the chances that they can impose themselves are weak. Let's not forget that such U-turns would require vivid popular movements. It is difficult to imagine how they could appear simultaneously in so many countries, and previous uprising experiences (1848, 1917, Latin America in the nineties, the 'Arab Spring') show that they never come to the front in the majority of the countries of a specific area.[75] The history of the EU project is one of adopting the main points of the corporate agenda in all its defining moments (Rome 1957, Single European Act, Maastricht, adoption of the Euro, Lisbon Agenda, etc.) and it demonstrates that there were never steps back from this 'acquis communautaire'.

For Friedrich Hayek – the other patriarch of neoliberalism – the main advantage of a 'European federation' is that it would strip trade unions of their capacity to impose on governments some protection of labour. The mere idea of industrial policy makes no sense when the main competitors of a member state's industry are under the same Union. 'The federation should have the power to prohibit to member states to interfere on economic activity', said Hayek. According to him, peoples with different cultures and histories will not accept a federal power capable of organising production and consump-

---

75    Vassalos 2014.

tion according to a plan.[76] 'A federation means that none of the government levels will possess the means for a socialist planning of economic life', he concluded.[77]

It is impossible to make structures established under this logic work for aims that are in direct opposition to it. The fact that reforms such as the economic governance, the Troika, and the ESM occur is not a product of some deviation from the project, but rather going all the way down the road opened up by the Single European Act (if not the Treaty of Rome). The attack on fundamental rights is just the explosion of the smokescreen under which the real content of the EU project has been promoted in the last decades.

The far-right can surf on the reactionary acquis of the EU (weakened trade unions and welfare state, discredit of democracy and the stigmatisation of immigrants) in order to accomplish its objective of transforming the EU into a reactionary intergovernmental co-operation. If it fails to take power everywhere, it will continue serving as a pressure to transnational elites to govern in a more and more authoritarian way. A far-right government among the 28 has much more margin to implement its agenda within the framework of the EU legal order than a radical left government. Syriza remained in government only after abandoning its entire political programme, while Fidezs in Hungary is allowed to proceed with its 'illiberal democracy' agenda. Far Right parties in government in Poland, Austria and Italy have been also allowed to implement an important – and not necessarily the least radical – part of their programme.

In reality, political forces that want to go in the direction of deepening democracy, increasing the commons, redistributing resources to cover modern social needs and apply social justice – and most of all Left forces in crisis-hit countries that urgently need to adopt such measures to save their societies from collapse – have few options available to them other than disobeying and making a rupture with the European Union.

The most powerful tools that the leadership of the EU has in order to prevent indebted governments radically changing policy is freezing the cohesion funds, blocking the loan disbursements and – the most important of all – that the ECB cuts liquidity to banks, thus creating bank-runs or bank closures at any moment. We saw these tools deployed many times and almost all of them together against Cyprus in 2013. The ECB closed down Greek banks in summer 2015 in order to force the Syriza government into accepting the continuation of harsh austerity.

---

76    Durand 2013, pp. 21–2.
77    Hayek 1939, p. 271.

The only way to disable these tools is to re-introduce national currencies under democratic control by sacking the 'independence' of their central bank and thus reappropriating the capacity to create their own liquidity.[78] Less indebted member states can also be pressured against abandoning neoliberalism by using the provisions of economic governance. More than the threat of fines, triggering excessive deficit or macro-economic imbalance procedures can be effective, since this has a direct impact on any country's access to the financial markets. Sectoral liberalisation and state-aid legislation can bring any government trying to break with neoliberalism into sharp conflict with the EU legal order.

But the basic principles of international law give to any country the right to prioritise the needs of its citizens over any other engagement. The UN Charter provides that '[i]n the event of a conflict between the obligations of the Members of the United Nations under the present Charter and their obligations under any other international agreement, their obligations under the present Charter shall prevail'. And – unlike the EU treaties – the UN Charter includes the objective of raising people's living standards. Disobedience to the EU can be in accordance with international law, while obeying the EU increasingly leads to disrespecting international law.

### References

Charter of Fundamental Rights of the European Union 2000 (2000/C 364/01), available at: http://www.europarl.europa.eu/charter/pdf/text_en.pdf

Cœuré, Benoît 2012: 'Towards a consistent, coherent and complete Economic and Monetary Union', available at: http://www.ecb.int/press/key/date/2012/html/sp121119.en.html

Corporate Europe Observatory 2011a, 'Business against Europe: BusinessEurope celebrates social onslaught in Europe', available at: http://corporateeurope.org/2011/03/business-against-europe

Corporate Europe Observatory 2011b, 'An undemocratic economic governance?', available at: http://corporateeurope.org/power-lobbies/2011/04/undemocratic-economic-governance

Corporate Europe Observatory 2011c 'Corporate EUtopia – how new economic gov-

---

78 A quite thorough description of the steps needed to be taken is contained in Lapavitsas 2014.

ernance measures challenge democracy' available at: http://corporateeurope.org/eu
-crisis/2011/01/corporate-eutopia-how-new-economic-governance-measures-
challenge-democracy

Corporate Europe Observatory 2012, available at: 'Inspired by big business: the EU Austerity Treaty' http://corporateeurope.org/news/treaty-inspired-big-business

Corporate Europe Observatory 2013, 'BusinessEurope and the European Commission:
in league against labor rights?'. Available at: http://corporateeurope.org/eu-crisis/
2013/03/businesseurope-and-european-commission-league-against-labor-rights#
footnote5_sagkyou

Council Regulation (EU) No. 472/2013, 'On the strengthening of economic and budgetary surveillance of Member States in the euro area experiencing or threatened with
serious difficulties with respect to their financial stability', available at: http://eur-lex
.europa.eu/legal-content/EN/TXT/PDF/?uri=CELEX:32013R0472&from=EN

Damo, Peter 2012, 'Romania: bad and good news from the EU periphery & social and
trade union situation in CEE', available at: http://cadtm.org/Romania-bad-and-good
-news-from-the

Durand, Cédric 2013, 'Introduction: qu'est-ce que l'Europe?', in *En finir avec l'Europe*,
edited by Cédric Durand, Paris: La fabrique.

ETUC 2015, The Functioning of the Troika, available at: http://www.etuc.org/sites/www
.etuc.org/files/press-release/files/the_functioning_of_the_troika_finaledit2
.pdf

EU Summit conclusions, December 2010 available at: http://www.consilium.europa.eu/
uedocs/cms_data/docs/pressdata/en/ec/118578.pdf#page=6

Euro Plus Pact 2011, available at: http://www.consilium.europa.eu/uedocs/cms_data/
docs/pressdata/en/ec/120296.pdf

Eurofound 2012, 'Hungary: Amended strike law one year on', available at: https://www
.eurofound.europa.eu/observatories/eurwork/articles/industrial-relations/
amended-strike-law-one-year-on

Europan Council 2012, 'Implementing decision of 22 June 2012 lifting the suspension
of commitments from the Cohesion Fund for Hungary' available at: http://eur-lex
.europa.eu/legal-content/EN/TXT/PDF/?uri=CELEX:32012D0323&from=EN

European Commission 2010, 'The Economic Adjustment Programme for Greece', available at: http://ec.europa.eu/economy_finance/publications/occasional_paper/
2010/pdf/ocp61_en.pdf

European Commission 2012, 'European Commission launches accelerated infringe-
ment proceedings against Hungary over the independence of its central bank and
data protection authorities as well as over measures affecting the judiciary', available
at: http://europa.eu/rapid/press-release_IP-12-24_en.htm

European Commission 2013a, 'Refocusing EU Cohesion Policy for Maximum Impact on
Growth and Jobs: The Reform in 10 points', available at: http://ec.europa.eu/regional

_policy/en/newsroom/news/2013/11/refocusing-eu-cohesion-policy-for-maximum-impact-on-growth-and-jobs-the-reform-in-10-points

European Commission 2013b, 'Headline scoreboard of 2013'.

European Commission 2013c, 'Two-Pack enters into force, completing budgetary surveillance cycle and further improving economic governance for the euro area'.

European Commission 2014a, Economic governance review Report on the application of Regulations (EU) n° 1173/2011, 1174/2011, 1175/2011, 1176/2011, 1177/2011, 472/2013 and 473/2013, available at: http://eur-lex.europa.eu/legal-content/EN/TXT/?uri=CELEX:52014DC0905

European Commission 2014b, 'A new EU Framework to strengthen the Rule of Law' COM (2014)158 available at: http://ec.europa.eu/transparency/regdoc/rep/1/2014/EN/1-2014-158-EN-F2-1.Pdf

European Commission 2013a, 'Report on the application of the EU Charter of Fundamental Rights secondary'

European Commission 2017, 'Proposal for a Council Regulation on the establishment of the European Monetary Fund' COM (2017)827

European Left 2013, 'Final political document 4th EL Congress', available at: http://www.european-left.org/positions/congress-motions/documents-4th-el-congress/final-political-document-4th-el-congress

European Parliament 2014a, 'Resolution of 13 March 2014 on Employment and social aspects of the role and operations of the Troika (ECB, Commission and IMF) with regard to euro area programme countries', available at: http://www.europarl.europa.eu/sides/getDoc.do?pubRef=-//EP//TEXT+TA+P7-TA-2014-0240+0+DOC+XML+V0//EN

European Parliament 2014b, 'Joint answer given by Mr Moscovici on behalf of the Commission on written questions: E-007535/14, E-007778/14', available at: http://www.europarl.europa.eu/sides/getAllAnswers.do?reference=E-2014-007535&language=EN

European Round Table of industrialists 2002, 'European Governance for greater competitiveness', available at: https://www.ert.eu/sites/ert/files/generated/files/document/2002-11_eu_governance_leaflet.pdf

European Social Charter 1961 available at: http://conventions.coe.int/Treaty/en/Treaties/Html/035.htm

FIDH 2014, 'Report on Greece unveils human rights violations stemming from austerity policy' available at: https://www.fidh.org/International-Federation-for-Human-Rights/europe/greece/16675-greece-report-unveils-human-rights-violations-stemming-from-austerity

Front National 2012, *Notre Projet. Programme politique du Front National*, Paris.

Front National, n.d., 'Grand Dossier: Tout ce qu'il faut savoir sur la fin de l'euro', available at http://www.frontnational.com/pdf/fin-euro.pdf

Hayek, Friedrich, 1939, 'The Economic Conditions of Interstate Federalism' in *Individualism and Economic Order*, Chicago: University of Chicago Press

Hodson, Dernot, 2011, *Governing the Euro Area in Good Times and Bad*, Oxford University Press.

Jones, Gavin 2011, 'ECB debates ending Italy bond buys if reforms don't come' available at: http://www.reuters.com/article/2011/11/05/us-ecb-mersch-italy-idUSTRE7A426720111105

Juncker, Jean Claude (in cooperation with Donald Tusk, Jeroen Dijsselbloem, Mario Draghi and Martin Schulz) 2015, 'Completing Europe's economic and monetary union', available at http://ec.europa.eu/priorities/economic-monetary-union/docs/5-presidents-report_en.pdf

*Kathimerini* 2012, 'Fuchtel critical of municipal staff', available at: http://www.ekathimerini.com/4dcgi/_w_articles_wsite1_1_14/11/2012_470051

Lapavitsas, Costas, 2014, *A radical program for Greece and the periphery of the Eurozone*, [In Greek], Athens: Livani.

Lega Nord 2013, *Programma Elezioni Politiche 2013*,

Locke, John, 1690, *Second Treatise of Civil Government*, available at: https://www.gutenberg.org/files/7370/7370-h/7370-h.htm

Lumina, Cephas 2013, 'Report of the Independent Expert, Cephas Lumina, after the Mission to Greece (22–27 April 2013)', available at: http://www.ohchr.org/EN/HRBodies/HRC/RegularSessions/Session25/Documents/A-HRC-25-50-Add1_en.doc

Memorandum of Understanding between the European Community and the Republic of Hungary 2008, available at: https://www.mnb.hu/letoltes/hungary-mou-for-publication-rev.pdf

New York Times 1993, 'Intervention by Bundesbank is detailed', available at http://www.nytimes.com/1993/01/21/business/intervention-by-the-bundesbank-is-detailed.html

Open Conference of Presidents of the European Parliament 2014, 'Hearing of Frans Timmermans', available at: http://www.europarl.europa.eu/hearings-2014/en/schedule/07-10-2014/frans-timmermans

Peers, Steve 2014, 'The CJEU and the EU's accession to the ECHR: a clear and present danger to human rights protection' available at: http://eulawanalysis.blogspot.be/2014/12/the-cjeu-and-eus-accession-to-echr.html

PODEMOS 2014, *Documento final del Programa colaborativo*, available at http://www.xixonpodemos.info/2014/05/podemos-documento-final-del-programa-colaborativo/

Ravanos, Aris 2014, 'Full retreat of the government on the exemption from the ENFIA tax' [In Greek], available at: http://www.tovima.gr/politics/article/?aid=650197

Schmitt, Carl 1988 (1922), *Théologie politique*, translated by J.-L. Schlegel, Paris, Gallimard.

Spiegel, Peter 2014, 'How the Euro was saved', available at: https://www.ft.com/content/
  e72db602-c6d8-4970-ab0c-9a408af464ae2

Syriza 2013, 'Political decision of the founding congress' [In Greek], available at: https://
  www.syriza.gr/article/id/32409/Politikh-Apofash-10y-Idrytikoy-Synedrioy.html

Tansey, Rachel 2014, 'The crusade against 'red tape': How the European Commission
  and big business push for deregulation', available at: http://www.foeeurope.org/
  sites/default/files/news/crusade_against_red_tape_oct2014.pdf

Ticlea, Alexandru and Tiberiu Ticlea 2011, 'Romania' in *The Right to Strike in the EU. The
  complexity of the norms and safeguarding efficacy*, edited by Carmen La Macchia,
  Rome: Ediesse.

Treaty establishing the European Stability Mechanism 2012, available at: http://europa
  .eu/rapid/press-release_DOC-12-3_en.htm

Treaty of the European Union, available at http://eur-lex.europa.eu/legal-content/EN/
  TXT/?uri=CELEX:12012M/TXT

Van Rompuy, (in close collaboration with: José Manuel Barroso, Jean-Claude Juncker,
  Mario Draghi) 2015. 'Towards a Genuine Economic and Monetary Union', available at: http://www.consilium.europa.eu/uedocs/cms_Data/docs/pressdata/en/ec/
  134069.pdf

Vassalos, Yiorgos 2014 "Pour une position claire sur la question de l'Euro" http://www
  .avanti4.be/debats-theorie-histoire/article/pour-une-position-claire-sur-la-
  question-de-l

VlaamsBelang 2013, Colloquium on the future of (Flanders in) Europe: 'For Europe,
  against this EU'.

Whelan, Carl 2012, 'The ECB's Secret Letter to Ireland: Some Questions', available at:
  http://www.forbes.com/sites/karlwhelan/2012/08/17/the-ecbs-secret-letter-to-
  ireland-some-questions/

CHAPTER 5

# Labour under Attack during the Period of Crisis and Austerity

*Giannis Kouzis*

## Introduction

The changes that have been underway in the Greek labour market as a result of the economic crisis and the policies of labour deregulation inscribed in the 'Memoranda of Understanding', in order to 'support the Greek economy', have not been a surprise. These changes in the condition of labour have been in the making for the past 20 years in Greece, through a series of gradual and inter-connected interventions that aimed at boosting competitiveness and lowering labour costs. The basic policy tool has been the introduction of a variety of measures in order to encourage and expand labour flexibility. Moreover, these policies have been part of the broader framework of the dominant policy at the European Union level. The EU has fully endorsed the need for a radical reform of the European labour market, with the explicit aim of enhancing competit-iveness and employment. At the same time, this creates a new situation in the field of labour relations, which, under the influence of neoliberal doctrines, has led to the deregulation of the postwar labour paradigm, by means of a new regulation of work and employment conditions. In the context of this new perspective regarding the functioning of the labour market and labour rela-tions, which valorises business competitiveness above labour and social rights, labour legislation has been viewed as an obstacle to the accomplishment of the above-mentioned targets. The basic consequence of the new conception is the fact that elements of Commercial Law and in particular of Competition Law have been introduced in Labour Law, in steady and increasing rhythms. The res-ult has been the mutation of the content of Labour law and its deviation from its essential role, which is the protection of the weak pole of the labour relation and the strengthening of the position of employers. The changes underway in the terrain of labour relations have been made manifest in five basic directions regarding the content of labour: the degradation of the role of full and stable employment in favour of flexible forms of labour that lead to reduced wages and rights; the dismantling of the process of negotiating collective agreements and contracts to determine wages and salaries; the flexibilisation of labour time with its full adjustment to the needs of business; the lowering of protection from lay-offs; and finally, the convergence in terms of labour conditions between the private and the public sectors in terms of a general degradation.

In Greece, the policies of enhanced labour flexibility have been in place from the beginning of the 1990s, and aim at labour cost reduction in the name of increased competitiveness. They have been combined with two traditional practices for keeping the labour costs at a comparatively low level in relation to the rest of Europe. First of all, the average yearly labour income from full employment in Greece was in 2009 at 68% of the EU-15 average and at 87% of EU-27. One should remember that in the latter we can find countries such as Bulgaria that have wages that were as low as one tenth of Greek wages. Moreover, there have been extended forms of illegal labour flexibility as a result of violations of labour and social security legislation, exemplified in the fact that employment off the books and without social security was at 22% in 2009. This has supported management policies of low labour cost in Greece. These developments meant that even before the full eruption of the symptoms of the crisis, one could speak of the 'dark sides' of the Greek labour market, especially for the 700 Euros generation that represented one fifth of the Greek workforce. During the same period, Greece maintained the lowest labour cost in the EU-15 alongside Portugal, and, again alongside Portugal, had the worst position regarding competitiveness, proving that truly competitive economies demand first of all high-class products and not reductions in labour costs.

During the 2010–15 period and as a consequence of the crisis and the Memoranda, the changes in the labour market have been sweeping. The content of these changes follows the same path as the changes that have been underway in the country in the past 20 years, albeit to a greater extent and with more intensity. However, the measures that have been adopted, in terms of their nature and content, are not a novelty in comparison to the rest of Europe. The reason is that within the measures that have been introduced in Greece during the period of the Memoranda, one cannot find measures that have been introduced solely in Greece. In contrast, these measures have been implemented in various forms in a series of European countries, at different moments in the past 25 years. However, it is significant that it is the first time in recent European history that we can see such an avalanche of measures to such an extent and in such a short time. This, indeed, points to the direction of a Greek novelty. Among the European countries where important changes in the terrain of labour relations have been underway one can count Germany, which has been the main beneficiary of the creation of the common currency, where wage labourers, producing the products that have fled the market, have not only suffered a 11% reduction in real wages during the first decade of the Euro, but have also had to face the extensive use of minijobs, with five million workers being paid with salaries of less than 600 Euros. This situation can justify Germany being at the top spot in Europe in relation to the percentage of low-paid workers, who amount to 23% of the total number of employees. This highlights the fact that labour is being degraded in the entire space of Europe as part of a broader design to lower labour costs through generalised deregulation, in institutional terms, of the European labour market in combination with the deregulation of the post-war welfare state under the attack of neoliberalism, which constitutes the most extreme expression of the current aggression of capital.

## 1    Labour Deregulation as a Political Strategy

The main direction of the measures that have been imposed by national and international economic and political power centres, as a consequence of the economic crisis and of the Memoranda of Understanding, has taken the form of specific interventions that deal first of all with the sharp fall in employment and the deregulation of labour relations in the public sector, in the context of the convergence of status of labour in both the public and private sectors, in terms of a general degradation. The deregulation of labour in the public sector has prepared the ground for the widespread deregulation of labour in the private sector, by means of the further enhancement of flexible and precarious labour, the easing of lay-offs, the flexibilisation of labour time and the dismantling of the system of collective bargaining. More specifically:

a) The reduction in public sector employment has been achieved by gradually establishing a 1:5 and 1:10 ratio between hiring and departures from the public sector force, by abolishing work posts, by introducing specific measures such as redundancies, pre-pension redundancies and mandatory mobility that equal indirect lay-offs, and by shrinking the number of temporary posts (most of them covering permanent needs). These measures have been accompanied by hardening disciplinary control and the expansion of the practice of automatic suspension and the introduction of a system of evaluation that had an already predetermined analogy between 'productive' and 'unproductive' civil servants. They created an asphyxiating climate of labour insecurity in the public sector as part of the commitment, undertaken in the Memoranda, for further personnel reductions of more than 150,000 in the 2012–15 period. These developments have reduced public sector employment by 22%, to 16% of total employment, which is well below the averages that we can see in most European countries. Moreover, there has been an across the board reduction in earnings, from 20–55%, by means of direct legislative intervention in salaries and benefits, of abolishing collective agreements and personnel regulations, and by lifting any extra protection from lay-offs public sector employees had in the past. Moreover, weekly work-hours have been raised from 37.5 to 40 hours in full conformity to the conditions in the private sector. This created an extra burden for employees and intensified the rhythm of work as a direct consequence of personnel shortage created by the policy of workforce shrinkage in the public sector. There has been an attempt to answer this personnel shortage in certain parts of the public sector by means of the subsidised programmes of social work that have been implemented through third parties (as a form of employee loaning). These included low-end labour relations and pay below the minimum wage of the private sector. More measures were expected, that pointed towards the equalisation of labour status between the public and the private sectors, such as the establishment of an introductory wage in the public sector at the same level as the minimum wage established for private enterprises.

b) The easing of lay-offs has taken place in a period of increased unemployment, thus intensifying labour insecurity. Lifting the workers' protection, both in relation to individual but also mass lay-offs, is another attack on the basic tenets of labour law. The measures adopted as part of the first Memorandum had reduced the cost of laying-off by reducing the maximum time of warning from 24 to four months and by halving the compensation for lay-offs for employees who have been with an employer for a long time (from 24 months' pay to 12), which means that the cost of lay-off per worker has been reduced for up to 14 salaries. Moreover, employers have gained the right to pay compensation for lay-offs in more and lower instalments than in the past, by limiting the amount for the first instalment for the compensation from six months to two months. Moreover, the minimum employment time necessary to be eligible for compensation in case of a lay-off in a contract of indeterminate duration has been raised from two months to 12 months. Regarding the limit to mass lay-offs, this has been raised from four to five employees for companies that employ 20–150 employees and from 2% to 5% for companies that are bigger. The need for a ministerial decree approving the percentage for mass lay-offs that are over these limits has been abandoned. Moreover, there had been some planning for extra measures regarding abolishing the limit to mass lay-offs for big enterprises, as part of the commitments included in the memoranda. This aims at offering an extra help to mass lay-offs expected in view of the restructuring of banks, mass media, and privatised companies.

c) The enhancement of flexible and precarious forms of employment has taken place through a series of measures included in the first Memorandum of Understanding. These include the lifting of any limits to the use of sub-contracted labour; extending from 18 to 36 months the maximum time for loaning an employee, along with introducing this form of employment into the public sector; raising from two to three years the maximum time of renewing temporary employment contracts; expanding from six to nine months per year the duration of alternate labour (four-day workweek, three-day workweek); abolishing any extra pay for part-time labour in case of overtime and in case of employment at less than 20 hours per week.

d) The dismantling of the system of collective bargaining and of collective agreements is the middle step aiming at individualising labour relation wage determination. With the first Memorandum a basic tenet of labour law was discarded, namely that of the priority of the regulation that is more favourable to the employee, through the legislation of the possibility to sign collective agreements at the company level, with worse conditions than those included in sectoral agreements, with the company-level agreement taking legal precedent. According to the provisions of the second Memorandum, the minimum wage was reduced by 22% (32% for youths under 25 years of age), through legislative intervention, thus abolishing the role of the national collective agreement as a policy tool to determine lower wages and replacing it with a ministerial decree. Moreover, maturity increases for long-term unemployed paid the minimum wage were also abolished. Pay rises through collective agreements in minimum wages, maturities, and benefits for duration of employment were suspended until the unemployment rate fell below 10%, an eventuality that under the austerity policies would not be possible before 2034, according to INE-GSEE/ADEDY estimates. Changes in the system of collective agreements not only affected general minimum wages, but in combination with the measures of the first and second Memoranda, they have contributed to the reduction in average wages towards the minimum level of earnings. This was accomplished through the following measures: Legislation regarding freezing pay rises because of wage maturities. By suspending the expansion of sectoral and professional collective agreements to cover all employees of a sector or a particular profession, we have seen business leaving the relevant employers' associations that have led hitherto binding collective agreements, while others have been relieved of the obligation to implement them by signing individualised contracts that force employees to accept only the general minimum. By offering the possibility of signing collective contracts at company level, that can respect only the minimum wage and the levels set at the sectoral level

and the ability to sign collective agreements with 'unions of persons', a caricature of union representation that does not enjoy the legal protection of union
activity and will be used by employers as a means of signing collective agreements with wage reductions. They limited the time of after-effects of collective
agreements after their end or their denunciation from six to three months.
This reduction regarding the regulating force of the content of collective agreements and the after-effects of collective agreement regarding individual terms
of labour, will only refer to the basic wage, child benefits, education benefits,
seniority and dangerous employment benefit. This change forced trade unions
to rush to sign collective agreements before the end of the three-month period,
under pressure from the employers, in order to avoid the danger of an individualised pay structure. The right of trade unions to ask for arbitrage in case
of a failure of the mediation process with the employers was abolished. This
development led to a further reduction in the role of labour relations' power
to deal with collective disagreements, obscured the process by which disputes
would be resolved, and increased employees' insecurity. Moreover, labour relations arbitrage no longer has the authority to decide on all the matters under
negotiation but only on the basic wage at any level of negotiation. These developments in fact discouraged labour from asking for arbitrage, because even
if the employers were to accept its ruling, this would only refer to the basic
wage and not all the other aspects of the labour relation, such as the structure
of benefits, the terms of employment, and all the gains that were guaranteed
by previous collective agreements. They could only lead to the unions being
forced to sign collective agreements under duress. It was made obligatory for
mediators and arbitrators to guarantee the reduction in unit labour cost and
the increase in the competitiveness of business in relation to the evolution of
labour costs. These measures attempt to fully dismantle the system of collective
agreements and of solving collective labour disputes through mediation and
arbitrage, and, at the same time, they strengthen excessively the position of
the employers.

e) The enhancement of the terms of flexibility of labour time is another aspect
of the Memoranda policies. There measures include the regulation that limits the cost of extending overtime by 20%, the abolishment of the five-day
working week for commercial shops, the expansion of work on Sunday to the
entire country (and not only in tourist locations), the facilitation of flexible
labour time by increasing and decreasing labour time at company level through
collective agreements with 'unions of persons' and in smaller businesses with
fewer than 20 employees based upon the consent of only two employees.

f) Finally, as part of the commitments of the Memoranda, there had been plans for fully liberating mass lay-offs, the reduction in special leaves of office for union officials and the attempt to introduce the condition of the absolute majority of all inscribed union members as a condition for strike action and the reintroduction of the possibility for management lock-out after its abolition in 1982. Moreover, there had been discussion of further reductions in the minimum wage (from 581 – and 511 Euros for employees under 25), the abolishment of the '13th' and '14th' salaries (Christmas, Easter and holiday benefits) despite the fact that wage reductions already equate to the loss of three salaries, the introduction of 'free economic zones' with a special wage, social security and tax status, the further reduction in overtime pay in tandem with further flexibility over labour time, a measure that aimed at not paying extra for overtime employment, thus leading to an extra decrease in labour costs.

## 2    The Social Consequences of the Measures Regarding Unemployment

The intensification of the economic crisis and the measures included in the Memoranda have created a new situation in the labour market and a new work landscape which was very different from the image before the eruption of the crisis and the signing of the loan agreements. The consequences of these measures have been the following:

a) The increase in unemployment that reached 27% in 2014 with 1,350,000 unemployed (up from 9% and 450,000, respectively, in 2009) has been a devastating consequence of the crisis, of the measures included in the Memoranda, and of recession. The level of unemployment is far beyond the historical high point of the end of the 1950s, a period of mass migration. There have been estimates that the real unemployment rate (not the one observed in statistical reports) is higher by at least 3% of the workforce in comparison to official statistics. We must also take into consideration that 150,000 have already migrated during the period of the crisis and some 30,000 have considered migrating. All this attests to the fact that real unemployment is much higher. Long-term unemployed represent the majority of the unemployed (75%, up from 58% at the start of the crisis). In the age cohort of youths up to 25, unemployment increased from 29% to 58% in just five years despite the labour cost reduction measures for this age cohort that had been introduced in 2012. We have to stress that unemployment benefits have been particularly low in Greece, in terms of both amount and duration, as a particular manifestation of the deficiencies of the Greek social security system, since the unemployment benefit does not represent a compensation for lost wages, since it is only at 57% of the minimum wage (which meant 367€ after a 100€ reduction that followed the reduction in the minimum wage) and its maximum duration is 12 months, not covering the long-term unemployed and including a long list of limitations as to who is eligible to receive it. The Memoranda also included the introduction of a system of individualised benefits according to which each unemployed person can receive the benefit for up to 400 days per three years. These developments have contributed to an important reduction in the number of unemployed people who actually receive unemployment benefits.

b) Wage reduction has been a major consequence of austerity politics. Wages have been reduced by 15% up to 60%. This is the result of across the board reductions in salaries in the public sector and in the wage reduction in the private sector due to the dismantling of collective agreements, in the individualisation of wages and the transformation of stable contracts into flexible labour. In the private sector, average wage reductions through collective agreements at enterprise level and individual labour contracts are at 22% and 24% respectively, much higher than the supposed target in the Memoranda for a reduction of 15% in unit labour costs. Moreover, the Inspectors of Employment have estimated that the tendency is for 80% of employment posts to be arranged by individual rather than collective bargaining, as a result of the significant changes that have disorganised the system of collective bargaining. This dramatic reduction in average wages has been affected by the immense strengthening of the position of the employers in relation to the facilitation of lay-offs and the ability to transform labour contracts into flexible and lower-paid employment.

c) The increased reduction in full employment – in terms of hiring, during the past few years full employment posts have been reduced by 63% – in favour of flexible work, which now represents 52% of new contracts, has been accompanied in the period of the Memoranda by the tendency to change full employment contracts into part-time jobs, a practice that has increased by 350%, and to alternate work arrangements, with fewer workdays per week. The occurrence of this change, which the employer can impose unilaterally, has increased by 13,000%! This development led to wage reductions of up to 60% and in the combined reduction in wages and work-time, since up to 15% of alternate work contracts refer to working for one day per week, thus increasing job insecurity and precariousness.

d) An aspect of the workplace insecurity is the rapid increase, during the past four years, of uninsured work, growing from 22% to 40%, something that has negative repercussions on both wage levels and social security finances.

e) The increase in unemployment, the violent reduction in wages, the tax increases against middle and low incomes, and the reduction in social benefits as a result of the undermining of even the modest Greek welfare state led to the increase from 21% to 33% in those living below the poverty threshold, to a 27% rise in the number of homeless people during the past four years, and to 3,000 suicides because of the economic crisis in the same period.

f) The dramatic reduction in wages along with maintaining the same or even higher prices in basic products, and the increased taxation along with the reduction in social spending, has contributed to a 50% reduction in the spending power of labour during the period of the crisis and the Memoranda. This process constitutes the pauperisation of labour that has contributed to the massive appearance of the 'new poor' strata.

g) The deterioration of the labour market has forced a large part of the labour force to seek employment abroad. According to the Europass network, more than 350,000 CVs have been sent in search of employment abroad and 150,000 people have already migrated during the period of the crisis. It should be noted the majority of those interested in employment abroad represent highly competent, educated and specialised persons. Consequently we have faced not only a social problem, but also a loss of productive capabilities, especially in a country that has strongly invested in education. The result is that the Greek labour market has been deprived of a particularly specialised and productive part of the labour force.

h) The deregulation of labour law is an important development because of the measures adopted during the period of the economic crisis and the Memorandum. This development is the result of the dismantling of the system of collective bargaining and of collective contracts, which intensifies the tendency to individualise labour relations, lifting the protection against lay-offs, and limiting the role of stable and permanent employment.

i) Undermining the role of collective agreements, and in particular of the central negotiation process, undermines the strength of the trade union movement and in particular the national and sectoral organisations, by moving negotiation to the company level that strengthens the negotiating power of the employers. Taking apart the system of collective agreements is a step in the strategy of the most aggressive expression of capital that aims at fully individualising the terms of the labour contract and limiting the role of the collective expression of employees by inflicting decisive wounds to the trade union institution. The tendency towards the idolisation of individuality at the expense of collective values was facilitated by the bureaucratisation of large segments of union representation, leading to the further decrease in the role and importance of unions, while things were made worse by the imposition of new limits to the ability to strike.

j) Creating a new work landscape aims at solidifying a new workplace environment with wages and rights that would lead to the balkanisation of labour relations, which is a commitment coming out of the second Memorandum aiming at the convergence of salaries in Greece with the salaries in other Balkan countries.

k) The crisis, the Memoranda, the deregulation of labour relations and the reductions in labour costs underway have not only induced the violent pauperisation of Greek society and undermined the content of labour; there have also been those who have benefited from the crisis. First of all, we have those who have invested – or intend to invest after the end of the recession – taking advantage of an environment of reduced labour costs that will guarantee a high profit-rate for capital. In the same context, we can see the expected advantage for investors who will attempt to buy public companies and organisations as part of existing privatisation plans. In particular, private investors have benefited not only from the important reduction in public sector employment that has been underway in recent years, but also from the important changes that have been accomplished in the terrain of labour relations. Labour conditions now in the broader public sector are much worse than before the period of the Memoranda. Moreover, the privatisations that will follow will lead to employees having to cope with a labour condition identical to that in the private sector where conditions are significantly worse than the period before the Memoranda. In sum, public sector employees in 2009 that then had to work for private enterprises in 2013, would have, as part of a deteriorating tendency, gone through three different work regimes. Finally, the reduction in income, in a negative feedback with the recession, enhances the shrinkage of the number of businesses (by 150,000 in two years), mainly small and medium businesses, which in large numbers have been forced out of the markets in favour of big corporate interests that attempt to take up their market share, thus intensifying the concentration and centralisation of capital.

l) The Greek example of the period of the crisis and the Memoranda, this attempt to make permanent the consequences of these measures regarding the labour market, has also been an experiment in relation to the broader proposed changes in the European labour market. It sets an example with regard to the evolving changes in the direction of austerity as part of the already adopted 'Treaty for the Euro' (2013) by European institutions and the attempts to constitutionalise the 'iron laws' of the Stability and Growth act. As an extreme example of labour relations deregulation, it can even be seen as an experiment of 'China-isation' of the countries of the European South in what concerns the position of labour, especially well-educated labour, as part of a broader process of labour deregulation in Europe.

### References[1]

Aliprantis, Nikos (ed.) 2008, *Social Right at transnational level around the world*. [In Greek], Athens: Papazisis.

Gavroglou, S. 2009, *Aspects of flexibility in Greece and Europe*, [In Greek], Athens: PAEP

Dedousopoulos, Apostolos 2000, *The crisis in the labour marker: regulation flexibilities, deregulation*, [In Greek], Athens: Papazisis.

Esping-Andersen, Gosta (ed.) 2000, *Why deregulate labor markets?*, Oxford: Oxford University Press.

European Commission 1998–2013, *Employment in Europe: Annual reports*.

European Commission 2007, *The modernization of labor legislation; Green Paper*, Brussels: Employment and Social Affairs.

European Commissio 2005, *The evolution of labor law in Europe*, Brussels: Employment and Social Affairs.

Zabarloukou, Stella and Maria Kousi (eds.) 2014, *Social aspects of the crisis in Greece*, [In Greek] Athens: Pedio.

INE/GSEE-ADEDY 1998–2014, *Greek Economy and Employment. Yearly Reports*, [In Greek] Athens: INE/GSEE-ADEDY.

INE/GSEE-ADEDY 2008–2014, *Labour Relations in Europe and Greece*, [In Greek] Athens: INE/GSEE-ADEDY.

Kouzis, Giannis 2001. *Labour relations and European Integration Flexibility and deregulation or enhancement of labour?* [In Greek] INE/GSEE-ADEDY Studies 14.

---

1   The references in this chapter include the books, articles and sources consulted for its preparation.

Kouzis, Giannis 2007, 'The Green Book on the modernization of labour law. Comments', [In Greek] *Epitheorisi Ergasiakwn Sxesewn*, 45.

Kouzis, Giannis 2008, 'Flexibility and Security (flexicurity) a critical approach' [In Greek], *Koinwniki Synochi kai Anaptyxi*, 3,1: 67–77.

Kouzis, Giannis 2010, 'The evolution of neoliberal deregulation of labour and the alibi of the crisis' [In Greek] in Leonidas Vatikiotis et al. *The 'map' of the crisis. The end of an illusion* [In Greek] Athens: Topos.

Kouzis, Giannis 2011, 'Labour in the vortex of the economic crisis and the Memorandum. Ten points' [In Greek], *Utopia* 97: 7–12.

Negreponte – Delivani Maria 2007, *Reforms: the tragedy of labour in Europe* [In Greek], Athens: Livanis.

Corps of Inspectors of Labour 2013, *Yearly Report* [In Greek].

# CHAPTER 6

# 'First Comes Indignation, Then Rebellion, Then We Shall See': Political Crisis, Popular Perception of Politics and Transformation of Consciousness amid the Rebellious Cycle of 2010–11 in Greece

*Eirini Gaitanou*

## Introduction

Indignation is a beginning. A way of rising up and getting going. First comes indignation, then rebellion, then we shall see.[1]

.<br>.

It is well known that the international crisis that emerged from the USA in 2008, a structural and historical crisis, affects Greece in a very particular and intense way. This crisis is not merely contained within the economic sphere, but pervades all aspects of the political spectrum, exacerbating a deep social crisis, a crisis of political representation and legitimation of the state and its apparatuses, which has finally led to a nascent organic crisis of the state.[2] The interventions of the IMF-EU-ECB 'Troika' since May 2010 have accelerated the neoliberal management of the crisis. The measures taken, under constant revision,[3] have taken aim at salvaging European capital; moreover, they have used Greece as a guinea pig in determining the specific form of neoliberalism in the new era.

These measures have induced a dramatic reduction in living standards for large social strata as well as the intensification of class polarisation (sharply diminishing the traditional petty-bourgeois strata), both in parallel with an intense authoritarian shift in the political system and the state. Resistance

---

1  Bensaïd 1994, p. 106.
2  Kouvelakis 2011e.
3  From 2010 to 2014, seven different packages of measures have been imposed, including the Memoranda and their revisions, analytically reviewed in Sakellaropoulos 2014, pp. 75–83.

© KONINKLIJKE BRILL NV, LEIDEN, 2018 | DOI:10.1163/9789004280892_008

at the social and the political level has also escalated in recent years; despite the cyclical and controversial nature of these protests and their relative recession during the period 2012–14, a deep rupture in society clearly looms.

Social movements in Greece have been a constant feature of the last few years, starting with the youth revolt of December 2008. The period after the official intervention of the Troika in April 2010, and up to early 2012, has been full of popular mobilisation, constituting what has been called *a rebellious cycle* (as explained in what follows). This period includes: the squares movement of May–June 2011; a significant wave of general strikes and many sectoral ones; various forms of civil disobedience (the most important being the 'I won't pay' movement); and the disruption of official festivities by protesters during national holidays and certain local movements (the most important being the mass protests in Keratea against plans for an environmentally disastrous landfill). These political practices share common features and stand at the margins of the traditional forms and the 'acceptable' political methods exercised in a parliamentary democracy. The main goal of this chapter is to study the crisis of the existing forms of political representation, alternative forms of political participation and transformation of people's consciousness in relation to this particular participation and experience, principally regarding (1) the objective circumstances; (2) their own social position in society; and (3) conceptualising the 'political'. What is of interest here is the development of new relations between people and politics, as well as their relationship with various forms of political representation (existing and/or new ones).

For this argument to be analysed, I shall start from a brief presentation of the basic mechanisms and structures of political representation over the last two decades during the implication of the restructuring process in the Greek state and society, the transformation of their dynamics prior to the crisis, and the potential impact of the movements in the collapse of their legitimation. This presentation is useful in order to understand the background of the current political crisis. Subsequently, I shall present the main theoretical point motivating this research, meaning the constitutive terms of subjectivity and class consciousness within specified conditions, based on a Marxist philosophy of praxis approach. Afterwards, I shall present the main conclusions from my fieldwork, conducted via in-depth interviews, regarding people's perceptions of politics and the transformation of consciousness in relation to participation in the movements discussed here.

1     The Restructuring Process and Political Representation Prior to the
      Crisis

In the last two decades of the twentieth century, a radical rearrangement of the
constitutional terms of capitalism took place in Greece, aiming at overthrowing
the acquired rights, but also at the dissolution of every form of collective organisation and bargaining. In parallel, radical transformations in labour relations
have a fourfold objective: (1) degradation of full and stable employment and its
replacement by flexible forms of employment with low wages and rights; (2)
dismantling of the pattern of collective bargaining and wage-setting; (3) flexibility of working hours; and (4) liberalisation of redundancies.[4]

The way out of the 1970s' crisis has been the commitment towards neoliberal management. This has signalled a continuous effort to shift the relation of
forces in favour of capital and against labour, including policies that serve the
restructuring of labour relations, the privatisation of public sector enterprises,
the liberalisation of the financial system, policies of low wages, an increase in
working time and labour flexibility, reforms to pensions and the tax system, and
the dismantling of social security. In parallel, capitalism has been continually
expanding into new fields and new social practices, which have not always been
directly subsumed into mercantile and capitalist relations. Insertion in the EU
has enabled the shift of the social cost of this entire process to the popular
strata, whilst the consequent dependence upon European funding has bound
the bourgeoisie but also segments of the new petit-bourgeois class to the ideology of Europeanism. The modernisation strategy of the '90s has thus signalled
a very aggressive bourgeois strategy of consolidating the rapid neoliberal transformation processes.

On the ideological and the political levels, and as far as the State is concerned, its role is not restricted but broadened (as the guarantor of the long-
term interests of the bourgeoisie), and shifted to the more immediate benefit
of forces of capital: State interventionism in the economy has grown, aiming at
an increase in business profitability. There is actually a shift from an interven-
tionist State to a headquarters-State, which includes the assignment of specific
functions to the private sector.[5] In this context, the separation of powers is challenged and the juridical mechanism's role is upgraded, being transformed into
an institution of normalisation of the restructuring process and of realisation of
authoritarianism. A transfer of power into supranational organisations contrib-

---

4   INE/GSEE 2012, p. 27.
5   Sakellaropoulos and Sotiris 2004, p. 101.

utes to the abolition of formed social alliances and compromises of a former period, whilst national bourgeois sovereignty basically assumes the shield of the State apparatus and the destruction of the 'internal enemy' (i.e. the popular movements).[6]

Besides, repression in the broader sense has been a constitutive element of the State in the post-civil-war Greece.[7] In examining the constitutive terms of political power, the post-civil-war State has been characterised by anti-communism, being staffed by collaborators of the German Nazis, while the resisters have been targeted and fully marginalised.[8] The bourgeois class as the winner of the civil war has adopted a tough stance towards the dominated classes, denying any economic or political concessions. In the latter, parliamentarism has been consolidated as a democratic response to the State of violence and arbitrariness, while those classes have gradually shifted ideologically from the left towards the centre, as the material consequence of the way they have experienced the collapse of EAM.[9] At the same time though, radical social struggles have developed, mainly throughout the whole post-dictatorship period, as a consequence of both the historical political consciousness and the contradictions of the bourgeois strategy.

In terms of political representation, the transition after the mid-1980s has been characterised by de-ideologisation and the professionalisation of politics. At this time, the political scene is relatively stabilised. The political system is structured on the basis of bipartisanship, which from the '80s until 2004 reached 85% of the electorate. The systemic political parties' character is transformed: they converge in terms of political programmes, and at the same time, they are strongly intertwined with private capital. Parties no longer function as forms of political agency that express the demands of the dominated classes, but mainly express an intra-bourgeois negotiation.[10] Technocrats and the media acquire an important political role. Clientelism between citizens and the State prevails, though not in the way corruption is usually perceived: clien-

---

6    Sakellaropoulos and Sotiris 2004, pp. 51–3.
7    Characteristically, apart from the constitution of the post-civil-war State of violence, exec-
     utives of the army who participated in the 1967–74 dictatorship have been incorpor-
     ated into the State apparatus after its fall, the police has been organised in paramilitary
     ways, while legal forms of violent repression have been implemented, both by the first
     right-wing government after the dictatorship, and by the Socialist Party governments sub-
     sequently (Charalampis 1985, pp. 348–51).
8    Meynaud n.d. (b), pp. 18–19.
9    Sakellaropoulos 1998, p. 256.
10   Sakellaropoulos 2014, p. 114.

telism is often the only way out for the popular strata in order to achieve their political representation and a regulation of their basic interests.[11] This relative political stabilisation is also reinforced through broad integration into the public sector, access to higher education, and the existence of intermediary channels between citizens and the political power (local power, official trade-unionism).

At the same time, ideological constructions of technocracy and productivism, developmentalism and liberal individualism are diffused into broader social strata, under the impact of the ideology of modernisation.[12] There is a shift in political self-determination and ideological placement: a detachment from politics, an increasing self-positioning in the centre, inter-class voting, and a transformation of classical opinions on certain issues (imperialism, socialism, economy of the market).[13] However, these political and ideological transformations are still contradictory, since the ruling class fails to propose a coherent and convincing strategic plan that would positively engage the popular strata.

## 2       Heading towards the Crisis

This landscape was reformulated while approaching the outbreak of the crisis in 2008. At the ideological level, the neoliberal hegemony of previous years came into question, due to certain factors: aggressive reforms in education and labour, the collapse of expectations of broader social strata and the exacerbation of the gap between these expectations and their material reality, economic crisis, constant austerity and political impasse. The market, which would supposedly function as a social regulator, is discredited in the consciousness of the poorest strata, who realise that the social cost is transferred onto their shoulders. Personal enrichment and consumerism no longer constitute an outlet; besides they are no longer feasible for the majority of the population. Expectations of social mobility collapse even for the larger part of the middle classes. Individualism is questioned, whilst social protest and collective struggles return to the political scene.

---

11    This is due to the fact that, as far as the Greek State in particular is concerned, and for reasons related to its historical and political constitution (as implied above), its relative autonomy from the ruling class is much more limited than in other western States.

12    Sakellaropoulos and Sotiris 2004, p. 153.

13    Loulis 2001, pp. 57–9.

At the political level, the collapse of the social contract of the previous decades, the hardening and intensification of State authoritarianisation and of
political management, the increasing connection of civil society institutions to
the State and political power, the collapse of social democracy and the adoption for its part of neoliberal management, bureaucratisation of official trade-
unionism, along with the burst of scandals, provoke a deep crisis of legitimation of the State and its institutions, and a crisis of political representation.[14]
Especially regarding official trade-unionism, the landscape is characterised by:
low union density; unified organisational expression, but also organisational
differentiation and fragmentation based on employment status; severe differentiation in trade-unionism between the public and the private sectors;[15]
State interference in unions' internal life; lack of alternative forms of worker
representation; lack of financial independence; severe influence of and close
interconnection between political parties; bureaucratisation and clientelism;
gradual decline of the confrontational character of the trade union movement;
developed trade-unionism in traditional social strata (men, the elderly, workers
on stable employment), but clearly more limited in the youth, women, flexible
workers, immigrants, the unemployed.[16]

The social fabric is disintegrating, since the petty-bourgeois strata, through
which was ensured the participation of the people in political and social life,
have been suppressed and/or proletarianised. Citizens have minimum opportunities of representation and political expression, a reality intensified by the
State's rigidity toward their demands. They face a State that is incapable of
reproducing basic linkages of citizens with politics, namely with daily life management and with political power; a State deprived of the capability to produce
new fields of hegemony and new positive consents (both material and symbolic
ones). The absence of public space, in which there would be the sense of an
ongoing political debate supposedly leading to socio-political changes, intens-

---

14    In autumn 2008, in a Eurobarometer survey, 77% of the participants claim that they do not
      trust the government (66% in spring 2007 and 61% in the EU). 68% do not trust the par-
      liament, 86% the political parties, 56% the judicial system. In the same survey, a general
      dissatisfaction is expressed. Only 53% feel relatively satisfied with their daily life (65% in
      spring 2007 and 76% in the EU), 66% predict that their economic situation will worsen
      in the following year, and 64% predict that the situation in labour will worsen in the same
      period. 64% state that their purchasing power has declined over the past five years, while
      63% face difficulties in paying their bills (Eurobarometer 2008).
15    18% in the private sector and 65% in the public sector.
16    Kouzis 2007a.

ifies this sentiment of political impasse. Any sense of the political is restrained to the official forms of political activity, ignoring, marginalising, and repressing any social claim.

Thus, broad social strata are politically, institutionally, but also socially marginalised. The intensification of a 'law and order' strategy intensifies this reality. Physical repression is exacerbated, while police violence and impunity constitutes its characteristic but not sole element. Changes in the legal system and the adhesion of the judicial and the executive power are also part of this strategy. A series of new laws aims at the restriction of protests and the intensification of surveillance. Repression is militarised and new special forces of persecution are created. Finally, paramilitary mechanisms and fascist groups act in direct or indirect coordination with the State and the police.

## 3     A Necessary Digression: Social Movement as a Rupture in Continuity

Thus, the reality described above and the severe socio-economic impacts of the crisis are becoming increasingly evident to large segments of the population since 2008, leading to, among other controversial processes, a significant rise in social movements. Since 2008, several different forms of mobilisation have emerged. If, however, the objective circumstances, the socio-political and economic reality, and the hardening of the State management serve to decisively influence the rise of the social movement, the subjective factor and class struggle itself rearrange its constitutive conditions. In other words, the development of social struggles transforms not only the consciousness of those participating, but also the society as a whole.

The theoretical point that arises here refers to the constitutive terms of subjectivity and class consciousness within specified conditions.[17] Our perspective is based on a philosophy of praxis approach, posed in the context of a broader Marxist tradition, as the theoretical affirmation 'that every "truth" believed eternal and absolute has had practical origins and has represented a "provisional" value'.[18] In other words, praxis itself transforms reality. This approach conflicts with a more 'orthodox', objectivist description of history as the process of the development of productive forces, in which the subjective factor has no space to act in the sense of transforming the circumstances themselves.

---

17     The argument of this paragraph is further developed in Gaitanou and Gousis 2015.
18     Gramsci 1972, p. 406.

It is, however, also in conflict with a voluntarist/subjectivist approach, deifying human action irrespective of objective conditions.[19]

According to the famous Marxian quotation, '[i]t is not the consciousness of men that determines their being, but, on the contrary, their social being that determines their consciousness'.[20] This thesis has been read in many different ways, implying multiple understandings of the relationship between objective conditions and consciousness. A rather dominant reading treats it as if the latter is a non-mediated and linear reflexion of the objective circumstances, in which people are forcedly subsumed. However, there are numerous references supporting the thesis that Marx himself thought of the role of consciousness as a catalyst. Highly important for that matter are the well-known *Theses on Feuerbach*, in which Marx breaks with existing materialism, in emphasising the perception of reality 'as *sensuous human activity, practice*, not subjectively' and 'not in the form of the *object or of contemplation*'.[21] Thus, the decisive element of praxis is established as a perceptive condition of reality. Revolutionary praxis is defined as precisely 'the coincidence of the changing of circumstances and of human activity or self-changing'[22] establishing the subject/object dialectic. This is the core element of our approach: posing the question of consciousness based on the dialectic subject/object unity.[23]

A basic concept, in order to approach this fundamental issue of consciousness formation, is that of organisation, in relation to its relationship with the spontaneous element. At this point, the role of the political party is indispensable, albeit not exclusive. Theories of an elitist orientation correlate the importance of the party to an alleged weakness of the masses to make politics for themselves, restricting their role to economic struggles. Contrarily, we think of the masses as perfectly capable of exercising politics, and indeed across all three levels: in the party, the front, and the movement. The mediation of the political subject as such is crucial for the working class to conceive the totality of its interests and their incompatibility with the socio-political system as a whole. Politics is perceived exactly in that sense: not as a sphere aside from others, but as the expression of the overcoming of fragmentation into separate spheres and of the possibility of a potentially unifying dynamics, of a hege-

---

19      Gaitanou and Gousis 2015, pp. 128–9.

20      Marx 1859, p. 11.

21      Marx and Engels 1968, p. 659.

22      Marx and Engels 1968, p. 660.

23      In the Lukácsian sense, in which the proletariat is perceived as 'the class which was able to discover within itself on the basis of its life-experience the identical subject-object, the subject of action' (Lukács 1971, p. 204).

monic dimension that enables the re-establishment of the whole towards the particular, in their internal articulation.[24] Thus, the concepts of political consciousness/ideological formation and of the self-activity of the masses are not perceived in antithetical terms, but in a dialectical unity.

If praxis transforms reality and the self-organisation of the masses is a necessary condition for social transformation, then the development, structures, and forms of the movement serve as a catalyst in this process. This development, however, is far from linear. This process is not an eternally evolutionary one: the actual movement of real people can intervene decisively in certain crucial moments, which encapsulate the substantive tendencies of this process (in the sense of Lukács's 'decisive moment'). It is in those moments that the role of class consciousness is fundamental. This active intervention transforms the balance of forces in the sense of a dialectical interaction of objective forces and the subjective factor.

Therefore, history as a process is defined as a field of possibilities, a vast structure of alternatives (according to Benjamin),[25] in which the objective conditions are also the conditions of that possibility. This broader relationship between the unpredictable and the objective conditions framing it goes back to the classic Marxian formulation: 'Men make their own history, but they do not make it as they please; they do not make it under self-selected circumstances, but under circumstances existing already, given and transmitted from the past'.[26] Choice within these possibilities is not premeditated, but includes the unintentional, the accidental, and the mistaken. Limits and degrees of freedom in this 'field of possibilities' are not prefixed: praxis itself transforms the very field and its limitations. Ultimately, class struggle is not an instantiated concept moving linearly towards a specific direction, but a real conflict of real people with determined positions in production and society, whose outcome is posited within a range of possibilities, and with a high degree of contingency.[27]

The emergence of these moments has a degree of indeterminacy, characterised by aleatory imponderables.[28] Leninist 'concrete analysis of the concrete situation' is necessary indeed in order to identify and seize the revolutionary moment. This concept is related to that of 'imputed consciousness': the gap between what the proletariat is and what it could be. And it is precisely the

---

24    Gaitanou and Gousis 2015, pp. 134–5.

25    In Löwy 2005, pp. 105, 107. Also according to Engels, as analysed in Bitsakis 2013, p. 178.

26    Marx 1963, p. 15.

27    Gaitanou and Gousis 2015, pp. 139–40.

28    Lukács 2002, pp. 54–5, 60.

masses' praxis that mediates the reducing of this gap (by producing new, collective knowledge) on the one hand, and the practical character of the party on the other. As Gramsci wrote: 'What "ought to be" is therefore concrete; indeed it is the only realistic and historicist interpretation of reality';[29] this interpretation aims exactly at dominating and thus overcoming reality. Therefore, the Lukácsian imputed consciousness and the Gramscian 'two theoretical consciousnesses (or one contradictory consciousness)'[30] are perceived as aspects of the same concept, as the expression of the two tendencies appearing at the same time in the working class, a tendency of emancipation and one of submission. Moreover, Gramscian elaborations are less vulnerable to elitist interpretations, since they suggest their articulation in relation to collective political mobilisation of the masses and forms of self-government, as essential conditions for the transformation of the 'common sense' and for a constituent process of social and political leadership formation.[31]

In relation to our argument here, we study the movements that have developed in Greece in the current period of crisis exactly as those decisive moments that bear contingently the possibility of resolutely transforming both reality and the subjects mobilised. Movement politics in that sense intervenes in and transforms temporality in a concrete manner. Thus, consciousness is not perceived as a kind of enlightenment but as a per se practical process, in the same way that objectivity does not exist abstractly in theory but must be proven in practice.[32] Practice in its turn cannot be perceived as constituted and developing linearly, but rather in leaps and ruptures. From this point of view, we have studied the transformative effects of action on the participants in the specific movements under study.

To this point, we should express the following thesis: although the 2010–11 movements in Greece had, in our estimation, the dynamics, scope, initial organisation and depth to accomplish the aforementioned role, and thereby to function as an overdetermined, decisive moment that could have changed the course of history, their effect has been more limited than it could have been, particularly in relation to people's organisation within a contemporary potentially revolutionary moment. The main reason for that is related to the weaknesses of the Left, and the absence of a political subject, and more specifically (but not only) of a party, that would surpass the fragmentation, fear, strategic deficiency, programmatic insufficiency, lack of vision and the absence

---

29    Gramsci 1971, p. 172.
30    Gramsci 1971, p. 333.
31    Thomas 2012b, pp. 129–30.
32  .  Marx and Engels 1968, p. 659.

of an alternative culture in a broader sense. Thus, the study of the transform-ative effects of action that follows should be read while keeping in mind both the potentialities and the weaknesses of that period.

## 4       Movements in Greece during the 2010–11 Period

The first organised reaction against the economic, social and political reality, as well as the first organised expression of the need for new ways of exercising politics, had been the youth revolt of December 2008. Greece's insertion into the Troika mechanism and the violent consequences of the Memoranda were accompanied by a severe burst of social mobilisation. A week after the inser-tion in the mechanism, hundreds of thousands of people participated in one of the biggest demonstrations in Greek history, during the general strike of GSEE (General Confederation of trade unions) on 5 May 2010. The rebellious cycle of 2010–11 had very unique features: and we speak of a 'rebellious cycle' due to the scale of mobilisation, their diversity, size and radicalism, the escalation of the confrontation, the means of struggle, the rearrangement of social alliances and of political representations and the ruptures produced. Those mobilisa-tions can be seen in the sense of a 'protracted people's war', as the strategy of aggressive defence, through the alternation of different forms and levels of struggle where expanding sections of the population are involved, as Stathis Kouvelakis has put it.[33]

In parallel, these mobilisations were highly politicised in the sense of a new politicisation: in the context of the rapid depreciation of the official polit-ical scene and its structures, broad social strata and especially the youth have sought new forms for exercising politics, often in direct contrast to traditional ones. These forms express a need for a reappropriation of politics; a need for collective participation, including that of independent structures, of public spaces, of spaces of social experimentation, of alternative counter-institutions, of meeting places.

The structures created during the various movements have had those nodal political characteristics. In the labour movement and the wave of strikes, the coordination of grassroots trade unions played a leading role in organising the struggle, whilst several initiatives and mobilisations were undertaken through horizontal organisation at a grassroots level. During the squares movement, a large segment of the masses mobilised in the squares and especially in Syn-

---

33    Kouvelakis 2011a.

tagma, functioning through a general assembly on a daily basis, whilst thematic assemblies were responsible for each field and sector of action. Moreover, the creation of working groups concerning broad fields of action and of everyday organisation (cleaning, feeding, information and alternative media, entertainment, composure, but also of thematic elaborations – e.g. of economists) signalled a large effort of self-organisation alongside the involvement of every participant in the decision-making and political process.

This mode of functioning was preserved to some extent in what followed. Local initiatives, labour clubs in neighbourhoods, solidarity structures, social clinics and pharmacies, local assemblies, anti-fascist initiatives and many relevant structures have flourished on the basis of the same logic (though with existing problems in organisation and functioning). What is expressed here is actually a need of a return to the political, but not in mainstream or institutional terms; a return to politics beyond its traditional forms of exercise; a form of *street politics*. This need is thus antithetical to movementist approaches, which tend to devalue politics per se.

As for the rebellious processes discussed here, they constitute forms of struggle that challenge, prevent, and disrupt political unity, the unification of social differences as organised under law, and reveal the latter's artificial nature. They thus manifest a potential crisis of hegemony, the failure of a successful coordination of interests within the State. At the same time, any expectation of partial settlements, moderate treatments, 'productive/creative' reforms and social, institutional dialogue no longer have any application, since political power does not allow for the emergence of such expectations, while the affected majorities cannot find a way out through them.

This reality is outlined within a landscape in which a *sui generis* totalitarianism and authoritarian Statism are exacerbated. State mechanisms' internal function is transformed; power is transferred towards the top of the executive mechanisms, in centres inaccessible to popular control. It is indicative that there is a constant circumvention of parliamentary procedure and constant violations of the country's laws and Constitution.[34] Moreover, the State is shielded from popular intervention, through the intensification of repression, the development of the concept of the 'enemy people', a growing lack of representativity, massive usage of strike prohibition and conscription of strikers.[35] Moreover, the transfer of power towards the Troika and supranational organisations has led to an anti-democratic shift, perceived by the people as such.

---

34    Sakellaropoulos 2014, pp. 119–21.

35    Sakellaropoulos 2014, pp. 125–6.

This choice should not, in our opinion, be acknowledged according to the traditional schemata of dependence. On the contrary, it has signalled a voluntary alliance of the national bourgeois class with certain bourgeois classes of the EU, aimed primarily against the Greek people, and secondarily against non-competitive capitals (i.e. at the reorganisation of the State and its economic functions to the benefit of certain sections of monopoly capital).

Having defined the beginning of the selected period for this research, we consider its ending in early 2012. After the pivotal mobilisation of 12 February 2012, when the legislation associated with the second Memorandum was voted for in parliament and tens of thousands of people took to the streets in militant and mass demonstrations, the social movement entered a new phase. We do not consider the cycle of mobilisations of that period as closed; nor do we adopt a fragmentary logic of partial social struggles studied as such. Instead, our approach treats every individual form, in its particularities and its special features, as part of the social movement as a whole. However, we do believe that the two-year period of 2010–11 marks a first phase, with certain common characteristics, especially with respect to the issues we are interested in, related to consciousness formation and transformation through political participation. The period that followed, from spring 2012 until the January 2015 election, has been defined more by the shift of the confrontation and of expectations towards the parliamentary level, beginning with the double elections of May–June 2012. This two-and-a-half year period was characterised by the imposition of violent social and political measures against the social majority and a decline in social mobilisation – although certain important struggles have developed in specific spaces, mostly against the closure of the Hellenic Broadcasting Corporation (ERT), in the student movement and certain education sectors, in part of the public sector, and in Skouries (Chalkidiki) against gold-mining.

## 5    Methodological Remarks and Empirical Results

Methodologically, the data presented in what follows are extracted from research in progress within a PhD thesis, including 40 semi-structured interviews conducted during the academic year 2013–14.[36] The sample was chosen in order

---

36    It is obvious that the conjuncture in which the interviews were conducted is of high importance for the tendencies and findings presented here. This period is characterised, as noted above, by a relative lack of social struggles (except for isolated cases), development of individualistic tendencies, intensification of the implication of neoliberal measures and of the social and economic impasses, and a sharpening of undemocratic deflections,

to offer the opportunity to investigate forms and effects of political participation, interviewing people who belong to different social groups, especially
with reference to their former participation and engagement. I have particularly focused on people who had little or no prior relationship with politics and
activism, and more specifically those who were not members of political organisations and parties at the time of their participation. This criterion guarantees
that the interviewees participated in the movements due to personal motiva-
tion and not as their common practice as members of a political group. It also
provides the opportunity to study the transformational effects of participation,
since the chosen sample has experienced its participation as a relatively new
experience.

The sample was chosen according to purposeful sampling (based on the
researcher's view of what is useful or interesting), and using the snowball
sampling method. Of course, even though in qualitative methodology we are
not interested in quantitative figures or a proportional distribution of the
sample, I have tried to achieve a relative representativity, in terms of gender,
age group, education level and region of residence (related to class position).
Having said that, I did not intend to represent all categories, but rather focus on
those that are of great importance in the composition of what we could call 'the
Greek people' (mostly in the sense of class structure and education level) and
those particularly significant for my research, related to questions of political
participation. Thus, as far as age groups are concerned, I have mostly focused
on those aged 26–35, since the youth has played an important role both in
the movements and in the constitution of new relationships with politics, and
those aged 36–45 and 46–55, who represent those strata formed in the context
of the relative stability of the 1990–2000 and now face an almost total collapse
of both their way of life and their political representations.

Before presenting the main tendencies emerging from this research, an
important first element related to the sample refers to the question of political
self-determination.[37] An intense hesitation to answer this question has been
identified. Certain participants stated their inability to posit themselves, others
claimed to deny or reject 'labels' or 'identities', others questioned the distinction between the Right and the Left, and a few denied it from an anarchist
perspective. This weakness in a relatively simple and classical question in ques-
tionnaires is, in our opinion, absolutely related to the broad crisis of political

---

in both the political and the civil societal level. The presentation that follows must be read
with those elements in mind.

37    'Speaking of politics in general, in which political space would you posit yourself, on a
scale from 1 to 10 in which 1 represents far-left and 10 the far-right?'

representation and reveals its depth, since the existing political identities are firmly relativised, without however new commitments being created, at least in the current understanding of the political distribution. A second respective finding is that, finally, participants tended to self-posit themselves towards the left part of the scale, to a larger extent than their general political perspective, at least in my judgement during the whole interview. This is also an interesting observation related to many social and historical factors (strong left historical narrative that has influenced the Greek society and especially its more militant segments, relative hegemony of the Left in certain sectors, particularly those related to social mobilisation,[38] wide social legitimisation of the militant, combative, and partly confrontational character of the Left, strong division and political polarisation of the society along historically established lines, etc.).

Moving on to the interviews, and starting with the dominant perception of politics, initially there is a relative inability to comprehend politics outside political parties. However, as the discussion unfolded, there was an almost universal emphasis on the fact that movement processes, and especially general assemblies and various structures (in the squares movement), had had a political character. The question on the definition of politics usually provoked a profound conversation. With regard to the political system, there is a very deep, almost indiscriminate, degradation. As for political parties, the majority locates the principal liability for the current socio-political situation in the two parties in power (PASOK and New Democracy), emphasising that the whole 'old political personnel' is thought to be included, even if part of it has moved towards new parties. This finding is important, given that in Greece the phenomenon of new parties being created, mainly by former executives of the two parties in power, has been one of the main channels used for the political system to advance its stabilisation.[39] However, we did detect a tendency (albeit an

---

38    This point partly explains the weakness of the far-right and the inability of the fascist Golden Dawn to acquire an important reference to the streets and to movementist processes.

39    This was the initial tendency, in order to deal with the deep crisis of political representation. Because of the viewpoint described here, however, those tactics have had poor results in integrating citizens into a new strategic plan of political power. Thus the emergence of new parties was linked to persons who had no prior relationship to politics. This has been far more effective for the political system, since it has incorporated the broad feeling that politicians are the main agents responsible for the current situation in Greece. The engagement in politics of technocrats, as well as journalists and persons related to the mainstream star system, has thereby been legitimated. It is indicative that the fourth party in the last elections (25 January 2015), with 6.05% of the vote, was a new one created

implicit one) of a broader distrust of all parties, even if theoretically most participants claimed that there are differences between parties ('ok, I cannot speak
of all the parties since they have not all been in power'). Others clearly attributed responsibility to all the parties in parliament, whilst others distinguished
between the Left (KKE and SYRIZA) and the rest. Moreover, several claimed that
obtaining power linearly leads to corruption: a characteristic statement concerning the Left was that 'Even if it initially has good intentions, it will become
one of the same if it acquires power', or 'When something is transformed into an
institution, it is incorporated in the system' (however, the benefit of the doubt
is generally maintained). In any case, the vast majority claimed that they would
not consider joining a political party as members.

However, contrary to a debate in the public discourse, the above perception
does not seem to lead to an overall depreciation of democracy as such. The
majority of participants claim that the problem is not located in the regime of
parliamentary democracy, but in the way it functions in Greece or its political
representatives (parties, politicians, etc.). This does not simply refer to scandals
or corruption: most interviewees claim that the official function of the political
system does not correspond to parliamentary democracy. The statement 'What
democracy? What we actually have today in Greece is a junta' is repeated aston-
ishingly often during the interviews. Almost all explicitly claim to be supporting
democracy as a regime, and indeed many negatively associate the rejection of
democracy as such to Golden Dawn and fascism, or their thoughts immediately
turn that way when the relevant question is posed.

As far as the Left is concerned, there is considerable scepticism and mistrust.
That refers to both its stance in parliament and its intervention in movements.
Most interviewees claim that the Left, when participating in the movements,
aims at satisfying its own interests and not those of the people, does not listen
to or care for what the people have to say, and is rigid and inflexible. We can
detect a contradiction within what is considered to be the role of the Left. The
majority claims that movements have faced certain problems and limitations,
and that the presence of an organised and experienced political force would
have been a catalyst for their organisation, political formulation, strategy and

---

by a former journalist of the mainstream media (Potami by Stavros Theodorakis), with a
clearly neoliberal political programme. In any case, because of the concrete political and
historical tradition and reality in Greece, this tactic has in no way been able to fully incorporate the political impasse of the masses. Rather, it is the Left that has more successfully
intervened into this crisis of political representation. This explains why in Greece it would
be far more difficult for phenomena to develop such as the Beppe Grillo party (Five Star
Movement) in Italy.

planning, persistence and determination. On the other hand, they denounce the existing leftist groups that have participated, based on the above criticism. Thus, for example, on the squares movement, a large debate had developed on whether the Left should have participated in the movement with its own symbols, based on the argument that people should participate without any political mediation. Most interviewees were indeed aware of this debate, and actually agreed that the Left should not participate as such (however, on the same debate concerning trade unions, the majority claims that, on the contrary, they should participate in the movement as such). Moreover, many detect a gradual degeneration of the Syntagma Square general assemblies, attributed by certain interviewees to the Left: 'they only sought to impose their views', 'they did not hear us ordinary people', 'they tried to impose their own way of functioning, usually in a subtle way', etc. Thus, we observe an overall recognition and legitimisation of the potential role of the Left at an abstract level, but the existing leftist organisations and parties appear suboptimal for that role. The main criticism towards them is that they are incapable of communicating with the people participating in movements, of hearing what they have to say and taking it under serious consideration. This general mistrust and lack of positive engagement of the Left is also expressed by many when discussing their stance on the electoral level.[40] In any case, many emphasise the need for unity on the Left, as a spontaneous reflection, without being actually concerned about any deeper elaboration (on the programme, the strategic goal, tactics, coalitions, etc.).

Discussing the State and the institutions, there has been an overwhelming delegitimisation, and at the same time participants acknowledge the transformation of their opinion after their participation in the movements, towards a deeper depreciation. The police is totally discredited as an instrument of repression that does not protect citizens. The majority claims that this has been clear to them even prior to their participation, but after the latter, they have realised 'the degree of brutality and of arbitrariness'. However, an important minority also claims that their opinion has clearly shifted when observing the police's stance in the streets, 'the unprovoked and irrational character of its action'. At the same time, it is characteristic that the vast majority claims that

---

40    This mistrust refers mainly to low expectations from a potential victory of the Left in the elections: actually, although the interviews did not at all focus on electoral representation, many participants stated at some point that they probably *would* vote for the Left, and especially SYRIZA, but with low expectations regarding its actual radicalism and potential.

although it considers that the police's presence discouraged 'others'/'the majority of the society' from participating in mobilisations, it did not discourage them personally. Thus, they recognise 'the efficacy of repression and of terrorisation', but for *others*. Almost everyone claims that they have felt fear; however, many say that the police's behaviour made them feel more determined as far as their participation is concerned, rather than discouraging them from participating. It is also significant that in response to a relevant question on the State, participants had had difficulty understanding what the question referred to, and often answered as if it referred to the police. This finding demonstrates a belief in the deep interconnection of the State and the police, and the identification of the State with repressive tactics.

As for official trade unionism, there is a considerable degradation of GSEE and ADEDY (the General Workers' Confederations in the private and public sector respectively), and generally of official trade unionism. Many participants identify it as 'bureaucratised', 'corrupted', whilst the most important element denounced by almost all is its dependence on political parties ('every single executive of them becomes a deputy afterwards'). The majority claims explicitly not to feel that they represent workers' interests. On the other hand, most people distinguish between tertiary confederations and grassroots unionism (irrespective of their actual knowledge on the action of the latter, as acknowledged by themselves), with grassroots unionism believed to be actually trying to represent workers' true interests, but having fewer opportunities to do so, and therefore being weaker. In general, the majority's stance towards trade unionism is better than expected: the necessity of union representation is widely recognised, and syndicalism itself is thought to be necessary and positive by principle.

There is also a deep delegitimisation of the media, as 'directly tied to political power, functioning as a propaganda mechanism'. Many claim that this has been clear after their participation in a mass rally, when, upon returning home, they witnessed the media presenting it contrary to their personal experience. In any case, almost all react as if the mainstream media is deeply delegitimated.

Finally, regarding the European Union, there is also an important devaluation concerning both its policies and its function. An important part of the responsibility regarding the situation in Greece is attributed to the EU. However, in response to the question of whether this responsibility rests more on external or internal sites of power, there is a tendency to attribute it equally to both: very few speak of the country's 'occupation' or of Greek politicians as simply 'pawns' of European elites. Actually, many perceive the question as a tendency to underestimate the liability of Greek politicians and react negatively. The majority claims that the EU functions in the interests of North Western countries (most of them refer to Germany and secondarily to France). Many claim to be sceptical but not negative about the idea of leaving the EU: certain respondents claim that, theoretically, there should be the possibility of a linkage between European countries to the benefit of their people, but very few consider this feasible in the current situation.

In questions related to consciousness transformation,[41] most participants self-detected a significant shift in themselves, describing the way they perceived the above, and stating that prior to their participation, they were either indifferent or had a rather blurred image. This primarily concerns the political system, the role of the State and their own social position (on this last point, most of them said that now they realise that they themselves, even as single individuals, '*do have power* and *can* offer something'). As for the police, they stated that they knew its role but only afterwards realised its brutality. The media seem to have been vastly delegitimised before the movements. Also, many have stated that they have a greater appreciation of 'the society' and 'the people' after their participation, a fact that, as they state, they did not expect to this extent.

Finally, regarding politics and movement structures – that is, the possibility of constituting new forms of exercising politics through movement processes – the majority claims that the respective forms of movements (structures, assemblies, focus and thematic groups) do have a political character, attributing to them both a practical contribution and a method of functioning as a political paradigm. Regarding general assemblies, there is a positive stance, especially concerning their democratic functioning and the ability of all to participate. However, there is a strong hesitation on their effectiveness in praxis. Many state that assemblies have functioned as 'a space of expression', 'a forum for everyone to say his/her problem', or as 'a psychological uplift', but with few opportunities to actually organise and concretely implement a political direction. Thematic and working groups, e.g. in the squares (cleaning, feeding, etc.), are thought to be generally more effective. However, there seems to be some reluctance as to the possibility of generalising this model as an example of exercising politics: the majority claims that they cannot understand how this could function on a large scale.

---

41    'Has the way you perceive the social reality / the political system / your social position / the role of the State / the media / the police changed after your participation in the protests, and if so, how?'

## Conclusion

In conclusion, this research – conducted through interviews with people who participated in the mobilisations of 2010–11, with no prior political commitment or concrete participation – confirms what was posed theoretically at the outset, namely that there is a very deep crisis of political representation. This reality refers to the political system, the political parties and their representatives, and also, more than what is implied in public discourse, to the political parties in power (PASOK and New Democracy). The legitimisation crisis of the State and its fundamental institutions (police, official trade unions, and mass media) is also confirmed. This tendency is undoubtedly deeply destabilising for the functioning of the political system. For several years, there has been a process of political destabilisation, a lack of political representation of the people, its interests, and its political behaviour, and little popular engagement in a positive strategic plan. During this period, the established political scene has collapsed, and efforts to restructure it have not been fully successful. Bipartisanship has fallen apart, new parties have emerged, the broader centre has not been able to be reconstructed, the Left has been reorganised, with its impact, political and electoral influence rising significantly, whilst the right-wing forces have witnessed many transformations and a fascist party (Golden Dawn) has appeared, representing in successive elections a percentage of people reaching approximately 7%.

Moreover, the theoretical point about consciousness transformation through political participation, and people's own *praxis* and autonomous political activity, is also confirmed. Indeed, political participation in movements induces an even more acute transformation of people's perception of the State, politics, the media and other institutional mechanisms and institutions like the EU. There is a certain radicalisation linked to participation, also proven by findings not presented here analytically (e.g. on popular belief in forms of struggle, the use of violence by protesters, the perception of their interests as competing against those of other social groups, etc.). There is also a deeper than expected[42] trust in social mobilisation, an optimism in relation to their potential, and a positive stance toward their meaning and effectiveness.[43]

However, in terms of their political function, there is a difficulty in forming, through this personal experience, a specific alternative potential of political

---

42   This lower expectation is due, among other things, to the specific conjuncture in which the interviews were conducted.

43   This conclusion comes from a part of the interviews that was not deeply examined in the context of this text.

constitution, even if it is acknowledged as a necessity. The sense of the weakness of the Left, of an alternative positive engagement and of a specific and convincing strategy and vision, both in terms of social organisation and of political function, contributes to this deficit. In any case, even if not specifically and organisationally formulated, there is a strong demand for a deepening of democratic functioning, greater involvement of people in politics and for forms and structures that would guarantee this participation.

At the start of 2015, Greek society has entered a new era, since SYRIZA, a party coming from the Left, has won the parliamentary elections and has formed a government in coalition with ANEL, a relatively newly established party of the Right, one with an anti-Memorandum viewpoint. Things have accelerated since SYRIZA was elected after a clearly anti-Memorandum campaign, only to retract from its commitment. It made clear right from the beginning that it did not intend to break ties either with the existing framework of the EU and the IMF mechanisms or with the broader framework in which the country had been operating in recent years. Thus, it proclaimed its commitment to respect every obligation of the country and maintain compliance with the terms of fiscal adjustment and stability, while it renounced any unilateral action and choice of rupture. At the same time, it removed from its political programme the most progressive and movementist claims, and, of course, in no way called for the people to stay active in the streets. Thus, soon the SYRIZA-ANEL government was obliged to face its inability to implement even minor aspects of its political programme, even failing in the protection of elementary civil rights.

A point of rupture in this course has been the conduct of a referendum on whether the Memorandum proposed by the troika mechanism was to be accepted by the Greek people. Over 61% of the population voted against the acceptance, in an astonishing response against all kinds of blackmail and five years of extremely unpopular Memorandum policies. It is not, of course, the object of this chapter to study this period. However, it should be stated that the lead up to and the result of the referendum has made evident the footprint of the social and class struggles of the last years, and especially of the biennial 2010–11 under consideration here. Moreover, it has made evident the footprint of the transformation of consciousness and a certain potential radicalisation shown here. Despite this result, the SYRIZA-ANEL government signed up to the Memorandum one week later, submitting to institutional blackmail. A triple coup, as it has been called, has actually been effectuated: first, by the EU towards the Greek people as a whole and the government in particular, blackmailing the latter to accept the agreement or else exit the EMU. Secondly, by the Greek bourgeois class against the popular classes, as it threatened to respond in various ways (including the threat of a coup) in case the pro-Memorandum and pro-EU policies were questioned. And thirdly, by the SYRIZA-ANEL government towards the Greek people, who voted against the agreement with the troika. A major organisational split in SYRIZA was to come. However, in the September 2015 elections that followed, SYRIZA managed to maintain its position, though it had fully incorporated the pro-Memorandum rhetoric and political programme. In the context of this chapter, we have not been interested analytically in partisan representations. In terms of political representation, the overall image seems currently to have changed since the two-year period of 2010–11, when it was much more fluid. The political scene and political affiliations appear at this point more stable and concrete. Politics in the official sense has resumed its dominant position in the public discourse. At the same time, movement practices and structures are less in the foreground, and their scope is limited more to material contributions (solidarity, coverage of basic necessities, defence against the aggressiveness of the State or capital) and less to the formulation of a different paradigm of exercising politics.

However, the social rift remains very deep and political representations, though more stable, do not seem to actively engage large segments of the society in a coherent, positive, strategic plan. Both the current management of the crisis and the political orientation of the SYRIZA-ANEL government offer neither a viable way out of the crisis nor some better perspective for the social majority. Thus, the socio-political rift is expected to deepen. Besides, independent of the politics intended to be followed by the SYRIZA-ANEL government, the dynamics liberated by its election are unpredictable and establish the possibility of a new emergence of the popular factor at the forefront. The research presented in this chapter, on the pre-existing crisis of political representation and of the legitimisation of the State and its mechanisms, as well as on the conception of politics and its various perspectives, aims at contributing to the comprehension of the people's mobilisation and potential, with an eye toward the future. It reinforces the belief that, since history is the history of class struggles,[44] its greatest moments shall be written in the streets, and the Greek paradigm is a unique manifestation of this potentiality. Keeping in mind, that if, according to Eagleton, hope 'is necessary precisely because one is able to confess how grave a situation is',[45] at the same time

44    Marx and Engels 2002, p. 219.
45    In opposition to optimism, which expresses 'a form of psychological disavowal', 'a moral evasion', underestimating the obstacles to tackling it, and thus ending up with a fairly worthless kind of assurance. Optimism does not take despair seriously enough (Eagleton 2015). Or else, 'There is no reason to despair, even under the most desperate situations', in

*'Hope is something too much. In my opinion, it is a great revolutionary force, namely the idea that you can reach something'.*[46]

### References

Bensaïd, Daniel 2001, *Les irréductibles. Théorèmes de la résistance à l'air du temps*, Paris: Textuel.

Bitsakis, Eftichis 2013, *Human nature. For a communism of the finite*, [In Greek] Athens: Editions Topos.

Charalampis, Dimitris 1985, *Army and political power. Power structure in post-civil war Greece*, [In Greek], Athens: Exantas.

Eagleton, Terry. 2015, 'The Banality of Optimism', pre-published extract from Terry Eagleton, 2015, *Hope Without Optimism*, by permission of the University of Virginia Press.

Eurobarometer (Standard) (2008). No. 70: Autumn.

Gaitanou, Eirini. and Costas Gousis 2015, 'The ultimate truth of First International is its own existence: Consciousness, subjectivity and the actuality of an absence (or what's missing, is it really missing?)', [In Greek] *Utopia* 110: 127–45.

Gramsci, Antonio 1971, *Selections from the Prison Notebooks*, New York: International Publishers.

Hobsbawm, Eric, 1994, *Age of extremes: The short twentieth century, 1914–1991*. London: Michael Joseph.

INE/GSEE 2012, *Greek economy and employment*, [In Greek] Annual Report, Reports 14, August.

Kouzis, Giannis 2007, *Characteristics of the Greek trade union movement. Divergences and convergences with the European area*, [In Greek] Athens: Gutenberg.

Kouvelakis, Stathis 2011a, 'Time of Crisis. Six positions for the revolt', [In Greek], *Dromos tis Aristeras*, 11 June.

Kouvelakis, Stathis 2011b, 'The invisible end of a winter. Towards the second phase of politico-social confrontation', [In Greek], *Epochi*, 25 March.

Loulis, Giannis 2001, *The twenty years that changed Greece: Winners and losers*, [In Greek] Athens: Nea Synora.

Löwy, Michael 2005, *Fire alarm: Reading Walter Benjamin's On the concept of history*, London: Verso.

---

the words of Leo Valiani, whom Hobsbawm cites in his discussion of the short twentieth century (1994, p. 2).

46    Sartre 1974, p. 205.

Lukács, Georg 1971, *History and class consciousness: Studies in Marxist dialectics*, Cambridge, Mass: MIT Press.

Lukács, Georg 2002, *A defence of history and class consciousness: Tailism and the dialectic*. London: Verso.

Marx, Karl 1977 [1859], *A Contribution to the Critique of Political Economy*. Moscow: Progress Publishers.

Marx, Karl 1963, *The 18th Brumaire of Louis Bonaparte*, New York: International Publishers.

Marx, Karl and Friedrich Engels 1968, *The German Ideology*. Moscow: Progress Publishers.

Marx, Karl and Friedrich Engels 2002, *Communist Manifesto*, London: Penguin.

Meynaud, Jean (n.d.). *Political forces in Greece*, Volume B. Athens: Editions Byron.

Sakellaropoulos, Spyros 1998, *The causes of the April coup 1949–1967. The social context of the course towards the dictatorship*, [In Greek] Athens: Nea Synora – Livanis.

Sakellaropoulos, Spyros 2014, *Crisis and social stratification in Greece of the 21st century*, [In Greek] Athens: Editions Topos.

Sakellaropoulos, Spyros and Panagiotis Sotiris 2004, *Restructuring and modernisation. Social and political transformations in Greece in the 1990s*, [In Greek] Athens: Editions Papazisi.

Sartre, Jean Paul 1974, *It is Right to Rebel*, [In Greek] Athens: Arsenidi editions.

Thomas, Peter 2012, 'The communist hypothesis and the question of organisation', [In Greek] *Utopia* 100: 117–34.

# CHAPTER 7

# Reshaping Political Cultures: the 'Squares Movement' and Its Impact

*Angelos Kontogiannis-Mandros*

## Introduction

Economic crisis was no doubt the main instigator of the socio-political developments that occurred in many of the countries of the European periphery in the course of the last six years. True as that may be, the reflections of the economic turbulences at the political level have varied significantly. Whereas in Portugal, Cyprus and Ireland the political systems remained relatively stable, in Italy, Spain and particularly Greece we have the emergence of rather deeper transformative processes that shook the very basis of the political status quo. What is more, while in Spain the political system is in a phase of fundamental but prolonged transformation, which is, only lately, manifested in its full capacity in the party system and the surge of separatism, in Greece we can rather speak of a ruptural break occurring in a very condensed period of time, between 2011–12.

The enlightening bit of this observation is the fact that despite being the common denominator, economic hardships and dead-ends constitute only part of the equation regarding political developments in these countries. In other words, in contrast to an economically reductionist view, we argue here that the key variable that actually determined the impact of the economic crisis at the political level was the particular character, the magnitude and intensity of social mobilisation. This variable was in itself determined by the specificities of the political and ideological articulations, characterising the social formations of the crisis-hit countries at the time of their encounter with the aftershocks of the 2007 global financial crisis.

It is here that we find the basis of the particularity and importance of the Greek case for the examination of the overall conjuncture. It was only in Greece that the economic crisis intersected with a prolonged crisis of political representation leading, under conditions of mass political mobilisation, to what Gramsci would call an 'organic crisis' of the system; a simultaneous rupture at the economic, political and ideological levels, a collapse of the hegemonic articulations and an intense contestation that radically transformed the means and 'nature' of political competition.[1]

Hence our objective here is twofold: on the one hand, to substantiate the claim about the catalytic impact of the 2010–12 cycle of contention in the political rupture that manifested itself in the legislative elections of 2012; and on the other, to examine the dynamics that emerged within the movement and their impact on the broader political culture (denoting here discourses and organisational forms) of both the left and the right. We believe that such an analysis will illuminate the short-term dynamics empowered by the movement and will enable us to evaluate the strength and importance of its 'ideological-cultural' traits that in reality constitute its long-term impact.

In this context this chapter is divided into three main parts. In the first one, we elaborate on the characteristics of the political system in the period preceding the crisis (i.e. 1996–2009) so as to put our subsequent analysis into context. Emphasis is placed here on the characteristics of party competition, the ideological contestation under the 'modernisation' project and the subterranean socio-political dynamics that characterise this period, such as the struggles against the educational reforms and the revolt of December 2008. Following on from this, we examine the cycle of contention and the dynamics that emerged in its course (sections 2 and 3), while in the third and final part we analyse its long-term political impact on the lines described above (sections 4 and 5).

## 1        Greece in the 'Modernisation' Era

As already stated in the introduction, understanding the particular impact of the economic crisis on the Greek social formation is impossible without examining the latent dynamics of the political system in the preceding period. Key parameters here are the structure and character of the party system and the position/status of the 'modernisation' narrative within the broader configuration of the ideological field.

The legislative elections of 1996 constitute a breakthrough regarding subsequent developments on both these analytical axes. The formation of Simitis's government and the launch of the 'modernisation' project were, in this respect, catalytic both for the political orientation of PASOK and the political

---

1   Although referring to the potential of 'organic crisis', Kalampokas's analysis is quite revealing of the dynamics at play (Kalampokas 2013a, pp. 13–14). A strong support to the 'organic crisis' thesis is also to be found in the writings of Kouvelakis throughout the period (e.g. Kouvelakis 2011c).

system more generally. The prevalence of the neoliberal, 'modernisation', faction ('eksygchronistès' in Greek) over the social-democratic establishment of the party in the struggle of succession after Andreas Papandreou's death, signified a definite break with the political project of 'Allagi' (i.e. 'change') and the social coalition of the non-privileged that constituted the kernel of PASOK's political strategy in the preceding period of 'interim metapolitefsi'.[2]

Modernisation as an ideological and political programme comes thus as the implementation of the ideological and political agenda of neoliberalism that already dominated Western-European politics. Its core elements are the active participation of Greece in the processes of European Integration and, especially at the time, the monetary Union, as a key means for the financialisation and liberalisation of economic policy and the transformation of political representation. According to the modernisation narrative, parties and in that case PASOK should not represent class/social groups' interests, but rather the interest of the nation as such.[3] This was of course the means through which the neoliberal restructuration of the economic and political system was going to be legitimised at the expense of what was characterised as 'corporatist interests'.

At the ideological level, modernisation remained somewhat vague and unsystematised. Centring on Europeanism[4]–in its actual practice, a very contested idea of consensual politics and the promise of a new, more rational and de-ideologised type of governance – it was in reality advancing a radical break with the political and social polarisation of the 'early' and 'interim' metapolitefsi. The seeming 'neutrality' of the modernisation discourse and its narrative insistence on the themes of 'progress' and 'powerful Greece' gave it the ability to draw cross class support. In a conjuncture of a relative economic boom, large parts of the popular social classes with historical links to the party were able to maintain the prospect of upward social mobility while the emerging middle classes and the bourgeoisie could envisage the implementation of neoliberal policies in a less conflictual and thus more effective way than the failed liberalisation endeavour of Mitsotakis's government back in the early '90s.

Here lies the base of the hegemonic character of the modernisation project. By incorporating the neoliberal agenda and an aggressive Europeanism, while retaining its grip on the lower social strata, in reality PASOK left no way for New

---

2  Givalos 2005; Vernardakis 2011.

3  Psimitis and Sevastakis 2000; Gravaris 2002.

4  For the strength of pro-European ideology throughout the period, see Mavris 2004; Vernardakis 2007.

Democracy apart from following suit. The so-called 'triangular' strategy of the 'middle space' that Karamanlis put forward after his 2000 electoral defeat was in reality nothing more than a promise for a more effective and accountable modernisation.[5] The political implications of that were tremendous indeed, and marked the passage from 'interim' to what Vernardakis calls 'late meta-politefsi'.[6]

The latter is mainly characterised by the policy and ideological convergence of the bipartisan system. This process, which can be traced back to 1985 and the first turn of PASOK towards more fiscally 'robust' economic policies, was accelerated during the late 1990s and led to the gradual cartelisation[7] of the party system. This was a significant development that reflected a decisive change in the bourgeoisie's strategy and transformed the nature of parties' competition as well as their function. Instead of representing social dynamics, in reality the two main parties ended up managing and implementing state policies. Particularly in the case of PASOK, this process necessitated a fundamental change of its internal structure. By pretending to open up the party into society, the party leadership liquidated the notion of membership and gave greater autonomy to the highest echelons of the party's bureaucracy. Despite maintaining a rather sizable membership, hereafter the political orientation of the party was almost exclusively determined by the professionalised party elite, that alternated between party and governmental posts. This trend which was always more apparent in New Democracy deeply transformed the relation of the parties to society.[8]

Hidden behind the supposed successes of modernisation, at the turn of the century these changes created significant tensions that, although latent, in reality undermined the long-term stability of the system. The cartelisation of the party system played a significant role in the emergence of a strong current of political apathy and discontent with the political system as such. Although political parties were still perceived as key pillars of the democratic process, as testified by the persistent strength of parliamentarian ideology and their dominance in the political milieu,[9] their political and organisational

---

5   Pantazopoulos 2005; Vernardakis 2005.

6   Vernardakis 2011, pp. XXII–XXIII, 57.

7   Katz and Mair 1995.

8   Givalos 2005.

9   Parties remained by far the main element of the Greek political system. Labour and student unions were under their tight control while other civil society organisations remained utterly marginal.

transformation simultaneously redefined and eroded their relation with their electorate. Partially decompressed during the legislative elections of 2000 and 2004 due to the canalisation of popular grievances to New Democracy,[10] this dynamic became evident in the 2007 legislative elections where there was a sharp decrease in electoral participation.[11] Even more interestingly for the subsequent developments one year later, in the months preceding the December 2008 events, PASOK's electoral support was in freefall with SYRIZA reaching in the public opinion surveys an unprecedented 18% of the vote.[12] This trend did not 'survive' the political turbulence of the months to follow, but it was the first manifestation of the crisis of representation at the basis of the two-party system.

Apart from the convergence and absorption of the two dominant parties by the State, underpinning this dynamic were the socio-economic effects and the ideological counter-movements that the modernisation project brought to the fore. With regard to the former, large parts of the popular social classes and the traditional petty bourgeoisie perceived their social and economic status to be under threat as a result of the liberalisation of the economy and the undermining of the corporatist provisions incorporated in the social contract of 'metapolitefsi'. Although public finances were growing fast and cheap credit boosted consumption to unprecedented levels, economic growth was not equally distributed. As the 2008 December revolt unequivocally manifested, the majority of the youth were faced with a very gloomy future.[13] The massive movement that finally cancelled the insurance reform put forward by Simitis's minister of Labour Tasos Giannitsis in 2001, amidst the height of the economic boom of the early 2000s, was another telling manifestation of the subterranean social dynamics that neoliberalisation and further integration into the EU's structures were provoking at the basis of the social formation.

However, the economic deficiencies of the modernisation project were not the only source of discontent. Despite its hegemonic status, throughout this period at the ideological and political level, modernisation faced significant challenges. First of all, the majority of the population remained in favour of social welfare and some level of state interventionism, in opposition to the neo-

---

10   Vernardakis 2011, pp. 60–1.

11   For a nice overview of the long-term trends regarding participation rates, see K. Poulakis 2011. Regarding the 2007 legislative election, the analysis of Y. Tsirbas is also informative. See Tsirbas 2009.

12   Romaios 2013, p. 324.

13   Voulgaris 2013, p. 168.

liberal narrative[14] (the movement against Giannitsis's reform is here telling). Moreover, as was the case in many countries around the continent, European integration – the actual cornerstone of the modernisation narrative – triggered in wide parts of the population sentiments of fear over the loss of national and cultural identity, a trend that was in turn reflected in the re-emergence of conservative and openly reactionary discourses and movements. The massive popular participation in the rallies and other popular initiatives, instigated by the Church of Greece in the course of 2000, against the government's decision to remove the recording of religious denomination from ID cards is one of the most characteristic examples in this respect. Although these types of mobilisation were characterised by a strong temporal element in their interplay with emerging issues, such as immigration, they laid the basis for the emergence of significant radical right currents in the following years. Indeed LAOS, the first radical right party to enter the parliament in decades, built up its support through an anti-immigration and anti-globalisation rhetoric based on the defence of Greek Orthodoxy and the Church as cornerstones of Hellenic identity.[15]

As we will see later on, blurred behind the mild centre-right rhetoric of Karamanlis's New Democracy, these ideological sub-currents burst out in the late 2000s when the crisis hit the country. However, not all reactions to the ideological and political impositions of modernisation were conservative; quite the opposite. The traditional Left, ideologically and politically weakened as it was after the collapse of the Socialist camp and its recurring splits, still managed to retain a significant and ideologically consequential presence in the social milieu. The role of the Communist Party (KKE) was very important in this regard. In contrast to the trajectory followed by many Western European communist parties, KKE stood firm in a rigid ideological line characterised by a fundamental rejection of the EU as a process of capitalist integration, confined within a broader anti-imperialist discourse. As a result of its particular symbolic and political weight[16] and despite its hard line sectarianism, KKE's stance on the matter played a key role in the political and ideological configurations that emerged within the Left in the period under examination. The strong anti-capitalist verbiage of the party and its firm rejection of any co-operation with the bipartisan system had, in this respect, two significant effects. On the one hand, it helped the reproduction of various smaller radical left currents and

---

14    Tsatsanis 2009.

15    Voulgaris 2013, pp. 336–7.

16    Let us not forget that it remained the major political power of the Left throughout the twentieth and early twenty-first century.

the dissemination of a radically oppositional discourse to the modernisation narrative; and on the other, it contributed significantly to the portrayal of the Left as an uncompromised political power external to the machinations of the 'system'.

In this context, and despite its self-imposed confinement, KKE's position had an effect on the political dynamic and development of the minor parliamentarian power of the Left, Synaspismos. Being currently the focal point of attention, the latter followed a very interesting political trajectory that reflected much of the dynamics of development of the political system. Founded in 1992, for the first decade of its life Synaspismos was a moderate party of the Left with a social-democratic agenda that incorporated many of the key aspects of what some years later would be the kernel of the modernisation project.[17] In this respect, the Synaspismos of the 1990s was in reality a systemic (i.e entirely confined within the ideological limits of the current political and economic system) political power. It thus comes as no surprise that many of its cadres were attracted by PASOK's agenda and left the party in consecutive waves in the late '90s and early 2000s; a fact that in itself is telling of the hegemonic status of the modernisation narrative.[18] However, simultaneously, its close relation with the social struggles and broader mobilisation processes of the period,[19] at a time when the modernisation project started showing its first cracks, reinforced the more leftist voices within the party. Under Alekos Alavanos's presidency (2003–8), this progressive radicalisation took on a more concrete form and led to the formation of SYRIZA. A political front that incorporated the bulk of the small far-left organisations of the extra-parliamentarian Left and gave Synaspismos a new political dynamic that proved to be decisive in the years to come. At the ideological level, this was reflected in the articulation of a rather critical Europeanism, the hesitant reintroduction of socialist transformation as a long-term goal in the party's political strategy and a partial but identifiable break with its consensual and rather co-operative stance towards PASOK and the modernisation camp. Although it remained in the shadow of KKE until the 2012 elections, SYRIZA's political openness, mild radicalisation and greater communication with the emerging social dynamics played a crucial role in positing the party as the main receptor of political discontent during the crisis.

---

17    Vernardakis 2011.

18    Sakkelaropoulos and Sotiris 2004, pp. 68–9, 93.

19    E.g. anti-globalisation movement, the anti-war movements that shook the country against NATO and the US's intervention in Yugoslavia and Iraq respectively, the recurring movements against the various educational reforms.

To sum up, in the period 1996–2009 and especially its first half, modernisation was not only the expression of the strategic interests of capital, but indeed a hegemonic ideological narrative. Despite that, and despite the inability of the traditional Left, as the only actual oppositional force (LAOS entered parliament in 2007), to articulate a counter-hegemonic political programme, modernisation seemed by the late 2000s to have in reality exhausted its initial dynamism. Its political deficiencies, the social resistances provoked by the contradictions of the economic and productive model that had been advanced, the persistence of anti-neoliberal discourses and cultural traits all played their role in this respect. The emphatic 45% of PASOK in the elections of 2009 clearly suggests that the collapse was not predestined to happen, but rather arose from the steady decline of political participation, the growing political apathy stimulated by the reproduction of a 'neutral', de-ideologised 'centrist' political discourse on the part of the two major parties and the sporadic appearance of strong mobilisation processes, with December 2008 being the most important and characteristic instance of this subterranean dynamic.[20] All this seems to suggest that by the time crisis hit the country, the political system was in a process of deep, although latent, crisis.

## 2        Facing the Crisis

On 23 April 2010, the then Prime Minister George Papandreou declared Greece's entrance into the Troika mechanism in the face of a severe public debt crisis. Anticipating widespread social discontent towards the austerity measures, the government quickly put forward the dilemma 'memorandum or bust'. This dichotomy that constituted thereafter the bedrock of governmental discourse, no matter the office holder, did not fit well with the reality of the Greek economy and society. According to INE-GSEE, until 2011 GDP had contracted by 14% (9% more from the estimates of the European Commission at the time),[21] while purchasing power had returned to 2002 levels, leading to a severe decrease in domestic demand further fuelling the recession.[22] At the same time official unemployment had gone up from 7.8% in 2008 (starting point of the global financial crisis) to 17.9 in 2011, reaching 24.5% the year after.[23] Salaries

---

20    Sotiris 2013a.

21    INE-GSEE 2012, p. 89.

22    INE-GSEE 2012, p. 91.

23    Eurostat, Unemployment rate, annual data, available at: http://ec.europa.eu/eurostat/

had gone down by 13.2% by 2011,[24] followed by a severe slash in social welfare benefits and pensions, while hospitals' financing was reduced by more than 40% in two years,[25] demonstrating the devastating impact of austerity upon core structures of the welfare system.[26]

With all economic indicators being in free fall and a contracting State unable to absorb or even restrain the reforms' negative effects on the social fabric, the polity experienced a fundamental transformation. At the ideological level modernisation had received a fatal blow. Its main pillars – integration into EU standards, efficient State, enhancement of the country's role in the global division of labour, political accountability – had all been washed away by the recession and the aforementioned chronic problems of the two-party system. What is more, clientelism, as the main means of absorption and canalisation of social grievances, was no longer sustainable, leaving the political establishment with nothing more to offer than the politics of fear.[27]

With one round of measures following the other, the narrative of collective responsibility was not good enough to dispel the mounting tensions.[28] In order to cope with that situation, and being unable to offer any positive identification with the Memorandum policies, the power system moved quickly towards the authoritarian shielding of the State. New crowd control units were formed in the police, the independency of the judiciary was significantly undermined, with legal rights regarding industrial action, etc. being repeatedly violated, while the parliament was systematically sidelined, with the government legislating through presidential decrees. The discourse of the government could not but follow suit. In an attempt to direct public attention elsewhere, intimidate the public and push the Left into a corner, PASOK resorted to a 'law and order' campaign with an aggressive anti-immigration rhetoric and a constant offensive against the unions' claims. Although this strategy was not sufficient to prevent the rapid disintegration of its electoral base, it was enough to unleash deep-rooted conservative and reactionary dynamics. Absorbed initially by the right-wing turn of ND under Samaras's presidency,

---

tgm/table.do?tab=table&plugin=1&language=en&pcode=tipsun20 (accessed 1 December 2014).

24    INE-GSEE 2012, p. 67.

25    Kentikelenis et al. 2011, p. 1457.

26    Poulopoulos 2014.

27    Some very telling examples of the governmental and media discourse are to be found in Zaroulia and Hager 2014.

28    Athanasiou 2012.

these currents were further radicalised and independently expressed during the following period.[29] Temporarily though, they enabled ND to stabilise its electorate and recover part of the losses it experienced after the 2009 elections and the subsequent revelations over the role of Karamanlis' governments in the deterioration of the public finances.

For the power bloc, the assumption was that a combination of an economic 'shock therapy', an aggressive authoritarian discourse and the immediate and severe repression of any emerging resistance would suffice to demobilise the popular and labour movement, both politically and ideologically. For the modernisers the objective here was not to retain their hegemonic grip but rather to achieve what Stuart Hall once called 'managed dissensus'.[30] The formation of a rather passive consensus won grudgingly and with discontinuities. The ruling bloc is no longer in a hegemonic position but it has the ability to rule and sustain a minimum of legitimacy. This strategy could have been successful were it not for the emergence of a wide and intense cycle of contention. As further elaborated in the course of this chapter, although social mobilisation proved unable to immediately cancel the so-called 'structural adjustment' programme, it nonetheless managed to raise significant obstacles to the implementation of the reforms, built up collective efficacy, produced strong alternative narratives regarding the crisis and its resolution, and accelerated the political crisis that brought about the collapse of the cartelised two-party system in the double elections of 2012.

## 3      The Cycle of Contention

The massive rally on 5 May 2010 against the signing of the Memorandum agreement marks the starting point of a protracted series of intense social mobilisations and episodes of contention that ended with the last big demonstration against the austerity measures on 12 February 2012.[31] Despite their

---

29    Key in this respect was ND's participation in Papademos's 'national unity' government in
      late 2011 and its official crossing to the Memorandum camp, which is to be discussed in
      the next sections.

30    Hall et al. 1988, p. 33.

31    We take the demonstration of 12 February 2012 as the terminal point of the cycle of con-
      tention due to the fact that it was the last massive rally that took place in the capital before
      the legislative elections of May. If we want to be precise though, the last episode of con-
      tention took place on 7 March on the island of Rhodes.

differences all these mobilisation events in reality constitute a unified cycle of contention centring on popular opposition to austerity policies, governmental authoritarianism, and what was perceived as a corrupted and delegitimised political elite.[32]

Unified and reliable aggregate data regarding the magnitude and the participation rate on the various rallies, sit-ins and strikes of the period are not available. Despite this, some estimates can be drawn from the number and the type of industrial actions that occurred as well as from public opinion research data regarding participation in the 'squares movement', which in a way constitutes the culmination of the entire cycle of contention.

For the year 2011, when the movement reached its height, INE-GSEE recorded 445 strikes and work stoppages throughout the country, including six 24-hour and two 48-hour general strikes co-organised by the General Confederation of Greek Workers (GSEE) and the Confederation of Civil Servants (ADEDY).[33] More telling than the rates of industrial action though is the magnitude of social mobilisation and popular discontent as recorded by Public Issue in the period before and during the emergence of the 'squares movement'. Asked in early May if they have participated in protest activities over the last 12 months, 28% of the respondents answered in the affirmative,[34] while on the ten-point scale measuring the intensity of social remonstration there is an average of responses at point 8.4.[35] These feelings of social discontent no doubt explain the sharp increase in mobilisation rates when the 'squares movement' made its appearance at the end of the month. According to Public Issue's estimates of early June, around 2,790,000 people above the age of 18, or 31% of the sample, stated categorically their will to participate in the movement, while an extra 21% declare a high probability of doing so.[36] 35% of the respondents stated that they had already participated in the rallies and other popular initiatives organised around the country at the time.[37] Taking these data into consideration and keeping in mind that the movement reached its peak at the massive

---

32    Even movements focusing on local demands, such as the one in Keratea against the creation of a landfill, were quickly coloured by the broader political conflict and incorporated into the symbolic matrix of the cycle of contention.

33    INE Papers 2012, pp. 91–9.

34    Public Issue 2011a, p. 80.

35    Public Issue 2011a, p. 78, point one of the scale denoting very low intensity and 10 extremely high.

36    Public Issue 2011b, p. 33.

37    Public Issue 2011b, p. 12.

rallies accompanying the 48-hour general strike on 28 and 29 June 2011, we can assume with a degree of certainty that at its height almost a quarter of the population actively participated in the mobilisations of the period.

In contrast to the union movement, which is more or less ascribed in the 'established' political culture both in terms of the repertoires of action and the political powers mainly involved, the 'squares movement' had a strong element of originality. First of all, it was a truly popular movement drawing support from the entire political spectrum. Being triggered almost spontaneously via social media as a solidarity campaign in support of the Spanish 'Indignados' with a call out on 25 May, the 'squares movement' was presented from the very start as a process outside of party politics and the traditional mobilisations of the Left. During the first weeks of its appearance, 41% of its participants were not positing themselves on the Left-Right axis, while 16% were identifying with the Right or the Center-Right and another 27% with the Left or the Centre-Left.[38] This catchall character of the movement was reflected in the strong anti-party and even anti-political frames and discourses initially circulating in the rallies at Syntagma Square. As time passed and the movement grew and organised more, the intervention of ANTARSYA's and especially SYRIZA's factions become more evident and had a significant impact in further politicising the discourse and the claims of the movement.[39] In reality the 'organised/political' Left remained till the end a supportive rather than a leading force within the movement, the actual motor of which was to be found in the popular assemblies and all the self-organised initiatives around them. In this respect, the movement of the 'squares' was probably the first of that magnitude to grow independently of parties' strategies and dynamics. True as that may be, the Left and especially SYRIZA remained the only political force that systematically tried to engage with the dynamics of the movement, a choice that would prove to be a determining factor in subsequent political developments.

Being in a way exogenous to the traditional politics and repertoires of social movements, the 'squares' proved to be highly innovative in organisational terms as well. At Syntagma Square, the symbolic and material heart of the movement, the popular assembly that operated daily decided the formation of various initiatives/groups regarding cleaning, 'calm' (i.e protection/defence),

---

38    Public Issue 2011b, p. 14.

39    For example, the 'we don't owe, we don't shell, we don't pay' slogan that became the benchmark of the movement was in reality a motto of the Coordination of Grassroots Unions; a trade-union initiative created and supported by the aforementioned political powers.

medical units, media and cultural activities as well as thematic assemblies and public talks regarding open democracy, education, crisis exit strategies, etc. Horizontal organisation was the norm and decision-making was always to take place in the assembly. This paradigm, which was to be followed at various degrees from demonstrators throughout the country, marked an entirely new way of popular organisation, that proved somewhat perplexing to even the more activist and politically 'open' parts of the Left. Based on a strong mentality of grassroots activism, self-organisation and direct democracy, the 'squares' managed to engage even with people of no previous political experiences or party alliances and boosted collective efficacy. According to public opinion data, 52% of the public believed that the movement would have a definite impact on the political developments, while 85% stated that it was a very or relatively important political event.

This increase in popular self-confidence brought about by the movement accompanied by the deepening of the crisis was the main instigator of the events of the 'hot' October that in reality constituted both the upshot of the 'squares' and the start of a new political cycle. Starting with days-long occupations of key ministries and public services by civil service unions and a surge of militant unionism in the broader public sector with repeated industrial actions on public transportation and especially the protest activities of GENOP-DEI,[40] mobilisations reached a climax with the 48-hour general strike on the 19–20 October[41] and the massive rallies that took place in Salonika on the 28 October (commemoration day of Greek resistance to the Axis), with masses of people interrupting the military parade and chasing politicians off the VIP stands. Trying to appease the public and blackmail New Democracy and the creditors for concessions, Papandreou opened Pandora's Box by proposing on the 27 October a referendum over the bailout terms. Unable to control internal opposition to his move and publicly humiliated by Merkel and Sarkozy at the G20 summit in Cannes, he resigned, giving way to the formation of a national-unity government under Loukas Papademos. With significant functions of the State apparatus brought to a halt in the wake of the strike, social

---

40    GENOP is the union of workers of the State Electricity Company and one of the biggest and strongest syndicates of the country. On 12 and 25 October, the union occupies respectively the Accounting Center and the IT Directorate of the company thus obstructing the implementation of the new taxes put forward by the government through electricity bills. See INE Papers 2012, p. 98.

41    It is estimated that approximately 500,000 people took to the streets nationwide during the days of the strike. See Kouvelakis 2011d, p. 18.

mobilisation being at its peak and the political centre internally divided and weakened,[42] we are confronted here with a political situation characteristic of what Gramsci would call an 'organic crisis'.


## 4      Between the Movement and the Ballot Box

The intensity and magnitude of the mobilisations of the period May–October 2011 made clear that PASOK had neither the necessary legitimacy to carry on the reform agenda nor even the ability to effectively manage the state apparatuses. Faced with the possibility of an immediate political collapse with unforeseen outcomes, the ruling elites pressed forward the idea of the national unity government. According to Kouvelakis, the latter constitutes a type of 'Bonapartism' in the context of contemporary parliamentary regimes that aims to construct '*a power bloc that bypasses, or significantly alters, representative arbitration and electoral legitimacy, without breaking explicitly with the existing parliamentarian framework*'.[43]

Successful as it was on temporarily bringing down social tensions, the move came at a significant mid-term cost. With New Democracy and the far-right LAOS entering the government and thus crossing to the Memorandum camp, the traditional Left remained the only actual opposition to austerity policies, while the anti-Memorandum conservatives were left with no political expression. With PASOK being in a phase of historical retreat and rapid electoral collapse, and with New Democracy taking responsibility for the continuation of the adjustment programme, SYRIZA was in a position to ride the wave of popular discontent.[44] Being the only parliamentarian power to be in close contact with the social movements of the period and especially the 'squares', the party experienced a steady growth in its electoral influence from July 2011 onwards. When it played out the strategy of the 'government of the Left', based on an aggressive anti-Memorandum discourse centred on the moto 'end to austerity – no sacrifices for the euro', its electoral scope skyrocketed. From 6% in March 2011, to 11% in March 2012,[45] SYRIZA went up to 16.8% in the May elections and

---

42      92% of the people were dissatisfied with the government and 85% stated that things in the country are going the wrong way. See Public Issue 2011c.

43      Kouvelakis 2011d, p. 25.

44      It is crucial to note in this respect that since the formation of the Papademos government in November 2011, SYRIZA took a steady lead in being the best oppositional party. See Lambrinou and Mpalampanidis 2014, p. 141.

45      Voulgaris and Nikolakopoulos 2014, p. 19.

26.9% in the by-elections of June. Its programme promised not only an end to austerity but also a radical break with the old political establishment that communicated the demands and the aspirations of the people participating in the movement. Although it did not lead the latter in any of its phases, SYRIZA had thus the ability to express its dynamic at the political level, taking advantage of both the entrapment of the Right by the Memoranda agenda and the inability of ANTARSYA and especially KKE to cope with the new dynamics. In other words, SYRIZA was the only force within the Left to understand that political power was the main issue at stake in the context of an ongoing 'organic crisis'. No matter the weaknesses and inconsistencies of its proposal, the mere articulation of the strategy of the 'government of the Left' sufficed to give it a definite lead in the anti-Memorandum camp.

According to Voulgaris and Nikolakopoulos, the double elections of 2012 constitute a characteristic type of 'earthquake elections', meaning elections that, under the impact of a 'trigger event', radically reshape the political landscape of the country under examination.[46] In this respect, the May elections marked the point of an extended dealignment with the established party affiliations (close to 3.3 million voters or 47% of the electorate changed party preferences with respect to the 2009 legislative elections),[47] while the elections of June signalled a process of realignment in the context of a new polarised multipartism with two main actors (SYRIZA and New Democracy). Apart from SYRIZA's impressive expansion, there occurred equally important developments at the other end of the political spectrum. As New Democracy took the lead as the guarantor of the reform agenda, significant parts of the petty bourgeoisie and popular social strata with conservative and anti-Memorandum orientations were seeking political expression. This was to be found in Independent Greeks, an anti-Memorandum split from ND, and the neo-fascist Golden Dawn. Taking advantage of the (re-)emergence of strong authoritarian and reactionary currents within the Greek social formation as a result of the authoritarian transformation of public discourse and the function of the State (along the lines described in section 2), these parties scored extremely high results,[48] at the expense of New Democracy and LAOS, which found itself below the 3% electoral threshold in both electoral contests. Opposition to the Memoranda had cut across and reshaped the entire political system, bringing a definite end to the politics of 'metapolitefsi'.

---

46    Voulgaris and Nikolakopoulos 2014, pp. 9–10.
47    Mavris 2012, p. 97.
48    Independent Greeks: May 10.6%; June 7.5%; Golden Dawn: May 7%; June 6.9%.

In social terms this was generally translated into a rift between on the one side the more dynamic and economically active segments of the population, especially of the urban centres, and on the other the economically inactive and those people living in rural and semi-urban areas. Mainly directed towards SYRIZA and secondarily towards Golden Dawn and Independent Greeks, the former were the backbone of the anti-Memorandum camp, while the latter constituted the main basis of support for the Memorandum powers. New Democracy and PASOK managed to retain their grip over the upper and upper-middle social strata and parts of the populace that had been less exposed to the mobilisation cycle (pensioners, housewives) and the economic decline (farmers), but they lost influence over wide parts of salaried labour, the unemployed and the younger generations of the cities who were heavily hit by the crisis and the austerity policies. This was particularly the case for PASOK, which saw the bulk of its working-class and lower-middle-class support, hence the core of its historical social bloc, move to SYRIZA and a significant portion of its upper-middle-class electoral basis move to the Democratic Left.[49] Not incidentally, the latter was the third party to join Samara's government after the elections. As in the case of LAOS though, the severity of the austerity programme and the intensity of political polarisation would soon exhaust its political capital in favour of its contesters.

Having given an abridged overview of the political developments and changes brought about by the cycle of contention in its immediate aftermath, let us now turn to the examination of its long-term impact upon the broader political culture.

## 5      The Legacy of the Movement

As elaborated above, the 'squares movement' marked a determining point in the development of the cycle of contention both in quantitative and qualitative terms. In quantitative terms, in the period of May–July 2011, the mobilisation rate was at its peak, while in qualitative terms, the 'squares' gave birth to a whole series of repertoires of action and opened up new fields of contestation and struggle.

Occupations as a means to reclaim the public space, although present in some cases in the December 2008 revolt,[50] were one of the key novelties of the

---

49    Mavris 2012, p. 104.

50    See the self-organised park at Navarinou Street in the district of Exarcheia, Athens, and

movement. Following the example of the Spanish Indignados and the mobilisations at the Puerta del Sol in Madrid, protesters organised months-long camps
at Syntagma Square in Athens, the White Tower area in Salonica, and other
sites across the country.[51] As already described in section 3, at the heart of the
'squares' organisation and discourse production were the popular assemblies.
This experiment in horizontal grassroots organisation and immediate democracy made a very strong impression since its very beginning. With thousands
participating almost daily at the assemblies at the lower end of the Syntagma
Square, this model of people's self-organisation was soon to be imitated not
only by other local assemblies, but also by collectives and thematic movements.[52]

Especially in the metropolitan centre of Athens where the movement experienced its greatest growth, popular assemblies were organised in many districts, especially of lower-middle-class and middle-class social composition.[53]
Being inspired by the self-organised collectives formed at Syntagma and taking advantage of their local character, many of these assemblies played a critical role in the creation of social solidarity initiatives such as social pharmacies, dispensaries and grocery stores. Inscribed within the movements' self-
organisation discourse, some of these initiatives managed to flourish and develop significant connections with the local communities, increasing social
confidence and collective efficacy by helping people to cope better with the
impact of the crisis and the retreat of the social welfare. At the peak of the
movement and in conditions of mass social mobilisation, some of them truly
constituted forms of dual-power experimentations.

Although many of them managed to survive the decline of the movement,
their initial political dynamic was soon partially exhausted. The key reason for
that was the retreat of the local assemblies. The latter in reality outlived the
big assemblies of the city centres and, at least until September 2012, there were

---

the similar events at the park on the crossroad of Cyprou and Patision Street in Kypseli,
Athens.

51  Bresta 2011.

52  Movements against the tolls on the national highways and the property taxes incorporated
in electricity bills all followed this pattern of horizontal organisation.

53  In the two-day event for the organisation of the popular assemblies put forward by the
Syntagma Assembly on 9 and 10 July 2011, from the 24 local assemblies that participated
from the metropolitan area of Athens, a clear majority was from the middle-class districts
of the north, east and south sectors of the city and not from the working-class areas of
Western Athens and Piraeus. It is also important to note here that a total of 38 assemblies
participated through representatives to the event.

clear indications that they could have been consolidated and help sustain popular confidence and local resistances at high levels. The problem was that none of the factions of the organised left or indeed any other political power chose to invest in this (rather idiosyncratic for the Greek political culture) social experiment. The only political power that attempted to actually engage with popular self-action was SYRIZA.[54] The months preceding the double elections of 2012 and in their immediate aftermath, the party organised some very impressive (in terms of participation) local gatherings at the prototype of the squares' assemblies. This move, though, that shared a lot of similarities with the practices of the Spanish Podemos was not meant to last long. The main reason for that was the choice of SYRIZA's leadership to follow a strategy of political moderation after the elections. The unprecedented polarisation that characterised the electoral debate, the campaign of fear launched by the Ideological State Apparatuses, and the crude foreign interventions that supported it, convinced the majority of SYRIZA's leadership that a frontal confrontation with the domestic and EU establishment was not a viable option, neither in electoral nor in economic terms.[55] In this context and despite internal opposition, SYRIZA made a decisive move towards electoral politics and away from the experimentation with forms of popular self-organisation and struggle.[56]

Having the 'maturity' and the ability to incorporate the main discursive frames and political objectives of the movement in the strategy of the 'government of the Left', SYRIZA was in a position to absorb the bulk of the movement's dynamic and demobilise its smaller political expressions. Political projects, closely related to the activism and discourse of the 'squares movement', such as the 'Kinima den plirono' (Won't Pay Movement) and EPAM, managed to garner support and build significant national networks within a few months. Confronted though with SYRIZA's dynamic, internal cleavages, political deficiencies

---

54    The Communist Party had from the very start a clearly negative approach to the movement. ANTARSYA on the other side found itself internally divided over the analysis of the movement's dynamic and was thus unable to make decisive moves. As SYRIZA's political strategy became more 'aggressive' and centred around the issue of governmental change as the immediate solution to the austerity packages and the neoliberal reforms, its introvert reflexes prevailed and it was thus unable to capitalise on part of the movement's dynamic and to fruitfully engage with it in the mid-term.

55    According to Yiannis Mavris, one of the leading pollsters in the country, 'the unabashed intervention in favour of the "pro-Europe parties" undoubtedly influenced the result on 17 June, perhaps by as much as 4 per cent' (Mavris 2012, p. 99). A percentage that in reality determined the outcome of the elections in favour of ND and the Memorandum bloc.

56    Sakellaropoulos 2014, p. 170.

and the lack of further stimulus as the movement entered a prolonged phase of retreat,[57] they soon faced decline. Unlike the Spanish case with the emergence of Podemos, in Greece the movement was not able to develop its own political expressions, and given the inability or the unwillingness of the political Left to fruitfully engage with its practices and organisational forms, its long-term impact on the broader political culture remained existent but not significant.

The parties' internal organisation did not change and their discourse was only minimally affected by the discourse of the movement, apart from an ephemeral turn of SYRIZA to a more critical discourse regarding the Eurozone during the period of May 2011–July 2012. With the organised Left soon incorporating the main projects that stemmed from the movement into its established structures and repertoires of action, the latter's impact was mainly to be confined to a renewed emphasis on local initiatives primarily centred on social solidarity.[58] In a way, the party system had once more prevailed over the independent expressions of civil society. Dialogical processes were as always at play but the balance of power was definitely in favour of the former.

It comes thus as no surprise that the majority of the local popular assemblies that still exist at various districts of the big urban centres of Athens (19, including Piraeus) and Salonica (4) now resemble more the local projects put forward by the organised Left and the anarchist collectives and already in place before the crisis, and less so the popular initiatives of the 'squares'. In a similar vein, under the influence of the political Left, local authorities, municipalities or prefectures have taken up much of the social solidarity projects that spread throughout the country in the course of the cycle of contention. The element of popular self-organisation is here either in decline or non-existent.

### Final Notes on the Conjuncture

As is often the case, social movements tend to have a latent, long-term effect not immediately observable after the events. In this respect, there is no doubt that the 2010–12 cycle of contention, its main political themes, and the organisational forms that emerged in its course have been inscribed in the collective memory and in the history of struggles of the Greek people.

---

57    Kotronaki 2014.
58    See, for example, the creation of the 'Ergatikes Lesches' (i.e. Labour Clubs) by the part of the forces of ANTARSYA, or the various solidarity initiatives taken over or launched by SYRIZA and small anarchist collectives.

Having experienced a significant left-wing turn under the impact of the mobilisation cycle in the first years of the crisis, Greek society has steadily moved towards the right in its aftermath. The power bloc may still lack a hegemonic political project, but the politics of fear and the severe hits to labour and democratic rights seem to have increased political apathy and demobilised the public. In this context, SYRIZA's electoral growth was more the outcome of people's disillusionment with the coalition government and the promised end to austerity advocated by Samaras time and again since 2012, and far less the result of any active mobilisation and increase in popular self-confidence. Given the overall balance of power at the present conjuncture, this seems to be a critical parameter, undermining the mid- and long-term potential of the 'government of the Left'.

## References

Athanasiou, Athena 2012, *Crisis as a "state of exception"*, [In Greek], Athens: Savvalas.

Bresta, Marina 2011, 'The entire Greece, a square', in *From the streets to the squares: Democracy under construction*, edited by Christos Giovanopolous and Dimitrris Mitropoulos, [In Greek], Athens: A/synecheia.

Givalos, Menelaos 2005, 'Transformations and differentiations of PASOK during the 1990–2000 decade. Comparisons of governmental policies and leading figures', [in Greek], in VPRC Institute, *Public opinion in Greece, 2004*, Athens: Savvalas.

Gravaris, Dionysis 2002, 'The demand for political modernization: Details from the functioning of a political ideology', in Sakis Karagiorgas Foundation 8th Conference Proceedings, *Ideological currents and tendencies of intelligentsia in contemporary Greece*, [In Greek] Sakis Karagiorgas Foundation.

Hall, Stuart 1988, *The hard road to renewal: Thatcherism and the crisis of the Left*, London: Verso.

INE-GSEE 2012, *Greek economy and employment: Annual report 2012*, Reports, No. 14, [in Greek] Athens: INE-GSEE.

INE-GSEE 2014, 'INE-GSEE's report for the Greek economy and employment', [in Greek], *Enimerosi*, Vol. 219.

INE Papers-Special Edition 2012, *Reforms in Greece: Strikes in 2011*, [in Greek] Studies, No. 37, INE-GSEE.

Kalampokas, Giorgos 2013, 'Political crisis, power and the Left', [In Greek] *Ektos Grammis*, 33.

Katz, Richard and Peter Mair 1995, 'Changing models of organization and party democracy, the emergence of the cartel party', *Party Politics*, 1, 1: 5–28.

Kentikelenis, Alexander, Maria Karanikola, IOrene Papanicola, Sanjay Basu, Martin

McKee, and David Stuckler 2011, 'Health effects of financial crisis: Omens of a Greek tragedy', *Lancet* 378, 9801: 1457–1458.

Kotronaki, Loukia 2014, 'Recapturing protest in crisis democracies: Paths of radicalization and deradicalization', [In Greek] Paper presented at the 10th Conference of the Greek Political Science Assosiation, 'Aspects and prospects of the 3d Hellenic Republic'.

Kouvelakis, Stathis 2011a, 'The Greek Cauldron', *New Left Review* 72: 17–32.

Kouvelakis, Stathis 2011b, 'The time of the crisis: Six positions over the revolt', [In Greek], in *From the streets to the squares: Democracy under construction*, edited by Christos Giovanopolous and Dimitris Mitropoulos, Athens: A/synecheia.

Lamprinou, Katerina and Giannis Mpalampanidis 2014, 'The unsteady transformation of the Greek Center-Left', [In Greek], in *The double election earthquake*, edited by Giannis Voulgaris and Ilias Nikolakopoulos, Athens: Themelio.

Mavris, Yiannis 2012, 'Greece's Austerity Elections', *New Left Review*, 2/76: 95–107.

Pantazopoulos, Andreas 2005, 'The right wing populism. The abstention phenomenon, New Democracy and LAOS before and after the EP vote', [In Greek] in VPRC Institute, *Public opinion in Greece*, 2004, Athens: Savvalas.

Poulakis, Costas 2011, 'Evidence and conclusions from the post-junta elections, 1974–2009', [In Greek] in VPRC Institute, 'Public opinion in Greece, 2008–2010', Athens: Savvalas.

Poulopoulos, Charalambos 2014, *Crisis, fear, disruption of social cohesion*, [In Greek], Athens: Topos.

Psimitis, Michalis and Nikos Sevastakis 2002, 'The irrational in Greek theoretical thinking', [In Greek] in Sakis Karagiorgas Foundation 8th Conference Proceedings, *Ideological currents and tendencies of intelligentsia in contemporary Greece*, Athens Sakis Karagiorgas Foundation.

Public Issue 2011a, 'The movement of the indignant citizens', [In Greek], Flash Barometer, No. 159.

Public Issue 2011b, *Political Barometer*, [In Greek] No. 92.

Public Issue 2011c, *Political Barometer*, [In Greek] No. 95.

Romaios, Giorgos 2013, *The adventure of parliamentarianism in Greece, Vol. 4, 1974–2009*, [In Greek], Athens: Patakis.

Sakellaropoulos, Spyros 2014, *Crisis and social stratification in 21st century Greece*, [in Greek], Athens: Topos.

Sakellaropoulos, Spyros and Panagiotis Sotiris 2004, *Restructuring and modernization: Social and political transformations in Greece during the 90s*, [in Greek], Athens: Papazisis.

Sotiris, Panagiotis 2013, 'Reading revolt as deviance: The Greek intellectuals and the December 2008 revolt of Greek youth', *Interface*, 5: 2: 42–77.

Tsirbas, Yannis 2009, 'The retreat of bipartisanship after the 2007 elections: The characteristics, the causes and the power of that phenomenon', [In Greek] in *Parties and politics in Greece* edited by Yannis Konstantinidis, Nicos Maratzidis, and Takis Pappas, Athens: Kritiki.

Voulgaris, Yannis 2013, *The post-junta Greece, 1974–2009*, [In Greek], Athens: Polis.

Voulgaris, Yannis and Ilias Nikolakopoulos 2014, *The double election earthquake*, [In Greek], Athens: Themelio.

Vernardakis, Christophoros 2005, 'Political parties and the "middle space". The ideological, political and cultural parameters of today's political powers', [In Greek] in *VPRC Institute, Public opinion in Greece, 2004*, Athens: Savvalas.

Vernardakis, Christophoros 2011, *Political parties, elections and the party system*, [in Greek], Athens: Sakoulas.

Zaroulia, Marilena and Phillip Hager 2014, 'Europhile or Eurosceptic?: Gaps in the narrative and performances of panic', in *Remapping 'crisis': A guide to Athens*, edited by Myrto Tsilimpounidi and Aylwyn Walsh, London: Zero Books.

# CHAPTER 8

# Political Crisis, Crisis of Hegemony and the Rise of Golden Dawn*

*Despina Paraskeva-Veloudogianni*

Even before 2008, when the effects of the global economic crisis started to appear in Greece, a gradual but ongoing transformation in the way governmental power was exercised seemed to emerge. The long-time vision of a strong European country, hegemonic among the Balkans, and the rhetoric of modernisation and economic growth, developed along with the 'neoliberalisation' of both public administration and the economy in the past decade, was replaced by a rhetoric of 'necessary sacrifices' and 'debt crisis', by economic tutelage and the absence of any prospect of upward social mobility; a transformation accompanied by a new political model.

## 1    An Unstable Stability

Until recently, the bourgeois strategy was not only to represent those social strata that would support its functioning; it was also to ensure the smooth reproduction of social hierarchy and stratification in a way that managed to eliminate or defuse class divisions and confrontations, thus presenting an image of social life in which these contradictions seemed to be absent. In short, the bourgeois strategy managed to remain hegemonic,[1] and finally to prevail against confrontational strategies, precisely because it succeeded in maintaining the unequal and hierarchical social stratification for its own benefit, without running the risk of being seriously questioned by the dominated strata's reactions.

---

* The chapter is based on the relevant chapter of the book *The Enemy, the Blood and the Punisher: Analyzing Thirteen Speeches of Golden Dawn's 'Leader'* [In Greek] (Paraskeva-Veloudogianni 2015).

1 For the concept of hegemony of a class or of a coalition of social classes within a social formation, see Gramsci 1971, pp. 123–205. For a short summary of the concept of hegemony as political and social 'leadership', see Thomas 2012.

Such a condition had become possible only after the establishment of alliances with the middle social strata, which play a special and cohesive role in relation to both the strata on which they dominate and those by which they are dominated. These alliances occasionally included some small material concessions as a result of the pressure of social struggles, but mainly signified the formation by the bourgeois strategy of a positive ideological project within which almost all social strata could recognise themselves. Within this ideological condition, most social classes were not only looking forward to a better future and working to improve their present living conditions, but also establishing bonds of trust with the political parties that were designing and implementing the bourgeois strategy and presenting this positive ideological project. In this sense, the parliamentary representation of these parties was credited with a positive-productive electoral mandate, a mandate that reflected the expectation of the voters for the implementation of the above-mentioned project.

The economic crisis and its consequences, as well as the deepening of the recession,[2] caused severe social turbulence. Of course, this social turbulence was not a kind of 'natural' development; rather it emerged as a result of the governmental choices about how to manage the crisis. These choices, aiming to maintain at all costs the hegemony of the bourgeois strategy, signified a change in the manner of exercising governmental power simultaneously as a result and as a prerequisite for the achievement of the bourgeoisie's objectives. Such an intention under conditions of crisis certainly presupposed that those social strata that had always been the direct and the basic props of the bourgeois strategy would not be affected, so as to be able to continue to reproduce themselves. This process, however, inevitably led to the rearrangement of the previous balance within the social stratification, namely to the cancellation of earlier alliances with the intermediate social classes.[3] Supporting the ruling classes in a time of crisis demanded the implementation of harsh austerity measures that would ensure the direct reproduction of their class interest.[4]

Within this context, we can see broad changes in social conditions as a result of the economic pressure put on the new and the traditional petit-bourgeois

---

2   See Labour Institute of the General Confederation of Greek Workers (INE-GSEE) 2013.

3   'The crisis is perceived as an opportunity for the rearrangement of the class relations in favour of capital, for decades' (Lapavitsas and Kouvelakis 2012, p. 23).

4   A key pillar of this policy was also the state support of the banks, as depicted in the grant of 28 billion Euros given to the Greek banks in 2008. For a breakdown of the profits of finance capital during the Greek crisis, see Bogiopoulos 2011, pp. 268–9.

strata,[5] which underwent a process of 'proletarianisation'. Not only did their material living conditions change, but also the positive ideological project, to which they were attached until recently and which gave them 'assurances' of upward social mobility, disappeared. Moreover, the classes that were even lower in the social stratification were further undervalued, being in poverty or below the limits of it, while they were constantly living 'in and out' of social institutions, even those for the protection of life itself.[6] Such a development demonstrated that the previous tactic of alliances with subordinate classes had already been abolished, constituting the turning point of the transformation of the political model. Actually, the material or ideological representation of almost all social strata, as well as the smooth management of the balance between class forces, as described above, were practices that rendered the bourgeois strategy hegemonic. When these practices disappear without being replaced by anything similar, then the ability of a political strategy to be hegemonic and socially legitimated also vanishes.[7]

These transformations decisively influenced the previous relations of political representation, contributing to the greatest rupture in the past 40 years in the relations of the masses to the traditional government parties,[8] and bringing about new political formations. This has been an active tendency in the past five years and and found its material and institutional expression for the first time in the Greek parliamentary elections of 2012. The results highlighted the political bankruptcy and the electoral collapse of bipartisanism, pointed out the social delegitimation of the neoliberal policy of the bail-out programmes, and led to the political emergence of the Left, with the impressive rise of SYRIZA.[9] In this sense, we can conclude that the crisis is simultaneously economic, political and ideological, ultimately referring to the Gramscian 'crisis of hegemony', which potentially retains the character of an 'organic crisis'.[10]

---

5     For the presentation of the analytical category of the 'new petty bourgeoisie', see Poulantzas 2001, pp. 237–417.
6     Lapavitsas and Kouvelakis 2012, pp. 24–5.
7     Lapavitsas and Kouvelakis 2012, pp. 23–4.
8     The traditional governing parties in Greece are New Democracy, the right-wing's representative par excellence, and PASOK, a former social-democratic party which gradually became a fundamental part of the neoliberal political project. PASOK and New Democracy had been alternating in governmental power, almost without interruption, since the establishment of the Third Greek Democracy. In the elections of 2012, PASOK was the party that lost the greater number of its supporters.
9     Mavris 2013a.
10    Sotiris 2012, pp. 26–9.

## 2      Authoritarianism as Management of the Political Crisis

Although the political forces that once prevailed are no longer hegemonic, during the period of 2012–14 these forces were still dominant. The bourgeois strategy seemed to maintain the initiative, and traditional government parties, though disconnected from a large part of their traditional audience, had occupied the government niches once again.

Seeking the factors that contributed to this development, one must first note the change in the exercise of governmental power. Since voter representation by the governmental parties, and the latter's positive relation to the former, had been largely diminished, it would be almost impossible for the bourgeois strategy to be implemented and to prevail mainly via social consensus and legitimisation. We could therefore estimate that during this period bourgeois strategy remained dominant less as a result of the hegemonic incorporation of almost the entire social formation, and more as a result of its being imposed by the institutions that represented it in a voluntaristic way. In addition, let us not forget that by this time other political powers failed to develop a counter-hegemonic strategy capable of penetrating the majority of social classes and of prevailing. Governments gradually rejected the model of gaining legitimisation by seeking and endorsing popular consent – a rather established political model since the fall of the Dictatorship and the establishment of the Third Greek Democracy – and went over to a more authoritarian model,[11] according to which the governmental measures had to be implemented even if they were in conflict with the governing parties' pre-election pledges, or even if they were in opposition to the popular will.[12] In this context, the relation between the governors and the governed was turning into a one-way command-obedience relation, which finally was established as a dominant form of the political. And this became another factor that intensified the ideological, political, and electoral rupture in the relation of the masses to the traditional governing parties.

---

11      This condition is described by Poulantzas under the term 'authoritarian statism' (Poulantzas 2000, pp. 203–47).

12      The condition of authoritarianism described here takes the form of an authoritarian entrenchment of the state itself. Of course, this is largely due to the lack of legitimisation faced by the government forces, which – being unable to implement their programme in a hegemonic way – treat every political formation in opposition as well as all the social groups that are mobilised against the government choices as political (and sometimes state) enemies.

The government's authoritarian turn during 2012–14 was accompanied by an additional tactic that would support the prevalence of the bourgeois strategy: the cultivation of fear; the fear of an impending catastrophe that was about to come if the government's programme – which was presented as a one-way solution – was not implemented; the fear resulting from the shock[13] caused by the economic crisis and the social transformations, a fear that could be allayed only if political experts, namely economists and technocrats, were allowed to take over in order to 'scientifically' implement the governmental programme. The government tried to show that the country was in a state of emergency, so as to prove that a series of typical political practices had to be suspended and replaced by 'emergency' procedures. Of course, this choice first affected the institutions of parliamentary democracy: the systematic and repeated resort to legislative procedures, the activation of which is appropriate only in cases of extreme urgency, the absence of parliamentary scrutiny, the one-article bills, the 'express' votes, etc. are typical examples.

At the same time, there was an attempt to overthrow the previous ideological status quo. The statement of Nikos Dendias, former Minister of Public Order and Civil Protection – namely, that the time had come for Greece to 'close accounts' with 1974[14] – meant exactly that it is was about time to abolish (not only in essence but also in form) the political and social condition that emerged during the post-dictatorship period, and the 'social contract' that became the norm at that time; that it was about time to inculpate even the political model which unequally represented the social interests under the bourgeois hegemony and aimed at the integration of the social dynamic.[15]

Consequently, the depreciation and the delegitimisation of the very concept of rights were necessary for accomplishing this purpose. During the supposed 'state of emergency', the notorious governmental 'responsibility' not only stopped responding to the needs of the subultern strata, but almost stopped recognising their very existence. According to the government, the only legal and moral claim were the 'necessary sacrifices' for the recovery of the markets, and the generalised need to 'save the country', which was a plan fully implemented by the government in the name of the whole nation. In this context, the demands of certain social groups were not considered as social rights, but as a reflection of the 'post-dictatorship corporatist conception of politics',

---

13    Klein 2008.

14    When the occupation of the Polytechnic School in Athens took place, resulting in the junta's fall and the establishment of the Third Greek Democracy some months later.

15    We can aptly describe this political model as a 'pro-popular break in the capitalist continuum' (Sakellaropoulos 2013, pp. 39–43).

which had to be curbed. In this sense, political organisations that were supporting the subaltern strata and their demands were arraigned; especially the
Left, which was presented as an irresponsible and catastrophic political power.
The concept of the right was baptised 'luxury' and 'unfair claim' in relation to
other social groups, and was presented as the proof of how spoiled the Greeks
had been all these years.[16]

Of course, the above-mentioned political model was not an entirely new way
of doing politics: instead, its goal-setting and characteristics were imprinted in
the way in which the forces whose prevalence is now to be ensured may exercise their power. What was attempted during this period was a change of the
previous 'balance', but this change created a new, post-hegemonic political condition of authoritarian governing, which did not promise anything concerning
the improvement of the social majority's status.[17] On the other hand, it would
be a rather one-sided approach if we concluded that social consensus – as a
political process that expresses the legitimisation of the governors and their
policies – was absent from this new political condition. We cannot overlook the
fact that the governmental insistence on the concepts of 'legality' – versus what
was baptised 'lawlessness' – and of 'social order' – versus what was presented as
disrupting social cohesion – was finding active allies in some social strata, who
believed that in this way their survival could be ensured and their economic
compression resisted.

However, the political and electoral support of the governing parties during this period was rather of a 'negative' nature: the electorate was not positively engaged with the governing parties' programme, but it rather voted for
them in the sense of a forced political choice, one which could minimise possible damages. In this context, the voters of the traditional governing parties
indeed consented, but they consented exactly because the ideological condition of fear and one-way salvation maintained its social efficacy. However,
such an ideological condition was 'negative' at its core: firstly, it was not aiming at providing the government with supporters, but rather it sought to limit
the electoral losses of the traditional governing parties as much as possible.
Moreover, the consensus gained proved to be a short-term one, as the governing parties failed to develop the necessary conditions for the engagement of
the electorate in an overall political plan promising a tangible positive future.
From this perspective, we can assume that it was impossible for the governing parties to claim a positive social consensus, since material concessions, or

16    Douzinas 2011, pp. 82–4.
17    Kalampokas 2013, pp. 64–7.

promises for such, were not on the table. Thus, under such a crisis management strategy, gaining the social consensus became an issue of minor importance ahead of the implementation of the recession measures, since these two elements – consent and budgetary changes – seemed mutually exclusive.

If, during the period before the crisis, victorious social struggles ensured several material victories, which the governing parties presented as 'concessions' from them, in order to gain the social trust, during 2012–14, when the terms of representation of the social interests had already changed, the political pressure created by the mass movements was no longer translated into the governmental position's rearrangement. The erstwhile 'carrot' of 'concessions' was converted into an interpellation for necessary sacrifices, the result of which would not promise the improvement of the social majority's status, but a vague 'country's salvation'. And for the ideological defence of such a governing strategy, the rhetoric of unjust but unavoidable measures, as part of the 'national effort', was usually conscripted. However, over time, even this rhetoric was replaced by an even more aggressive one, according to which the government measures were not unjust; they just aimed at transformations that had already taken place in other European countries, and which Greece had, at last, to follow.

## 3    The Movements as an Answer

However, the changes in social stratification, the absence of the political representation of all social strata and the transformation of the way central power was exercised were only some aspects that led to the crisis of hegemony. The other factor was the simultaneous emergence of mass movements. The first signs of the crisis and the new socio-political period were accompanied by the launch of an insurrectionary circle with a series of social struggles with continuities and discontinuities, which nevertheless had a common component: the questioning of and the opposition to the political model which had been shaped during the crisis. Once again, youth played the role of a catalyst; in fact, youth 'opened' the circle of protests after a long period during which mass and nationwide movements were absent.

The turning point for the emergence of the insurrectionary circle was the student movement of 2006–7; a movement of unprecedented magnitude, intensity and geographical spread, which was developed in two phases. Initially, it articulated its opposition to the 'neoliberal transformation' of the university, to the restriction of student freedoms, to the intensity of control and discipline; and then it fought against the repeal of Article 16 of the Greek Constitution, which ensured the public character of Higher Education. The importance of that movement was reflected not only in the fact that government had to withdraw its initial proposals, but also in the fact that this movement managed to connect to other social strata under attack, thus enjoying a broader appeal and support during the entire course of the movement. Consequently, the movement of 2006–7 managed to shape collective representations of mass and victorious struggles as well as a new version of 'the political', inspiring a different way of claiming rights. On the other hand, it showed that such movements could indeed be victorious, especially when they connected to the social majority. The importance of these developments is even more obvious if we consider that they occurred just two years after the Olympic Games of 2004 that took place in Greece, namely at a time when mass social struggles did not thrive and when the prevailing impression was one of perpetual progress without social divisions and social contradictions.

If these simmering conflicts were expressed creatively in the student movement of 2006–7, 2008 was about to change the social situation even more abruptly. Far from the organised protests of the 'traditional' labour or student movements, the outbreak of December highlighted new forms of struggle, of externalising anger and of opposition to a system that determined all aspects of everyday life. It also suggested a new collective, fighting subject: the youth, which, once again, connected to the most affected social strata, such as immigrants, young workers and the unemployed.

It is often written that the murder of Alexandros Grigoropoulos by a police officer was the straw that broke the camel's back of social indignation; of the indignation caused by the continuous deterioration of living standards, the systematic rise in unemployment, the crisis that was just around the corner, and of course the authoritarianism of state power. December seemed to articulate no specific demands perhaps because it was rather clear that the receiver of these demands was missing:[18] the state and the government seemed not only to disregard the social demands, but also to taunt and suppress them. Such authoritarianism took place because of the government's efforts to impose intensive control, fear and discipline aiming at developing a strict 'social normality' in the context of an extreme neoliberal economic management.

Of course, the 2011 Movement of the Squares cannot be missing from this equation. Once again, Greek society was rocked for a long time because of these nationwide demonstrations; demonstrations that were also original on

---

18    Gaitanou 2011.

account of both the multifaceted forms of struggle undertaken and their social composition. This movement expressed even more clearly its opposition to the political system: its slogan, request, and modus operandi was 'Direct Democracy'. Furthermore, the Movement of the Squares became even more politically effective when it connected to the protests and strikes of trade unions, thus succeeding in becoming one of the most critical factors that would determine the stability of the government's planning and of the government itself.

It is notable that both December 2008 and the Movement of the Squares highlighted simmering trends in Greek society, giving expression to the need for the reclamation and the re-appropriation of 'the political'; of 'the political' as a process coming from the masses and addressing the masses, that focuses on self-organisation and the collective shaping of everyday life. So it is understandable why these movements insisted on reclaiming public space and public discourse: the occupations of squares, universities, theatres, town halls, television stations and the self-managed radio and online information centres highlighted a new approach to the concept of 'public space', as a place where the social majority is being socialised and shaped as a collectivity, far from the intervention of the state. We could say that these movements were, to some extent, challenging the 'social normality' itself, while, at the same time, reflecting the absence of the erstwhile 'social normality' that could incorporate the tensions from class confrontations and successfully interpellate ideologically the social majority.

## 4     The Contradictory Results of an Indecisive Battle

However, the influence and the importance of these movements were defined not just by their political content and their penetration into society, but also by the way they were treated by the government itself. In a period of transition to a post-hegemonic political governance, these movements confronted a condition of extreme state repression both in the sense of the physical repression of the mobilisations and of the political non-response to their demands. Being the first to encounter the new period of harsh police repression, the student movement of 2006–7 was an exception regarding the extent to which a movement could induce shifts in policy. In all other cases, the government did not integrate the demands of the movements; rather it denounced the demonstrations as corporatist, minor, vandalism, undemocratic and subversive. It is certainly noteworthy that struggles of unprecedented magnitude, intensity and social legitimisation – i.e. the demonstration of 15 June 2011, and especially the general strike on 20 October 2011 – failed to reach their declared goal, the abolition of the Memorandum: The implementation of the bourgeois strategy should be achieved even at the cost of the current government's survival: the Medium-Term Plan (part of the Memorandum) was signed in June 2011, and after a few months a coalition government was established; the new leadership did not aim at changing the existing political project, but at presenting it as having the approval of the majority, by means of government reshuffling. A shift in the governing personnel was the response to a real political crisis.[19]

In fact, how the government confronted the movements of 2006–14 clearly expresses the above-mentioned transformation of the political model.[20] When the social movement is not represented as the number one domestic terrorist, it is stigmatised as an immature, irresponsible and mischievous child, who asks for more than it deserves and who disturbs the smooth running of the house. And because the period during which it expresses its demands is not like any other – when once the circumstances allowed the 'parent' to be more flexible and sometimes to succumb to the children's requests – but a period of an extraordinary crisis, where there is no margin for mistakes and child's play, children must refrain from the discussions of the grownups, even if they need to stay locked in their room for a long time.

Thus, a social reality in which many of its previous features had been deeply transformed was emerging. On the one hand, the changes in social stratification led to a great part of the population being unable to meet its basic living needs, bringing together the sense of injustice and anger as well as the conviction that a great marginalisation of the masses was underway. Moreover, the authoritarian turn of governmental power, the criminalisation of the very concept of social rights and the repressive treatment of social demands sometimes led the masses to turn away from politics in general – by representing politics as a heinous activity – while at other times it intensified their disengagement from the governing parties. At the same time, the legitimisation of authoritarianism and of the attitude that the governmental authority should be beyond criticism, as if it drew its correctness from a 'natural law' of politics and economy, was leading to social conservatism. Moreover, the inability of the social movements to reverse in whole or in part the implemented policies

---

19    Following Gramsci, Kouvelakis notes that, in times of generalised political crisis, the political scene tends to draw away from the representation relations and the rules of parliamentary change; it is when 'Bonapartism' or 'Caesarism' trends emerge. And a 'Caesarean solution' can exist without necessarily the existence of 'Caesar'. In times of parliamentary democracy, such solutions take the form of coalition governments (Kouvelakis 2011).

20    Sotiris 2011, pp. 157–63.

was creating a psychological frame with two key determinants: political frustration and commissioning of hope to the 'last chance'.[21]

On the other hand, the emergence of the movements contributed to the radicalisation and the cultivation of a different pattern of everyday life, as well as encouraging political engagement and further intensifying the disengagement of the subordinate strata from the traditional bourgeois parties. It is therefore clear that all the factors described induce new forms of practice and representation, creating multiple subjectifications synthesised from elements often different and contradictory, and leading to the emergence of a new balance of class forces. Similarly multiple were the transformations on the ideological level: the groups that were turning away from bipartisanism were seeking a new political project in which they would be able to recognise themselves. In this sense, even the 'punitive vote' of the 2012 elections, involved, besides punishment, the quest for a different perspective, and an intentional act of 'destabilisation' of the existing balance of political power.

Finally, to return to the original question, the bourgeoisie remained dominant, but only in the context of the struggles for hegemony, of the struggles that were in progress and that had not yet reached a stable equilibrium. At the same time, new political formations were emerging, staking out their political role and transforming the existing political being.

## 5    Golden Dawn's Rise and Its Causes (2012–14)

The question of the governmental power and the quest for new political projects were deeply reflected in the strengthening of the Left, as recorded in the impressive rise of SYRIZA. But if this is one aspect, then another is the rise of the extreme-right and more specifically the explosive emergence of Golden Dawn onto the political scene. As aptly noted, Golden Dawn's strategy is one of 'developing a hegemonic socio-political bloc, although not yet a majority one', which relates to what could be called a 'new fascist version of hegemony ... Golden Dawn builds its fascist hegemony in an exemplary manner, by stepping up and conquering positions both within the formal political arena, state institutions and mechanisms, and by constructing popular institutions which correspond to its own version of everyday social being within "civil society"'.[22]

---

21    Vernardakis 2013.
22    Kalampokas 2012, pp. 31–2.

To support this approach, let us describe in detail the elements that outline Golden Dawn's activity and profile during 2012–14, as well as its role within a balance of political power which has not yet been stabilised.

As Wilson and Hainsworth note, far-right parties seem to flourish when the traditional right parties change their policy and practice,[23] enabling the first to promote themselves as the novel and unique anti-systemic political formation and as those who dare to say publicly what the 'silent majority' only manage to think.[24] Similarly, Golden Dawn emerged during the authoritarian turn of the governmental power and the devaluation of Greece's democratic institutions; consequently it emerged on a ground fertile for the development of extreme-right attitudes, indeed in a political conjuncture where the implemented government policies were legitimising racism, xenophobia and social Darwinism.

During the same period, the government was highlighting immigrants as a basic problem of the Greek economy, and was shifting the responsibilities of the crisis onto them. Undocumented immigrants were now stigmatised as 'illegals', as illegal entities who do not deserve to exist, and as invaders during a military invasion, who have to be faced by the country accordingly. Alongside, on the northern border of the country, a barrier was being built in order to stem the entry of immigrants, and the immigration policy programme called 'Hospitable Zeus' was launched: Detention centres were also being built, the police was unleashing raids in immigrant neighbourhoods on a daily basis, and hundreds of complaints about beatings of immigrants by police officers in prisons and detention centres were being recorded. At that time, the Prime Minister publicly stated that we must 'recapture our cities', adopting Golden Dawn's motto, while one of his Ministers, Adonis Georgiadis, stressed that the goal is 'to make their lives as difficult as possible'. The social cannibalism, orchestrated by the government itself, culminated some days before the elections of 2012: Police arrested several sex workers, who were forced into mandatory medical exams. A few days later, the women found to be HIV-positive were being accused of intending bodily harm, and the press released their photos. The Minister of Health described the migrant sex workers as a 'health bomb' that 'infects the Greek paterfamilias' and the Greek family.[25]

Under these circumstances, we could assert that the political attitude Golden Dawn promoted was not far from the government's practice and rhetoric;

---

23    Wilson and Hainsworth 2012.
24    Betz 2003, pp. 193–210.
25    For more, see Athanasiou 2012.

it was more of a radical sequel to the dominant narrative than a dissonance within the neoliberal political model.

Based on the already existing narrative, according to which politics is almost like a metaphysical and inevitable event, Golden Dawn explicitly states that its positions are not political in the current sense, but shaped by the eternal natural law, which defines the 'worthy blood' and structures the good society. Moreover, the 'There Is No Alternative' doctrine is also a structural element of Golden Dawn's worldview: the party indicates that the nation is on the brink of destruction and that the only chance of recovery is to implement natural law, namely the destruction of non-nationals and of the 'others', and the predominance of the white race.

In this sense, Golden Dawn also declares a state of emergency, an emergency concerning the nation's survival. Due to that, there is no time for thought, but only for blind action under the authority of the 'Leader'. How far is the very concept of the 'Leader' who holds the absolute truth from the government's declaration about the necessity for 'specialists' in politics, really? Moreover, the pattern of sacrificing oneself for an unspecified cause is also present: Golden Dawn's members are eternally sacrificed for a 'higher purpose', which is never named and perhaps never understood. Of course, we cannot omit the two main elements common to both Golden Dawn's strategy and the strategy of the government: Firstly, the attribution of political responsibility to the weakest links of the society – immigrants in our case – on the one hand, and to the deadly political 'enemies', namely the Left, which is 'behind all state structures', on the other. Secondly, similarly to the government, Golden Dawn denounces the post-dictatorship era and presents it as the period of lawlessness par excellence. Golden Dawn, of course, aims at showing that parliamentary democracy per se means chaos and anarchy, that it has failed, and that there is a need for a new national regime.

However, long before Golden Dawn's legitimisation and parliamentary representation, Popular Orthodox Rally (LAOS), a racist and anti-Semitic far-right party,[26] the leader of which was previously a member of New Democracy, had already made its appearance. A few years later, LAOS's political positions, from right opposition to New Democracy, will be upgraded to official government positions: In 2011, LAOS will claim its participation, next to PASOK and New Democracy, in the transitional government headed by Prime Minister Lucas Papademos. LAOS will be accepted into the government coalition, although

---

26    Psarras 2010.

that was not parliamentarily necessary.[27] At the following elections, Golden Dawn will reap not only the parliamentary consolidation of racism and anti-Semitism, but the majority of LAOS's voters as well; LAOS suffered electoral ruin, mainly because of its participation in the coalition government at a time when the party proclaimed that it was one of protest.

Golden Dawn's electoral emergence is also due to a series of other factors. As Vernardakis states, New Democracy, as a key pillar of the coalition government (New Democracy, PASOK, DIMAR)[28] that emerged from the 2012 elections, was a mixture of neoliberalism and state, right-wing authoritarianism; as a consequence, large parts of the traditional Right were released from the interior of New Democracy, and turned either to the extreme-right or to the so-called middle ground.[29] However, before that, New Democracy had already accepted as members several politicians coming from other political parties: In 2011, Makis Voridis, Adonis Georgiadis, and Thanos Plevris, three leading members of LAOS, switched to New Democracy, where they became ministers of the government and also undertook the party's public representation. In his former political life, Makis Voridis had served as secretary general of the youth of EPEN, namely of the party founded by George Papadopoulos, head of the 1967 dictatorship. Makis Voridis's predecessor in this position was Nikolaos Michaloliakos, current leader of Golden Dawn. On the other hand, Adonis Georgiadis maintains to this day a publishing house, which openly propagates books of nationalist, anti-communist and pro-Nazi content.

The extreme-right tendencies do not stop there though. It is rather obvious that far-right political operatives, who not only were closely associated with Golden Dawn but also promoted the co-operation with this party, had occupied positions within the government's narrow leadership core. The political course of important government officials is indicative: Takis Baltakos, government Secretary General, had systematic secret contacts with Golden Dawn's spokesman, Ilias Kasidiaris, about many important issues, including that of the juridical developments referring to the prosecutions of Golden Dawn's leading members.[30] Chrysanthos Lazaridis, the Prime Minister's right-hand man,

---

27    Mavris 2013b.
28    The group of people that formed DIMAR (Democratic Left) had seceded from SYRIZA in 2010. As a part of the coalition government since 2012, DIMAR voted for all the laws dictated by the Memorandum until 2013, when it left the government. In the elections of 2015 it failed to enter parliament.
29    Vernardakis 2013.
30    Kasidiaris secretly recorded his meetings with Baltakos, and at the right time released

conceived and recommended the 'two extremes theory' that the government centralised during 2012–14 as its main ideological rhetoric. Failos Kranidiotis, member of New Democracy and the Prime Minister's close friend, did not hide his admiration for the junta's leaders. All of them had previously served as members of the nationalist formation 'Network 21', set up in 1997 aiming at the 'patriotic awareness' of Greeks on foreign policy issues. Of course, the Prime Minister himself, Antonis Samaras, was inspired by similar political beliefs, which he attempted to represent independently in 1993, when he left New Democracy and founded the 'Political Spring', on the occasion of his disagreement on the naming of FYROM and the use of the term 'Macedonia'.

In addition, we must acknowledge some special features of Greek society, related to specific historical conditions, namely the post-civil-war and the pro-dictatorship era. Peloponnese, Central Greece, Attica and Central Macedonia proved to be the best constituencies for Golden Dawn. As Mavris mentions, 'at the level of the electoral base, Golden Dawn (and "Independent Greeks"-ANEL as well) is a social split of the conservative wing', while its 'increased influence in the regions of "Old Greece" clearly indicate the party's political-ideological continuity with the state apparatuses and its close relation to them'. In fact, Laconia, a region with a strong anti-communist tradition, proved to be the best county for Golden Dawn (and the second best for New Democracy), while it is characteristic that in the referendum of 1974,[31] Laconia was the best county for the monarchy with a 59.5%.[32] It is obvious that Golden Dawn steadily appeals to, among other things, social strata that were formed in the post-civil-war period (collaborationists, etc.) and maintained their conservatism, authoritarianism and anti-communism, a tendency intensified by the cracks in the relations of representation of the main right-wing formations.

These actual tendencies were evident in a poll conducted before the murder of Pavlos Fyssas; 10% of respondents answered that they would view positively the possibility of a Nazi-fascist party taking power via democratic processes. Similarly, almost 11% of respondents 'partly agreed' or 'strongly agreed' with those who believe that Nazism-fascism in pre-war Europe was quite positive.[33] These percentages reflect to some extent the ideological transpositions that have already taken place in Greek society because of Golden Dawn's penetration. On the other hand, it seems that a large part of these percentages

---

these videos to the press in order to blackmail New Democracy and avoid being arrested like the other members of Golden Dawn in the same period.

31    Crown Democracy vs Republic.

32    Mavris 2013b.

33    VPRC 2013d.

consists of people who are ideologically linked to Nazism and fascism in a non-serendipitous way; rather they seem to be part of a social group that historically emerged already before the Civil War, and continues to be reproduced, though without being able to publicly support its positions – at least until recently.

It is also important to note that throughout the electoral rise of Golden Dawn, as indicated by the polls, the party was on permanent display in the media, as an equal and perfectly legitimate political partner. In fact, the media overemphasised the local political activities of Golden Dawn members, which were presented as having strong pro-popular characteristics. The 'breaking news' about the Golden Dawn members protecting old ladies who wanted to receive their pension from the bank but feared being robbed is widely known. Of course, such 'news' proved to be cheap constructs often created by Golden Dawn members themselves.[34] This, combined with Golden Dawn's huge self-promotion business – internet sites, newspaper, magazine, public presentation of the recorded activities of the party, daily and systematic presence in social media, promotion of the party by other media with which Golden Dawn maintain elective affinities – further contributed to the social acceptance and the legitimacy of the party.

However, as mentioned before, Golden Dawn also constitutes its hegemony by claiming and conquering positions within the state apparatus itself.[35] The political and organisational relations with the police, the security forces,[36] and the army[37] not only bring to light the long-term relation between the extreme Right and key state institutions,[38] but also eloquently imprint the party's systematic attempt to become an important political player that is going to exercise political pressure that will affect the development of government strategy.

At the same time, the party's parliamentary strategy proved its close relations with major business circles. Being from the beginning in line with the

---

34    Psarras 2012, pp. 378–9.

35    As Gramsci notes, fascists were supported by 'thousands of functionaries of the State ... [who] have become their moral and material accomplices' (Gramsci 1978, p. 44).

36    After the arrest of the Golden Dawn members on 28 September 2013, a lot of information about the organisation's activities came to light. A policewoman was among the first to be arrested; what's more, another policeman was subsequently arrested as a Golden Dawn co-operator, who, until a year ago, was the Commander of Agios Panteleimonas Police Station. Those facts make the suspicions about the concealment of Golden Dawn's criminal activities more than valid.

37    O Ios 2013.

38    Christopoulos 2014.

government, Golden Dawn did not hesitate to vote in favour of bills that were crucial for the bourgeois strategy (i.e. the bill about the sale of Greek islands to civilians), to publicly defend ship-owners over the employees of the Perama Shipbuilding Zone, to object to the taxation of ship-owners and to pay lip service to Latsis and its shipping company during a parliamentary debate, and of course to vote against SYRIZA's proposal to convene the Economic Affairs Committee of the Parliament, which would investigate the overnight sale of the Agricultural Bank to the Piraeus Bank.

But if this is the one aspect of Golden Dawn's consolidation, the aspect that refers to the central political scene, then the other side refers to the so-called 'civil society' and the representation relations that the organisation constitutes with its electoral base, mainly in the neighbourhoods but also in workplaces. By June 2014, Golden Dawn had increased its local nuclei to 61; it used them both as bases for its criminal activities and as territories for the development of actions that would contribute to the constitution of representation relations with the residents. Local nuclei aimed at the political mobilisation of the residents on the basis of the political perceptions of the organisation; thus, these concepts started taking shape as they were being converted into everyday practices. These practices, implemented by the organisation's electoral basis, were gradually and methodically developing political relations of trust and recognition between the party and its base, while, at the same time, they were strengthening and widely spreading Golden Dawn's programmematic message. It is this perspective under which we should evaluate actions such as the food distribution 'just for Greeks', the voluntary blood donation of exclusively 'Greek blood', the 'Greek Doctors' group, the groups of the so-called 'indignant residents', who were chasing immigrants and demanded their expulsion from the neighbourhoods, as well as the 'anonymous' attacks on immigrants and non-Christians.[39]

Of course, such activism did not just aim at politically mobilising the residents; it also aimed at the imposition of their material dependence on the organisation. As became widely known after the arrests of the organisation's leading members, a large part of Golden Dawn's funding sources came from nightclubs' protection rackets, from the sale of clothing with Golden Dawn's logos mainly to members of the Security Forces and football clubs, as well as from entrepreneurs who 'hired' Golden Dawn's members to perform controls in the labour market, making sure that the employees were Greeks and that their hunger wages were also Greek.[40]

---

39    See more in Ellinas 2014.
40    Civil Action Petition 2014.

Nevertheless, we should not remove from the above described picture two important elements: On the one hand, Golden Dawn's local activities were not only a direct implementation of a fascist and racist political programme; they were also a (neo-)Nazi party's response to current social problems. Under such a perspective, Golden Dawn sought to give tangible answers to the social demand for 'security' – a demand constructed by government rhetoric about immigration – but also to show that the party, unlike the governing ones, was interested in covering basic social needs (food, health, etc.) in practice and immediately.

In this context, Golden Dawn was systematically attempting to present itself not only as an opposition party, but mainly as an anti-systemic one; and it managed to communicate that to a large extent, resulting in the proliferation of its followers. Aiming at increasing its audience's anger over social problems, but also at depoliticising it, Golden Dawn systematically reproduces a vague accusation of 'treason' made towards the governing personnel, thus hiding the real causes of social inequality and denouncing 'the political' per se. In this respect, Golden Dawn invites the audience to set up an army-avenger that would execute instructions; this is Golden Dawn's answer to the social need to participate in political decision-making. Thus, the organisation also manages to provide its followers with an identity, answering to their quest for fixed reference points in a society of constant change.

Moreover, it is obvious that Golden Dawn tries to incorporate the social radicalisation of recent years. For this purpose, it insists on punishment as the only means of salvation and as the only way of externalising the social discontent; thus avoiding the transfer of anger into productive proposals for social relief. As a result, the audience obtains a mistaken sense that it is acting in a revolutionary way. The frequent references of Golden Dawn to the concept of 'rights' are part of such a strategy: but the 'rights' here are not meant as social ones, but as 'the rights of the Greeks' and of the white race, converting social and class differences into racial ones, in order to address Golden Dawn's programmatic massage. But generally Golden Dawn seeks to usurp old concepts by giving them a new content: thus, being a racist means defending rights, being a killer means defending life, being Nazi means being a lover of ancient Greece. It is all about an aestheticised anti-systemic attitude, which in fact is nothing but the reproduction of elements already registered in the practices and the perceptions of a section of society, such as racism and conservatism, and of a masculine model of wounded pride, which will rise up and restore law and order.

However, the construction of Golden Dawn's 'antisystemism' is based on the systematic depreciation of the democratic institutions: The organisation

accuses these institutions of being responsible for social problems and highlights that they act against society because they only serve governmental interests. As a result, such an 'antisystemism' always leads to the emergence and
the reproduction of Golden Dawn's fundamental political position: the desire
to abolish democracy and to replace it with a 'national regime'. It is certainly
no coincidence that democracy is being denounced at a time when the democratic institutions are in crisis, and the public confidence in them seems to
wane.[41] This is an opportunity for Golden Dawn to denounce not only the governmental strategy, but also democracy itself as a social system. As Adorno
mentions, the far-right demagogue correctly understands its audience's psychological situation and tries to maintain its intensity in order to depoliticise
it and use it for their own purposes.[42]


## 6      Crisis, Fascism, and Political-Economic Interests

At this point it is important that we refer to an apparent contradiction. On
the one hand, it is obvious that Golden Dawn's strategy by no means aims at
changing the existing relations of social production and social organisation,
nor does it require from its audience any rejection of the dominant practices
and ideological forms; instead Golden Dawn systematises and reproduces the
already existing trends and perceptions, contributing to the further authoritarian shift of the dominant rhetoric. Thus, we can assert that Golden Dawn
represent radical continuity in relation to existing right-wing policy. However,
the new 'national regime' that the organisation envisions is clearly contradictory to the existing state form of parliamentary democracy, the maintenance of
which is still a strategic choice of the bourgeois strategy. It is in this sense that
we can conclude that Golden Dawn is both a continuity of and a rupture with
the right-wing politics today, especially if we take into account the fact that
Golden Dawn is the only political force that clearly speaks about the superiority of the white race and transforms its rhetoric into practice.

Therefore the question arises: What is Golden Dawn's relation to the bourgeois political system in general and to the government in particular, during
2012–14? Was Golden Dawn a dissonance in the social reality, an outcome of
the unexpected economic crisis, or did it become the system's 'golden reserve',
namely a means that the system itself triggered during the crisis in order to

---

41    See Public Issue 2010; Mavris 2010; Mavris 2014.
42    Adorno 2000.

restore 'law and order', acting with due authoritarianism that could not be applied by the government?

Regarding the first part of the question, Ignazi notes that the intensity of the emergence of extreme right-wing parties cannot be reduced mechanically to the financial crisis: the development of these parties can already be identified in the 1980s and 1990s, when the crisis was still far away.[43] Similarly, Ellinas mentions that the political opportunities for the promotion of the extreme-right in Greece occurred in the 1990s, when issues of national identity came to the fore, on the occasion of the 'Macedonian issue'.[44] Indeed, racism, xenophobia, anti-Semitism, authoritarianism and ethnocentrism, the key elements fuelling fascism,[45] already existed as latent trends in Greek society – and, of course, not only in Greek society. In this sense, it would be wrong to claim that the crisis gave birth to fascism, but undoubtedly the economic and political crisis acted as a catalyst in the emergence of right-wing formations. In this respect, the social stratification of the organisation's electoral basis is characteristic.

Regarding the second part of the question, let's return to the example of Golden Dawn. It is true that for quite some time the organisation's electoral influence was complementary to the government's strategy: what the anti-immigrant policies could not achieve was achieved by Golden Dawn's local activities; the extra social conservatism that the 'law and order' doctrine could not induce was indeed projected by Golden Dawn on the sidewalk; the bills that had to be voted through were approved; and the particular employers and businesses (e.g. ship-owners and repair shipyard owners in Perama) found a friendly voice in parliament.

Historically, the fascist formations had a catalytic function in the struggle for the restoration and the stabilisation of the bourgeois regime. And in this sense, their relation with capital, the state and the bourgeois strategy is crucial and bidirectional.[46] However, it would be rather shortsighted to approach the fascist formations as if they were simply subservient to the bourgeois governments, which start functioning or cease operating after a government order. Their emergence is rather the result of more complex political and social processes. According to Poulantzas, fascism grows amid political crisis (which is a crisis of hegemony) and it is also expressed through the crisis of party rep-

43    In Wilson and Hainsworth 2012.

44    Ellinas 2010, p. 126.

45    Kouzelis 2014, pp. 111–21.

46    Paxton 2004, pp. 145–8.

resentation. Also, it is developed amid a generalised ideological crisis, which mainly corresponds to the crisis of the dominant ideology but indirectly affects both the petty bourgeoisie – which is in economic crisis – and the very working class – which faces a long period of defeats.[47] In this context, fascist formations, beyond street-armed groups or political organisations supported by capital, can develop relations of political representation with the people. And the critical moment is when the fascist formation tends towards or is about to operate in terms of a widespread movement; namely, in terms that enable it to claim hegemony sometimes confrontationally or complementarily to the existing political leadership.

Let us stay with the example of Golden Dawn. During January–July 2013 its polling rates, around 11–15%,[48] were the party's highest since the 2012 elections. During the same period, Golden Dawn was involved in a multitude of violent physical attacks against immigrants, attempted homicides and homicides. From January 2012 until April 2013 the independent authority 'The Greek Ombudsman' had recorded 71 racially motivated attacks, in which Golden Dawn's members were involved:

> [T]he escalating intensity of the applied violence has also to do with the political developments which allowed Golden Dawn's party to achieve parliamentary representation in the twin national elections in May and June 2012 ... Which, among other things, seems to have encouraged the general exculpation of racist rhetoric as well as the adopting of related practices from various other organised groups.[49]

Gradually, Golden Dawn was increasing its legitimisation; its political project tended to be expressed and implemented in the streets by the party's audience itself, which was gradually increasing too. At the same time, no Golden Dawn member was either tried or investigated for possible connection with the attacks and the attempted murders. This provided the organisation's members with a belief in their own omnipotence; the confidence to proceed to the next stage of their action. It was at this stage that both the rhetoric and the practice of Golden Dawn would be further hardened, revealing its pure ideological vision. It was exactly the period when the organisation would begin to speak publicly about the need for the overthrow of the existing state and the

---

47    Poulantzas 2006, pp. 77–97, 157–66, 271–81.

48    VPRC 2013a; 2013b; 2013c; 2013d; 2013e.

49    The Greek Ombudsman 2013.

transition to a non-democratic regime. It was precisely the moment when the murderous fury of the organisation would turn from migrant workers to the Left: the murder of Pavlos Fyssas, a few days after the attack against members of the Communist Party, was the tragic expression of the launching of this new phase in Golden Dawn's action.

Based on these data, the subsequent arrests of Golden Dawn's leading members can be interpreted in two ways. First, the anti-fascist movement was getting bigger and bigger during that period, intensifying its activities, increasing its appeal and managing to play a crucial role in political developments. In this context, it was exercising political pressure on the government and its institutions to deal with a fascist formation, the activities of which had been known for a long time. On the other hand, the government could no longer control or limit the increase in Golden Dawn's electoral percentage and social impact. Rather, it was evident that Golden Dawn was able to undermine the integrity of the government both electively and politically. For this reason, a more radical solution was required. Of course, the solution was none other than to properly address the members of an organisation that was committing crimes publicly and daily. The fact that it took so long for these arrests to occur, is in fact evidence of a certain 'political protection' and reflects Golden Dawn's complementary role to the government strategy.

## 7        Fascism Remains Unarrested

The prosecution of Golden Dawn's leading members resulted in the decline of the organisation's criminal activity during this period. Moreover, as far as its public presence is concerned, the party withdrew its acute ideological references and adopted a 'milder' profile. Does this process mean the beginning of the end for the fascist phenomenon in Greece during the crisis?

It is characteristic that even after the accusation of Golden Dawn being a criminal organisation, as well as after the murder of Pavlos Fyssas and the disclosure of numerous of criminal activities, the party's polling rate increased from 6.92% (parliamentary elections of 2012) to 9.39% at the Euroelections of 2014. At the parliamentary elections of 2015, Golden Dawn's rate declined to 6.28% amid a huge political polarisation and a mass anti-fascist movement. Of course, the fact that, since the prosecutions, the media had changed their attitude towards Golden Dawn, now openly accusing them, also played a significant role. Still, 6.28% is almost the same percentage Golden Dawn gained at 2012, and a huge percentage for a (neo-)Nazi party anyway. What has happened?

Dimitris Psarras emphasises: 'Those who are attracted to the rhetoric of Golden Dawn are ready to turn a blind eye to violence and the worship of blood, even to its fanatical dedication to German National Socialism, because they believe that only an extreme response can be given to extreme political and social conditions'.[50] So, are those who still support Golden Dawn just angry but not fascists? No matter how important the previous citation, we cannot over-look the fact that the shift to fascism requires time and entails people's engage-ment with fascist practices and discourses. Consequently, the long-standing support of Golden Dawn under these circumstances highlights the political development and stances of its voters, reflecting that the bonds with that party are quite deep and tend to acquire characteristics of ideological identification of the voters with it.

On the other hand, throughout this process and amid the general socio-political developments in Greece, the movements and the positions occupied by the political and social subjects are neither fixed nor given. In this sense, we are not entitled to deal with the question of a potential fascist transformation of Greek society as if it were a kind of linear development or repetition of history. Although great losses had already occurred in social goods (shrinkage of the welfare state, dismantling of labour relations, retreat of the labour movement to a deeply unfavourable socio-political balance of forces), the dynamics and the underground processes of the social struggles were still able to intervene and change the balance of forces.

The rise of SYRIZA to power was one of the results of these processes. It was a development that rapidly rearranged the central political scene and expressed the need of the majority of Greek society to stop the austerity measures, but also for a re-establishment of democratic institutions. However, the fact that SYRIZA is now in government does not mean that the project that is confronta-tional to bourgeois strategy has managed either to acquire the necessary social penetration or to win the struggles for hegemony; not only because SYRIZA does not seek to break with the bourgeois strategy as expressed within the European Union, but also because the overthrow of bourgeois strategy is a much longer-term process, which refers to much more than the government: the state itself and its ideological mechanisms, the society and the class and ideological balance that defines it.

It is therefore clear that the maintenance of a condition of reduced pop-ular sovereignty and democracy as well as the continuation of austerity and declining living standards that the Third Memorandum brings, in the period

---

50    Psarras 2014.

during which a left party governs, will give the kiss of life to the forces of reaction, which remain active and plan their counterattack. On the other hand, as shown by the referendum of 5 July 2015, the radical dynamic in Greek society is profound and confrontational. In this sense, the confrontation between the forces working to recover the hegemony of the bourgeois power and the forces trying to change the existing social and political model in a radical direction proves that despite the fact that the bourgeoisie remains the dominant side of the dominant contradiction,[51] the outcome of this struggle has not yet been written.


## References

Adorno, Theodor 2000, *The Psychological Technique of Martin Luther Thomas' Radio Addresses*, Stanford: Stanford University Press.

Athanasiou, Athina 2012, *The Crisis as a Condition of "State of Emergency". Critiques and Resistances*, [In Greek] Athens: Savvalas.

Betz, Hans-Georg 2003, 'Xenophobia, Identity Politics and Exclusionary Populism in Western Europe', in *Socialist Register 2003 Fighting Identities: Race, Religion and Ethnonationalism*, edited by Leo Panitch and Colin Leys, London: The Merlin Press.

Bogiopoulos, Nikos 2011, *'It's Capitalism, You Idiot'. Those Responsible for the Crisis and the 'Debt' for their Overthrow – A Kind Answer to the Praetorians of the Memoranda*, [In Greek] Athens: Livanis.

Christopoulos, Dimitris (ed.) 2014, *The "Deep State" in today's Greece and the Extreme Right. Police, Justice, Army, Church*, [In Greek] Athens: Nissos.

Civil Action Petition 2014, 'Civil Action Petition regarding the Golden Dawn Trial' [In Greek] https://jailgoldendawn.com/wp-content/uploads/2014/11/YPOMNHMA_POL AGWGHS_TELIKO.pdf

Douzinas, Costas 2011, *Resistance and Philosophy amid the Crisis: Politics, Ethics and Syntagma Station*, [In Greek] Athens: Alexandreia.

Ellinas, Antonis A. 2010, *The Media and the Far Right in Western Europe. Playing the Nationalist Card*, Cambridge: Cambridge University Press.

Ellinas, Antonis A. 2014, 'Neo-Nazism in an Established Democracy: The Persistence of Golden Dawn in Greece', *South European Society and Politics*, 20: 1–20.

Gaitanou, Eirini 2011, 'Fuck December '08 – Fight Now!', [In Greek] available at: https://ilesxi.wordpress.com/2011/12/14/fuck-december-08-fight-now/

---

51    Poulantzas 2006, p. 68.

Gramsci, Antonio 1971, *Selections from the Prison Notebooks*, New York: International Publishers.

Gramsci, Antonio 1978, *Selections from Political Writings (1921–1926)*, London: Lawrence and Wishart.

Kalampokas, Giorgos 2012, 'Hegemony as a Sum, Hegemony as a Transformation', [In Greek] *Ektos Grammis*, 31: 30–3.

Kalampokas, Giorgos 2013, 'The Deletion of the Post-Junta era: From Consensus to Post-Hegemonic Authoritarianism', [In Greek] *Ektos Grammis*, 34: 64–7.

Klein, Naomi 2008, *The Shock Doctrine: The Rise of Disaster Capitalism*, London: Picador.

Kouvelakis, Stathis 2011, 'The Great Turning Point', [In greek], available at http://www.e-dromos.gr/%CE%B7-%CE%BC%CE%B5%CE%B3%CE%AC%CE%BB%CE%B7-%CE%BA%CE%B1%CE%BC%CF%80o%CE%AE/

Kouzelis, Gerassimos 2014, 'How Fascism is Constructed', in *Fascism and Democracy*, [In Greek] Athens: Nissos.

INE-GSEE 2013, *The Greek Economy and Labour: Annual Report 2013*, [In Greek] Athens: INE-GSEE.

Lapavitsas, Kostas and Stathis Kouvelakis 2012, *The Crisis and the Left Way Out: Positions for a Social and Political Front*, [In Greek] Athens: Livanis.

Mavris, Yannis 2010, 'The Deep Crisis of the Representative Institutions Remains', [In Greek], available at: http://www.publicissue.gr/1378/institutions-analysis-2009/

Mavris, Yannis 2013a, 'The Party System a Year After the Elections', [In Greek], available at: http://www.mavris.gr/3424/party-system-one-year-after/

Mavris, Yannis 2013b, 'The X-Ray of Golden Dawn. The Emergence and the Consolidation of the Right-Wing Phenomenon', [In greek], available at: http://www.mavris.gr/3625/aktinografia-xa/

Mavris, Yannis 2014, 'The Crisis of Trust in Institutions is Deepening in Greece', [In Greek], available at: http://www.efsyn.gr/arthro/vathainei-i-krisi-empistosynis-stoys-thesmoys-stin-ellada

O Ios 2013, 'The Reverse of the Post-Junta Era', [In Greek], available at: http://vathikokkino.gr/archives/60549

Paraskeva-Veloudogianni, Despina 2015, *The Enemy, the Blood and the Punisher: Analyzing Thirteen Speeches of Golden Dawn's "Leader"*, [In Greek], Athens: Nissos.

Paxton, Robert 2004, *The Anatomy of Fascism*, [In Greek] Athens: Kedros.

Poulantzas, Nicos 2000, *State, Power, Socialism*, London: Verso.

Poulantzas, Nicos 2001, *Classes in Contemporary Capitalism*, [In greek] Athens: Themelio.

Poulantzas, Nicos 2006, *Fascism and Dictatorship. The Third International and the Problem of Fascism*, [In Greek] Athens: Themelio.

Psarras, Dimitris 2010, *The Hidden Hand of Karatzaferis. The Televised Rebirth of the Greek Far-Right*, [In Greek] Athens: Alexandreia.

Psarras, Dimitris 2012, *The Black Book of Golden Dawn*, [In Greek] Athens: Polis.

Psarras, Dimitris 2014, 'The Rise of Golden Dawn is a Political Defeat of the Left', interview to Loucas Chalandritsanos, [In Greek], available at: http://popaganda.gr/anodos-tis-chrisis-avgis-ine-mia-politiki-itta-tis-aristeras/

Public Issue 2010, 'Greek Confidence Index in Institutions 2009', [in Greek], available at: http://www.publicissue.gr/1375/institutions-3/

Sakellaropoulos, Spyros 2013, 'The Organization of the State Power during the Post-Junta Era: A Pro-Popular Rapture in the Capitalist Continuity', [In Greek] *Ektos Grammis*, 34, pp. 39–43.

Sotiris, Panagiotis 2011, 'The Age of Uprising. Thoughts about the "Squares" and Politics', [In Greek] in Christos Yovanopoulos and Dimitris Mitropoulos (eds), *Democracy Under Construction*, Athens: A/sinexia.

Sotiris, Panagiotis 2012, '"State of Exception" or organic crisis? Theoretical Issues about the Authoritarian Transformation of the Bourgeois State', [In Greek] *Ektos Grammis*, 31: 26–9.

The Greek Ombudsman 2013, Special Report: *The racist violence phenomenon in Greece and How to Deal with It*, [In Greek] http://www.synigoros.gr/resources/docs/eidikiekthesiratsistikivia.pdf

Thomas, Peter 2012, 'Confronting the Crisis: Gramsci and the Politics of Hegemony Today', [In Greek], available at http://ektosgrammis.gr/website/antimetopoi-me-tin-krisi-o-gkramsi-kai-i-politiki-tis-igemonias-simera

Vernardakis, Christoforos 2013, 'The Contradictory Advance of the Left', [In Greek], available at: http://tvxs.gr/news/egrapsan-eipan/i-antifatiki-proelasi-tis-aristeras-toy-xristoforoy-bernardaki

VPRC 2013a, 'Political Situation and Governance. January 2013', [In Greek].

VPRC 2013b, 'Political Situation and Governance. March 2013', [In Greek].

VPRC 2013c, 'Political Situation and Governance. April 2013', [In Greek].

VPRC 2013d, 'Political Situation and Governance. June 2013', [In Greek].

VPRC 2013e, 'Political Situation and Governance. July 2013', [In Greek].

Wilson, Robin and Paul Hainsworth, 2012, *Far-Right Parties and Discourse in Europe: A Challenge for Our Times*, Brussels: European Network Against Racism (ENAR), available at: http://cms.horus.be/files/99935/MediaArchive/publications/20060_Publication_Far_right_EN_LR.pdf

# CHAPTER 9

# The Crisis and the Strategy of the Greek Ruling Class

*Spyros Sakellaropoulos*

## Introduction

This chapter aims at highlighting the basic parameters of the strategy of the Greek ruling class, following the eruption of the present crisis. Moreover, we also deal extensively with the two preceding strategies elaborated in the period from the founding of the Greek state in 1828 up until 2009. There are two reasons for this: The first has to do with the need to present the differences between the three strategies; the second with identifying the factors inherited from the past that have made the most decisive contribution to the current crisis.

## 1    The Strategy of the Megali Idea

The basic strategy adopted by the Greek ruling class following the establishment of the Modern Greek state was that of the *Megali Idea* (Great Idea). The 'Megali Idea' amounted to the notion that the fledgling Greek state was a temporary bridgehead from which free Greeks would launch an offensive to liberate their enslaved compatriots living in various regions of the Ottoman Empire.[1] The essential point is that following the Greek Revolution (1821–7), the limited territory of the new State was experienced by the Greek elite as something traumatic because it had not been feasible to create a state comparable to that of the old Byzantine Empire. This was a corollary of the national ideology which had prevailed in the decades prior to the revolution, according to which modern Greeks were the direct descendants of the ancient Greeks and consequently of the Byzantines (at least from the point after which the Byzantine polity had separated itself from its Roman origins). This also had to do with the existence, in parts of the Ottoman Empire, of populations considered

---

1    Petropoulos–Koumarianou 1977, p. 82.

© KONINKLIJKE BRILL NV, LEIDEN, 2018 | DOI:10.1163/9789004280892_011

Greek on account of either their language (Greek) or their religion (Christian Orthodox). In any case, as Costas Vergopoulos notes:

> All of the internal life of Greek society was predicated on the positioning of all organizations and classes vis-à-vis the national integration question ... [C]onsequently the Greek irredentist issue became something like a catalyst for activating the dynamic of Greek society. Governments were formed and fell, the throne, the parties, the intellectuals, the army, the Great Powers were sanctioned or rejected on the basis of their real or assumed stance on this issue.[2]

It is impressive how overwhelming was the consensus on the need to achieve this objective. Even the bitter conflicts of the last decades of the nineteenth century between the parties of Charilaos Trikoupis and Theodoros Deligiannis centred on different variants of the same strategy. Trikoupis believed that it would be achievable if Greece acquired institutions and structures analogous to those existing in Europe, whereas Deligiannis thought that the realisation of the *Megali Idea* required transformation of the country into a kind of bridge between Europe and the East.[3]

The primacy of the *Megali Idea* overshadowed the question of Greece's economic development. The Greek economy was agrarian, with around two-thirds of the active population in 1870 being farmers and the great economic centres situated outside the country (Constantinople, Smyrna, Thessaloniki), with the exception of Patras and Syros. There was no processing industry until the 1860s; exports were confined to agricultural products, chiefly raisins, tobacco and oil. The 1870s saw the gradual emergence of the first processing plants, primarily – again – engaged in treatment of agricultural products (food, textiles, drinks, tobacco). There was one exception to this anaemic situation and that was in commerce, and above all shipping. Ship-owning capital underwent rapid growth, rising from a capacity of 85,000 tons in 1838 to 404,000 tons in 1870. This made Greece the world's fifth maritime power, controlling half the shipping to and from the Ottoman Empire.

A series of setbacks were to lead the country to bankruptcy in 1893 and to the imposition of international financial regulation in 1898: exports of currants would plummet, the sailing ships of the merchant navy would be exposed to

---

2   Vergopoulos 1978a, pp. 33–4.
3   Vergopoulos 1978a, p. 168.

competition from steamships, the high expenditures on infrastructural works but also on the military's priorities generated soaring rates of external indebtedness.

However, the basic point to be stressed is that above and beyond economic shortcomings and politico-military failures (British and French military intervention in reprisal for Greece's pro-Russian stance in the Crimean war, Greek non-participation in the Congress of Berlin, where the allocation of the territories of the Ottoman Empire was designed following Ottoman defeat in the war with Russia, severe defeat in the Greco-Turkish war of 1897), the strategy of the *Megali Idea* was gaining ground: in 1864 the Ionian Islands, and in 1881 Thessaly, were incorporated into Greece. Of course, there were aspirations for greater territorial expansion but the annexations actually achieved show that the strategy under implementation had the potential to produce results, even if this took place within a contradictory context including elements of financial and political crisis.[4]

The transition to the new century was to be accompanied by two important developments: The first has to do with the dynamic entrance of the popular masses into the scene that was to lead to the Goudi movement in 1909, and the emergence of new political forces untainted by the failures of the past and with the ability to make concessions to the subaltern classes (land grants to the landless, the first social policy measures) for the sake of ensuring national unity, an absolute prerequisite for continuation of the effort to realise the *Megali Idea*. The second was the deterioration of the crisis of the Ottoman Empire, culminating in the Balkan Wars of 1912 and 1913. These two developments in conjunction were to result in the even further extension of Greek territory, with the acquisition of Macedonia, Epirus, the islands of the central Aegean and Crete. Achievement of the *Megali Idea* was beginning to appear an ever more tangible possibility.

In this context, we must also account for an extra factor: slow but real economic growth. The number of business enterprises grew from 210 in 1879 to 1,213 in 1909 and 33,811 in 1920. This can be attributed to a variety of factors, such as the fall in interest rates, the entry of Greek Diaspora capital into the market, and the widening of the internal market as a result of a rise in urban population. Nevertheless, it should be noted that this increase in industrial activity remained one-sided, given that more than two-thirds of the industrial installa-

---

4 One characteristic fact is that there were continual changes of government in the first years of the twentieth century.

tions handled foodstuffs (1917), with limited liability companies, numbering 13 in 1896, rising to a figure of only 56 by 1918.[5]

The country's participation, albeit delayed,[6] on the side of the victors in the First World War, made it possible for Greece to extend its influence into the Near East: apart from Western and Eastern Thrace and the islands of the Eastern Mediterranean, the country achieved the status of occupying power in Smyrna for a period of five years, after which a referendum was to be held on whether the region could be incorporated into Greece. The 'Greece of five seas and two continents' had become a reality.

However, this balance of power was soon to be overturned, as the Greek government opted for the continuation of the war with Turkey aiming at an ever-growing expansion of the territory under Greek control. What the Greek side had not taken into account was, on the one hand, the determination of the Young Turks to defend their country, and, on the other, the stance of the Great Powers, which did not desire further reinforcement of the role of Greece in the Eastern Mediterranean, particularly now that a strong Turkey was seen as a necessary bulwark against the newly-established Soviet regime.

## 2      The Asia Minor Disaster and the Turn towards Economic Development

The defeat of the Asia Minor expedition was to mark the beginning of a new historical period for the Greek ruling class.[7] It was becoming clear that possibilities for further expansion were limited to certain areas (Cyprus, Northern Epirus, Dodecanese), which were not under Turkish rule. This led to a new strategy whose basic characteristic was to attempt to improve Greece's position in the international division of labour through economic growth. Geograph-

---

5  Milios 2010, p. 263.
6  The delay was a by-product of the conflict between the Prime Minister E. Venizelos and King Constantine, with the former desiring participation in the war in the side of the Entente and the latter supporting neutrality that would favour Germany. The conflict assumed dramatic dimensions when for a short time two separate Greek states coexisted: the Greece of Thessaloniki led by Venizelos and the Greece of Athens led by the King. The deadlock was resolved through military intervention in Athens by the French.
7  'The politics of the Megali Idea was terminated once and for all. The period that had commenced with the Revolution of 1821 came to a close. The dream of creating a new Greater Greece was extinguished ... But the Asia Minor disaster did not mark just the ending of one period. It was at the same time the beginning of another. From 1923 onwards Greece became something new' (G. Dafnis, quoted in Rigos 1988, pp. 16–17).

ical expansion was now relegated to secondary status. We should in any case remember that one of the significant consequences of the defeat in Asia Minor was the geographical unification of Greek capital, a development which in itself injected a new dynamic into domestic capital accumulation.

An important role in this development was played by the arrival of approximately 1.5 million refugees from Turkey, comprising an impressively specialised labour force with low salary requirements. Their arrival also boosted internal demand. Between 1923 and 1939 industrial production doubled in value, with a 68% increase in volume. At the same time, unprecedentedly for a country with chronic balance-of-payments deficits, there was a large trade surplus: rising from a figure of 41.6% in 1923 to 75.4% in 1939.[8] This can be explained by the fact that while imports remained at the same level, exports rose by 45%.[9] A significant role in this connection was played by restructuring of the credit policies of the banks and of the state, along with the monetary stabilisation of 1928, which contributed to the creation of a climate favourable for private investment. Of course, the process was largely based on an upgrading of infrastructures (communications, transport, projects of accommodation provision for refugees) which became possible thanks to the influx of substantial loans from home and abroad: It is estimated that between 1923 and 1932, 1.168 billion gold French francs entered the Greek economy in the form of state loans (approximately 150% of GDP), with 144,100 million gold French francs as internal loans.[10] Other contributing factors were the policy of devaluing the currency, the policies of tax breaks for large enterprises and notably low wages,[11] along with the protectionist measures taken by the Greek state.[12]

The shipping sector also saw rapid growth, notwithstanding the losses it had suffered during the First World War. Shipping capacity rose from 563,353 tons in 1919 to 1,837,000 tons in 1940.[13]

---

8     Vergopoulos 1978b, p. 86.
9     Vergopoulos 1978b, p. 99.
10    Rigos 1988, pp. 51–2.
11    Between 1922 and 1935, the consumer price index rose by 207% whereas average wages rose by only 83%. Labour productivity rose by 43% in the 1928–38 period, whereas wages rose by only 24% (Milios 2000, p. 418). The State in essence pursued a twofold strategy vis à vis the popular strata: on the one hand, introduction of certain social welfare measures (no work on Sundays, abolition of child labour, introduction of the 8-hour day), and on the other, maintenance of a low ceiling on wages and political persecution of the Communist Party and its members.
12    Rigos 1988, p. 70; Milios 2000, pp. 412–13.
13    Milios 2000, p. 410.

The general conclusion is that a significant dynamic emerged in the Greek economy following the shock of the Asia Minor disaster. It is noteworthy that industrial production between 1929 and 1938 registered the highest growth rates in the world after the USSR and Japan.[14] However, this dynamic continued to be marked by a number of anomalies: it was based on low wages, low-tech commodities for domestic consumption, repeated currency devaluations and a high level of external debt to cover the cost of necessary infrastructures, not to mention the payment of war reparations. Consequently, in conjunction with the repercussions of the global economic crisis of 1929, the country was led into bankruptcy in 1932. A rapid recovery followed, however, thanks to a series of well-targeted state interventions such as further strengthening of tariff protection and a policy of preference for local industries in public sector procurements,[15] indicating that the preceding economic restructuring had not been superficial.

At the political level, the protagonists were faced with the task of resolving a number of conflicts and problems: the most crucial, to start at the beginning, was that of coming to terms with the new situation that had been dictated by the change in strategy, the economic consequences of the Asia Minor disaster and the reality of a latent international over-accumulation crisis. To put it differently, the bourgeois political personnel were saddled with the task of achieving economic growth in a country that had been at war between 1912 and 1922, facing the social deterioration and loss of social status that had been experienced by the refugees and the newly annexed populations, the fact that a large part of the population was not represented politically, the emergence of labour unionism and the tensions of class struggle as a result of intervention by the newly constituted Communist Party of Greece (KKE) but also of escalation of the international economic crisis.

One consequence of all the above was the appearance of a multitude of individual and conflicting micro-strategies among the entire bourgeois political personnel (the Palace, factions of the army, parliamentarians) culminating in a succession of political confrontations (alternations between democracy and Bonapartist regimes, military pronunciamentos, government crises, party splits) whose end-product was the military dictatorship of I. Metaxas that was to last until the occupation of the country by the Germans in 1941.

Essentially, in its attempt to deal with the new realities, the Greek bourgeoisie was frequently in the position of being attracted to prospects of abol-

---

14    Milios 2000, p. 415.
15    Chadziiosif 2002, p. 275.

ishing parliamentarianism. It was in any case a time that favoured such orientations. In the final analysis, the change in strategy did not take place without internal frictions and conflicts for the dominant power bloc.

## 3 Postwar Developments

The occupation of the country by the Germans, the growth in influence of the Greek Communist Party (KKE) through participation in the resistance to the occupier, the unstable political situation in which the country was left following liberation (on the one hand, the bourgeois bloc enjoying the support of the British troops, and on the other, the National Liberation Army (ELAS) that was controlled by the KKE and its allies) precluded continuation of any effort to upgrade the country's position in the international division of labour. The first priority for the Greek ruling class until the end of the 1940s was to save the bourgeois regime.

Defeat of the Communists in the Civil War (1947–9) enabled the bourgeoisie to continue the policy of economic development it had initiated after the Asia Minor disaster, the more so because, apart from Cyprus, the remaining geographical claims had, in one way or another, lapsed. Dodecanese had been incorporated into Greece (1947). Northern Epirus was part of Albania, with which Greece, until 1947, was on a war footing.

Thus a new period of growth started in which the state was to play a significant role: interventions for the rationalisation of the monetary system, the undertaking of infrastructural works, and the implementation of a credit framework for cost-effective financing of processing facilities.

The construction sector was to occupy a central position by virtue of internal emigration to the cities, encompassing lower petty-bourgeois social layers whose economic strength was boosted through utilisation of income from land ownership. As far as industry was concerned, a coalescing of activity could be observed in sectors such as textile manufacturing, foodstuffs, tobacco, drinks, clothing, footwear, chemical goods, and metalworking machinery.[16] As a result, the share of industrial products in total exports was to rise from 2.1% in 1954 to 14% in 1966.[17] It is also worth underlining that there was an internal restructuring of Greek processing towards sectors with greater dynamism: the more traditional products (foodstuffs, drink, tobacco, clothing, shoes) contrac-

---

16    Samaras 1986, p. 55.
17    Fotopoulos 1985, p. 260.

ted from 63.2% of the total in 1950 to 42.4% in 1970, with chemicals rising from 3.7% to 11.2% and metallurgy/transport from 2.8% to 12.7%.[18]

Seen as a whole, the postwar Greek economy registered very high growth rates: between 1952 and 1961 it was as high as 5.7%, and this continued into the 1963–73 period, during which it fluctuated between 5.3% and 10.3%.[19] Consequently, between 1937 and 1966 Greece had the highest rate of growth in per capita income of any of the Western countries (5%, as against 2.0% for the UK, 4.9% for France, 4.0% for the USA, 4.9% for Western Germany and 3.7% for Japan).[20]

Of course, it should be noted that a significant parameter in these developments was the low wages and the whole regime of repression of social rights, a by-product of the bourgeois camp's victory in the civil war, which discountenanced any manifestation of trade-union activism. We might mention characteristically that the income distribution between wage earners and enterprises in Greece in 1963 was 41% for wage earners and 59% for enterprises, whereas in France it was 62% and 38%, in the USA 70% and 30%, in the UK 74% and 26%, and in West Germany 61% and 39%.[21]

Overall expansion of the economy reinforced the degree of enterprise concentration. In 1963 there were seven industrial enterprises employing more than 1,000 workers, with 13,700 workers employed in them. By 1971 there were 24 such enterprises, employing 42,000 workers.[22] In 1958 enterprises employing more than 50 workers accounted for 44.1% of the total workforce. By 1973 they had come to account for 65.8% of those in employment. At the same time there was a continuation of the development of Greek shipping, the most internationalised sector of Greek capital, whose tonnage underwent a threefold increase between 1962 and 1973.

It was in the midst of this upwards trajectory of the Greek economy that the strategy of a potential membership in the European Economic Community was adopted. This choice was made as part of an attempt to make Greece part of advanced Western capitalist countries. Participation in the EEC was viewed as a mechanism of transmitting pressures into the interior of less competitive capitals which could at the same time function as political and ideological safeguard for capitalist power relations.[23]

---

18    Karabelias 1989, p. 187.
19    Milios 2010, pp. 278–80.
20    Bambanasis and Soulas 1976, p. 225.
21    Sakellaropoulos 1998, p. 226.
22    Karabelias 1982, p. 149.
23    We should bear in mind that apart from the fear that pervaded the ruling classes following

The 1967–74 dictatorship came as the dominant classes' response to the challenge from the popular strata to the post-civil-war power structure (hyper-exploitation of the working classes, a very prominent role for the forces of repression and particularly the army, continual anti-parliamentary and anti-democratic irregularities) as conveyed through the mass political and social mobilisations of the 1960s.

Economic growth was to continue throughout the seven years of the dictatorship, aided not only by the favourable international conjuncture but also by suppression of all forms of collective action. The period following the global economic crisis of 1973, but also the fall of the dictatorship (1974) was to be characterised by a continuation of the growth dynamic, but at a more moderate pace, until the end of the 1970s, nevertheless retaining its dynamism by comparison with other European countries (average annual increase in GNP 4.7% as against 3.0% for the countries of the EEC in the period between 1975 and 1979). There were two reasons for this: one of them has to do with industry's turn in the 1973–80 period towards more traditional sectors of low-tech consumer goods production.[24] The second relates to the development of economic relations with the Arab countries, either in the form of commodity exports or in that of undertaking large construction projects in these regions.

The restoration of parliamentary democracy took place in a conjuncture deeply marked by the anti-dictatorial sentiments of the people, both on account of the seven years of tyranny culminating in the massacre of the National Polytechnic uprising of November 1973 and on account of the coup in Cyprus carried out by the Greek junta, followed inexorably by the Turkish invasion and occupation of 40% of the island. The ruling class was forced to make certain concessions to the subaltern classes to avert the possibility of popular discontent transforming into an open challenge to capitalist power relations: abolition of the monarchy, legalisation of the Communist Left, unimpeded functioning of parliamentary institutions, restrictions on the role of the Army, wage increases. Nevertheless, in addition to certain institutional safeguards (assignment of a wide array of functions to the President of the Republic, con-

---

the experience of civil war, only three years before, in 1958, the Left party EDA, in which the illegal KKE participated, received 24% of the vote and emerged as official opposition.

24    As has been shown in a relevant 1977 study by T. Giannitsis, in West Germany, France, Holland and Italy 55% of investment was channelled into 'heavy' industrial sectors (chemicals, machinery, means of transport, paper), whereas the corresponding percentage for Greek industry was 17.6%. By contrast in traditional sectors (textiles, clothes, shoes, non-metallic mining, and tanning) the percentage in the industrial countries is 14.8%, whereas in Greece it is as high as 47.6% (Giannitsis 1988, p. 76).

centration of powers in the executive branch, adoption of laws hampering independent trade union action), there was also a second route towards the desired fortification of the bourgeois regime, namely the country's EEC membership application, in continuation of the previous Association Agreement.

Undoubtedly, entry into the EEC would mean transference to the interior of the Greek social formation of pressures from the more productive European capitals, with the danger of the consequent closure of the less competitive units, a prospect which would be viewed as positive by the monopolistic faction of the Greek ruling class. On the other hand, there were the advantages of inclusion of the powerful Greek merchant fleet, which could function as a link between Western Europe, the Middle East and North Africa, in addition to the further strengthening of the bourgeois political regime.

## 4        From the Entry into the EEC to the Outbreak of the Crisis

The country's entry into the EEC coincided with the assumption of power by PASOK, Europe's most leftist Socialist party, but also with the beginnings of a period of significant economic downturn. The sectors of the economy which had been sustained by domestic demand (consumer goods, the building industry) appeared to be reaching the limit of their potential. On the other hand, wage increases that were conceded in response to the development of the workers' movement in the '70s, in conjunction with increases in the prices of inputs (raw materials, energy) tended to reduce profitability.[25] Higher inflation, and the subsequent increase in the cost of money, was also an important contributory factor to emergence of a climate of recession. Thus between 1978 and 1982 there was a 55% increase in the number of loss-making enterprises, with private investments declining from a figure of +8.2% by 7.8% in 1980, 9.9% in 1981, 5.0% in 1982, and 13.3% in 1984. Corresponding fluctuations were to be noted in GNP rise, which stood at 6.4% in 1978, 3.8% in 1979, 1.9% in 1980, −0.2% in 1981, −0.1% in 1982, and 2.2% in 1984.[26]

PASOK was called upon to govern in this situation, attempting on the one hand to manage the consequences of the recession (disinvestment-deindustrialisation), and on the other to respond to popular expectations, above all, from the social layers that had brought it to power. Moreover, it was called to gov-

---

25    Note that wage labour's share of domestic income rose from 48.8% in 1974–5 to 62.2% in 1981–2 (Karabelias 1989, p. 273).

26    Karabelias 1989, p. 119.

ern within a more competitive EEC context and against a bourgeoisie whose attitude ranged from scepticism to open enmity. In the first four-year term, a contradictory policy was pursued, with nationalisations of loss-making enterprises, wage and pension increases, a expansion of the welfare state, an attempt to find some balance both with the Greek ruling class and with international imperialist mechanisms (EEC, NATO). In the post-WW2 context it was arguably the first time since 1922 that such a strategy had been pursued, and it was later questioned on account of both the recession and the radical programme on the basis of which PASOK had won the 1981 elections. It is worth stressing that after the Asia Minor disaster, despite the political crises, the emergence of armed forces movements, the dictatorships, and the political crises, there had never been any questioning of the orientation towards economic development as the decisive tool for upgrading the country's position within the capitalist West, but also as a counterweight to Turkey.

Nevertheless, given that PASOK had never intended to embark on a transition to a different set of social relations, the inherent imperatives of the capitalist system itself were to determine subsequent developments. As a result a sudden deficit in the current account balance (attributable primarily to conjunctural factors such as the price of petrol and revenue from tourism), which took it from 4.9% of GNP in 1982 to 10.0% in 1985, led to PASOK and the New Democracy governments that followed it (1990–3, 2004–9) adopting a set of policies that in the Greek Marxist bibliography was designated as *capitalist restructuring*: austerity in perpetuity, with the overall trend being one of reducing labour's share in the proceeds of production, the introduction of flexibility in labour relations, privatisation, not only of nationalised and formerly private enterprises but also of public utilities, increases in private consumption through unimpeded access to consumer debt. If we add capitalist restructuring to the politics that had prevailed from 1973 onwards, along with international developments, we arrive at a restructured version of the strategy adopted from 1922:

a)  Low labour costs, falling even further given the hyper-exploitation of the immigrants who started coming to Greece in 1990 and afterwards.
b)  Gradual implementation of all forms of flexible labour relations.
c)  Revival of the construction sector as the motive force of the Greek economy, both through implementation of the so-called major works projects (harbours, roads, airports, stadia for the 2004 Olympic Games) and through new house construction.
d)  Continuing presence of cosmopolitan shipping capital as the most powerful sector of the Greek ruling class.

e)   Increased role of private banking capital through expansion of the money
     flow to businesses and households.
f)   Use of European funds for various purposes (infrastructures, vocational
     training, support for industry), which made a decisive contribution to
     the creation of social alliances (bourgeois and petty-bourgeois strata who
     benefited from this funding).
g)   The importance of low- and medium-technology enterprises remained in
     place, along with further development of services (tourism, banks, tele-
     communications, insurance companies, consultancy, etc.).
h)   The reorientation of the commercial sector towards the countries of the
     EEC (the share of Greek exports to the nine EEC countries of the time
     increased from 47.6% in 1980 to 61.4%, with non-petroleum imports
     rising from 56.8% to 71.5%).[27]

All the above comprise elements in an overall intensification of state authoritarianism: displacement of a significant proportion of political decision-making
towards the technocratic administrative bureaucracy, a transfer of powers conducted by agreement between Greek governments and the EU bureaucracy,
strengthening of the ideological apparatuses of the state, above all the mass
media, reinforcement of the machinery of repression.

   This orientation was initiated with relative success following Greece's entry
into the Economic and Monetary Union. It was successful because throughout
of the 1990s the country had an annual average growth rate of 1.9% and in most
years it has varied between 2.0% and 4.5%. The fall in share of labour in the
GDP from 65%–70% in 1984–90 to 62% in 1994[28] made a significant contribution to this. An important role was also played by the increase in direct transfers
from the European Union, which rose from an annual average of 1,147.5 million
Euros (2.2% of the GNP) to 3,725 million Euros for the 1990–9 period (4.2% of
GNP).[29] Greek-owned shipping retained its powerful presence, amounting to
15% of the world's commercial fleet, 20% of the tanker fleet and 23% of the
fleet for transport of dry cargos.[30]

   However, the success was relative because it was not accompanied by profound transformations in production with the potential to increase the competitiveness of the Greek capitalist economy from a structural perspective.

---

27   Giannitsis 1988a, pp. 313–14.
28   Milios 2010, p. 282.
29   Manassaki and Colchida 2010, p. 235.
30   Milios 2010, p. 283.

Thus, in 1994, 6.6% of added value was produced by high-technology and 53.1% by low-technology industries, and in 2003 the corresponding figures were 7.3% and 46.5%. As far as the spread of investment is concerned, in 1994 high-technology industries were responsible for 6.6% of total investments and low-technology industries for 58.8%. In 2003, the corresponding figures were 6.0% and 45.9%.[31] By contrast, in 1994, 10.5% of exports were agricultural products and raw materials, 34.5% low-technology industrial products and only 1.6% high-technology. In 2002, the corresponding figures came to 8.9%, 29.6% and 5.4%.[32] Investment of innovative capital for expansion and product substitution as a percentage of GNP in Greece increased from 0.006 in 1995 to 0.007 in 2003, at a time when the corresponding figures for the EU-15 saw an increase from 0.038 to 0.088.[33] Parallel to this, we also had the further increases in the balance of trade deficit, with the export/import ratio falling from 43% in 1995 to 35.1% in 2000. We note that there is a slow but very real shift towards employing high technology, but against the prospect of a single market with a single currency, this does not cut much ice, on the one hand because the gap between Greece and the developed EU countries is so wide and not bridgeable by this frail tendency towards modernisation, and on the other because the common currency precludes the devaluation of national currency and the offsetting of the technological advantages by countries with higher productivity of capital. The transformation, in short, would be too slow to counteract the deterioration in the trade balance (see below).

In any case, Greece's entry into the Economic and Monetary Union (EMU) was opted for by the country's ruling class on the basis of exactly the same criteria as had been applied in the case of the decision to enter the EEC. The objective was for the Greek social formation to be subjected to an 'iron cage' of capitalist modernisation. This would entail the liquidation of non-competitive capitals and the strengthening of the higher-productivity enterprises of monopoly capital, in conjunction with a further contraction of labour's share of the proceeds of production. There would also be the advantage, from this perspective, of the comparatively more reactionary regulations being introduced at the level of the EMU and EU institutions (austerity policies, expansion of flexible labour relations, raise of retirement age, etc.).

However, it very soon became evident that participation in the EMU would exacerbate an already unsound and problematic situation. While the techno-

---

31    Giannitsis, Zografakis, Kasteli and Mavri 2009, pp. 45–6.
32    Giannitsis, Zografakis, Kasteli and Mavri 2009, p. 133.
33    Stassinopoulos 2005, p. 152.

logical gap between Greece and the other countries in the EMU was part of the given situation, there was no determination to pursue drastic measures that might reduce it. In 2005 expenditure on Research and Technology in Greece came to 0.59% of GNP, in comparison to 1.82% in the EU-25, 1.89% in the EU-15 and 1.84% in the 16 countries of the Economic and Monetary Union.[34] The business sector in Greece spent 0.18% of GNP on Research and Technology in 2005, at a time when the average for EU-27 was 1.15%, for EU-15 1.20%, and for the 16 EMU countries 1.16%.[35]

Moreover, there was a further deterioration in the export/import ratio, which went from more than 35.1% in 2000 to 29.5% in 2009 (in 1980 prior to Greek entry into the EEC the corresponding figure was 48.8%).

What had happened was that existing deficiencies in the competitiveness of Greek capitalism had merely escalated with entry into the EMU. The strategy opted for in the light of this development was to reorient exports to countries outside the capitalist West. Thus, whereas in 1991 77.1% of Greek exports were channelled to OECD countries, 67.2% to EU-15 countries, and 6.3% to North America, in 2001 the corresponding figures were 61.6% to OECD countries, 47.7% to EU-15 countries, and 5.9% to North America. By 2009 exports to OECD countries had fallen even more, to 52.9% of the total and the same applied for EU-15 countries – 37.1% of the total, and for North America, 5.7% of the total. By contrast the Balkans became a prime recipient of Greek exports, rising from 4% of the total in 1991 to 16.6% in 2001 and 17.2% in 2009.[36]

Thus we have a economy which is having difficulty coping with intensified international competition and is being called upon to manage a high level of public debt: from 22.5% of GNP in 1980 to 71.7% in 1990 and 104.4% in 2000, after which it will remain relatively stable until 2007 (107.2%). The basic reason for the debt undergoing such excessive increases is an accumulation of chronic balance of payments deficits (–5.3% of GNP in the 1983–6 period, –2.2% between 1987 and 1996,[37] –5.6% between 1997 and 2000 and subsequently skyrocketing to –9.1% between 2001 and 2009). This development is attributable first and foremost to the permanent deficit in the trade balance, which from –13.2% of GNP in the 1983–6 period was to rise to –13.6% between 1987 and 1996, –14.6% between 1997 and 2000 and –15,4% between 2000 and

---

34   Lykos 2012, p. 166.

35   Lykos 2012, p. 168.

36   Sakellaropoulos 2014.

37   The fall is mainly attributable to the reduction in the balance of payments deficit for fuels from 4.5% to –2.0%.

2008.[38] Of course, the international tendency from the 1970s onwards towards increases in public debt to underwrite local accumulation must be factored into this tendency.

In any case, prior to the crisis the overall picture was as follows: there was an economy which up until its entry into the European Monetary Union was based on production of low- and medium-to-low-technology products along with certain types of services (tourism, banks, trade, communications, transport). The external orientation was basically towards the countries of the West, and in particular the countries of the European Union, with the result that the technological deficit generated significant problems of competitiveness, which in turn contributed to an accumulation of public debt. As far as profitability was concerned, this was handled through a policy of relatively low wages and hyper-exploitation of immigrants, maintenance of a high level of local consumption through heavy lending to households by the banks but also through gradual reorientation of exports to countries outside the capitalist West. This situation worsened with the country's entry into the EMU, despite the prolongation of low labour costs and exports to non-Western countries, not to mention a state policy of reducing public expenditure (from 43% of GNP in 2000 to 38.3% in 2009). One key factor behind the problem was the reduction in the tax rate for large companies from 29.9% in 2000 to 18.6% in 2006, with the result that in 2010 taxes comprised only 28.7% of total revenue from income tax receipts, whereas in 2004 the corresponding figure had been 46%.[39] From an overall perspective, the regime of capital accumulation in Greece was underpinned by a fragile equilibrium that would be drawn into question with the advent of the crisis.

5      The Period of the Crisis

The crisis was to affect Greece as follows: on the one hand the deficits in the trade balance and the current accounts balance rose sharply, while on the other the GNP underwent contraction, resulting in a deterioriation in the debt-to-GNP ratio from 107.2% in 2007 to 129.7% in 2009. This triggered an avalanche of pressures from speculative capital gambling on the county's impending bankruptcy, or in other words its inability to continue servicing its debt. Thus, step by step, the climate in the international markets became very unfavourable for

38    Manassakis, Katiforis and Vasardani 2010, pp. 103–4.
39    Sakellaropoulos 2014.

Greece, with the government judging it difficult for the country to borrow at low interest rates. The course of action chosen was resort to the Troika (IMF, EU, ECB) and implementation of the politics of the Memoranda.

In the face of this, after the initial shock, the Greek ruling class began to perceive the necessity for a radical change of strategy, even if this change would mean on the one hand liquidating a sizeable segment of less productive capitals, and on the other accepting the stifling embrace of institutions of the imperialist centres and international capital. The Troika for its part (basically the social and institutional forces that it represents) decided for two reasons to intervene in the Greek problem: on the one hand there was the danger that the consequences of the Greek crisis would spread into the interior of the EMU (given that French and German banks were holding a large proportion of Greek bonds), and on the other there was the temptation to strive for the establishment of a new high-profit model of accumulation that might contribute to overcoming the global crisis of capital.

This project, which was under implementation during the Memoranda period, is moving along the following path: Very significant transformations are underway at the level of social alliances. Up until the onset of the crisis, with the exception of the 1940s, a period that was anomalous on account of the spread of influence of the Communist Party, the bourgeois class had elaborated a stable alliance with the traditional petty-bourgeoisie, elements of the rural population and the new petty-bourgeoisie. As a result of the economic policies being implemented, this alliance had undergone significant changes. The economic crisis had devastated not only a great part of the traditional petty-bourgeoisie (small traders, light industry),[40] but also significant factions of the bourgeoisie,[41] even segments of its monopoly sector. This meant that on the one hand a number of businesses had not succeeded in coping with the new conditions and had dropped out of the market, and on the other the dynamic enterprises possessing the necessary strength began to diverge from the others (see below). Above and beyond the ruin of traditional bourgeois and petty-bourgeois strata, this led to a dissolution of the alliance between the bourgeoisie and the traditional petty-bourgeois class, given that the latter was beginning to sense the prospect of its impending degradation. And the pressure was also exercised upon the new petty-bourgeoisie, and the rural strata. In the

---

40    It is entirely indicative that the number of companies registered with the Athens Chamber of Small and Medium industries fell from 49,180 in 2009 to 41,433 in 2013 (−16.7%).

41    The ICAP business services group, which records the evolution of Greek capitalist enterprises, had 29,852 companies on its books in 2009 and 17,279 in 2012 (a fall of 41.1%).

case of the new petty-bourgeoisie this is explicable by the high level of unemployment (rising from 9% in 2009 to 27% in 2014), which was taking a heavy toll within these strata. However, another crucial factor was the steep reduction in their income that was one of the consequences of the Memoranda policies. For the rural population a key consideration was the unprecedented taxation not only of income but also of their real assets (i.e. land). What appeared to be emerging in the final analysis was largely a monopoly bourgeoisie devoid of any social alliances to support it, so that the question arose as to how it was going to be able to remain dominant. The answer to this is not unrelated to the new role that the bourgeois state was being called upon to play.

In the state of this new type, the mechanisms for integration, representation and the securing of consent are steadily receding. The reference here is not to the process of an incremental transfer of powers from the parliament to the government and from there to the administrative bureaucracy, an evolution that has been part of the political history of the twentieth century. It is something altogether different: the transfer of virtually the entirety of the central mechanisms of state politics to centres independent of the relations of representation, centres embodying a pure politics of capital, without any recognition of the popular demands that are conveyed through representative institutions. In this way non-elected international institutions (such as the European Commission, the IMF, the European Central Bank) in collaboration with local agencies (business associations, mass media, governmental consultants) shape a new institutional reality (along the lines of the various Memoranda), which *a posteriori* receives ratification from the Hellenic parliament. But for this new institutional framework to become operative an unprecedented (in a parliamentary democracy) further hardening of the mechanisms of the bourgeois state's hard core is indispensable: harsh repression, repeated institutional coups and violations of the constitution, routine civil mobilisation orders for civil servants on strike, indifference towards implementation of court decisions that are not to the liking of the government, shutting down of the public television because of its alleged hostility towards the government, followed by introduction of a new public broadcaster unconditionally pro-government in orientation, curtailment of trade-union rights, continual monitoring of the functioning of local government to ensure its compliance with Memoranda policies. And all this was predicated on something very basic: that no government could, even if it wanted to, deviate from the edicts of the Troika. What was being constructed was essentially a vassal state, an inverted protectorate, as it were, where foreign policy remains the province of the central government and domestic policy is ceded to international organisations. Nevertheless, the lack of flexibility in the institutions of state is offset by increased profitability of the largest enterprises (see below) and assessments that this profitability is going to continue and even accelerate in the immediate future.

At the same time, attempts have been made to construct a new framework for labour relations, the functioning of which will likewise make a decisive contribution to increasing profitability: a drastic reduction in the number of public service employees with corresponding transfer of their tasks to private companies, extension of flexible labour relations (job rotation, part-time work, seasonal work), opening of shops also on Sundays, institution of 'apprenticeship' arrangements with reduced salaries for those under 25, withdrawal from recognition of collective agreements, drastic reductions in the minimum wage, toleration of *de facto* abolition of extra overtime pay in the private sector, lengthening of working hours in the public sector, reduction in the number of occupations that are categorised as 'hazardous', cutbacks on insurance and pension rights.

Or course, a key role in the overall strategy is played by the politics of permanent and absolute austerity. In other words, we are not speaking of income policies where wage increases fail to keep pace with increases in productivity in the economy, with the result that capital's share of the proceeds from production increases proportionately to that of labour. The reference is a drastic reduction in the wages and incomes of the popular strata. To be specific, the purchasing power of wage earners fell by 37.2% between 2010 and 2013, the share of wages fell from 64% of GNP in 2009 to 54% in 2013. The purchasing power of Greeks compared to that of the EU-15 countries fell from 84% of the average to 65% of the average.[42] Social inequality increased, as evidenced by the fact that in 2012 the income ratio between the richest fifth of the population and the poorest rose to 6.6, whereas in 2009 it had been 5.8. Correspondingly, the proportion of the population living in relative poverty rose from 19.7% in 2008 to 23.1% in 2011, with material deprivation indicators in 2012 reaching levels of 19.5%, by comparison with 11.2% in 2008.[43] What is most serious is that this situation was designed to continue indefinitely, given that according to the Memoranda no increases would be conceded unless unemployment falls under 10% (bear in mind that in 2014, the fifth year of Memoranda policies, its stood at 27%).

The objective is the greatest possible implantation of monopolised structures in the Greek economy. Existing statistical data confirm the presence of

---

42    INE/GSEE 2013.

43    Sakellaropoulos 2014.

this tendency in the midst of the crisis. In 2009, the 20 most profitable enterprises accounted for 45% of overall profits. By 2012, this had risen to 48.5%. In 2012, the 500 most profitable enterprises would register total profits of 10 billion Euros, with all the other profitable enterprises realising only two billion Euros. The 300 enterprises with the highest volume of sales (outside the financial sector) between 2009 and 2012 would increase their turnover from 53.6% of the total to 62.9% and their assets from 42.2% to 49.4%. Last but not least, in 2011, 445 people were living in Greece who each possessed a fortune of over 30 million dollars and owned in aggregate a total of 50 billion Euros or 24% of the GNP. In 2013, there would be 505 people with a fortune of over 30 million dollars and owning an aggregate of 60 billion Euros or 32% of the GNP in that year.[44]

The acuteness of the crisis has triggered significant intersectoral changes. There are sectors which notwithstanding the crisis are projecting considerable dynamism and other sectors in conspicuous decline. Summarising the findings of a relevant study[45] and focusing on specific sectors and subsectors, the banking sector is on the borderline of survival, primarily as a result of the policies of over-lending that the banks had pursued in previous years but also because of the losses sustained through the haircut of Greek bonds.[46] The construction sector has also experienced difficulties (from 3.4% of total turnover in 2009 it drops to 2.1% in 2012), non-metallic minerals (from 1.45 to 0.8%), car sales (from 4.5% to 1.6%), publishing (from 1% to 0.6%), the subsector of recreation – sport – culture (from 3.6% to 2.8%), *other business activities*[47] (from 3% to 2.5%) from the sector *Other services*. By contrast, a noteworthy dynamism can be seen in the sectors of energy and water supply (from 4.3% to 8.9%), and the sub-sector of petroleum products (from 4.9% to 10.8%), with satisfactory participation from basic metals (from 1.5% to 2.2%), food and drinks (from 5.5% to 6.4%) and telecommunications (from 3% to 3.5%). These developments highlight the preferences of capital in the current period, with an especially prominent role being assigned to energy and water supply and petroleum goods. Energy – water supply is the sector that includes renewable energy sources, a branch of production that has been particularly privileged by the current terms of the institutional framework (high compensation figures for energy), with the result that profit margins went as high as 50%. The increase

---

44    Sakellaropoulos 2014.

45    Ibid.

46    From a figure of 35 billion Euros of their own capital in 2009 the banks had by 2012 fallen to a figure of −5 billion Euros.

47    Egnatia Odos SA, Thessaloniki International Fair, etc.

in the share of petroleum goods is largely attributable to the export dynamism they demonstrated when exports went up from a figure of around 3.5 billion in 2009 to reach 10.5 billion in 2012.

Another aspect of the strategy being pursued is the transformation in the structure of Greek exports. This has to do with both intra-sectoral and geographic restructuring. At the level of intra-sectoral changes, existing data[48] indicate that there is a significant dynamic in the category 'minerals, fuels, lubricants', which rose from being 20.3% of total Greek exports in 2009 to reach a figure of 39.9% in 2013. It is noteworthy that no other sector has been comparably dynamic. On the contrary, categories such as 'food and animals', 'drinks and tobacco', 'chemical products', 'industrial goods classified on the basis of raw materials', 'machines and transportation materials', 'miscellaneous industrial goods' all fell sharply. We are therefore led to conclude that the acuteness of the crisis depressed most categories of exports, but brought forward an extraordinary dynamism of petroleum products. In terms of geographical reorientation, we note that exports towards OECD countries fell from 45.3% of total Greek exports in 2009 to 35.1% in 2013. Correspondingly, exports to the 11 countries that initially comprised the European Monetary Union fell from 31.5% to 24.4%. The same applies for the EU-25: exports to these countries went down from 47.8% to 36.5%. By contrast, exports to the Balkan countries increased from 22.2% to 25.1%, to the countries of North Africa and the Middle East from 8.5% to 12.1% and to 'other' countries from 6.1% to 12.4%. The conclusion that emerges is that a pre-existing tendency for Greek exports to move beyond the province of the capitalist West is continuing unabated. This is related to differences in competitiveness, which on the one hand are not fully counterbalanced by the drastic fall in salaries, and on the other are more perceptible in relation to the countries of the EMU where there is the common currency. At the same time, countries that are closer geographically become a significant destination for exports. If now we endeavour to establish a linkage between intra-sectoral changes and geographical reorientation, we will see that the basic export item, petroleum products, between 2009 and 2013 was increasingly channelled to locations outside the West: thus the 23.5% that went to OECD countries falls to 11%, to EU-25 from 25.2% to 12.3% and to the EMU-11 countries from 12.3% to 7%. By contrast, to the Balkans it increases from 26.6% to 31.7%, to other countries from 18.5% to 27.3% and to North Africa and Middle East from 14.3%

---

48    All the relevant information on restructuring of imports comes from unpublished data of the Greek National Statistical Service. Many thanks to Phaedon Papadimoulis for his important contribution to processing the primary data.

to 17.9%. That said, there is an interesting increase in exports to North Africa and the Middle East of 'machines and transportation materials', from 7.8% to 12.2% and 'miscellaneous industrial goods' from 5.4% to 10.3%. This development is explicable, in the case of the 'machines and transportation materials', by the fall in exports to OECD countries from 48.8% to 38% and in the case of the 'miscellaneous industrial goods' from the reduction for the EU-25 countries from 59.4% to 54.6%. Finally, it is worth noting that Turkey is the country to which most Greek exports go, presenting a remarkable increase: from 5% in 2009 to 11.7%[49] in 2013 (whereas in 2009 Italy was the country with 10.1%).

Another aspect that has not received the attention it warrants concerns direct Greek investment abroad. According to Bank of Greece data, in 2001 this amounted to 8 billion Euros or 5.5% of GNP; by 2005 it had risen to 11.4 billion Euros or 5.9% of GNP, in 2009 to 29.8 billion or 12.9% of GNP and in 2012, despite the crisis, to 34.1 billion Euros or 17.5% of GNP. In the years prior to the crisis, this development was interpreted as an extroverted movement of powerful units of Greek capital searching for high levels of profitability abroad while retaining their presence in Greece. Nevertheless, for the 2009–13 period our view is that it was more a movement of removing the consequences of crisis, a process of effecting a separation from the morbid economic situation within Greece, an abandonment of locally-based activity and initiation of a more permanent orientation towards activity abroad. Geographically, Greek foreign investment is directed towards Cyprus (28.5% of total Greek investment in 2009 and 25.9% in 2012), Holland (14.9% and 15.8% respectively), Turkey (13.7% and 10.9%), Romania (11.3% and 8.2%) and Bulgaria (5.1% and 5.8%). We note that with the exception of Holland there is a preference, with investment as with exports, for countries neighbouring Greece. At the sectoral level, the great majority involve the sector 'financial and insurance activities', accounting for 74.5% of total Greek investment in 2009 and 73.9% in 2013. Closely following come 'information and communication,' with 9.7% in 2009 and 5.7% in 2013, 'other processing industries', with 2.5% in 2009 and 5.7% in 2013 and 'commerce and repairs and maintenance', with 5.4% in 2009 and 5.4% again in 2013. The presence of the broader finance and insurance sector appears to be not unrelated to a more general rise of the finance sector at the end of twentieth and beginning of the twenty-first century; the stagnation of the Greek banking sector must have caused unease for companies

---

49    Such that in 2013, 8.7% of Greek exports or 74% of total exports to Turkey involved exports
       of petroleum products, rising from 1.7% of total Greek exports or 34% of total Greek
       exports to Turkey in 2009.

managing capital, insurance services, and so on, prompting them to establish themselves abroad and/or to expand their presence in places abroad where they are already active.

One question emerges: what is the position of foreign capital amid this whole process? Implication in the Greek crisis is undoubtedly motivated by a concern to forestall the spread of the consequences of the crisis to the powerful Western economies, but also to elaborate a new model of accumulation with a potential for export to other social formations as a model for a general over-coming of the international economic crisis. Our view is that all this is clearly valid, but for foreign investing circles other material priorities prevail, evid-ently taking two forms. The first concerns the investment potential opened up through the implementation of the Memoranda. One part of the country's pro-ductive fabric is destroyed, leaving a gap to be filled by foreign capital. At the same time, the plummeting of labour costs, the expansion of the reserve army of labour, the extension of flexible work arrangements, all conspire to shape an environment of particularly favourable regulation. The second involves the field of real estate. For a number of historical reasons that cannot be outlined within the parameters of the present chapter, Greece has the highest propor-tion of home ownership in Europe, around 75%. This Greek 'peculiarity' has from the outset been in the sights of the consecutive Memoranda: property taxation at very high rates so that small proprietors, who at the same time have seen their incomes drastically fall as a result of other aspects of Memorandum policies, will find themselves unable to pay their taxes and will be obliged to sell one or more of their properties. The same applies, more dramatically, to those who have taken out a loan to buy a house and, in the new conditions, are not able to meet the payments, so that they risk having it put up for auc-tion. Such a development will benefit not only sections of the bourgeoisie who will be able to buy property at new bargain-basement prices. It will also benefit foreign real estate companies who will exploit the new situation by buying up private residences *en masse*. But this prospect will have another side to it: it will contribute to an overall drastic fall in land prices that will be very attractive to the foreign financial conglomerates that want to invest in infrastructures: ports, airports, the construction of corridors for the passage of natural gas and oil pipelines, wind parks and other installations for the introduction of Renewable Energy Resources, for producing electricity and conveying it to central Europe, for the cultivation of organic crops, and so on.[50] It should nevertheless be noted that these prospects are for when the planned arrangements have been eco-

---

50    Chatzimichalis 2013.

nomically and politically consolidated. For as long as there is a continuation of Greece's economic crisis and the concomitant political instability, foreign investors will remain very wary about coming to Greece. In this light it is characteristic that whereas in 2009 cumulative direct foreign investment in Greece came to 28.1 billion Euros, by 2012 the figure had fallen to 18.8 billion Euros.[51]

### Conclusion

In this chapter we have attempted to highlight the basic elements informing the Greek ruling class's strategy throughout the current crisis. Our key argument has been that neither the reasons for the crisis nor certain aspects of the strategy for overcoming it can be seen in isolation from bourgeois strategies of the past, starting from the period of establishment of the Greek state.

Thus the strategy of the *Megali Idea* prioritised geographical expansion of the country into all areas where there was a significant Greek presence. This had as one of its consequences a downgrading of the importance of economic development and the retention of distinct traditional agrarian characteristics up until the first years of the twentieth century. (The substantial development of ship-owning capital modifies this picture but does not basically change it). This evolution was not just the outcome of adequate state planning. It was to a great extent a by-product of the fact that on the one hand the most important Greek capitalists lived outside Greece, and on the other the perennial political upheavals and multifarious military entanglements had a dampening effect on private investment. It should not be overlooked, of course, that this strategy notched up some notable successes, for within a space of 80 years Greece expanded its territory not just once but a number of times.

Nevertheless, the situation changes after the Asia Minor disaster, which marked the end of the *Megali Idea*. From that point on, a new strategy would be adopted, focusing on economic development but also including a subordinate element, namely the demand for integration into the country of certain additional regions (Dodecanese, Cyprus, Northern Epirus – of which finally only the Dodecanese would become part of Greece, in 1947). This new strategic orientation was to yield certain economic benefits, which were, however, curtailed by the German occupation and the ensuing civil war.

---

51    Characteristically, direct foreign investments are either falling or static in all sectors with the exception of 'electricity, gas and water', which go from a figure of 389 million Euros in 2009 to 1,250 million Euros in 2012, and the sector of 'Agriculture, Mines', which rises dramatically from 69 million Euros to 564 million Euros.

The bourgeoisie's victory in the civil war symbolised continuity of the strategy of economic development based on the following parameters: construction, shipping, tourism, low salaries, emigration of working people, trade, low- and medium-tech industrial production. Association with the EEC (1961) aimed at utilising the country's advantages in exchange for bringing the country into an international framework that was clearly more competitive, without at the same time overlooking the potential eliminatory functions for some sections of capital. On the other hand, it is true that from the beginning of the 1960s up until the international economic crisis of 1973, there was something of a turn towards production of high-technology products, but this was reversed from 1974 onwards.

Factors such as the increase in wages for working people (on account of the post-junta social contract and the evolution of workers' struggles), increase in the cost of imported production goods, not to mention the rise in oil prices, led Greece into a recession after 30 years of growth. As for PASOK, for all its initial hesitations owing to the radical profile it possessed in its early years, from 1985 onwards it inaugurated the orientation of capitalist restructuring, which would continue up to the advent of the crisis. The strategy of upgrading the country's position in the international division of labour was supplemented with elements such as hyper-exploitation of migrants, reduction in labour's share of the fruits of production, adoption of flexible forms of labour, upgrading the role of banks, and the utilisation of European funding.

But the major problem is going to persist. The competitiveness deficit by comparison with the stronger European countries remains a reality, notwithstanding some perfunctory attempts to reduce it, on the one hand through a slight shift towards high technology, on the other through gradual reorientation towards countries outside the capitalist West. Moreover, it has become more acute since Greece entered the Economic and Monetary Union. Inside the Union there is no longer the option of moderating external pressures through recourse to devaluation because of the existence of the common currency. Internal and external mechanisms exist (as they did before the establishment of the single currency) for containment of the consequences of international competition. The internal mechanism is linked to enterprise profitability and includes austerity policies, the distribution of European funding and the reduction of taxation on capital. The external mechanism concerns financial management of the state and includes recourse to borrowing to cover the deficit in the balance of trade and the balance of current accounts.

The salient point is that when the international crisis broke, Greece was particularly seriously affected. GNP began to fall and that in turn increased the debt in percentage terms and gave the impression that Greece would find it impossible to service its debt. Faced with these realities, the Greek ruling class opted for the policies of the Memoranda. What it seeks to do via this Memoranda politics is to establish a different regime of accumulation in Greece, elements of which will also be useable in other social formations, with a view to attempting to overcome the international economic crisis. The first element in the strategy is the break-up of the traditional alliance between the bourgeoisie and the two groupings of the petty-bourgeoisie. A new framework is created of continual downgrading of the role and the position of the petty-bourgeoisie but also of the non-competitive sectors of the bourgeoisie. For this to be accomplished, changes must be made to the internal functioning of the state in the direction of undermining institutions of representation and strengthening centres that are inaccessible to popular control, in conjunction with a general hardening of the repressive mechanisms of the state. The second element is immiseration of broad sectors of the population, exacerbation of social inequalities and an unprecedented expansion of flexible labour relations. The third is the transformation of the Greek state into an idiosyncratic form of inverted protectorate, with a consequent loss of important elements of national sovereignty relevant to the functioning of the economy. This amounts to a 'trade-off' for adoption of measures contributing to a rise in the profitability of domestic capital. The fourth element has to do with the continuation of a process of delinkage from the countries of the West and identification of new markets. Greek direct investment abroad is following more or less the same trajectory.

### References

Babanasis, Stergios and Costas Soulas 1976, *Greece on the periphery of the developed countries*, [in Greek], Athens: Themelio.

Chatziiosif, Christos 2002, 'The refugee shock, constants and changes in the Greek economy' [in Greek], in *History of Greece in the 20th century* edited by Christos Chatziiosif, Volume II, Part I.

Chatzimichalis, Costas 2013, 'Why is the Troika interested in land and real estate?', [In Greek], available at http://enthemata.wordpress.com/2013/09/29/kostisx

Fotopoulos, Takis 1985, *Dependent Development*, [in Greek], Athens: Exantas.

Giannitsis, Tassos 1988, *Greek Industry*, [in Greek], Athens: Gutenberg.

Giannitsis, Tasss 1988b, 'Foreign exchange and the position of Greece in the international division of labour: the perspective for 2000', [in Greek], in *Politics and Society, Economy, External Relations*, edited by Tassos Giannitsis, Ilias Katselis and Panos Kazakos, Athens: Papazisis – Friedrich Eberg Stiftung.

Giannitsis, Tasos, Stavros Zografakis, Ioanna Kastelli and Despoina Mavri – 2009, *Competitiveness and Technology in Greece*, [in Greek], Athens: Papazisis.

Karabelias, Giorgos 1982, *Democracy of the Small-to-Medium*, [in Greek], Athens: Commouna.

Karabelias, Giorgos 1989, *State and society in the post-junta period*, [in Greek], Athens: Exantas.

INE-GSEE 2013, *The Greek economy and employment. 2013 Annual Report*, [in Greek], Athens: INE-GSEE.

Lykos, Martinos, 2012, 'Research and Technology in the Greek Regions;' [in Greek], In *Exit from the Crisis*, edited by Napoleon Maravegias, Athens: Themelio.

Manassaki, Anna, Christos Katiforis and Melina Basardani 2010, 'International competitiveness and the current accounts balance in Greece,' [in Greek] in *The Greek current accounts balance. Causes of imbalance and policy proposals*, edited by Georgios Oinokomou, Isaac Sabethai and Georgios Symigiannis, Athens: Bank of Greece.

Manassaki, Anna and Eleni Koltsida 2010, 'The contribution of EU transfers to the balance of payments and economic growth', [in Greek], in *The Greek current accounts balance. Causes of imbalance and policy proposals*, edited by Georgios Oinokomou, Isaac Sabethai and Georgios Symigiannis, Athens: Bank of Greece.

Milios, John 2000, *The Greek Social Formation*, [in Greek], Athens: Kritiki.

Milios, John 2010, 'The Greek Economy in the 20th century', [in Greek], in *Greece in the 19th and 20th centuries*, edited by Antonis Moissidis and Spyros Sakellaropoulos, Athens: Topos.

Petropoulos, Ioannis and Aikaterini Koumarianou 1977, 'The Period of Othon's Kingdom 1833–1862', [in Greek], *in History of the Greek People*, Vol. XIII, Athens: Ekdotiki Athinon.

Rigos, Alkis 1988, *The Second Greek Republic 1924–1935*, [in Greek], Athens: Themelio.

Sakellaropoulos, Spyros 1998, *The causes of the April coup*, [in Greek], Athens: Livanis.

Sakellaropoulos, Spyros 2014, *Crisis and social stratification in 21st century Greece*, [in Greek], Athens: Topos.

Samaras, Giannis 1986, *State and Capital in Greece*, [In Greek] Athens: Synchroni Epochi.

Stasinopoulos, Giorgos, 2005 'Entrepreneurship: the deficient development parameter in the Greek economy', [in Greek] in *Economic changes and social conflicts in Greece*, edited by Giorgos Argeitis, Athens: Typitheto-G. Dardanos.

Vergopoulos, Costas 1978, *State and Economic Policy in the 19th Century*, [in Greek], Athens: Exantas.

Vergopoulos, Costas 1978a, *Nationalism and Economic Development*, [in Greek], Athens: Exantas.

# CHAPTER 10

# From Resistance to Transitional Programme: the Strange Rise of the Radical Left in Greece

*Christos Laskos and Euclid Tsakalotos*

> Communism is for us not a state of affairs which is to be established, an ideal to which reality [will] have to adjust itself. We call communism the real movement which abolishes the present state of things. The conditions of this movement result from the premises now in existence.
>
> – KARL MARX and FRIEDRICH ENGELS, *The German Ideology*, 1845

∴

SYRIZA's rise has been nothing short of extraordinary. From its uncertain start in 2004, as a coalition of leftist parties and movements, when it received a little over 3% of the vote, and thus just scraped into parliament, few would have predicted its serious challenge for power in the two general elections of 2012,[1] where it received 17% of the vote in May and just under 27% a month later when it became the official opposition in parliament. By the European Parliament elections of 2014 it was the first party, and at the time of writing (January 2015) it seems certain to repeat that performance in the general election, although it is uncertain whether it will achieve an overall majority. How can we account for such a meteoric a rise?

No doubt the severity of the Eurozone crisis, the devastating social and economic effects of the successive structural adjustment programmes imposed by Greece's creditors after 2010, and the usual corrosive effects of IMF involvement on domestic elites would all feature prominently in most accounts. But this leaves unanswered why the Left should be the main beneficiary. After all, elsewhere the beneficiaries from the effects of austerity have more often than not been parties, or movements, of the radical right. And more specifically, why SYRIZA?

---

1  For an accessible account of the 2012 elections, see Mavris 2012.

© KONINKLIJKE BRILL NV, LEIDEN, 2018 | DOI:10.1163/9789004280892_012

Our answer is essentially Gramscian[2] in spirit. SYRIZA understood that it must engage in all forms of resistance to the policies of austerity if it was to create an effective opposition and promote a hegemonic project. To be sure, the 'common sense' of the wider society was difficult to challenge comprehensively – even when SYRIZA started to lead in opinion polls, the qualitative aspects of the same polls still showed considerable support for the dominant narrative of the crisis which had been supported by Greek elites and their supporters in the media: Greece had been living beyond its means and therefore consumption had to be cut; the fault lay with a bloated public sector and the inefficiency of the Greek state; sectionalist forces, once again mainly in the public sector, had blocked essential supply-side reforms and thus had severely impaired the competitiveness of the private sector.[3] Despite this, SYRIZA was able to achieve a more localised hegemony and become the central anti-austerity party of the Left, offering coordinated support to all forms of opposition to the policies of successive austerity governments.

If we can delineate a turning point, then it was surely the decision of Alexis Tsipras, and the leadership of the party, to publicly announce before the May elections of 2012 that SYRIZA had set its sights on forming the next government. This acted as a radical political catalyst, energising those who had participated in multiple forms of social resistance and social solidarity, that had achieved local victories, had brought down two previous austerity governments, but had been unable to change the relentless implementation of austerity policies. Having created multiple ruptures within civil society, the Left was seeking to take the challenge to the state itself.

In this sense SYRIZA seemed to have an intuitive grasp of the concept of the 'integral state', and the fact that without a political challenge at the level of political society, the widespread forms of social resistance were likely, sooner or later, to dissipate. Correspondingly ruling elites had lost considerable ground within civil society and their hold on power was now slanted considerably towards their ability to control the reins of state power. The balance of their hegemony had shifted to an over-reliance on coercion, rather than consent, with the politics of fear playing a central role in periods between elections, but especially so during election campaigns: fear of financial markets, of bank-

---

2   See, in particular, Ian McKay's excellent discussion of Peter Thomas's *The Gramscian Moment* (McKay 2014).

3   The general tenor of what we term the dominant narrative can be seen in Meghir et al. 2010 and Mitsopoulos and Pelagidis 2011. We offer a comprehensive critique of this openly ideological perspective in Laskos and Tsakalotos 2013.

ruptcy and Grexit (that is Greece's expulsion from the Eurozone), of people's savings being lost, and so on. SYRIZA's response by the summer of 2014 was to promote a transitional programme not only to renegotiate its non-sustainable debt, but also to address the growing humanitarian crisis confronting Greece and to kick-start the economy. Moreover, the transitional programme included a set of institutional reforms to break the stranglehold of elites on the state, and thus confront the problems of tax evasion, corruption and lack of transparency. In short, SYRIZA realised that without such interventions within the state itself, ruling elites would in time re-establish their hegemonic project within society, and create new forms of consensus for that hegemony.

Thus at one level SYRIZA's strategy was defensive – to block further austerity and the ability of ruling elites to pursue their neoliberal project in a more hegemonic manner. But at the same time, the transitional strategy was intended not just to block a further deterioration of the position of labour, but also to open new ground for a new political economy to challenge the neoliberal order.

## 1      The Economic and Political Context

Elsewhere,[4] we argue strongly against the exceptionality thesis of the Greek crisis. It is certainly true that Greece was one of the few cases in which widening fiscal deficits and a growing public debt *preceded* the crisis. In other countries, these fiscal problems followed as a result of sorting out the financial crisis and/or the effect of adopting austerity policies. But this is to remain at the surface of things.

Since the mid-1990s, neoliberal apologetics notwithstanding, modernising Greek governments had launched a full panoply of supply-side reforms; including an impressive privatisation programme and a wide range of precarious employment arrangements in both the public and private sectors. To be sure residual leftist and social-democratic sentiment, and organisation, had blocked 'reform' in certain areas, notably pensions, but before the crisis there was little doubt on whose side the momentum lay. But momentum is one thing and a hegemonic project quite another. In short, Greece was open to the same forces that lie behind the crisis of democratic capitalism that has been so brilliantly analysed by Wolfgang Streeck in a series of articles.[5] The neoliberal economy has been unable, as yet at least, to spread economic well-being to

---

4   Laskos and Tsakalotos 2013.
5   See in particular Streeck 2011 and Streeck 2012.

large enough sections of the working and middle classes. Stagnating wages and inequality have been the major signposts of this phenomenon; rising levels of debt the main response. The major difference in the Greek case was that this debt was more public than private. Thin and underdeveloped financial markets meant that Greece could not go down the road of 'privatised Keynesianism' that was more characteristic of the Anglo-Saxon economies. In the latter, private debt shored up stagnating incomes, and thus demand, in the years before the crisis of 2008. So in a very real sense the fiscal crisis in Greece represents a similar phenomenon to the financial crisis elsewhere, with common roots in the attempt to stave off distributional struggle through increased levels of debt.

And of course this commonality extends to responses to the crisis. If the proximate causes of the crisis were macroeconomic imbalances, social inequalities and financial 'excess', it cannot be said that any of these were seriously addressed in the period after 2008. Especially within the Eurozone, the dominant response was austerity. This approach not only misdiagnosed the causes of the crisis; it severely underestimated the threat of the Eurozone entering a poverty trap, disinflation and seemingly endless stagnation or worse. It also ignored the almost self-evident deficiencies of the economic and financial architecture of the Eurozone: the absence of Eurozone debt in Euros, the lack of a large central budget to act as a fiscal stabiliser, the inability of the ECB to act as a lender of last resort, and much else besides. If anything, the political shortcomings were even more acute. Rather than dealing with the financial crisis and peripheral debt at the EU level, the dominant response was bilateral, with the involvement of the IMF in such cases merely underlining the absence of a coordinated response based on European-wide priorities.

To be sure the dominant response was not without a strong political rationale: the crisis as an opportunity to finish off the neoliberal programme of permanently sidelining labour and cutting back social and democratic rights. But this class instinct does not automatically translate into a hegemonic political project. For that to be the case, some sections of the working and middle classes would need to feel that their interests are partly incorporated into the elite project. And in many member states, this just was not the case, leading to widespread disaffection with the European project, and centrifugal political forces, nationalist and secessionist movements, and so on. But, of course, it also led, in some places, to more promising political reactions with the phenomenon of the town squares, and the rise of the political Left, especially in Spain and Greece.

The failures of the Eurozone are well documented and well understood, even if ignored in Berlin and the Commission, and there is little point in rehearsing the arguments here. What needs emphasising is that the response to the economic crisis underlined the crisis in democratic capitalism that had been developing since the previous crisis in the 1970s. In the countries of the periphery of the Eurozone, the economic crisis turned more quickly into a political one. It is important to stress that this political crisis was one of political representation. Thus first in Greece, and then in Spain, the stranglehold of the parties of the centre-left and the centre-right was loosened as they could no longer be seen to be representing important, and more popular, sections of their traditional social base. The most obvious indication of the political crisis was that when the ruling party was in trouble this did not automatically translate into an increase in support for its traditional opponent.

In short, the game had been opened up to those political forces that could credibly argue that they could represent those sections of society that had been abandoned by the parties of the centre-right and centre-left that had converged on neoliberalism before the crisis, and refused to abandon it even afterwards.

## 2      Resistance

SYRIZA had started off as a coalition of eurocommunist, more orthodox but reform-inclined communist, left-social-democratic, maoist, and trotskyist currents, together with a wide range of activists who had been involved in various social movements. As elsewhere, the Greek left was at a low ebb for most of the 1990s, following the demise of the orthodox communist experiment in the East, and the seemingly irrepressible dynamic of neoliberalism in the West. But by the end of the decade, a new potential could be detected with the rise of the anti-war and the anti-global movements. SYRIZA's foundation was built on this new potential and it was crucial to its future development.

For whereas Synaspismos, the largest of the parties in the eventual coalition, had constituted a significant, if small, presence in Greek politics, it too had been affected by the neoliberal juggernaut: frequently, even if often unfairly, it was seen as a mere morally conscious or political corrective to the 'Blairite' transformation of the social-democratic party, PASOK, under Kostas Simitis. A significant minority within Synaspismos had felt uncomfortable with the party's concentration on the central political scene,[6] and its alliance with

---

6    For left-wing currents, 'governmentalism' and its close cousin 'legalism' were seen as mortal
     sins for the Left. Legalism implied a belief that major social change could be achieved merely
     by winning the government and changing laws, while ignoring the need to change the bal-

PASOK in union or local elections, at the cost of grassroots activism and a more openly confrontational ideological and activist stance. By the end of 2004, all this had changed. SYRIZA had stood in its first national election, not with great success to be sure and with considerable backtracking from the Synaspismos leadership after the event. But by the end of the year at the Synaspismos party congress a new leader, and leadership, was elected on a platform of 'turning left' and deepening the commitment to the SYRIZA experiment.

In the period after 2004, and before the Greek crisis entered its troika-dominated phase in the spring of 2010, SYRIZA cut its teeth in a succession of emblematic social struggles, that underlined its radical turn, while, at the same time, providing valuable experience for what was to follow.[7] Significantly, some of these interventions led to successful outcomes. Thus the student and university movement was able to block New Democracy's attempt to change article 16 of the Greek constitution that does not permit private universities. A few years later, students were also instrumental in ensuring a compromise for a large number of immigrants who went on hunger strike to support their right to remain and work in Greece. Other conflicts, such as the violent response by young people to the police murder of Alexis Grigoropoulos in December 2008, which opened up a host of issues to do with education, precarious employment, and the overall predicament of young people in contemporary Greece, led to more uncertain outcomes.

All the above protest movements divided not only Greek society in general, but the parties of the Greek Left. It is difficult to believe that the rise of SYRIZA would have been anything like as impressive if it had not openly supported these, and similar, movements vigorously. To be sure other non-parliamentary parties, and radical organisations, including those of the anarchists and anarchist affinity groups, were heavily involved as well. But SYRIZA was supposed to be a more conventional party, on the right of the orthodox communist party, the KKE. The support of SYRIZA at the time seemed risky (even foolhardy, to some commentators). It was not an easy choice given the conservative nature of Greek society. But SYRIZA managed to keep a fine balance. It refused to accept that one should focus on the violence of the confrontations without examining the nature of the discontent that underlay the violence. It accepted that social movements always have spontaneous elements and a degree of autonomy from political parties. It argued that the role of the radical Left was

---

ance of social forces necessary to impose such changes, and the active social collectivities which could ensure that such changes were transformed into social reality.

7   For a full account of this engagement, see Laskos and Tsakalotos 2013, ch. 5.

not to oppose social polarisation as such, but to provide a more political, and of course non-violent, vehicle for channelling protest towards strategies for social transformation.

The KKE's stance was radically different but hardly radical. Continuing a long tradition of not supporting social movements it does not control, the KKE was hostile to the December events. It sought to ridicule all talk of 'uprising', and attacked SYRIZA as opportunistically seeking to make overtures to anarchist elements. It was a mistake that it was to repeat later with the phenomenon of the town squares with even more fateful political consequences. It seriously underestimated the scale of the polarisation that was to come, and the fact that those not taking sides in such episodes of polarisation face the risk of polit-ical marginalisation. The KKE was also seemingly unaware that social protests were bringing to the fore new actors, new means of political mobilisation and new goals.[8] There would be no need for any Left party to incorporate all these innovations in an uncritical fashion. But to ignore them was a sign of political sclerosis.

For years the KKE had been the dominant party on the Left – SYRIZA and before that Synaspismos were often the poor relation. In any fuller account of the eventual reversal of this relationship, the KKE's stance with respect to the protests discussed here will have to figure prominently.

In the period after the spring of 2010, when the first structural adjustment programme was agreed, and the troika[9] became a seemingly permanent fea-ture on the Greek political landscape, SYRIZA was able to build on its above experience. We cannot go into all the examples here, but it was involved in a huge variety of protest initiatives, from opposing poll taxes, and preventing poor people having their electricity supply cut off, to blocking prescription and hospitable charges to uninsured citizens; and from resisting water and electri-city privatisation to fighting the sacking of some of the poorest public sector workers (including cleaners and high school security guards). And of course SYRIZA gave its full support to the phenomenon of the town squares that was so prominent in the summer of 2011 and contributed greatly to the fall of the first austerity government of George Papandreou in the autumn of the same year.[10]

---

8    See Seferiades and Johnston (eds.) 2012 for a balanced assessment of these new forms of
     political struggle.

9    The troika was the enforcing agent of the structural adjustment programme imposed by
     Greece's creditors, with representatives of the EU, the IMF and the ECB. In many ways this
     was an ad hoc institution, of dubious legality, that underlined the willingness of EU elites
     to by-pass existing, and more democratic, institutions.

10   Douzinas 2011.

TABLE 10.1   *400 initiatives in 60 Greek cities, in around 70 areas of Athens*

| | |
|---|---|
| c. 45 | social clinics and pharmacies |
| c. 60 | solidarity networks, kitchen collectives, exchange bazaars, etc. |
| c. 35 | co-operative coffee shops and restaurants |
| c. 35 | working collectives (web-radios, web-sites, civil engineers and architects collectives, accountants, computer engineers, web-designers, educational crammers, music schools, etc.) |
| c. 15 | time banks |
| c. 40 | social and cultural spaces including ΕΜΠΡΟΣ theatre |
| c. 70 | 'No intermediaries' and 'solidarity trade' initiatives Networking services – providing consulting, good practices, legal support, etc. Publishing initiatives |

For our purposes it is perhaps more important to emphasise the wide range of initiatives that developed after 2010 in the area of social solidarity and the social economy. Some of these are listed in Table 10.1.

Whether or not these initiatives were directly productive activities, SYRIZA embraced them from the beginning. Once more, other leftist currents, notably the KKE, were outflanked. Given the scale of the humanitarian crisis and thus of unmet social needs, the claim that such initiatives at best were inadequate, and at worst diverted workers from the immediate task of overturning the government, could not but ring a hollow note. And this for a number of reasons:

1.  Such initiatives constituted a direct intervention at the level of social needs. In terms of Lebowitz's analysis,[11] they supported the 'logic of labour' in contradistinction to the 'logic of capital' (i.e. the profit motive). In any transitional programme they could potentially mesh with the Left's supply-side policy for the productive economy by promoting not only other operating principles but also more diverse social productive collectivities.
2.  They were able to show that the Left could be effective even in opposition. Thus, to give just one example, by the summer of 2014, even the austerity government of Antonis Samaras was forced to bring to parliament meas-

---

11   Lebowitz 2003. The schema of the 'economy of needs' had been worked out in some detail in a programmatic congress of Synaspismos, held in 2009, and it subsequently provided a major input into SYRIZA's programme.

ures to deal with those workers who had lost access to medical service as a result of losing their job and thus (after a period) their social insurance. This social issue was brought to the fore by the social clinics and pharmacies, which in the early days had dealt mostly with immigrants, but which eventually had to support large numbers of Greek citizens as well.

3.  They were able to influence the environment beyond their immediate scope. Thus, to stick with the example of the social clinics, they aspired not to replace the National Health Service but to imbue it with a new ethos of social solidarity and a sense of public service. It is difficult to underestimate the potential of this force, given the widespread distrust of the Greek state that has been riddled with bureaucratic practices and clientelistic politics.

4.  Finally, such initiatives have the ability to intervene more directly at the level of ideology. For such alternative practices have the ability by operating on the external environment (i.e. social needs) to change those involved in them – the values of solidarity, collective action and egalitarianism are learnt through participation in political structures that can lead to concrete results.[12] In successful cases this also helps to reverse the 'hollowing-out' of democracy that has been such a feature of the neoliberal era.[13]

It is certainly the case that the above dynamic would have been strengthened if at the same time there had been more examples of co-operatives, self-managed firms and worker occupations of failing companies. In many sectors, such as agricultural co-operatives or manufacturing production, the wider Left, and not just SYRIZA, just did not have enough of a presence to be able to take such initiatives. Indeed the active presence of PASOK in such sectors in the period after 1981 had given co-operatives and self-management a bad name, almost synonymous with corruption and inefficient management. But this should not detract from the overall impact of the initiatives that did spring up. It contributed to a widespread belief within SYRIZA that any transitional programme would need to give space to such alternatives as part of a strategy for social transformation.

---

12    For a theoretical defence of this point, see Suchting 1983, pp. 119–20.
13    Mair 2013.

3        Transitional Programme

The turning point for SYRIZA's fortunes, as we have said, was the explicit goal of winning governmental power before the elections of 2012. This was based on an assessment that without such power, whatever gains had been made by social protest movements, or alternative social practices, could collapse as easily as they had grown. Furthermore SYRIZA was in a good position to make this shift, precisely because it was the left-wing force that had argued for the greatest possible unity amongst the Left. Its first party congress in 2013 argued that common ground could be found: stretching from left social democracy to the KKE and the non-parliamentary left (especially the forces of ANTARSYA).[14] While critics, such as Kouvelakis,[15] claimed that SYRIZA's appeal rested on the narrow grounds of anti-austerity, this was clearly unsustainable.

Significant differences aside, SYRIZA's appeal had more in common with the Comintern's shift towards the strategy of the United Front in the early 1920s.[16] By the early autumn of 2014, SYRIZA had presented a set of immediate measures that could aspire to unite working people, irrespective of political differences, stop the further deterioration of their position and their ability to organise, while at the same time opening fissures within the austerity coalitions in Greece and Europe. In this sense the strategy was both defensive and offensive. It relied on three pillars: firstly, measures to respond to the humanitarian crisis, such as access to energy for heating, social housing and food coupons; secondly, measures to kickstart the economy through increasing the minimum wage and addressing people's inability to pay back their mortgages and tax arrears; and thirdly, a set of institutional interventions aiming to begin the transformation of the Greek state: to address corruption and the lack of transparency, to limit the ability of Greek elites to pay taxes only on a voluntary basis, and to introduce elements of social accountability and direct democracy. If we add to this the commitment to redistribute income, to begin to reverse the commodification of social services especially in the areas of health and education, and support the initiatives discussed in the previous section, then we can see

---

14    ANTARSYA is also a coalition of disparate Maoist, Trotskyist and more orthodox communist groupings. While more willing than the KKE to co-operate in the forms of resistance described in the previous section, they ruled out more central political co-operation, mainly, but not exclusively, because of their disagreement over SYRIZA's more pro-European stance.

15    Kouvelakis 2011d.

16    Riddel 2012.

that the concept of a transitional programme is a fair description of the overall approach in question.

More contentious, amongst the Greek Left at least, was SYRIZA's commitment to working towards a solution to Greece's massive debt problem within the EU. From early on in the crisis, SYRIZA had argued that the problem of debt was a European problem that needed a Europe-wide response.[17] Its argument that Greece could be treated in the same manner as Germany had been at the 1953 London Conference was appealing to many outside observers. After all the 1953 solution, which had included a debt haircut, repayment of the remaining debt in line with the performance of the economy, and the Marshall Plan investment programme, had paved the way for Germany's postwar economic miracle. Moreover, SYRIZA was suggesting that a mutualisation of European debt was one element in addressing the Eurozone's continuous stagnation and its ineffective economic and financial architecture. It was hoped that such an approach could lead to wider alliances throughout Europe for those forces searching for an exit from the policies of austerity. While such arguments were marginal in the elections of 2012, things had changed by early 2015; not only with the rise of Podemos in Spain and Sinn Féin in Ireland, but also at the level of intellectuals throughout the EU.

Furthermore, SYRIZA had argued that a 'national road to socialism' had little to say on how Greece, or any other economy for that matter, could take on the power of financial markets and MNCs – capital outflows, the relocation of manufacturing, not to mention tax evasion and avoidance were all issues that could be better dealt with at the supra-national level. Finally, the fear was that the collapse of the euro could be better embraced by the radical right than the Left, as the examples of Farage in the UK and Le Pen in France testify. The fear was for a straight re-run of the interwar period of rival nationalisms, competitive devaluations, and so on.[18]

The strategy of exiting the euro had one further major blind spot. It suggested that the euro, and the EU in general, were unreformable since the balance of class power was too strongly in favour of the pro-austerity and neoliberal reform forces.[19] A return to the drachma, while difficult in the short-term as it was sanguinely expressed, could allow for the rapid imposition of capital controls, the nationalisation of the banks and the implementation of an alternative

---

17  And there was no shortage of proposals for such a solution – see Varoufakis and Holland 2012.

18  For an opposing view, see Kouvelakis 2011d and Lapavitsas 2012. For our critique of their arguments, see Laskos and Tsakalotos 2013, ch. 6.

19  Lapavitsas et al. 2010.

industrial policy. In one sense this constituted an alternative transitional programme. In another it suppressed such a programme, replacing it with a quick
transition to a very traditional conception of what constitutes a socialist economy.

From the standpoint of SYRIZA, this approach had two further drawbacks.
Firstly, it relied heavily on the ability of the existing state to take a central role
in the quick succession of moves necessary to arrive at the new arrangements.
At the same time, the overall conception was underworked with respect to
how the nationalised banks would work, or how industrial policy was to transform the productive base of the Greek economy. Anybody familiar with the
discussions of the British Alternative Economic Strategy in the '70s, or French
discussions with the Common Programme of the Left in the '80s, might be for-
given for expressing some surprise that there had been no development of the
Left's conception in the intervening period. But, secondly, and perhaps of more
importance, this alternative approach assumed what needed to be shown: that
beyond the desire to stop austerity and experiment with a new approach, there
was a widespread popular consciousness in favour of more openly socialist
solutions. Earlier we expressed some scepticism concerning this, and argued
that during the period of resistance the 'common sense' of the age continued
to be affected by ruling ideas about the inefficiency of the state and the importance of the competitiveness of the private sector economy.

However, SYRIZA's strategy was transitional in a more robust sense. It saw the
need to defend labour's interests in the short run; in the first instance blocking more austerity, and in the second beginning the process of recovery. At
the same time it realised that changing people's consciousness concerning the
superiority of collective solutions, in terms of both social justice and economic
efficiency, was a matter to be demonstrated by practical experience. Its support
for all those initiatives of social solidarity and the social economy must be seen
in this light. There was a strong Poulantzian undercurrent in this conception.
Poulantzas, in his later writings at least,[20] held that the state was essentially
a relation that expressed the existing balance of class forces. For the Left, the
state must be transformed in the direction of deepening representative democracy, as well as establishing forms of direct democracy, while at the same time,
encouraging self-managed, co-operative and collective enterprises within society and the economy as a whole.

---

20      Poulantzas 1980.

### Conclusions

If SYRIZA's progression from protest and social interventions at the level of civil society to seeking the extension of its hegemony within political society (the state) can be conceptualised within a Gramscian problematic of the 'integral state', then its concept of what to do with the state is more in the spirit of Poulantzas. But this Poulantzian element was also based on an understanding of the 'real movement' of things, to return to the quote at the beginning of this essay. After all, the desire for more participation, and experiments in direct democracy, was also a central feature of the demands of the indignados of the town squares. Thus SYRIZA's call for unity, as well as its overall strategy, sought to build not just on its own theoretical insights and experience but also on what it detected as the autonomous movements stemming from society that it needed to support and embrace.

Not surprisingly, the whole strategy was not without its blind spots or unknowns. One set of questions has to do with SYRIZA's European-wide strategy. Would SYRIZA be able to renegotiate a deal over the Greek debt and thus have the time to show the first elements of a different approach to exiting the crisis? Would its election and firm stance in any such negotiation lead to widespread movements of solidarity in the rest of Europe? Would more centrist forces see the new government as an opportunity to attempt to break the austerity stranglehold operating within the EU as a whole, and not just the Eurozone? At one level, EU elites would have every interest in crushing a government of the Left in Greece 'pour encourager les autres'. But on the other hand, such a stance would display a contempt for the democratic process in member states that would surely further undermine support for the European ideal. A reaffirmation, on the part of the powers that be in the EU, that any democratic shift to a more socially just Europe is permanently off the agenda would form an unstable basis for any future hegemonic project.

A second set of questions is more internal to the Greek context. Could a SYRIZA government inspire the notoriously bureaucratic and inefficient Greek state to operate differently? Could it generalise the good examples, of which there are many, to imbue public servants with a sense of public service? At the same time, would it be able to take on powerful private sector interests and their unhealthy umbilical ties to the state? These are all important questions, as they all relate to the issue of changing the 'common sense' of ruling ideas within Greece. Most important, in this respect, is demonstrating that a reformed, and more accountable, public sector, could become part of the solution and not the problem.

A final set of questions concern the relationship between the state and society, the state and the economy. Would SYRIZA's institutional reforms at the level of the economy find social collectivities willing to take the new framework and run with it? Would SYRIZA's support for a pluralistic range of social forms in production and finance harmonise with such collectivities and promote a new political economy? Perhaps these are the most difficult questions of all, as the Left as a whole has struggled throughout the period of neoliberal hegemony to articulate an alternative vision for the real economy.

But asking the right questions is a crucial step in developing such alternative visions. As Hall and Massey have argued,[21] the current crisis of capitalism is one of many 'moments', of which the economic is just one. And SYRIZA's strange rise is in part a function of its ability in the last few years to ask the right questions that go beyond the economic moment. There has been a certain dialectic at play in SYRIZA's rise to power. In its early period, it was critical of the strategy of aspiring to governmental power without intervening to change the balance of social forces before such an event, or understanding the role of wider participation in the aftermath of any electoral victory. This, we would argue, was the crucial element in their success story to date. Whether there will be a happy ending remains, at the time of writing, uncertain. But whatever the outcome, there are surely valuable lessons for the Left beyond Greece.

### References

Douzinas, Costas 2011, *Resistance and Philosophy in the Crisis: Greece and the Future of Europe* [In Greek], Athens: Alexandreia.

Hall, Stuart and Doreen Massey 2010, 'Interpreting the Crisis', *Soundings*, 44: 57–71.

Kouvelakis, Stathis 2011, 'The Greek Cauldron', *New Left Review*, 2/72: 17–32.

Lapavitsas, Costas 2012, 'Default and Exit from the Eurozone: A Radical Left Strategy', *Socialist Register 2012: The Crisis and the Left*, 288–97.

Lapavitsas, Costas, A. Kaltenbrunner, D. Lindo, J. Michell, J.P. Painceira, E. Pires, J. Powell, A. Stenfors, and E. Teles 2010, *Eurozone Crisis: beggar thyself and thy neighbour*, Research on Money and Finance, Occasional Report.

Laskos, Christos and Euclid Tsakalotos 2011, *No Turning Back: Capitalist Crises, Social Needs, Socialism*, [In Greek], Athens: KaPsiMi editions.

Laskos, Christos and Euclid Tsakalotos 2012, *22 things that they tell you about the Greek crisis that aren't so*, [In Greek], Athens: KaPsiMi editions.

---

21    Hall and Massey 2010.

Laskos, Christos and Euclid Tsakalotos 2013, *Crucible of Resistance: Greece, the Eurozone and the World Economic Crisis*, London: Pluto Press.

Lebowitz, Michael 2003, *Beyond 'Capital': Marx's Political Economy of the Working Class*, London: Macmillan.

Mair, Peter 2013, *Ruling the Void: the Hollowing-Out of western Democracy*, London: Verso.

Mavris, Yannis, 2012, 'Greece's Austerity Election' *New Left Review*, 76: 95–107.

Mckay, Ian 2014, 'Escaping the Throne Room: Peter Thomas and the Gramscian Moment', *Historical Materialism*, 22:2: 63–98.

Meghir Costa, Dimitri Vayanos and Nikos Vettas 2010, 'Greek reforms can yet stave off default', *Financial Times*, 23 August.

Mitsopoulos, Michael and Theodore Pelagidis 2011, *Understanding the Crisis in Greece*, London: Macmillan.

Poulantzas, Nicos 1980, *State, Power, Socialism*, London: Verso.

Riddell, John 2012, *Toward the United Front. Proceedings of the Fourth Congress of the Communist International, 1922*, Chicago: Haymarket Books.

Seferiades, Seraphim and Hank Johnston (eds.) 2012, *Violent Protest, Contentious Politics, and the Neoliberal State*, London: Ashgate.

Streeck, Wolfgang 2011, 'The Crises of Democratic Capitalism', *New Left Review* 2/71:5–29.

Streeck, Wolfgang 2012, 'Markets and Peoples: Democratic Capitalism and European Integration', *New Left Review* 2/73: 63–71.

Suchting, Wallis Arthur 1983, *Marx: An Introduction*, Sussex: Wheatsheaf Books.

Varoufakis Yanis and Stuart Holland 2012, 'A modest proposal for resolving the Eurozone crisis', *Intereconomics* 47, 4: 240–47.

# CHAPTER 11

# In Search of the Modern Prince: a Critical Absence Reconfirmed through the Greek Experience

*Alexandros Chrysis*

## 1    Defining the Problem

There is no doubt that we are still living in a period of a global capitalist crisis, the concrete identity of which is quite difficult to define. Since, however, it is not the aim of this article to analyse the character of the crisis, which started in 2008 and was rapidly transferred from USA to Europe, let's take for granted that this is not a regular cyclical capitalist crisis. It is an ongoing process, the causes of which lie deep within the structure of the capitalist social formation and its results embrace social life as a totality.

As far as Greece is concerned, it must be admitted that what is often characterised as a 'Greek public debt crisis' is a specific aspect and a crucial outcome of the broader EU capitalist crisis, a crisis due to an over-accumulation of capital, that provoked a neoliberal austerity policy on behalf of the dominant bourgeois classes and, more or less, massive protests from the part of the dominated social classes and strata. Actually, the Greek experience is not an exception to, but an expression of, the general socio-economic, political and cultural dynamics that push the European Union and Eurozone countries towards systemic turmoil. Moreover, it is worth noting that the Greek case reveals, in a dramatic manner, how social movements or protests and demonstrations appear, develop and die during the hard days of crisis.

In the following analysis, it will become evident that any optimistic interpretation of the given situation leads to a false conclusion. Listen, for example, to Antonio Negri: 'The more the crisis advances and the movements mature, the more one feels that something decisive is being produced in the consciousness of the workers'.[1] While in abstracto such an argument sounds banal, in concreto it proves to be nothing more than wishful thinking. At least, for the time being, the more the crisis advances, the more one feels that the radicalisation of the working masses becomes a myth.

---

1  Negri 2013, p. 30.

On the other hand, Alain Badiou's quite pessimistic interpretation of the Greek case seems closer to reality. While offering a sceptical take on the optimism of Costas Douzinas, who discerns the emergence of a new political subject on the terrain of the crisis,[2] Badiou recognises a feeling of 'general political impotence' and insists that the resistance movement on a European level 'looks more like a delaying tactic than the bearer of a genuine political alternative'.[3]

According to the French thinker, not only in Greece, but also in France and other countries as well,

> what is striking ... is the manifest impotence of the progressive forces to compel even the slightest meaningful retreat of the economic and state powers that are seeking to submit the people unreservedly to the new (though long-standing and fundamental) law of thoroughgoing liberalism.[4]

As Badiou suggests, it is wrong to explain this political impotence of the masses in terms of a lack of courage. Although there was a strong popular resistance across Europe, and especially in Greece, 'no new thinking of politics has emerged on a mass scale from these attempts, no new vocabulary has emerged from the rhetoric of protest, and the union bosses have finally managed to convince everyone that we must wait ... for elections'.[5]

In the analysis that follows, I am going to argue that there are two ways of dealing with the mass demonstrations and protests which took place in Greece and elsewhere during the recent years of the economic, socio-political and cultural crisis. From an anti-capitalist point of view, the ups and downs of recent activism can be studied and interpreted in either a Marxist or a post-Marxist way.[6]

---

2  Douzinas 2013, particularly pp. 137 ff. and 176 ff. In an optimistic direction, under the influence of John Holloway's theory, see also Katerina Nasioka (Nasioka 2014). For an analysis of the social and psychological effects of the Greek crisis using the terms of Erich Fromm's philosophy of hope, see Panayota Gounari's work (Gounari 2014).

3  Badiou 2013, p. 44.

4  Ibid.

5  Ibid.

6  It is worth explaining from the outset that I use the term 'post-Marxism' and its derivatives in a rather loose and descriptive way and not in a strictly academic or scholastic sense. In this article I define as 'post-Marxist' thinkers like Negri, Badiou and Žižek, who, despite their differences: (a) come to the ideological forefront after (i.e. post) Marxism's classical period; (b) remain in permanent tension with the Marxist tradition and Marx's own writings; while (c) moving against and going beyond Marxism.

In the next part of this chapter, I will proceed with a critical presentation of how post-Marxist thinkers like Negri, Žižek and Badiou evaluate the people's struggles against the capitalist crisis and the neoliberal austerity policy of the European Union and its states, with special emphasis on the case of Greece. This brief critical presentation will reach its decisive point while commenting on the issue of the political subject and the so-called 'organisational question' as confronted by philosophers like those mentioned above. Then, I will juxta-pose post-Marxist arguments, whose popularity intensified during the years of the Greek crisis, with the Gramscian theory of the Modern Prince as the Marx-ist theory of a modern revolutionary party.

In fact, the current chapter will discuss the hypothesis according to which the Greek case reconfirms an almost forgotten truth as regards the strategy and tactics of the Left: as long as a Modern Prince, namely a modern Marxist revolu-tionary party, is absent, there is no hope for mobilisations, demonstrations and protests to be transformed into a social and political movement, there is no hope for a revolt to become a revolution, there is no anti-capitalist/communist way-out of the blind alley of capitalism.

## 2      Post-Marxist Politics and Social Movements in the Age of Crisis

It is impossible to evaluate post-Marxist interpretations of the anti-capitalist movements and their perspectives, unless we take into consideration how par-ticular thinkers or currents of thought confront capitalism in our time. From this point of view, it is worth distinguishing between post-Marxist thinkers such as Negri and Žižek who insist that twenty-first century capitalism is, in fact, a postmodern or an already radically changed capitalism, and other thinkers like Badiou who, despite their post-Marxist views in crucial issues of political the-ory and practice, believe that capitalism still retains the fundamental features of its classical period.

According to Negri, we are living in a postmodern capitalism, grounded on the terrain of the metropolis. This means that we are acting in terms of 'biopol-itical capitalism',[7] within the global frame of which a new form of class struggle occurs, a 'biopolitical' kind of class struggle.[8] As Negri points out,

---

7   Negri 2013, p. 26.
8   Negri 2013, p. 28.

whereas, in the past, it fell upon the factory to centralize the organization of labour, today it is the metropolis that is saddled with this task: it is the metropolis that centralizes the networks of co-operative labour, whether cognitive or not, and that, through the contacts it allows, heightens the degree of tension and fusion of production and struggle.[9]

Through such an interpretation of contemporary capitalism, Negri draws the conclusion that the social movements of our times try and succeed, to a considerable degree, in reshaping the potential of the past revolt and revolution experience into a new strategy. According to this post-Marxist theory, protests, riots and every other sort of social mobilisation aim at 'constituting the multitude institutionally', that is, at 'transforming the social experience of the multitude into a *political institution*'.[10] But what kind of a political institution would that be?

[T]he current movements demand ... that we go beyond the constitutional model of modernity of the eighteenth, nineteenth, twentieth centuries – that is, the constitutional model that effaces every trace of constituent power as soon as the revolutionary phase has come to an end ... Since the spring of 2011, every movement has expressed the desire for a conflictual 'counter-democracy' ... These movements state their demand for biopolitical democratic constitutions that do not immediately transform themselves, by playing on legality and juridical formality, into mechanisms of oppression.[11]

No one can deny the fact that social movements and protests, not only in Europe, but also across the Arabic countries as well, raised the issue of democracy with intensity; actually, it is the Greek case that absolutely reconfirms the significance of democracy as a central demand for the fighting people. Nevertheless, the struggle for a 'real democracy',[12] a postmodern type of direct democracy, the fight for an open-ended radicalisation of politics through the creative and subversive *potentia* of the multitude does not seem to meet Negri's optimism. Unfortunately, the political efficiency and the institutional outcome of these battles are extremely poor.

---

9    Negri 2013, p. 31.
10   Negri 2013, p. 30.
11   Ibid.
12   Hardt and Negri 2011.

On the other hand, Negri's theoretical attempt to combine the internationalist content of contemporary social movements with radical political-institutional forms proves to be problematic. In my opinion, his self-evident conclusion that 'a political path which lacks continental dimensions in the midst of globalization' is nothing more than a blind alley[13] comes into conflict with his claim that 'the European Union is necessary and irreversible'.[14] At the end of the day, Negri's international anti-capitalist tactics and strategy of constructing 'new institutions of commons' is incompatible with his analysis of the European Union. At this point, it is worth mentioning that the Greek case is revealing indeed. On the basis of the Greek experience, it has been definitely reconfirmed that it is impossible for a European anti-capitalist movement to reach its targets without confronting both the institutions and the policies of the European Union as the main enemies of the people's movement.

Besides, it is really important to notice that, in full opposition to his argument on the necessity and irreversibility of the European Union and in open contradiction to his post-Marxist decentred methodology and politics, Negri comes up with a kind of traditional tactics, as he proposes a frontal attack against a concrete power centre, against the institutional nucleus of the European Union; he insists that 'the crux of the discussion today no doubt consists in coming up with an action against the European Central Bank, in so far as in Europe today it is the ECB that incarnates, in its own way, the Winter Palace'.[15] Needless to say, once again his optimism betrays him: there is not even the slightest indication that such an anti-capitalist mass action is on the way.[16]

For his part, Slavoj Žižek, without endorsing Negri's frame of analysis, admits that capitalism has changed dramatically during the last few decades. Following his own theoretical path, Žižek believes that 'the bourgeoisie in the classic sense ... tend to disappear: capitalists reappear as a subset of salaried workers – managers who are qualified to earn more by their competence ...'.[17]

Referring to the 'new bourgeoisie' as a class of 'salaried managers', Žižek focuses his attention on the so-called 'surplus-wage', the function of which is mainly not economic, but political, since it contributes to the survival of the

---

13    Negri 2013, p. 32.

14    Ibid.

15    Ibid.

16    From his own point of view, however, the libertarian post-Marxist thinker John Holloway, commenting on the Greek demonstrations and protests, seems to converge with Negri's optimism (Holloway 2012).

17    Žižek 2012, p. 10.

'middle class' and the maintenance of social cohesion.[18] In other words, according to Žižek's approach, the social structure of capitalism has already changed, given the fact that a new bourgeois class appeared whose members are paid above the minimum proletarian wage and fight to guarantee their economic position and social status.

At this point it is worth noting that the Slovenian thinker takes advantage of the concept of 'surplus-wage' in order to evaluate the anti-capitalist movements and protests of our times. Although these protests appear to be directed against the vulgar logic of the market, Žižek has no doubt that they are really turning against the downgrading of the economic and social position of the salaried bourgeoisie's lower strata. While admitting that the rebirth of the protests during the recent capitalist crisis must not be reduced to the mobilisation of the salaried bourgeoisie, Žižek believes that the anti-capitalist protests of our times

> are not proletarian protests, but protests against the threat of being reduced to a proletarian status ... This also accounts for the new wave of student protests: their main motivation is arguably the fear that higher education will no longer guarantee them a surplus-wage in later life.[19]

It is exactly in this framework that Žižek places and analyses the Greek case. He insists on the existence and dynamic activity of a Greek new bourgeoisie as a new salaried class fighting to maintain its economic and social privileges:

> Greece is a special case here: over the last few decades, a new salaried bourgeoisie (especially in the over-extended state administration) has been created, with EU financial help, and much of the ongoing protest is a response to the threat of losing these privileges.[20]

I am not going to comment at length on Žižek's concept of a new 'salaried bourgeoisie', though his approach sounds to me rather unsubstantiated. Particularly as far as Greece is concerned, just a few special elements of its social structure, such as a rather high percentage of a self-employed, petty bourgeois and rural population in relation to a relatively poor industrial sector, are not adequate to

---

18    Žižek 2012, p. 11.
19    Žižek 2012, p. 12.
20    Ibid.

refute the fact that the main social antithesis remains the one between capital and labour, bourgeoisie and working class.[21]

Actually, the proletarianisation of the middle class, despite its intensity during the years of the ongoing capitalist crisis, is not a recent social phenomenon. Suffice it to say that, in the pages of *The Communist Manifesto*, Marx and Engels already provide an accurate description of the proletarianisation process, arguing that capitalist development leads to a frontal conflict between bourgeois and proletarian. Žižek, however, adopts a rather narrow definition of the proletariat and draws a wrong conclusion as regards the existence and activity of a non-existent 'new bourgeoisie'. Under the impact of a post-Marxist eclecticism, he confuses the objectively determined class position(s) of the protesters as proletarians with the ideological illusions many of them share as former members of the middle class and petty bourgeoisie.

Contrary to philosophers and political thinkers such as Negri and Žižek, Alain Badiou faces the revival of anti-capitalist movements and riots in connection to his clearly expressed view that capitalism of the twenty-first century remains the same in relation to its fundamental characteristics:

> Contemporary capitalism possesses all the features of classical capitalism ... Basically, today's world is exactly the one which, in a brilliant anticipation, a kind of true science fiction, Marx heralded as the full unfolding of the irrational and, in truth, monstrous potentialities of capitalism.[22]

According to Badiou, we are now living in an 'intervallic period', which means that we are living in a period during which 'the revolutionary idea of the preceding period ... is dormant. It has not yet been taken up by a new sequence in its development. An open, shared and universally practicable figure of emancipation is wanting'.[23] Following this rather realistic and, at the same time, quite pessimistic approach, our epoch is characterised by an *aporia*, by a lack of transition from capitalism to a society practically inspired by and oriented towards the communist Idea.

While making a crucial distinction between three types of riots – immediate, latent, and historical – Badiou focuses his analysis on the historical type of riot. A 'historical riot' is not a revolution, since, contrary to a revolution, historical

---

21    For a recent critical approach to the Greek class structure in relation to the current anti-capitalist movement, see Gaitanou 2014.

22    Badiou 2012, p. 11.

23    Badiou 2012, p. 39.

riots (for example, the riots of the Arab Spring) do not offer an alternative to the question of political power. In an intervallic period such as ours, when 'the riot is the guardian of the history of emancipation',[24] Badiou defines the historical type of riot as the transition from 'limited localization to the construction of an enduring central site', from 'imitation to qualitative extension', from 'the nihilistic din of the riotous attacks to the invention of a single slogan that envelops all the disparate voices'.[25]

In terms of this typology, it is obvious that the Greek experience does not correspond to the historical type of riot. In my opinion, the application of Badiou's criteria leads to the definite conclusion that the Greek protests and demonstrations fit better into a kind of 'immediate riot', which 'can only combine weak localizations (at the site of the rioters) with limited extensions (through imitation)'.[26]

At this point, it is, therefore, worth taking a closer look at Badiou's description of the immediate riot:

> The subject of immediate riots is always impure. That is why they are neither political nor even pre-political. In the best of cases – and this is already a good deal – they make do with paving the wave for an historical riot; in the worst, they merely indicate that the existing society, which is always a state organisation of Capital, does not possess the means altogether to prevent the advent of an historical sign of rebellion in the desolate spaces for which it is responsible.[27]

I am afraid that the current situation proves even worse than the most pessimistic version of immediate riot as defined by Badiou. Just a few years after the mobilisation of the Greek people reached its climax, there is not even a sign of rebirth; there is not even a sign of a forthcoming anti-capitalist historical riot or uprising not only in Greece, but all over Europe as well. The existing capitalist society, organised and fortified through the mechanisms of the bourgeois state, seems invincible.

There is no doubt that post-Marxist political theories, such as those mentioned above, face serious difficulties in their attempt to determine and evaluate the deeper reasons of this socio-political immobility. On the other hand, the narrow limits of this chapter do not favour an extensive analysis of the prob-

---

24    Badiou 2012, p. 41.
25    Badiou 2012, pp. 33–5.
26    Badiou 2012, p. 25.
27    Badiou 2012, p. 26.

lem. That is why I prefer to focus my attention on the issue that turned out to be of critical significance for thinkers like Negri, Žižek and Badiou; it is the issue of the political subject, strictly related to the 'organisational question'. In fact, the following analysis will make clear that this is the nodal point of a contemporary anti-capitalist theory and practice from either a post-Marxist or a Marxist point of view. An anti-capitalist theory of the political subject and its organisation is the central point where post-Marxism and classical Marxism meet and fight each other in order to take the lead on the ideological terrain, while trying to interpret as accurately as possible the absence of a massive and efficient resistance against the capitalist neoliberal policy of our times.

It is all-important to notice, however, that, through personal paths and despite their differences, post-Marxist thinkers converge on the rejection of the party as regards both its historical and its theoretical classical Marxist connotations.

One of the most striking examples of such a rejection is, of course, Michael Hardt's and Antonio Negri's argument as presented in a series of articles, written during the recent years of crisis, and exposed in detail in their *Declaration*; commenting on the Arab revolts and the 'Occupy Wall Street' movement, the two post-Marxist thinkers find the opportunity to defend the horizontal network-type of organisation and openly attack not only the political representative system in general, but, especially, what they call the 'Bolshevik theory' of the party: 'No, the old Bolshevik theory of passage of political consciousness from spontaneity to organization no longer has place here',[28] argue Hardt and Negri and declare without hesitation that

> as singularities we gain free mobility in networks ... The form of political organization is central here: a decentralized multitude of singularities communicates horizontally ... Demonstrations and political actions are born today not from a central committee that gives the word but rather from the coming together of and the discussion among numerous small groups.[29]

According to Hardt and Negri, the classical political party, both in its parliamentary and in its vanguard form, is out of date.[30] In their opinion, the anti-capitalist movements of our times must continue to deny this vertical and

---

28    Hardt and Negri 2012, p. 35.

29    Hardt and Negri 2012, p. 36.

30    Hardt and Negri 2012, p. 61.

hierarchical type of organisation and proceed to the construction of horizontal networks in order to fight as absolutely autonomous political subjects.

Hardt and Negri show no mercy to the parties of the Left, those corrupted and delegitimised 'parties of lament', as they ironically call them.[31] They denounce without any reservation the passive stance of those parties with regard to the ongoing destruction of the welfare state and their inability to react effectively against the neoliberal policy of international and national capitalist institutions. So far so good; it is worth underlining, however, that this post-Marxist critique turns against not only the social-liberal politics of the European parties of the Left, but also the fundamental positions of the classical Marxist theory of the party.

Moreover, the two post-Marxists philosophers argue against the 'traditional political thinkers and organisers' of the Left who defend a pessimistic interpretation of the anti-capitalist riots and revolts of the twenty-first century all over the world. Hardt and Negri believe that those thinkers, stuck in their theoretical and political past, face the party like a church and the masses as believers without critical thinking and political initiative of their own.[32]

Following this post-Marxist interpretation, political theorists and cadres who still think and act in terms of classical Marxism, have no alternative but to express, one way or another, their disappointment as regards the content and form of the recent struggles. For their part, Hardt and Negri insist on the use of the 'party-church' comparison and attack with bitter irony all those Marxists who believe that without a vanguard party there will be no revolution. For the authors of the post-Marxist *Declaration*, the aim is not to refute the need for organisation; it is a matter of rejecting the organisational model of the party, while defending the horizontal-network organisation of the multitudes. Hardt and Negri reassure us that they are against anarchy, if by anarchy we mean chaos. Nevertheless, they are absolutely convinced that an anti-capitalist movement has the power to imagine and create new types of organisation by its own forces without submitting to the ruling ideology and practice of any party-vanguard. That is why they declare with emphasis:

> We need to empty the churches of the Left even more, and burn them down! These movements are powerful not despite their lack of leaders but because of it. They are organized horizontally as multitudes, and their insistence on democracy at all levels is more than a virtue but a key to

---

31   Hardt and Negri 2012, p. 76.
32   Hardt and Negri 2012, p. 90.

their power. Furthermore, their slogans and arguments have spread so widely not despite but because the positions they express cannot be summarized or disciplined in a fixed ideological line. There are no party cadres telling the people what to think, but instead there exist discussions that are open to a wide a variety of views that sometimes may even contradict each other but, nonetheless, often slowly, develop a coherent perspective.[33]

For his part, Alain Badiou proves equally sure that 'the party-form has had its day, exhausted in a brief century its state avatars'.[34] As he believes, the communist parties were suitable to the conquest of the state, but nowadays a new type of 'revolutionary political discipline' is needed. This revolutionary political subject will defend the 'dictatorship of the True', writes Badiou,[35] because Truth is not an issue of numbers, but the political outcome of a 'self-legislated' and a 'self-legitimated' collectivity.[36] Furthermore, inscribing his theory of the political subject within his analysis of the Event, Badiou defines the political organisation as the 'Subject of a discipline of the event', that is, a Subject aiming at the preservation of the characteristics of the event, when the event has exhausted its dynamics.[37] From this point of view, it is worth emphasising that, contrary to classical Marxism's theory of the party, Badiou's theory of political organisation is more interested in the *postfestum* maintenance of a revolt than in the preparation of a revolutionary break.

Since, however, it is not the purpose of this chapter to present and criticise Badiou's theory of the political subject, let me focus on the way the post-Marxist philosopher of the Event combines his interpretation of the riots and protests of our times with the organisational question. Thus, it is important to notice that Badiou not only rejects the outdated party-form, in agreement with Hardt and Negri, but also insists that one of the most serious problems facing us today is the invention of this revolutionary political organisation, which 'born with the historical riot, does not follow the hierarchical, authoritarian and quasi-mindless model of armies or storm troopers'.[38]

I really wonder where in the world appeared such a 'revolutionary political discipline' as the one conceived or imagined by Badiou. Leaving aside for the

---

33   Hardt and Negri 2012, pp. 91–2.
34   Badiou 2012, p. 65.
35   Badiou 2012, p. 66.
36   Badiou 2012, p. 59.
37   Badiou 2012, p. 70.
38   Badiou 2012, p. 66.

moment the Greek case, which, as I have already admitted, in no way meets
Badiou's criteria for a 'historical riot', I confine myself to writing down his theoretical and political *aporia* as expressed in the following comment on the
Egyptian uprising: 'The popular uprising we are talking about is manifestly
without a party, a hegemonic organisation, or a recognised leader. There will
be time enough to determine whether this characteristic is a strength or weakness'.[39]

For his part, Slavoj Žižek is unwilling to accept without reservation 'horizontalism' and is sceptical toward all those who distrust both vertical structures and
the notion of 'vanguard'. 'The opposition between centralized-hierarchic vertical power and horizontal multitudes', writes Žižek, 'is inherent to the existing
social and political order; none of the two is a priori "better" or "more progressive"'.[40] Nevertheless, as far as the party-type of organisation is concerned,
Žižek's overall approach to the organisational question is no different from that
of Hardt, Negri, and Badiou.

According to Žižek, the political subject, required while fighting against capitalism in our time, is not a revolutionary party founded in terms of classical
Marxism. During a global capitalist crisis, argues Žižek, a Master is needed, in
order to 'enact the authentic division – division between those who want to
drag on within the old parameters and those who are aware of the necessary
change'.[41] No doubt, this Master, a 'Thatcher of the Left'(!) as Žižek calls him
(her),[42] is nothing more than a 'vanishing mediator who gives you back to yourself'.[43] In fact, such a Master, who looks like a postmodern offprint of Rousseau's
Legislator, does not aim at cultivating and transforming people's spontaneity
into revolutionary consciousness and practice. Contrary to a Marxist political
vanguard, the Master, whom Žižek introduces, does not work dialectically on
the spontaneous will of the masses; he obeys his own desire and appeals to the
people to follow him.[44]

---

39    Badiou 2012, p. 111.
40    Žižek 2014, p. 35.
41    Žižek 2014, p. 32.
42    Žižek 2014, p. 38.
43    Žižek 2014, p. 42.
44    Žižek 2014, pp. 43–4: 'A true leader does not do what people want or plan; *he tells the people
      what they want*, it is only through him that they realize what they want. Therein resides
      the act of a true political leader: *after listening to him, people all of a sudden realize what
      they always-already knew they wanted*, it clarifies to them their own position, it enables
      them to recognize themselves, their own innermost need, in the project he proposes to
      them' (emphasis added).

Hence, interpreting the riots and the protests of our century, Žižek forms a political subject-rhetoric with a strong flavour of philosophical voluntarism and political messianism. Needless to say, in countries like Greece, with an ideological background significantly determined by populist and even fascist political practices, a Master-type theory of the political subject, such as that proposed by Žižek in the midst of the capitalist crisis, seems quite risky and is widely open to adventurism.

After this brief survey of post-Marxist politics with an emphasis on the political subject issue and the organisational question, it is now time to proceed to a Marxist critique of the post-Marxist discourses we have already dealt with, discourses which proved to be quite influential, if not hegemonic – especially in the ranks of the young activists and protesters during the Greek crisis – mainly on account of the absence of a Gramscian Modern Prince.

## 3 A Gramscian Critique of Post-Marxist Politics: Political Subject and Organisational Question in the Age of Crisis

Obviously, the Gramscian Modern Prince is opposed to the post-Marxist versions of the political subject, which we have already dealt with in the previous section. Recognising the anti-capitalist political subject in the form of a 'decentralised multitude of singularities [who] communicate horizontally' (Negri), or in terms of the 'Subject-dictator of the Truth' as inscribed in Badiou's philosophy of the Event, is nothing less than a 'change of paradigm' compared to a Marxist and, more specifically, to the Gramscian theory of the political party. No doubt, the same conclusion can be drawn while comparing Žižek's 'Master', this postmodern 'Thatcher of the Left', to the modern prince as defined by Gramsci:

> The modern prince, the myth-prince, cannot be a real person, a concrete individual. It can only be an organism, a complex element of society in which a collective will, which has already been recognised and has to some extent asserted itself in action, begins to take concrete form. History has already provided this organism, and it is the political party – the first cell in which there come together germs of a collective will tending to become universal and total.[45]

---

45    Gramsci 1971, p. 129 (see also pp. 147, 252–3).

For the moment, let me confine myself to pointing out the absence of a Gramscian Modern Prince during the anti-capitalist struggles of the last decades; on the other hand, I would like to stress the significance of this absence both on the global level and in the case of the Greek crisis.

Regarding Gramsci, however, it is worth noting that, writing in prison during the hard years of the 1929–30 world economic crisis, the Italian Marxist leader does not pass up the opportunity to remind us of the fact that, although such a structural capitalist crisis does not automatically produce 'historical events', it nevertheless creates 'a terrain more favourable to the dissemination of certain modes of thought, and certain ways of posing and resolving questions involving the entire subsequent development of national life'.[46]

The Gramscian Marxism leaves no room either for economism or for voluntarism. What actually matters in relation to the *political* confrontation with the crisis, argues Gramsci, is 'the permanently organised and long-prepared force which can be put onto the field when it is judged that a situation is favourable ... Therefore the essential task is that of systematically and patiently ensuring that this force is formed, developed, and rendered ever more homogeneous, compact and self-aware'.[47]

In fact, Gramsci proposed and defended a theory of the revolutionary party as the political vanguard of a broad inter-class anti-capitalist movement. From his point of view, however, such a movement cannot be efficient unless a Marxist political party *directs* the proletarian struggle against capitalism. In other words, according to Gramsci, there can be no revolutionary transcendence of capitalism without a party acting as 'the proclaimer and organiser of an intellectual and moral reform, which also means creating the terrain for a subsequent development of the national-popular collective will towards the realisation of a superior, total form of modern civilisation'.[48]

At this point, the Gramscian theory of the Modern Prince proves incompatible with the postmodern analysis of the political subject. This means that in order to interpret or rather intervene theoretically in the ongoing crisis, we are obliged to choose either the Gramscian theory of the party or the post-Marxist versions of political organisation. I will return to this theoretical and ultimately political dilemma; for the time being, however, I would like to insist on the way Gramsci himself conceives of the revolutionary party and its leading role in the class movement.

---

46   Gramsci 1971, p. 184.
47   Gramsci 1971, p. 185.
48   Gramsci 1971, p. 133.

According to the Italian Marxist leader, and contrary to what post-Marxist thinkers like Negri or Badiou believe, the political party is not a bureaucratic organisation by definition. A party can be either progressive or regressive: 'When the party is progressive it functions "democratically" (democratic centralism); when the party is regressive it functions "bureaucratically" (bureaucratic centralism). The party in this second case is a simple, unthinking executor'.[49]

It is worth emphasising the Gramscian distinction between a progressive party, an organism which functions according to the principles of the democratic centralism, and a regressive party, an organism which functions according to the principles of the bureaucratic centralism. From this Marxist point of view, a party of the Left is not a bureaucratic party *per se*. The fact that the so-called 'communist parties' all over postwar Europe, the eurocommunist ones included, functioned in a bureaucratic way, does not mean that a Marxist party is predetermined to become a bureaucratic institution, more or less integrated in the bourgeois political system as post-Marxist thinkers of our times believe.

Opposed to the bureaucratic parties and their own centralism, Gramscian Marxism supports the historical possibility of creating a revolutionary party, a political collective intellectual and leader functioning in terms of democratic centralism. Contrary to the bureaucratic centralism, which refuses to accept any kind of initiative with regard to the rank and file of the collective subject, democratic centralism

> is so to speak a 'centralism' in movement – i.e. a continual adaptation of the organisation to the real movement, a matching of thrusts from below with orders from above, a continuous insertion of elements thrown up from the depths of the rank and file into the solid framework of the leadership apparatus which ensures continuity and the regular accumulation of experience. Democratic centralism is 'organic' because on the one hand it takes account of movement ... and does not solidify mechanically into bureaucracy; and because at the same time it takes account of that which is relatively stable and permanent, or which at least moves in an easily predictable direction, etc.[50]

It is important to pay attention to the Gramscian defence of democratic centralism. Democratic centralism – fundamentally alien to the network-function,

---

49    Gramsci 1971, p. 155.
50    Gramsci 1971, pp. 188–9.

which characterises most of the current anti-capitalist movements and organ-isations – requires instead the dialectical combination of a vertical with a horizontal party-structure. Such a combination, Antonio Gramsci insists, is an 'elastic formula' flexible enough to be adapted both to the logic of historical necessity and to the variety of social conditions.[51] In dialectical terms, demo-cratic centralism does not work for an 'apparent uniformity';[52] democratic centralism does not represent the extermination but rather the *transcendence* of diversity within the life of the concrete universal, within the organisational life of the Modern Prince.

As a matter of fact, following Gramsci's analysis, both the party as the organ-isational form of a political vanguard and the democratic centralism as its operational mode are the necessary means to guarantee the permanent and escalating unfolding of the anti-capitalist movement; without a Marxist Mod-ern Prince, functioning in terms of a democratic centralism, there is no way to activate the class consciousness and practice of the proletariat in a revolu-tionary direction, there is no way to form a class movement able to fight and overturn capitalism. To what extent the revolts of our times and the Greek experience give right to the Marxist theory of the political party or to the post-Marxist theoretical approaches to the political subject remains to be evaluated in the last section of this chapter. Until then, it is worth noting a few more crucial remarks on the role of the Gramscian Modern Prince as the political vanguard of an anti-capitalist movement.

Following Gramsci's analysis, a Marxist political party does not come out of the blue. The formation of a political party is not a matter of pure will and arbitrary decision; rather it is the organic outcome of extremely complicated social conditions and long-term 'molecular phases'.[53] On the other hand, Gram-sci insists that there can be no effective anti-capitalist movement without a collective political leader. From his Marxist point of view, the existence (or absence) of a political vanguard in the form of the party is a crucial index of the social movement's maturity.

This is even more the case, since the revolutionary party, as conceived by Gramsci, is not only the organiser, but also the collective educator-intellectual, without whom there is no transformation of proletarian spontaneity into revo-lutionary class consciousness. It is exactly in this sense that Gramsci draws the conclusion that 'innovation cannot come from the mass, at least at the

---

51    Gramsci 1971, p. 189.
52    Ibid.
53    Gramsci 1971, p. 194.

beginning, except through the mediation of an *élite* for whom the conception implicit in human activity has already become to a certain degree a coherent and systematic ever-present awareness and a precise and decisive will'.[54]

In terms of a post-Marxist approach, it seems quite easy to criticise the Gramscian theory of the Modern Prince as an outdated element of the equally outdated 'grand narrative' of Marxism. At the end of the day, however, Gramsci's own analysis proves rather resistant. Defending Marxism as a 'modern theory' and stressing the need for a Marxist political vanguard, the author of *The Prison Notebooks*, argues as follows:

> Can modern theory be in opposition to the 'spontaneous' feelings of the masses? ... It cannot be in opposition to them. Between the two there is a 'quantitative' difference of degree, not one of quality ... Neglecting, or worse still despising, so-called 'spontaneous' movements, i.e. failing to give them a conscious leadership or to raise them to a higher plane by inserting them into politics, may often have extremely serious consequences. It is almost always the case that a 'spontaneous' movement of the subaltern classes is accompanied by a reactionary movement of the right-wing of the dominant class, for concomitant reasons. An economic crisis, for instance, engenders on the one hand discontent among the subaltern classes and spontaneous mass movements, and on the other conspiracies among the reactionary groups, who take advantage of the objective weakening of the government in order to attempt *coups d'état*. Among the effective causes of the *coups* must be included the failure of the responsible groups to give any conscious leadership to the spontaneous revolts or to make them into a positive political factor.[55]

I openly admit that I tried to resist quoting at length the Gramscian argument. It was impossible. The passage above seems to come from the future or rather from the present, especially from the still lasting present of the Greek experience. Actually, Marxism, this modern theory of the revolution, which, as Gramsci rightly pointed out, is not in opposition to the spontaneity of the masses, was not organically connected with the more or less spontaneous anti-capitalist movements and protests of our age. No doubt, the critical link for such a connection was and remains missing. The Modern Prince, the vital mediator of the theory-movement relation, is absent. As a result, the spontaneous revolts failed to become a conscious class movement.

---

54  Gramsci 1971, p. 335.
55  Gramsci 1971, p. 199.

On the other hand, as the leading Italian Marxist thinker accurately recognised in his own time and forecasted for our own, in the midst of an economic crisis, the unfolding of a multiform right-wing reactionary movement is not a surprise. It suffices to mention the Greek 'Golden Dawn' as a special case among a variety of extreme right political parties and other organisations, which try to turn the discontent of the working classes in a reactionary direction.

From their point of view, post-Marxist thinkers like Negri, Badiou and Žižek may feel confident to write and happily declare that the Marxist theory of the political party, its Gramscian version of the Modern Prince included, is dead. As I will argue, however, in the concluding section of this chapter, the Greek experience confirms that as long as the Gramscian Modern Prince is absent, there is no promising future for the anti-capitalist movements not only in Greece, but all over Europe as well.

## 4    The Greek Social Experience and the Missing Modern Prince: Conclusions and Perspectives

Focusing our analysis on the Greek experience, the theoretical and political absence of a Modern Prince in the form of a Gramscian political party becomes evident. Regarding the specific versions of the Greek political Left – i.e. SYRIZA, KKE and ANTARSYA – it is worth noting that there is no political organisation corresponding to a modern Marxist revolutionary party.

Despite its effort to be transformed into a coherent and united political party, SYRIZA functions as a social-liberal political trust, mainly influenced and inspired not by modern Marxist revolutionary theory, but by post-Marxist narratives. On the other hand, the Communist Party of Greece (KKE) endorses a neo-Stalinist ideology organically linked to an absolutely sectarian policy. Finally, ANTARSYA, a fragile front of the extra-parliamentary anti-capitalist Left, in spite of the remarkable activism of its members, functions as a loose and rather divided coalition, confirming how critical is the absence of a modern communist party as a collective leader of the masses and an efficient coordinator of their movements.

Given their rejection of the Marxist political party as a political vanguard organisation, it should be no surprise that distinguished post-Marxist thinkers like Negri, Badiou and Žižek, turning their analysis to the Greek case, seem content with – or fail to take into serious theoretical and political consideration – the fact that such a Modern Prince is missing.[56]

---

56    The most overt negation of the Marxist theory of the revolutionary party in our time is

Despite the fact that they consider the organisational question crucial, Hardt and Negri are pleased to realise that the recent protests and encampments, the Syntagma Square occupation included, 'have all developed according to ... a "multitude form" ... and express themselves through horizontal participatory structures without representatives' in terms of a 'real democracy'.[57]

From his point of view, Badiou, commenting on the 'Greek symptom' and the activism of the Left, openly admits that both in Greece and all over Europe we are acting as 'militants without a strategy of emancipation'.[58] Moreover, it is worth remembering that while acknowledging the political impasse of the recent movements and protests, Badiou insists on his consideration of the party as an outdated type of political organisation. Confronting the organisational question within his analytical frame of the 'radical generic-state' opposition and assigning to the 'organised politics' the responsibility for keeping alive the radicalised generic in the struggle against the state,[59] the French thinker confines himself to repeating the problem without proposing a solution in terms of a collective political subject:

> But if the party-form is obsolete, what is an organised process that lives of the kind of rectitude and genuine fidelity to the struggle of the politically generic – whose norm is equality – against state identity, which separates and suppresses? This is the main problem bequeathed to us by the state communism of the last century. Its terms are reactivated by the riots – immediate, latent or historic – that are in process in reopening History. This problem is manifestly as difficult to resolve as a problem of transcendental mathematics, if not more so.[60]

There is no doubt that the Greek experience brought to the fore once again the urgent need for a modern political organisation. The problem Badiou describes is a real one and explains, up to a point, the failure of the protests and demonstrations in Athens to be upgraded to a strong and effective anti-capitalist movement. Nevertheless, the question remains without an answer.

----

expressed by John Holloway in his *Change the World without Taking Power* (see, in particular, Holloway 2002, pp. 83–8). I had the opportunity to criticise Holloway's positions in my study 'On the dialectics of power and revolution: a few reflections on the work of John Holloway "Change the World Without Taking Power"'.

57    Hardt and Negri 2011.
58    Badiou 2013, p. 45.
59    Badiou 2012, pp. 78–82; for an interesting critique of Badiou's 'generic communism-state' opposition and his 'aporia of democracy', see Sotiris 2014a.
60    Badiou 2013, p. 80.

Obviously, the post-Marxist philosopher is disappointed not only by out-dated political parties like the traditional or neo-Stalinist so-called 'communist parties', but also by social-liberal political parties like SYRIZA, which are practic-ally oriented towards the electoral road to government and politically endorse a mainstream social and economic policy. Meanwhile, analysing the Greek symptom, the philosopher of the Event bends the stick in the direction of *irra-tionalism* and brings us face to face with an *aporia* as if we were condemned to expect a miracle, an event that would give rise to a new type of political organ-isation.

For his part, Slavoj Žižek, however, seems willing to argue that SYRIZA is the answer to the organisational and, ultimately, to the political problem of the subject as posed by the capitalist crisis in Greece, this 'testing ground for the imposition of a new socio-economic model … [that means] the depoliticized technocratic model wherein bankers and other experts are allowed to squash democracy'.[61]

According to Žižek's post-Marxist analysis, SYRIZA – a party and, in my opin-ion, an opportunistic political trust that aims at a mild reform of neoliberal capitalism – represents a true opposition to the Greek establishment and its parties. Nevertheless, it is Žižek himself who regards the 'return to the authen-tic Welfare State' as a 'moronic idea'![62] In fact, there is an open contradiction between Žižek's positive approach to SYRIZA and his negative evaluation of Welfare State politics. Describing Welfare State politics, Žižek seems to ignore the fact that he is actually describing SYRIZA's proclaimed and deceitful polit-ical agenda. At the end of the day, he succeeds in rejecting the former, while promoting the latter![63]

At the same time, the post-Marxist philosopher argues that the Syntagma Square demonstrations were a kind of self-organised protest, which created 'a space of an egalitarian freedom with no central authority, a public space where all were allotted the same amount of time to speak, and so on'. Žižek acknow-ledges, however, that such a type of organisation is not enough; there is a need for a new form of political organisation, since communism in the sense of fight-ing for the commons is not 'a carnival of mass protests in which the system is brought to a halt; it is also and above all a new form of organisation, discipline and hard work'.[64]

---

61  Žižek 2012, p. 13.
62  Žižek 2012, p. 15.
63  Žižek 2012, pp. 15–16.
64  Žižek 2012, p. 82; for an extreme libertarian version of dealing with recent protests in

It is worth insisting, of course, on Žižek's argument that the protests, especially in Greece, created a 'vacuum in the field of hegemonic ideology', a vacuum which cannot be filled without 'a strong body able to reach quick decisions and realise them with whatever force may be necessary'.[65] Actually, the Slovenian thinker moves even further, since he does not hesitate to praise Lenin for being conscious of the need for new forms of organisation. Nevertheless, he must not be misunderstood; he remains far away from a Marxist theory of the revolutionary party. Trapped in his own postmodern eclecticism and moving like a pendulum from his 'Thatcher of the Left' to a 'strong body able to reach quick decisions and realise them', Žižek proves unable to draw a coherent and persuasive conclusion in relation to the missing political subject of our times.

Neither the Greek experience nor the European one can be effectively interpreted in terms of post-Marxist theoretical variants. In the midst of the capitalist crisis and despite their efforts, distinguished thinkers such as Negri, Badiou and Hardt fail to set out a theoretically and politically convincing response to the political subject and the organisational question. Severing the links with Marxist dialectics and Marxist theory of revolution, post-Marxism, in its various alternatives, bypasses the critical significance of the missing Modern Prince, the absence of modern revolutionary Marxist parties not just in Greece, but throughout Europe.

According to the hypothesis I have presented and defended here, the theoretical frame of reference concerning the political birth of the much-needed Modern Prince is still included in the Gramscian *Prison Notebooks*.[66] The Greek experience adequately proved that insofar as social movements, riots or revolts are not directed by a political subject, firmly grounded and dialectically operating according to the principles of a modern Marxist theory of the party, there is no hope for the proletariat and its allies to overcome the dramatic consequences of the crisis and win the war against capitalism.

Surely, I do not suggest that the absence of the Modern Prince in terms of Gramscian-type political parties is the only factor we must focus on while analysing what is going wrong with the Greek and the international anti-capitalist

---

terms of 'horizontalism' and 'experimental communism', see Bonefeld and Holloway 2014, pp. 213–15.

65      Ibid.

66      It is worth mentioning that the most recent and exhaustive approach to the Gramscian philosophy and Marxist theory of hegemony is Peter D. Thomas's *The Gramscian Moment: Philosophy, Hegemony and Marxism*. Nevertheless, as Martin Thomas accurately points out, 'the question of the revolutionary working-class political party is almost entirely absent in [Peter] Thomas's discussion' (Thomas 2014, pp. 158, 162–4).

movement. Nevertheless, as the Greek case has reconfirmed, the existence of such a party is a necessary prerequisite to not only interpreting but changing the world.

### References

Badiou, Alain 2012, *The Rebirth of History*, translated by Gregory Elliott, London: Verso.

Badiou, Alain 2013, 'Our contemporary impotence', *Radical Philosophy*, 181: 43–47.

Bonefeld, Werner and Holloway, John 2014, 'Commune, Movement, Negation: Notes from Tomorrow', *The South Atlantic Quarterly*, 113, 2: 213–15.

Chrysis, Alexandros 2012, 'On the dialectics of power and revolution: a few reflections on the work of John Holloway "Change the World Without Taking Power"', available at: https://www.ssoar.info/ssoar/bitstream/handle/document/32298/ssoar-2012-chryssis-On_the_dialectics_of_power.pdf?sequence=1

Douzinas, Costas 2013, *Philosophy and Resistance in the Crisis*, Cambridge: Polity Press.

Gaitanou, Eirini 2014, 'An examination of class structure in Greece, its tendencies of transformation amid the crisis, and its impact on the organizational forms and structures of the social movement'.

Gounari, Panayota 2014, 'Neoliberalism as Social Necrophilia. Erich Fromm and the Politics of Hopelessness in Greece', in *Reclaiming the Sane Society. Essays on Erich Fromm's Thought*, edited by Seyed Javad Miri, Robert Lake and Tricia M. Kress, Rotterdam: Sense Publishers.

Gramsci, Antonio 1971, *Selections of the Prison Notebooks*, edited and translated by Quintin Hoare and Geoffrey Nowell Smith, London: Lawrence & Wishart.

Hardt, Michael and Negri, Antonio 2011, 'The Fight for "Real Democracy" at the Heart of Occupy Wall Street', *Foreign Affairs*, October 11, available at: http://www.foreignaffairs.com/articles/136399/michael-hardt-and-antonio-negri/the-fight-for-real-democracy-at-the-heart-of-occupy-wall-street

Hardt, Michael and Negri, Antonio 2012, *Declaration*, available at: https://antonionegriinenglish.files.wordpress.com/2012/05/93152857-hardt-negri-declaration-2012.pdf

Holloway, John 2002, *Change the World Without Taking Power*, London: Pluto Press.

Holloway, John 2012, 'Greece shows us how to protest against a failed system', *The Guardian*, 17 February, available at: http://www.theguardian.com/commentisfree/2012/feb/17/greece-protest-failed-system

Nasioka, Katerina 2014, 'Communities of Crisis: Ruptures as Common Ties during Class Struggles in Greece, 2011–2012', *The South Atlantic Quarterly*, 113, 2: 285–97.

Negri, Antonio 2013, 'From the end of national Lefts to subversive movements for Europe', *Radical Philosophy*, 181: 26–32.

Sotiris, Panagiotis 2014, 'Alain Badiou and the aporia of democracy within generic communism', *Crisis & Critique*, 1, 1: 116–35.

Thomas, Martin 2014, 'Gramsci without the Prince', *Historical Materialism*, 22, 2: 158–73.

Thomas, Peter D. 2009, *The Gramscian Moment: Philosophy, Hegemony and Marxism*, Leiden: Brill.

Žižek, Slavoj 2012, *The Year of Dreaming Dangerously*, London: Verso.

Žižek, Slavoj 2014, 'The Impasses of Today's Radical Politics', *Crisis & Critique*, 1, 1: 9–44.

CHAPTER 12

# From Resistance to Hegemony: the Struggle against Austerity and the Need for a New Historical Bloc

*Panagiotis Sotiris*

## Introduction

The aim of this chapter is twofold. On the one hand, it treats austerity as a class strategy attempting to answer a structural capitalist crisis. On the other hand, it uses the Gramscian concept of the historical bloc in order to rethink the question of strategy for the Left, taking the Greek case as a point of departure.

## 1 Austerity as a Class Strategy

### The Battle Cry of Austerity

Austerity has been the main battle cry from the forces of capital after the eruption of the global capitalist crisis in 2007–8. The call for budget cuts and deficit reductions has been accompanied by calls to abolish whatever has been left of labour rights. The supposed 'rigidities' of the labour market and the 'privileges' enjoyed by public sector employees and certain segments of the workforce are being targeted all over the world. Deregulating markets and removing obstacles to entrepreneurial activity have been at the centre of political debates. Saving the banking system has led to a massive redistribution of income towards capital.[1] Regarding the capitalist crisis, there has been a vast literature on a potential Marxist interpretation of the crisis.[2] It was never simply a banking crisis, nor was it simply the result of a lack of regulation of financial markets or of a lack of prudence in public spending. Rather it was:

---

[1] On the centrality of the policies of austerity in contemporary capitalist societies, see Schäfer and Streeck (eds.) 2013 and Lapavitsas et al. 2012. For an overview of austerity policies in various countries, see Hill (ed.) 2013.

[2] Konings (ed.) 2010; Mavroudeas 2010; Mavroudeas 2010; Duménil and Lévy 2011; Panitch and Gindin 2012; Lapavitsas 2013.

(a)   The condensation of the crisis of the regime of accumulation, which
      became dominant after the monetarist, neoconservative and neoliberal
      counter-revolution launched in the 1980s. This regime of accumulation
      was based upon mass devaluation of fixed capital and unemployment
      in the first phase, violent changes in class balance of forces, workplace
      flexibility, introduction of new technologies, trade and capital flows lib-
      eralisation, and increased financialisation of the economy.
(b)   The crisis of neoliberalism as a political strategy, dominant ideology and
      hegemonic discourse, since it was more than obvious that free markets,
      instead of being automatic mechanisms of economic rationality, are in
      reality intrinsically irrational and prone to exacerbating catastrophic eco-
      nomic trends. In fact, we can say that it was a crisis of neoliberal govern-
      mentality.[3]
(c)   The crisis of globalisation. All the imbalances of the global system came
      into view along with the systemic violence of international money and
      capital markets.

All these imply that we have been witnessing the profound crisis of an entire
social and economic paradigm. Consequently, the exit from such a crisis requires the implementation of a new social, economic and technological paradigm aiming at guaranteeing sustained accumulation and profitability. However, this is not a technical question; it is a question of the balance of forces
in the class struggle. Until now, the forces of capital have not presented a new
social and technological paradigm. They have presented austerity not only as
an attempt at boosting profitability, but also as a political strategy for changing
the balance of forces by means of a 'fuite en avant' tactic of even more aggressive neoliberal measures.

### The Eurozone as the Epicentre of the Crisis

Austerity and aggressive neoliberalism have been the main characteristics of
the 'European Integration' process since the 1980s, exemplified in the deficit
and debt limits incorporated in the Maastricht Treaty as criteria for acceptance into the Eurozone. The country that seems to have suffered less during
the period of the crisis, in terms of recession, Germany, is also the country
that had been the first to impose aggressive measures of austerity, real wage
reductions and workplace flexibility, in the first half of the 2000s, under social-

---

3   Dardot and Laval 2013.

democratic governments.[4] However, despite the ambitious declaration of the Lisbon strategy at the beginning of the 2000s, the European Union lagged behind its competitors in most benchmarks and important aspects of the European 'social model' and aspects of a 'welfare state' remained in place. Therefore, for the dominant elites in the European Union, the conjuncture of the economic crisis offered the opportunity for a violent change in the balance of forces.[5]

The Eurozone, designed as it was with a view to monetary stability, was one of the most aggressive attempts to create an iron cage of capitalist modernisation. In the Eurozone, a country cedes certain forms of sovereignty (in particular monetary sovereignty), undertakes an obligation to lower protective barriers against foreign competition, accepts the priority of European legislation and directives in most aspects of economic and social policy, from budget restrictions to forced privatisations, and is subject to constant pressure to adjust to a particular and aggressively neoliberal social and economic model. As part of the turn towards 'European Economic Governance', there is constant supervision of budgetary performance and monitoring of deficit targets. We can say that since the Single European Act of 1986 and a little later the Maastricht Treaty, the defining aspect of European Integration has been an embedded neoliberalism.[6]

The introduction of the euro as a single currency, controlled by a supranational Central Bank, in an economic area marked by important divergences in productivity and competitiveness, offered an extra comparative advantage to the high productivity and competitive countries of the European core. However, it was also the choice of the economic and political elites of European periphery countries, who thought of this exposure to increased competition without protective barriers as a means of inducing capitalist restructuring and modernisation, and of using, to that end, the legitimising appeal of the 'European road'.

This kind of monetary union between countries, which diverge to such an extent in terms of productivity and competitiveness, could only create imbalances. Initially, this could be tolerated because of the flow of relatively cheap

---

4   Schäfer and Streeck (eds.) 2013.
5   On the crisis of the Eurozone and the response of European economic and political elites, see Lapavitsas et al. 2012 and Schäfer and Streeck (eds.) 2013.
6   On the embedded neoliberal character of the European Integration process, see van Apeldoorn 2002; van Apeldoorn 2013; Cufrany and Ryner (eds.) 2003; Moss (ed.) 2005; Durand (ed.) 2013.

credit to fuel consumer spending and property bubbles. However, in a period of global economic crisis and subsequent recession, it could only make things worse. Especially, it made the debt crisis even worse, since on top of increased indebtedness because of recession there was increased indebtedness in order to cover trade and current account imbalances. Moreover, the very mechanism of the Eurozone and the fact that the euro is a single currency, not a national currency, meant that countries could find themselves in a condition of sovereign insolvency and potential default, creating the conditions for serious forms of sovereign debt crisis.[7]

The answer chosen from the EU was not solidarity in the form of a bailout against default. Rather, the sovereign debt crisis of Greece, but also that of Ireland, Spain and Portugal, offered a unique opportunity to experiment with a version of 'shock therapy' and a new and original form of imposed reduced sovereignty. The infamous 'Memoranda of Understanding' were aggressive 'structural adjustment programmes' with loans explicitly conditional upon implementation of the measures included in them. This represented an aggressive disciplinary form of neoliberal social engineering.[8] Chief IMF economist Olivier Blanchard described this in an article from 2006–7 as a strategy of internal devaluation.[9] Since member states of the European Union cannot use traditional methods of restoring competitiveness, such as currency devaluation, they have to lower both real and nominal wages and drastically change their institutional framework, in order to be competitive in a single currency area.

## 2      The Greek Experiment

### Greece as a Testing Ground for Austerity Policies

The Greek debt crisis reflected, on the one hand, the explosive contradictions of the Eurozone, and on the other, the crisis of the 'developmental paradigm' of Greek capitalism that was based upon low labour cost, the exploitation of immigrant labour, precarious forms of employment, the use of European funds, socially useless public works such as the ones constructed for the 2004 Olympic Games, increased household consumption fuelled by debt, and widespread tax

---

7      On the role of the financial and monetary architecture to the debt crisis, see Lapavitsas et al. 2012.

8      Schäfer and Streeck (eds.) 2013.

9      Blanchard 2007. See also Ioakeimoglou 2012.

evasion on the part of big business.[10] The dependence of important sectors of the Greek economy (construction, tourism, and shipping) upon the tendencies of the economic cycle and the global economic conjuncture only made things worse. As a result, Greek capitalism, after a period of constant growth, entered a prolonged economic downturn.

In Greece, the aim of the austerity packages went beyond the debt crisis, and had more to do with testing the ability to impose a violent change of 'social paradigm'. This was obvious in the violent imposition of wage competitiveness, in the deleting of a century's worth of labour law, in laying the ground for mass privatisations, in using OECD 'policy' recommendations such as the infamous 'OECD toolkit' for market liberalisation,[11] in abolishing collective bargaining, in enabling the lay-offs of civil servants, in introducing extreme precariousness regarding labour, in redistributing income in favour of capital, in neoliberal reforms in education, and in opening up the way for mass evictions and fore-closures. The extent and the speed of both the change in the relation of forces in favour of capital and of the implementation of neoliberal reforms have been without precedent.

In social terms, Greece plunged into a vicious circle of austerity, recession, unemployment and debt, comparable in terms of economic and social consequences only to the Great Depression of the 1930s. Total recession from 2008 to 2013 was close to -25%, and remained in recession until 2014, official unemployment peaked at 27.4% at the end of 2013 and was 26% at the end of 2014, youth unemployment remained over 50%, real wages were reduced by more than 25%.[12] There is also evidence of a deteriorating health situation as a direct result of both the social effects of the economic crisis and prolonged recession, but also of severe cuts in public health spending.[13]

### Political Crisis

This violent and aggressive neoliberal policy, along with the authoritarian undermining of popular sovereignty, led to a profound political crisis. This political crisis was first evident in the fall of the Papandreou government in 2011 as the result of 18 months of mass protests, which included the 'Movement

10 Sakellaropoulos and Sotiris 2014. For Marxist interpretations of the crisis of Greek capitalism, see Mavroudeas (ed.) 2015.
11 OECD 2014.
12 See data at the Hellenic Statistic Authority (www.statistics.gr), Bank of Greece (www.bankofgreece.gr) and INE/GSEE the Research Institute of the Confederation of Trade Unions (www.inegsee.gr).
13 Basu and Stuckler 2013.

of the Squares' in the summer of 2011, when, according to estimates, some 2.6 million people took part in some form of public protest.[14] It was also evident in the entire social and political sequence of early 2012, from the general strike of 12 February 2012 to the general elections of May and June 2012, when we had an impressive fall of the vote in favour of both PASOK and New Democracy and the meteoric electoral rise of SYRIZA.[15] The rise of the neo-fascist Golden Dawn from a marginal position to parliamentary representation was also an expression of a deep political crisis and of the re-emergence of reactionary, authoritarian and xenophobic tendencies.[16] Although the period from 2012 to 2015 was not marked by movements of the same magnitude, with notable exceptions such as the battle over the public television corporation (ERT), the elements of a deep organic crisis remained.

This is a manifestation of the broader crisis of neoliberalism as hegemonic discourse, strategy and 'methodology', and of the inability of the Greek bourgeoisie to articulate a coherent, *positive*, hegemonic discourse and narrative. This creates the potential for a crisis of hegemony.

> And the content is the crisis of the ruling class's hegemony, which occurs either because the ruling class has failed in some major political undertaking for which it has requested, or forcibly extracted, the consent of the broad masses (war, for example), or because huge masses (especially of peasants and petit-bourgeois intellectuals) have passed suddenly from a state of political passivity to a certain activity, and put forward demands which taken together, albeit not organically formulated, add up to a revolution. A 'crisis of authority' is spoken of: this is precisely the crisis of hegemony, or general crisis of the State.[17]

However, it is important to note that the political crisis reached the intensity of a hegemonic crisis exactly because of the emergence of forms of collective struggle and resistance that reached such intensity. This has been part of a global change in protest and contention movements. Since 2010 (or 2008 if we are going to include December 2008 as a 'postcard from the future'), we have entered, on a global scale, into a new phase of social and political contestation, a phase with an almost insurrectionary quality. From the struggles in

---

14    Public issue 2011.

15    Mavris 2012.

16    Sotiris 2015.

17    Gramsci 1975, p. 1603 (Q13, § 23); Gramsci 1971, p. 210. On the extent of the hegemonic crisis in Greece, see Kouvelakis 2011d.

Greece since 2010, to the Arab Spring, the various student movements (Britain, Chile, Canada), the Indignados movement and Occupy!, and more recently the Gezi Park protests in Turkey, there is an increase in the scale and scope of mass protests.[18]

Of particular importance during this cycle has been the fact that we see not only struggles and resistance, but also forms of popular unity during the protest movements. This new form of unity and common identity between different segments of the forces of labour and other subaltern classes is very important. It accentuated the political crisis, facilitated tectonic shifts in relations of political representation, and in certain cases helped certain forms of political radicalisation. Moreover, it created alternative forms of a public sphere. In Greece, this combination of social crisis and social mobilisation led to the deepest political and even hegemonic crisis since the 'Revolution of the Carnations' in Portugal.

### The Electoral Earthquake of February 2015

The electoral earthquake of February 2015 marks a crucial turning point in social and political developments in Greece. After five years of devastating austerity, a social crisis without precedent in Europe, and a series of struggles that at some points, especially in 2010–12, took an almost insurrectionary form, there has been a major political break. The parties that were responsible for putting Greek society under the disciplinary supervision of the so-called Troika (EU-ECB-IMF) suffered a humiliating defeat. PASOK, which in 2009 won almost 44% of the vote, now received only 4.68%; and the splinter party of Giorgos Papandreou, the PASOK Prime Minister who initiated the austerity programmes, got 2.46%. New Democracy came in at 27.81%, almost 9% below SYRIZA. The electoral rise of the fascists of Golden Dawn has been halted, although they still maintain a worrying 6% of the vote. Another pro-austerity party, the RIVER, representing the neoliberal agenda (although nominally coming from the centre-left) took only 6.05%, despite intensive media hype. SYRIZA won an important electoral victory, with 36.34% of the vote and 149 deputies (it needed only two more to have an absolute parliamentary majority). For the first time in modern European history, a party of the non-social-democratic Left formed a government.

The importance of the victory of SYRIZA was that in a certain way it made evident the possibility of a 'political translation' of broader social and movement dynamics into a political intervention that can indeed enable a confront-

---

18    On recent movements, see Solomon and Palmieri (eds.) 2011; Dean 2012; Douzinas 2013; Sotiris 2013b; Rehmann 2013.

ation with the question of political power. It showed that despite the many forms of political and ideological insulation of the political system from the aspirations of the subaltern classes, it is possible to have the rise to power of political parties that at least aspire to a radical break with the existing social and political order, and in particular with aggressive austerity as the condensation and epitome of the contemporary bourgeois offensive.

However, it was also evident at that time that SYRIZA lacked the kind of organic relation to its electorate that is associated with the emergence of an historical bloc. Rather it seemed like a traditional form of electoral representation. SYRIZA was well rooted in movements, of course, and people that were active militants in important struggles voted in massive numbers for SYRIZA. It is also true that in the social base of SYRIZA one can see the broad spectrum of the subaltern classes. However, it lacked that kind of organic relation to the everyday life and aspirations of broad segments of society that could make it the leading force of a potential new historical bloc, even though it managed to articulate the collective demand for an end to austerity.

### From Negotiation to Capitulation

From the start, the SYRIZA government came under great pressure from the EU and the IMF, despite the initial rhetorical expressions of defiance. The strategy of the Greek government was mainly to try and reach a compromise with its creditors, based upon the assumption that the economic and political fall-out from a Greek default would force the Troika to be more rational. However, from the beginning the demand on the part of the EU and the IMF was for Greece to fully comply with their demands, insisting that there should be a completion of the previous loan agreement before a new loan. The main forms of pressure from the Troika were the dependence of the Greek banking system upon European Central Bank liquidity injections and the fact that Greece needed a continuation of the loan agreement in order to meet its debt payment obligations. On 20 February, the Greek government was forced to accept terms that meant a negation of its electoral promises and acceptance of the basic demands of Greece's creditors regarding austerity measures and privatisations. This was followed by a long period of negotiations that went well into the summer of 2015, with the Greek government constantly postponing decisions on pieces of legislation that the Troika might consider unilateral actions (e.g. legislation on the reinstatement of collective bargaining that was never introduced) and struggling to meet the loan payments, especially to the IMF. The Greek government made even more concessions and fully accepted the logic of what seemed like a new Memorandum. However, even those concessions did not seem enough to the Troika representatives, and towards the end of June 2015 there was an impasse in the negotiation. This led to the decision to hold a referendum on the latest set of proposals from the Troika.

Although for the leadership of SYRIZA the referendum was seen as a negotiation tactic and not as the beginning of a process of rupture with the Eurozone, in reality it led to one of the most contested electoral processes of the last decades. On the one hand, there was an impressive display of economic and political pressure, in fact something close to blackmail. Due to the decision of the European Central Bank not to expand the liquidity cap for the Greek banking system, one week before the referendum the Greek government had to impose a bank holiday and capital controls. This actual material pressure, which led to long queues at ATMs, was accompanied by political pressure. European officials repeatedly stated that a NO vote in the referendum would lead to a forced exit from the Eurozone and their tone was echoed in similar statements not only by opposition parties but also by the mass media, with private TV channels abandoning any pretext of impartiality and openly blackmailing the electorate against voting NO. At the same time, many employers openly campaigned in favour of the YES vote, making it clear to their employees that in case of a NO win, there would be mass lay-offs. Not only did all the pro-Memoranda parties campaign in favour of the YES vote, but also the Communist Party called for abstention from the referendum.

However, and despite this social and political pressure, in the end there was a massive mobilisation of the subaltern classes. This was evident during the 3 July mass rallies all over Greece and especially in Athens, with a huge turnout, especially by people from a working-class background. The result was a massive 61.3% vote in support of the NO vote, despite the political and ideological pressure to the contrary. What is important is the degree of class polarisation that the result of the referendum showed. More than 70% of salaried employees, in both public and private sector, more than 70% of the unemployed, 85% of 18–24 year olds, 85% of students voted for the NO and in geographical terms there was a clear divide between working-class neighbourhoods and better-off regions.[19] In a certain way, the demographics of the NO vote were close to a radiography of a potential new historical bloc.

There has been a great debate in the Greek press regarding the question of whether all the voters who supported the NO vote were ready for an exit from the Eurozone, or they voted in favour of the explicit position of the Greek government, which was to oppose specific proposals while at the same time insisting on negotiating within the Eurozone framework. I think that the very

---

19    Public Issue 2015.

terms of the pre-referendum debate, and in particular the ideological tone set by both Greek media and European Union representatives, meant that most voters who voted NO at least accepted as a risk a broader rupture with the Eurozone.

However, the reaction of the Greek government was not to take advantage of the result of the referendum and the immense political momentum inside Greece. In contrast, it opted for a tactic of first building some form of consensus with the pro-austerity parties, in the name of 'national unity', and then trying to reach some form of compromise. In the end, in the early hours of 13 July, after a long weekend of negotiations and despite an international wave of solidarity, sympathy and protest, exemplified in the popularity of the #ThisIsACoup twitter hashtag, the Greek government fully capitulated to the demands of Greece's creditors and accepted a new Memorandum. The result was a devastating set of commitments to an aggressive neoliberal programme that entails privatisation and fire sale of state assets, additional austerity and budget cuts, pension reform, further curtailing of the right to collective bargaining, repeal of whatever legislation SYRIZA had already introduced, a humiliating condition of limited (or even non-existent) sovereignty, and disciplinary supervision from the EU.[20] On 14 August, the new loan agreement was voted through by the Greek Parliament with the votes of SYRIZA and the other pro-austerity parties, with more than 30 SYRIZA members of parliament voting against and announcing their decision to leave the party.

The leadership of SYRIZA presented the entire political sequence after the referendum as an unavoidable bitter compromise and insisted that any other choice would have led to a catastrophic exit from the Eurozone. In contrast to this position, we can say that the moment after the referendum was optimal for such an exit. The initial difficulties of the transition process to the new national currency would not have been much greater than the hardship already imposed by capital controls following the liquidity crisis, and could be answered by the increased politicisation and mobilisation of society. Consequently, and contrary to the rhetoric that there was no alternative to capitulation, we can say that not only was an alternative available, but it was also a political choice on the part of the SYRIZA leadership, the result of a deeply rooted Europeanism and a decision to avoid any rupture with the pro-euro position of most segments of the Greek bourgeoisie.

The reaction of the SYRIZA leadership was the resignation of the government, which led to the calling of an early election for 20 September. Despite an

---

20     Varoufakis 2015.

important split in SYRIZA, with thousands of members abandoning the party and the formation of a new political front, Popular Unity, by the left wing of SYRIZA and some groups of the anti-capitalist Left, SYRIZA managed to win the election and form a new SYRIZA–Independent Greeks government. In contrast, Popular Unity did not manage to pass the 3% electoral threshold whereas ANTARSYA had an increase but still fared below 1%, and the Greek Communist Party (KKE) remained electorally stagnant. Moreover, there was also an important increase in abstention, in contrast to previous elections.

The reason for this electoral victory had to do with the fact that the leadership of SYRIZA was successful in setting the terms of the electoral debate, namely that the question facing voters was not 'for or against the new Memorandum', which in a certain way was presented as an objective and almost inescapable reality, but 'who can manage it in the best manner'. This had also to do with the inability of the left opposition, in particular Popular Unity, to offer a feasible alternative, to offer some form of explanation and self-criticism for the capitulation of SYRIZA and to counter the 'nothing can change' mentality that prevailed. However, it was obvious that in contrast to the 2012 election, there was no 'pole of hope' in the political landscape, since SYRIZA's electoral success was more like the result of a 'lesser evil' choice on the part of the electorate, rather than the expression of a belief in the possibility of change.

## 3    Rethinking Strategy

### The Challenge ahead of Us

The Greek experience shows that today, thinking simply in terms of anti-austerity, anti-neoliberal progressive governance, is not enough. It will easily fall prey to all forms of blackmail and extortion from the forces of capital and international organisations, something exemplified in the Greek case. In contrast, what is needed is a more profound rethinking of a strategy for potential revolutionary sequences, uneven and contradictory sequences based upon the combination of government power and a strong autonomous movement from below, in a process that can perhaps be described as a form of permanent dual power, aiming at not only ending austerity but also initiating processes of social transformation, with the rupture and break with processes of capitalist internationalisation being the overdetermining factor. This means that we should at the same time distance ourselves from a 'governmentalism' that can only lead to capitulation and neoliberal policies, and the tendency to avoid strategic questions in the name of the conditions not being ripe.

From the tragedy of the 'Arab Spring' to the defeat and surrender of SYRIZA to the 'realist' turn of PODEMOS, to the inability of much of the European Left to respond to the capture of the question of sovereignty by the far right – all these attest to the urgency of this discussion. All these experiences and conceptualisations suggest that the challenges we face refer to both the ability to use state power as part of the rupture with capitalist strategies and imperialist pressures, and the importance of the autonomous role of movements and forms of popular counter-power both as an excess of power from below to counter the excess of force inscribed in the materiality of state apparatuses and as sites of experimentation and collective learning. Consequently, we need to rethink both a democratic and emancipatory recuperation of popular sovereignty as a means to impose a strategy of ruptures against the pressure of global markets and the forces of capital, and the 'molecular' aspects of social mobilisation and experimentation for the formation of a new historical bloc.

### Historical Bloc Revisited

One of the contemporary temptations regarding this necessary rethinking of strategy is to mainly think in terms of electoral strategies or in general of interventions at the level of the political scene. The meteoric electoral rise of SYRIZA has been taken to suggest that creating an electoral front at the right moment can have an impact, fill a political gap and open up new vistas for the Left. In a more modest form this takes the form of an anxiety regarding the existence of a political point of reference. I do not underestimate the importance of such initiatives, or the necessity to experiment with the radical Left front as a venue for the recomposition of the Left as a force of radical social change. However, an historical bloc is not formed simply by the existence of a political front or party that claims to represent its possibility. Nor can we deduce its formation from the analysis of the electorate of a party. The historical bloc is a strategic notion pointing to profound changes in the collective practices, consciousnesses, ideologies, and relations of the social classes which create the possibility of adherence to a common strategy and narrative, along with the collective practices that turn these 'encounters' into lasting 'organic' relations and alliances. As such it is not a process that can simply evolve 'from above', it cannot be simply a question of political and ideological interpellations or of the simple articulation and proposal of a 'programme'.

For Antonio Gramsci, the historical bloc is a strategic concept, not a descriptive or analytical one. It defines not an actual social alliance, but a social and political condition to be achieved. Historical bloc does not refer to the formation of an electoral alliance or to various social strata and movements fighting side by side. It refers to the emergence of a different configuration within civil society, namely to the emergence, on a broad scale, of different forms of politics, different forms of organisation, alternative discourses and narratives, that materialise the ability for society to be organised and administrated in a different way. At the same time, it refers to a specific relation between politics and economics, namely to the articulation not simply of demands and aspirations but of an alternative social and economic paradigm.

> Structures and superstructures form an 'historical bloc'. That is to say the complex, contradictory and discordant ensemble of the superstructures is the reflection of the *ensemble* of the social relations of production. From this, one can conclude: that only an all-encompassing (*totalitario*) system of ideologies gives a rational reflection of the contradiction of the structure and represents the existence of the objective conditions for the revolutionising of praxis. If a social group is formed which is one hundred per cent homogeneous on the level of ideology, this means that the premises exist one hundred per cent for this revolutionising: that is that the 'rational' is actively and actually real. This reasoning is based on the necessary reciprocity between structure and superstructure, a reciprocity which is nothing other than the real dialectical process.[21]

Therefore, a new historical bloc defines that specific historical condition when a new social alliance not only demands power but is also in a position to impose its own particular economic form and social strategy and lead society.

> An appropriate political initiative is always necessary to liberate the economic thrust from the dead weight of traditional policies – i.e. to change the political direction of certain forces which have to be absorbed if a new, homogeneous politico-economic historical bloc, without internal contradictions, is to be successfully formed. And, since two 'similar' forces can only be welded into a new organism either through a series of compromises or by force of arms, either by binding them to each other as allies or by forcibly subordinating one to the other, the question is whether one has the necessary force, and whether it is 'productive' to use it.[22]

---

21   Gramsci 1975, pp. 1051–2 (Q8, § 182); Gramsci 1971, p. 366 (translation altered).

22   Gramsci 1975, p. 1120; Gramsci 1977, p. 1612 (Q9, § 40; Q13, § 23); Gramsci 1971, p. 168.

It also includes a particular relation between the broad masses of the subaltern classes and new intellectual practices, along with the emergence of new
forms of mass critical and antagonistic political intellectuality

> If the relationship between intellectuals and people-nation, between the
> leaders and the led, the rulers and the ruled, is provided by an organic
> cohesion in which feeling-passion becomes understanding and hence
> knowledge (not mechanically but in a way that is alive), then and only
> then is the relationship one of representation. Only then can there take
> place an exchange of individual elements between the rulers and ruled,
> leaders [dirigenti] and led, and can the shared life be realised which alone
> is a social force with the creation of the 'historical bloc'.[23]

Regarding political organisations, the notion of the historical bloc refers to that
particular condition of leadership, in the form of actual rooting, participation,
and mass mobilisation that defines an 'organic relation' between leaders and
led – which when we refer to the politics of proletarian hegemony implies a
condition of mass politicisation and new forms of political intellectuality. It
also implies the actuality of the new political and economic forms, and the full
elaboration of what we can define as 'dual power' conceived in the broadest
sense of the term.

Christine Buci-Glucksmann has stressed that the historical bloc is mainly
an attempt to rethink a revolutionary strategy within the transition period and
summarises the importance of this notion:

> Compared with Bukharin's worker-peasant bloc of 1925–26, the Grams-
> cian historic bloc demonstrates a major new feature. This bloc is cultural
> and political as much as economic, and requires an organic relation-
> ship between people and intellectuals, governors and governed, leaders
> and led. The cultural revolution, as an on-going process of adequation
> between culture and practice, is neither luxury nor a simple guarantee,
> but rather an actual dimension of the self-government of the masses and
> of democracy.[24]

---

23    Gramsci 1971, p. 418.
24    Buci Glucksmann 1980, p. 286.

### *Rethinking Sovereignty*

Why is the question of sovereignty important? Because the European experience shows that today reduced and limited sovereignty within institutional forms, such as the European Union, is one the basic mechanisms for the imposition of austerity, neoliberalism and capitalist restructuring. We are witnessing the pervasive effects of the internationalisation of capital: the exposure of national banking systems to the international money markets; the emerging new forms of international division of labour and increased reliance on imports; the series of Treaties aiming at safeguarding investments against environmental concerns or labour rights, at opening up markets, and at undermining all national regulatory procedures; and the evolution of forms of economic integration and the 'embedded neoliberalism' of the EU, especially in the form of disciplinary austerity and restructuring packages, such as those imposed upon Greece.[25]

Consequently, such a delinking from processes of the internationalisation of capital with a recuperation of sovereignty is an indispensable aspect of any attempt towards a radical exit from the crisis. However, this delinking is becoming increasingly difficult. To take a simple example, the extensive privatisation programmes, all of them safeguarded by TTIP-style international arbitration processes, are becoming even more difficult to reverse and to replace with re-nationalisations, and the same goes for the legal framework of debt agreements. Moreover, this delinking is even more difficult in countries that do not have the luxury of exportable natural resources such as oil or energy.

Despite these difficulties, the Greek experience and the extremely aggressive and violent character of the supervision and tutelage of the Greek economy and society that the European Union attempts to implement, attest to the necessary and even inevitable character of this process of rupture for any radical and emancipatory exit from the crisis. Moreover, the relation of forces inside the EU and its embedded disciplinary neoliberalism make it clear that it is impossible to mount a challenge to the EU 'from the inside'. The EU cannot be reformed. Only a series of ruptures and exits can open up the way for new forms of co-operation and new forms of solidarity and perhaps new progressive alliances in Europe.

We have to understand that this predator-like practice of the European Union is not an exception. This combination of aggressive neoliberalism and

---

25    Cafruny and Ryner (eds.) 2003; Moss (ed.) 2005; van Appeldoorn 2002; van Appeldoorn 2013; van Appeldoorn et al. (eds.) 2009; Blanchard 2007; Sotiris 2014a; Baldassari and Melegari 2015.

limited sovereignty, this 'permanent economic emergency',[26] is the 'new normal' in Europe. In this sense we can follow Cédric Durand and Razmig Keucheyan in talking about a 'bureaucratique caesarism … a caesarism that is not military, but financial and bureaucratic',[27] that represents the 'organic crisis' of bourgeois strategies and of the European project and the inability of neoliberalism to create a 'historical bloc'. According to Durand and Keucheyan, the problem is that finance, as the dominant bourgeois fraction, can only represent a condition of a 'pseudo historical bloc'. When markets become the dominant relations that bring cohesion at the European level, the authoritarian and disciplinary bureaucratism becomes the only possible form of governance. This process is fundamentally authoritarian and undemocratic. Jean-Claude Juncker, the president of the European Commission, made manifest the antidemocratic cynicism that is deeply rooted in the institutional fabric of the European Integration Process when he declared that 'there can be no democratic choice against the European treaties'.[28]

Consequently, we have to admit that today the question of sovereignty becomes a class issue, a question around which we see the condensation of the antagonistic class relations. We need a democratic and popular sovereignty as a recuperation of democratic control against the systemic violence of internationalised capital.

We all know the problems associated with the notion of sovereignty, in particular its association with nationalism, racism and colonialism. However, here we are talking about a form of sovereignty based upon a social alliance that is different from that of bourgeois 'sovereignty': we are talking about an alliance based upon the common condition of the subaltern classes, their solidarity and common struggle. As Fréderic Lordon has stressed: 'Democracy and popular sovereignty: one and the same idea, that a community masters its own destiny'.[29]

In this sense, the recuperation of sovereignty is a necessary condition for a profound change in the relation of forces and represents the collective and emancipatory effort towards another road, an alternative narrative for a potential hegemony of the working classes.

What about the nation? It is obvious that the institutional aspects of national sovereignty are necessary in order to address many of the problems associ-

---

26    Žižek 2010.
27    Durand and Kucheyan 2013.
28    Soudais 2015.
29    Lordon 2013.

ated with the violence of globalised capital. At the same time, we understand that the crucial question has to do with the social alliance and the class strategy behind this recuperation of sovereignty. Does this mean that we have to revisit the lines of nationalism? Does this recuperation of sovereignty necessarily lead to nationalism, ethnic exclusion and racism, the dark sides of the modern democratic state? I think we need to go beyond and rethink both the people and the nation in a 'post-nationalist' and post-colonial way as the emerging community of all the persons who work, struggle and hope on a particular territory, as the reflection of the emergence of a potential historical bloc. This is not just a recuperation of the 'national reference'. Rather it is a way to rethink the possibility of a new unity and common reference point for the subaltern classes. The following phrase from Gramsci exemplifies this point:

> The modern prince must be and cannot but be the proclaimer and organizer of an intellectual and moral reform, which also means the creating of the terrain for a subsequent development of the national-popular collective will towards the realization of a superior, total form of modern civilization.[30]

What is interesting in this passage, one of the most dense of the *Notebooks*, is that it combines the reference to the modern political party or front, the organisation of 'intellectual and political reform' – a phrase that is not only a dialogue with Croce but also with the notion of cultural revolution in the late texts of Lenin – and the notion of a superior and modern civilisation, which in a certain way reminds us of the references to communist civilisation (civiltà communista) in texts from the youth of Gramsci.[31]

In this sense, the national-popular element is not a remnant of nationalism, but rather the result of a hegemonic project on the part of the subaltern classes. Moreover, it is interesting how Gramsci, in a very extensive note from Notebook 19, attempts to show how the reformulation of the national-popular element on the part of the subaltern classes is in opposition to bourgeois nationalism and is in reality a kind of proletarian cosmopolitanism.

---

30    Gramsci 1971, pp. 132–3; Q13, § 1.

31    'The workers will carry this new consciousness into the trade unions, which in place of the simple activity of the class struggle will dedicate themselves to the fundamental task of stamping economic life and work techniques with a new pattern; they will elaborate the form of economic life and professional technique proper to communist civilization' (Gramsci 1977, p. 101).

Italian expansion can only be that of humanity-as-labour and the intellectual who represents this humanity-as-labour is no longer of the traditional type, a rhetoric ... The Italian people is that people which is 'nationally' more interested in a modern form of cosmopolitanism ... Nationalism of the French variety is an anachronistic excrescence in Italian history.[32]

### Political Power: the Strategic Question

Any attempt towards a confrontation with questions of strategy, entails dealing with the question of power. In a post-democratic condition, it is not possible for movements to wage struggles and achieve compromises or pressure bourgeois governments in progressive reforms. A political break is necessary. However, thinking in terms of political power does not mean thinking simply in terms of a change of government. It means a process of breaks and transformations, and radical reforms, which in some cases also means a constituent process of changes and radical reforms in legislation, including the basic aspects of contemporary constitutions, which increasingly tend to constitutionalise austerity, private investment and international trade liberalisation agreements. It also requires the rupture with the embedded neoliberalism of EU treaties and commitments. Otherwise, the pressure for compromise and defeat will be overwhelming. This means that we start again thinking about a *communist* strategy for advanced capitalist formations.[33] Not only in the sense of going back to old debates, such as the 4th Congress of the Third International and the whole debate on workers' government, or Gramsci's attempt to rethink the United Front strategy in terms of a war of position for hegemony.[34] But also to try and learn from experience, both negative and positive, the successes and the shortcomings of contemporary events such as the attempts in left-wing governance in Latin America,[35] and naturally those coming from contemporary mass movements, both of their upsurges but also of their downturns.

Affirming that the state is not an instrument but a material condensation of a class balance of forces, as Poulantzas has suggested, does not mean that a simple change in the electoral balance of forces can change the role and function of State apparatuses. The State is also the materialisation of class strategies.

---

32    Gramsci 1996, p. 253; Q19, § 1.

33    On the recent re-opening of the debate on communism, see Douzinas and Žižek (eds.) 2010 and Žižek (ed.) 2013.

34    On these debates, see Riddell (ed.) 2012; Thomas 2009.

35    Webber 2011.

In the case of political movement that is not a systemic 'party of the state', we can see a contradiction between political will and the force of the strategy already inscribed in State apparatuses. Historically, this was the tragic experience of the Allende government. However, there is also the possibility of a 'postmodern' coup, in the form of a constant pressure and blackmail for compromises. In the 1970s, Althusser warned against this, insisting that

> The relative stable resultant (reproduced in its stability by the state) of the *confrontation* of forces (*balance* of forces is an accountant's notion, because it is static) is that *what counts is the dynamic excess of force* maintained by the dominant class in the class struggle. It is *this excess of conflictual force, real or potential, which constitutes energy A* which is subsequently transformed into power by the state-machine: *transformed into right, laws and norms.*[36]

Consequently, the question of the transformation of the state in relation to the exigencies of a new form of popular sovereignty cannot be conceived as a simple 'democratisation' of the state. As Althusser insisted, this '*is not to add the adjective "democratic" to each existing state apparatus*'.[37] This transformation must be conceived as the result of a necessary 'constituent process' which must include new forms of democratic participation at all levels, new forms of democratic social control, the institutional recognition of self-management, the imposition of limits to property rights, new forms of transparence and democratic supervision of coercive apparatuses.

Facing the excess of force of the dominant classes that is already inscribed in the materiality of contemporary States, we need an excess of force on the part of the subaltern classes. The flourishing of autonomous radical movements, the expansion of autonomous forms of popular organisation and of 'counter-institutions' of popular power, is more than necessary in a conjuncture of left-wing governance, even if, as Poulantzas stressed in 1979, this also means an 'implacable *tension* between workers' parties and social movements' as a 'necessary condition of the dynamic of a transition to democratic socialism'.[38] Althusser, in 1978, in an interview with Rossana Rossanda, referring to the big debate within the ranks of the European communist movement on the subject of a potential left-wing government stressed that '*the fact that class struggles*

---

36     Althusser 2006, p. 109.
37     Althusser 1977, p. 17.
38     Poulantzas 1980, p. 183.

(*bourgeois and proletarian*) *have at stake the State* (*here and now* [*hic et nunc*]) *does not mean in any way that politics is defined in relation to the State*.[39] It is exactly this *new practice of politics*, to which Althusser and Balibar refer,[40] that has been one of the major challenges facing the Left. It is the question of what practice of politics befits a new form of popular sovereignty, along with the question of a new relation between the parties of the Left and the State. It is what Althusser defined in terms of the position that even if the parties of the Left arrive in power, they cannot be 'an ordinary *"party of government"*' and must have an 'altogether different "political practice" than bourgeois parties'.[41]

It is exactly this new practice of politics, along with a programme of ruptures, a freeing of experimentations with a new productive paradigm, based upon the experiences of collective struggles and the collective political ingenuity of the masses that can transform contemporary dynamics into a new 'historical bloc'.

Consequently, the notion of 'dual power'[42] acquires a broader significance. It is no longer a question of catastrophic equilibrium, during which there is an antagonistic coexistence of two competing state forms. Dual power refers to the emergence of new social and political forms as part of the elevation of struggle and the fight for power and hegemony on the part of an alliance of the subaltern classes. It is a process of constant struggle, and of experimentation based upon the collective ingenuity of the people in struggle.[43]

### Alternative Narratives

Regarding demands and political programmes, we cannot think in terms of simply rejecting austerity measures. We must think in terms of radical alternatives, new social configurations, and new forms of a socialist alternative. The very intensification of the contradictions of the neoliberal strategy and choice of an even more aggressive neoliberalism means that the distance between urgently needed responses to social disaster and socialist strategy is diminished. It impossible to counter an unemployment rate of 27–28% without a sharp increase in public spending plus forms of self-management plus an increased role of the public sector, plus – in order to achieve the above – nationalisation of banks and strategic enterprises and reclaiming monetary sovereignty. At the same time, the only way to make a potential exit from the

---

39    Althusser 1998, p. 287.

40    Balibar 1974.

41    Althusser 2014, p. 226.

42    For the initial formulation of the notion of 'dual power', see Lenin 1964.

43    In this sense Negri and Hardt's reminder in *Declaration* (Hardt and Negri 2012) of the necessary *externality* of social movements and progressive governments is a welcome one.

Eurozone feasible would require a series of radical measures such as nationalisation of the banking sector and strategic enterprises. The experience of the SYRIZA government in Greece has made evident that the choice is indeed between radical solutions and capitulating to neoliberal norms.

More generally there is an urgent need to rethink the very notion of the transitional programme.[44] This has nothing to do with a theology of the programme – in the sense of battles over words and phrases – but, at the same time, we must not think of the programme as simply a set of demands coming from the movement. Nor do we need to fall into some form of 'realism' and just search for ways to do things without fundamental changes. We must focus on the main aspects of the current attack and offer alternatives, not only demands – that is, present concrete radical proposals for how we can run education, health, infrastructure, on how to finance public spending, on how to achieve food sufficiency, on energy saving in order to reduce dependence upon foreign markets, and so on. Elaboration of this programme necessarily requires the experience and the knowledge coming from struggles, coming from the collective ingenuity of the people engaged in struggle. A crucial aspect of every major and prolonged struggle is that people start to think about their sector, their enterprise, their workplace, how it is run, how the decisions that affect them are being taken, how their work can be more socially useful, how resources could be used in a more socially useful manner, and how destructive the role of 'private enterprise' can be. Consequently, from finding ways to deal with fuel shortages, to expanding the experience of networks of solidarity or of self-managed enterprises, we can see the importance of treating movements as learning processes for an alternative paradigm that would have social needs and environmental protection as main priorities.

This would also require a new ethics of collective participation and responsibility, of struggle and commitment to change, a transformed and educated *common sense* that becomes 'good sense'.[45] In this sense, the promise of left-wing politics cannot be a simple return to 2009, not least because it is materially impossible, but because we want to go beyond confidence in the markets and debt-ridden consumerism. In such a 'worldview', public education, public health, public transport, environmental protection, non-market collective determination of priorities, and quality of everyday sociality, are more important than imported consumer goods and cheap credit.

---

44    For an early confrontation with the questions of the transitional programme, see Trotsky 1938.

45    On 'common sense' as a battleground, see Rehmann 2013.

### Rethinking the Collective Subject of Struggle

Regarding social alliances, it is important to note that austerity measures, especially the extremely violent attempts at changing the social model, have brought different social strata closer together in terms of the deterioration of working and living conditions and increased insecurity, indebtedness and precariousness. In particular, they bring closer together those people in precarious, manual, low-end manufacturing, service or clerical posts with the better-educated segments of the workforce, which previously might have been more attached to ideologically supporting aspects of the neoliberal strategy. Youth has been at the epicentre of the attack because of increased youth unemployment and neoliberal educational reforms.[46] At the same time, the contemporary workforce, despite increased precariousness and fragmentation, new hierarchies, new polarisations, is at the same time more educated, qualified, skilled and with increased alphabetisation than any other previous generation. It combines higher literacy with communicative and affective skills that can help it articulate its demands and grievances in a more effective way. These collective skills have been more than evident in the communicative and information technologies of contemporary movements. We are talking about a workforce that is in a position to realise its role in the production of social wealth. Consequently, we are dealing with a contradiction at the very heart of the reproduction process of the contemporary labour force, especially when austerity and recession mean that it is not possible to compensate for job insecurity and overworking through the promise of debt-fuelled consumerist hedonism. This is one of the most important contradictions traversing contemporary advanced capitalist societies and offers the possibility to ground, in actual terms, a potential socialist and communist political project in important aspects of the contemporary ontology of labour.

This offers the possibility of new working-class hegemony, a social and political project for the prospect of contemporary societies based upon the directive role of the working class. Today the question facing us is: what social forces are going to shape the future of our societies: the forces of capital and in particular finance capital with its violence, cynicism and indifference towards the reality of life of the mass of populations, or the alliance of the forces of labour with all their cognitive, intellectual, affective and creative potential?

At the same time, it would be a mistake to take the current aspects of the composition of the labour force as given and think that they can be directly

---

46    On the strategic character of neoliberal reforms in education, see Solomon and Palmieri (eds.) 2011; Sotiris 2012b; Fernández, Sevilla and Urbán (eds.) 2013; McGettigan 2013.

transformed into a radical political composition. This is the mistake made by many representatives especially of the post-workerist trend that tend to present the current forms of communicative and affective labour as inherently offering the possibility of radical politics.[47] We should not underestimate the importance of the political forms of constitution of the social and political collective subject of resistance and emancipation. The 'traces of communism' in the collective practices, demands and aspirations of the contemporary labour force go hand in hand with the pervasive effects of fragmentation, insecurity, precariousness, along with various forms of ideological miscognition. Therefore, whether or not these potentialities can take a particular radical and anti-capitalist political form is a political stake; it needs a political intervention, it requires a conscious attempt to intensify political contradictions, it has to be combined with stressing particular political exigencies, and it forces us to face the question of political organisation. It is not – nor could it ever be – an unmediated process, in sharp contrast to spontaneist traditions.

These are not simply sociological trends. The *differentia specifica* of the conjuncture has been a series of mass movements and collective practices of protest and resistance that have brought together all these different segments of the forces of labour, creating material and symbolic forms of popular unity in struggle. Such protests facilitated the reinvention of the people as a collective subject of resistance, solidarity and transformation, as the alliance of all those women and men who, one way or another, depend upon selling their labour power in order to survive. Consequently, this conception of the re-emergence of the *people* attempts to ground it in actual material dynamics that have to do with the condition of labour today and the conjuncture regarding class antagonisms within and outside the workplace. Although this process also has discursive manifestations and effects, it is not fundamentally a discursive process and this marks the difference of our approach from that adopted by writers following Laclau's conception of populism and populist discourse, which in our opinion runs the risk of distancing the moment of political constitution from class antagonisms traversing regimes of capitalist accumulation.[48]

---

47    See, for example, Hardt and Negri 2000; Virno 2004; Roggero 2010. It is interesting to note that in *Commonwealth* (Hardt and Negri 2009), the authors pay more attention to questions of political organisation.

48    For an example of this approach, see Stavrakakis and Katsiabekis 2014 and Katsiabekis 2014. At the same time, we have to stress our agreement with the political insistence of writers from this tradition on radical democracy as a crucial aspect of potential (counter-) hegemonic projects that could expand the democratic and anti-hierarchical aspects of contemporary movements. For such an example, see Kioupkolis 2014.

This re-emergence of the people as a collective subject gives a new dimension to the demand for democracy and popular sovereignty.[49] Austerity takes the form of a perverse erosion of democracy and popular sovereignty. It seems like a move towards a post-democratic condition.[50] The radical demand for democracy coming from contemporary movements is not simply a demand for more 'deliberation', but rather calls for participation at all levels and deals with the actual exercise of power, the need to impose new forms of democratic social control, the need to make all the important aspects of social and economic policy subject to the collective decision of the forces of labour. This requires a profound rethinking of what a demand for popular sovereignty means: it means the demand for social transformation and justice based upon collective decision instead of the contemporary perverse market 'shareholder democracy'. In this sense it is indeed a conception of politics that points to a confrontation with the forces of capital. Jodi Dean has captured this aspect:

> The 'people as the rest of us' designates those of us who are proletarianized by capitalism, the people produced through the exploitation, extraction and expropriation of our practical and communicative activities for the enjoyment of the very, very rich. When communism is our horizon of political possibility, the sovereignty of the people points to a view of the state as what *we* see to govern for *us* as a collectivity. It is our collective steering of our common future for our common good.[51]

Rethinking the very notion of the people as a collective subject of emancipation and transformation is also a way to answer the divisive effects of racism within the forces of labour. This reinvention of the people as collective subject of struggle draws a line of demarcation from nationalism and racism, since instead of 'imagined communities', it is based on actual communities of struggles and resistances, offering the possibility of forging an inclusive common popular identity based upon the collective will to live, work and struggle within a particular society.

### Rethinking the Question of Organisation Today

A final point refers to the question of political organisation. What kind of political organisations do we need in order to be able to attempt such a revolution-

---

49     On this argument, see also Sotiris 2011a.
50     Crouch 2004.
51     Dean 2014, p. 79.

ary process? The traditional model that viewed, in a schematic and mechanical way, the confrontations with the question of power in terms of a military logic, placing all the emphasis on discipline, is of course inherently inadequate, and moreover runs the risk of imitating the model of the bourgeois state. It is necessary to think that in the struggle for a different society, based upon principles and practices antagonistic to the bourgeois/capitalist logic, we need organisations that reflect the emerging new social forms. In contrast to the traditional view – according to which the exigencies of the struggle and the need for disciplined commitment to the revolutionary process justify limits to intra-party democracy, suppression of free discussion, and rigid hierarchy – we want political organisations that are at the same time laboratories for the collective elaboration of new projects and new mass forms of critical political intellectuality, and experimental sites for new social and political relations. In this sense, they have to be more democratic, more egalitarian, more open than the society around them. Gramsci stressed this in the 1930s:

> One should stress the importance and significance, which, in the modern world, political parties have in the elaboration and diffusion of conceptions of the world, because essentially what they do is to work out the ethics and the politics corresponding to these conceptions and act as it were as their historical 'laboratory' ... The relation between theory and practice becomes even closer the more the conception is vitally and radically innovatory and opposed to old ways of thinking. For this reason one can say that the parties are the elaborators of new integral and all-encompassing intellectualities and the crucibles where the unification of theory and practice understood as real historical process takes place.[52]

However, this should not be considered an abstract exigency, but as an urgent task which also entails the whole process of reconstructing and reinventing political organisations. Contemporary radical political organisations reflect not only the dynamics of the conjuncture and current struggles; they are also the result of a whole period of crisis and retreat of the communist and revolutionary socialist movement. This is also evident today in the limitations of the main organisational forms suggested: the 'horizontal coordination' of movements, which is indispensable in order to create alliances and open spaces of struggle, but at the same time does not aid in the necessary elaboration of

---

52      Gramsci 1975, p. 1387 (Q11, § 12); Gramsci 1971, p. 335 (translation modified). On this question, see also Thomas 2009; Thomas 2013.

political programmes, and usually does not permit any discussion of questions of political power and hegemony; the left-wing 'electoral front' that usually is based on a minimum programme of immediate anti-neoliberal reforms that can easily take the form of a reformist agenda for progressive social-democratic governance; the classical model of the revolutionary group or sect (along with the respective international currents) that tend to reproduce fragmentation, sectarianism, and a parochial authoritarian version of an 'imaginary Lenin'. In contrast, 'repeating Lenin' today means thinking in terms of maximum originality, of trying not just to reproduce some model but to create laboratories of new political projects.

This is even more urgent, especially if such political fronts are going to face the challenge of government. The necessary autonomy of political organisations in relation to the state, the insistence on mass militancy and pressure to the government, the escalation of movement practices, all these are important exigencies.

### Conclusion

In sum, thinking about a new historical bloc means thinking both in terms of new inclusive social movements and new left fronts as political laboratories. It comprises both the ability to take advantage of conjunctures of intensified hegemonic crisis, but also the patient work of realignment and recomposition where the defeat of the labour movement is the prevailing condition. It is, in a way, war of position and war of manoeuvre at the same time, or a contemporary version of a 'prolonged people's war'.

*In sharp contrast to treating, for a relatively long time, questions of strategy in theoretical or even philological terms, we have the opportunity to discuss these questions under the pressure of actual historical exigencies and possibilities. We may feel overwhelmed by the scale of the challenge, we may feel tragically incapable of dealing with it, we may have to deal with open questions and unchartered territory, but the politics of social emancipation could never be easy.*

### References

Althusser, Louis 1977, 'On the Twenty-Second Congress of the French Communist Party', *New Left Review*, 1/104: 3–32.

Althusser, Louis 1978, *Ce qui ne plus durer dans se Parti Communiste*, Paris: Maspero.

Althusser, Louis 1998, *Solitude de Machiavel*, Paris: Actuel Marx / PUF.

Althusser, Louis 2006, *Philosophy of the Encounter. Later Writings 1978–86*, translated by G.M. Goshgarian, London Verso.

Althusser, Louis 2014, *On the Reproduction of Capitalism. Ideology and Ideological State Apparatuses*, translated by G.M. Goshgarian, London: Verso.

Balibar, Étienne 1974, *Cinque études de matérialisme historique*, Paris: Maspero.

Baltassari Marco and Diego Melegari 2015, 'Gramsci e Althusser a Bruxelles. Alcune note su diritto, Stato e ideologia nell'ambito dell'Unione Europea', (presentation at the Seminario (2) egemonia dopo Gramsci una reconsiderazione, Urbino, 6–8 October2015).

Basu Sanjay and David Stuckler 2013, *The Body Economic. How austerity kills*, London: Allen Lane.

Bensaïd, Daniel 2006, 'On the return of the politico-strategic question', available at: http://www.marxists.org/archive/bensaid/2006/08/polstrat.htm#p5

Berlinguer, Enrico 1977, *Historical Compromise*, [In Greek], Athens: Themelio.

Blanchard, Olivier 2007, 'Adjustment within the euro. The difficult case of Portugal', *Portuguese Economic Review* 6:1–21.

Buci-Glucksmann, Christine 1980, *Gramsci and the State*, London: Lawrence and Wishart.

Cafruny, Alan W. and Magnus Ryner (eds.) 2003, *A Ruined Fortress. Neoliberal Hegemony and Transformation in Europe*, Lanham: Rowland and Littlefield.

Comintern 1922, 'Theses on Comintern Tactics' (Fourth Congress), available at http://www.marxists.org/history/international/comintern/4th-congress/tactics.htm

Dardot, Pierre and Christian Laval 2013, *The New Way of the World: On Neoliberal Society*, translated by Gregory Elliot, London: Verso.

Dean, Jodi 2012, 'Occupy Wall Street: after the anarchist moment', *Socialist Register 2013*, 52–62.

Dean, Jodi 2014, 'Sovereignty of the People', in *Radical Democracy and Collective Movements Today. The Biopolitics of the Multitude versus the Hegemony of the People* edited by Alexandros Kioupkolis and Giorgos Katsiabekis, Farmham: Ashgate.

Douzinas, Costas 2013, *Philosophy and Resistance in the Crisis. Greece and the Future of Europe*. London: Pluto.

Douzinas, Costas and Slavoj Žižek (eds.) 2010, *The Idea of Communism*, London: Verso.

Duménil, Gerard and Dominique Lévy 2011, *The Crisis of Neoliberalism*, Cambridge Mass.: Harvard University Press.

Durand, Cédric (ed.) 2013, *En finir avec l'Europe*, Paris: La Fabrique.

Durand, Cédric and Razmig Keucheyan 2013, 'Un Césarisme bureaucratique', in *En finir avec l'Europe* edited by Cédric Durand, Paris: La Fabrique.

Fernández, Joseba, Miguel Urban and Carlos Sevilla (eds.) 2013, *De la Nueva Miseria. La universidad en crisis y la nueva rebelión estudiantil*, Madrid: Akal.

Gramsci, Antonio 1971, *Selections from Prison Writings*, edited and translated by Quintin Hoare and Geoffrey Nowell Smith, London: Lawrence and Wishart.

Gramsci, Antonio 1977, *Selections from the Political Writings (1910–1920)*, edited by Quintin Hoare and translated by John Mathews, London: Lawrence and Wishart.

Gramsci, Antonio 1978, *Selections from Political Writings 1921–1926*, edited and translated by Quintin Hoare, London: Lawrence and Wishart.

Gramsci, Antonio 1978–1994, *Cahiers de Prison*, 5 vols., Paris: Gallimard.

Gramsci, Antonio 1996, *Further Selections from the Prison Notebooks*, edited and translated by Derek Boothman, London: Lawrence and Wishart.

Gramsci, Antonio 1975 *Quaderni di Carcere*, edited by Valentino Gerratana, Torino: Einauidi.

Hardt, Michael and Antonio Negri 2000, *Empire*, Cambridge: Harvard University Press.

Hardt, Michael and Antonio Negri 2009, *Commonwealth*, Cambridge: The Belknap Press of Harvard University Press.

Hardt, Michael and Antonio Negri 2012, *Declaration*, New York: Argo Navis.

Hill, David (ed.) 2013, *Immiseration Capitalism: Austerity, Resistance and Revolt*, Brighton: Institute for Education Policy Studies.

Husson, Michel 2013, 'La "sortie sèche" de l'euro: une triple erreur stratégique', *Contretemps* 19, available at: http://hussonet.free.fr/videstract.pdf

Ioakeimoglou, Ilias 2012, *Internal Devaluation and Capital Accumulation. A Critical Approach*, [In Greek] Athens: INE GSEE/ADEDY.

Katsiabekis, Giorgos 2014, 'The Multidinous Moment(s) of the People: Democratic Agency Disrupting Established Binarisms', in *Radical Democracy and Collective Movements Today. The Biopolitics of the Multitude versus the Hegemony of the People*, edited by Alexandros Kioupkolis and Giorgos Katsiabekis, Farmham: Ashgate.

Kioukpkiolis Alexandros, and Giorgos Katsiabekis (eds) 2014, *Radical Democracy and Collective Movements Today. The Biopolitics of the Multitude versus the Hegemony of the People*, Farmham: Ashgate.

Kioupkolis, Alexandros 2014, 'A Hegemony of the Multitude: Muddling the Lines', in in *Radical Democracy and Collective Movements Today. The Biopolitics of the Multitude versus the Hegemony of the People* edited by Alexandros Kioupkolis and Giorgos Katsiabekis, Farmham: Ashgate.

Konings, Martijn (ed.) 2010, *The Great credit crunch*, London Verso.

Kouvelakis, Stathis 2011, 'The Greek Cauldron', *New Left Review* 2/72:17–32.

Kouvelakis, Stathis 2012, 'Introduction: the end of Europeanism', in Lapavitsas et al. 2012, pp. xiv–xxi.

Lapavitsas, Costas 2013, *Profiting without Producing. How Finance Exploits us All*, London: Verso

Lapavitsas, Costas et al. 2012, *Crisis in the Eurozone*, London: Verso.

Lenin, Vladimir Illich, 'The Dual Power', *Collected Works*, vol. 24, Moscow: Progress Publishers.

Lisa, Athos 1933, 'Informe de Athos Lisa sobre las opiniones políticas de Gramsci. Informe pedido por el Centro del partido', available at: http://www.rebelion.org/noticia.php?id=100128

Lordon, Frédéric 2013, 'Ce que l'extrême droite ne nous prendra pas', http://blog.mondediplo.net/2013-07-08-Ce-que-l-extreme-droite-ne-nous-prendra-pas

Mavris, Yiannis 2012, 'Greece's Austerity Election', New Left Review 2/76: 95–107.

Mavroudeas, Stavros 2010, 'Greece and the EU: capitalist crisis and imperialist rivalries', Paper presented at the IIPE and Greek Scientific Association of Political Economy First International Conference in Political Economy, Rethymnon, Crete, September 10–12 2010, http://www.iippe.org/wiki/images/b/b4/CONF_GREEKCRISIS_Mavroudeas.pdf

Mavroudeas, Stavros (ed.) 2015, Greek Capitalism in Crisis, London: Routledge.

McGettigan, Andrew 2013, The Great University Gamble, London: Pluto.

Moss, Bernard (ed.) 2005, Monetary Union in Crisis. The European Union as a Neo-Liberal Construction, London: Palgrave/Macmillan.

Negri, Toni and Sandro Mezzandra 2014, 'Breaking the Neoliberal Spell: Europe as the Battleground', http://www.euronomade.info/?p=1417

OECD 2014, OECD Competition Assessment Reviews: Greece. Paris: OECD.

Panitch, Leo and Sam Gindin 2012, The Making of Global Capitalism. The Political Economy of American Empire, London: Verso.

Porcaro, Mimmo 2012, 'Occupy Lenin', Socialist Register 2013: 84–97.

Poulantzas, Nicos 1980, Repères, Paris: Maspero.

Public Issue 2011, Political barometer 92 ( july 2011), [In Greek], available at: http://www.publicissue.gr/wp-content/uploads/2011/07/varometro-07-2011.pdf

Public Issue 2015, 'Greek Referendum 2015: "NO" voter demographics', available at: http://www.publicissue.gr/en/2837/greek-referendum-2015-no-voter-demographics/

Rehmann, Jan 2013, 'Occupy Wall Street and the Question of Hegemony: A Gramscian Analysis', Socialism and Democracy, 27, 1: 1–18.

Riddell, John (ed.), Toward the United Front. Proceedings of the Fourth Congress of the Communist International, 1922, Chicago: Haymarket.

Sakellaropoulos Spyros and Panagiotis Sotiris 2014, 'Postcards from the Future: The Greek Debt Crisis, the Struggle against the EU-IMF Austerity Package and the Open Questions for Left Strategy', Constellations, 21, 2: 262–73.

Roggero, Gigi 2010, 'Five Theses on the Common', Rethinking Marxism 22:3, 357–73.

Schäfer Armin and Wolfgang Streeck (eds.) 2013, Politics in an Age of Austerity, London: Polity.

Solomon, Clare and Tania Palmieri (eds.) 2011, Springtime. The New Student Rebellions, London: Verso.

Sotiris, Panagiotis 2011, 'Rethinking the notions of "people" and "popular sovereignty"', available at: http://greekleftreview.wordpress.com/2011/11/15/rethinking-the-notions-of-%E2%80%98people%E2%80%99-and-%E2%80%98popular-sovereignty%E2%80%99/

Sotiris, Panagiotis 2012, 'Theorizing the entrepreneurial university. Open questions and possible answers', *The Journal of Critical Education Policy Studies*, 10, 1: 112–26.

Sotiris, Panagiotis 2013a, 'Guest post: The new "age of insurrections" is far from over! Thoughts on the political significance of the Turkish movement', http://international.radiobubble.gr/2013/06/guest-post-new-age-of-insurrections-is.html

Sotiris, Panagiotis 2013b, 'Hegemony and Mass Critical Intellectuality', *International Socialism Journal* 137: 169–182.

Sotiris, Panagiotis 2014, 'The Left and the European Union. On the need for an anti-euro and anti-EU position', http://lastingfuture.blogspot.gr/2014/04/the-left-and-european-union-on-need-for.html

Sotiris, Panagiotis 2015, 'Political Crisis and the Rise of the Far Right in Greece. Racism, nationalism, authoritarianism and conservatism in the discourse of Golden Dawn', *Journal of Language Aggression and Conflict* 3, 1:173–99.

Soudais, Michel 2015, 'Juncker dit "non" à la Grèce et menace la France' available at: http://www.politis.fr/Juncker-dit-non-a-la-Grece-et,29890.html

Stavrakakis, Yannis and Giorgos Katsambekis 2014, 'Left-wing populism in the European periphery: the case of SYRIZA', *Journal of Political Ideologies*, 19, 2: 119–142.

Thomas, Peter D. 2009, *The Gramscian Moment. Hegemony, Philosophy and Marxism*, Leiden: Brill.

Thomas, Peter D. 2013, 'The Communist Hypothesis and the Question of Organization', *Theory and Event*, 16:4.

Trotsky, Leon 1938, *The Death Agony of Capitalism and the Tasks of the Fourth International: The Mobilization of the Masses around Transitional Demands to Prepare the Conquest of Power. The Transitional Program*, available at: https://www.marxists.org/archive/trotsky/1938/tp/transprogram.pdf

van Aperldoorn, Bastian 2002, *Trasnational Capitalism and the Struggle over European Integration*, London: Routledge.

van Aperldoorn, Bastian 2013, 'The European Capitalist Class and the Crisis of its Hegemonic Project', *Socialist Register 2014*, 189–206.

van Apeldoorn Bastiaan, Jan Drahokoupil and Laura Horn (eds.) 2009, *Contradictions and limits of neoliberal European governance: from Lisbon to Lisbon*, London: Palgrave.

Varoufakis, Yanis, 2015 'Greece's Third MoU (Memorandum of Understanding) annotated by Yanis Varoufakis', available at: http://yanisvaroufakis.eu/2015/08/17/greeces-third-mou-memorandum-of-understading-annotated-by-yanis-varoufakis/

Virno, Paolo 2004, *A Grammar of the Multitude*, New York: (Semio)texte.

Webber, Jeffrey R. 2011, *From Rebellion to Reform in Bolivia. Class Struggle, Indigenous Liberation and the Politics of Evo Morales*, Chicago: Haymarket.

Žižek, Slavoj 2010, 'Permanent economic emergency', *New Left Review* 2/64: 85–95.

Žižek, Slavoj (ed.) 2013, *The Idea of Communism 2. The New York Conference*, London: Verso.

# Index

2010–2011, period   141

Alavanos, Alekos   161
Allagi   157
Althusser, Louis   285
ANTARSYA   166, 169, 238, 238n14, 261, 277
Androulakis, Giorgos   26
Argitis, Giorgos   23–24
Asia Minor   206, 206n7, 207, 208, 209, 213, 225
Austerity   267
Authoritarian Statism   142, 180n11

Badiou, Alain   245–6, 250–2, 254–6, 258, 261–2, 264
Banking Union   89
Blanchard, Olivier   270
Bonefeld, Werner   263–264n64
Bourgeoisie   68, 82–83, 248, 249, 250
   'new bourgeoisie'   248–50
   petit-bourgeoisie   250
   salaried bourgeoisie   249
   bourgeois class   244, 249
   bourgeois political system   258
   bourgeois state   251
Buci-Glucksmann, Christine   280
bureaucracy   258
   bureaucratic organisation   258
   bureaucratic centralism   258
   bureaucratic party   258

Centralism   258
   bureaucratic   258
   democratic   258–9
class   244, 260
   bourgeois   244, 249
   consciousness   259
   middle class   249–50
   movement   257, 259
   new salaried class   249
   of salaried managers   248
   position   250
   structure   250n21
   struggle   246
   working class   250, 261
Collective bargaining   123

Communism   246, 250, 258, 261–3
Communist Party of Greece (KKE)   160–161, 169, 207n11, 208, 209, 211n23, 218, 235–236, 261
Consciousness   138, 244, 252, 255, 259
   Political   139
   Imputed   139
Contract, social   136
Crisis   244–6, 249–50, 252, 255–7, 260–61, 263–4
   Organic   131, 179
   Of political representation   150, 179
Cyprus   113

Dean, Jodi   290
December 2008 riots   234
Decisive moment   139
de-Europeanisation of trade   59–62
Delegitimisation, of the State   147
democracy   106, 247, 262–3
   democratic centralism   258–9
   democratic institutions   247, 253
   Greek case   247
Democratic Left (DIMAR)   170
Dendias, Nicos   181
Dictatorship   190, 208, 211
Douzinas, Costas   245
Dual power   286
Durand, Cédric   282

Eagleton, Terry   152
Economakis, Giorgos   26
Economic Adjustment Programmes   13, 17, 31–33
Economics
   Keynesian   14
   Mainstream   14
   Marxist   14
Eksygchronistès   157
Elections
   2012   187, 190
   Euroelections 2014   198
   February 2015   273
Employment
   Public Sector   69, 71, 74–77, 121–122
Engels, Friedrich   229

Eurogroup / ECOFIN   90
European Central Bank   88, 232, 235n9
European Commission   88, 92, 100–101
European Economic Community/ European
    Union   13, 210, 212, 213, 214, 215, 217, 218,
    244, 246, 248
European Exchange Rate Mechanism   87
European Stability Mechanism   98, 100
European Union Charter of Fundamental
    Right   102–103
Eurozone / European Monetary Union   13,
    214, 215, 216, 217, 222, 226, 226, 232, 268–
    270
Exit from the Eurozone   35
Exit from the EU   35–36
Extraverted and autocentric economy   47–
    50, 56–57

Far-Right   106–108
Financialisation   20–22
Fiscal deficits   67–68, 73, 76–77
Front National   106–107

Gaitanou, Eirini   250n21
General government expenditures   76–77
General government revenues   76–77
Golden Dawn   2, 108, 187–199, 261, 272
Gounari, Panayota   245n2
Greek public debt   1, 72–75
Gramsci, Antonio   137, 140, 230, 278–280,
    283, 291
    critique of Post-Marxism   256–61
    defence of democratic centralism   258–9
    Marxism   257–8
    Modern Prince   246, 256–7, 259–61, 264
    theory of the political party   256–9
Greece   244–6, 250–1, 256, 261–4, 270–277
Greek economic crisis   50–63, 217, 270–271
Greek ruling class   203, 206, 209, 210n23, 211,
    212, 213, 215, 218, 225, 227
Grigoropoulos, Alexis   184, 234

Hall, Stuart   164
Hardt, Michael   247n12, 252–5, 262, 264
Hayek, Friedrich   112
Hilferding, Rudolph   20
Historical bloc   274–275, 278–280
Hegemony   177, 179, 256, 264, 288
    Crisis of   179, 272, 292

Holloway, John   245n2, 248n16, 262n55,
    264n64
Hungary   87, 97

Imperialist exploitation   43–47, 56
Income elasticity of demand for imports
    54–56
Income taxes   78–80
Indirect taxes   78–79
Industrial relations   71, 74–77
International inter-sectoral competition
    45–46
International intra-sectoral competition
    46–47
Intersectoral linkages   49, 56
International Monetary Fund   87, 229, 232
Inverted protectorate   219, 227

Juncker, Jean Claude   282

Kaldor's paradox   19, 50
Karamanlis, Kostas   158, 169, 164
Keucheyan, Razmig   282
Kouvelakis, Stathis   167n41, 168, 186n19

Labour cost   19
Labour flexibility   120
Labour deregulation   121–125
Labour Law   119
Laclau, Ernesto   289
LAOS   162, 168–169, 189–190
Lapavitsas, Costas   20–21, 267n1
Laskos, Christos   20
Left   246, 253, 255–6, 258, 261–2, 264
Loan Agreement
    August 2015   276
Lordon, Fréderic   282
Lukács, Georg   139

Maastricht Treaty   17
Maniatis, Thanassis   25–26
Markaki, Mania   26
Marx, Karl   138, 229
Marxism   13, 245, 252–6, 260
    Gramscian   257–8
    classical   252–3
Megali idea   203, 204, 205, 206n7, 225
Memoranda of Understanding   68, 74–76, 82,
    87, 92–95, 119, 270

Metapolitefsi  157–159, 169
Michaloliakoa, Nicos  190
Middle classes  68, 80–83
Milios, John  22–23
Mouvement  244–8, 259–62
    anti-capitalist  246, 248–50, 252–3, 257,
        259–61, 263–5
    right-wing reactionary  261
    Mouvement structures  149
Multitude  247, 252–3, 255–6, 262

Nasioka, Katerina  245n2
Negri, Antonio  244, 245n6, 246–8, 250,
        252–6, 258, 261–2, 264
Neoliberalism  268, 281
    Crisis of  268
New Democracy  169–170, 189, 233,
        272–273
New Public Management (NPM)  71, 74, 82

Organisation  138, 247, 251–6, 258–9, 261–4,
    organisational question  246, 252, 254–6,
        262, 264, 290–292

Paitaridis, Dimitris  27
Papandreou, Andreas  157
Papandreou, George  1, 93, 162, 167, 235
party  252–5
    Bolshevik theory  252
    bureaucratic  258
    communist  254, 258, 261
    Gramscian  261, 264
    Greek establishment  263
    Marxist party  246, 253–4, 257–61, 264
    modern revolutionary  246, 257
    of the Left  253, 258
    outdated type of political organisation
        262
    party-structure  259
    progressive/regressive  258
    reformist  263
    revolutionary  246, 255, 257–9, 261,
        264
    working-class  264n65
PASOK  189, 212, 213, 272
Passas, Costas  25–26
PODEMOS  109–110, 278
Politicisation, new  141
Popular Assemblies  166, 171, 171n53, 173

Popular Unity  277
Possibilities, field of  139
Post-hegemony  185
Post-Marxism  245–8, 250–3, 256–61, 264
Poulantzas  180n, 240, 284, 285
Power  245, 247–8, 251, 253–5, 284–286
Praxis  137
Price elasticity of demand for imports  54–
        56
Privatizations  128
Proletariat  249–50, 257, 259, 264
Protest  244–247, 248n16, 249–251, 254, 256,
        260, 262–4
Psarras, Dimitris  198
Public enterprises  72, 73, 76
Public utilities:  69, 74–75
Purposeful Sampling  144

Radical Political Economy  14–15
Rebellious / Insurrectionary cycle  141, 183
Recession  178, 271
Referendum of July 2015  151, 275
Restructuring process  133
Revolt  246–7, 252–4, 259–60, 264
Revolution  246–7, 250, 253, 255, 257, 259,
        260, 264
Riot  247, 250–51, 253–6, 262, 264
Rossanda, Rossana  285

Samaras, Antonis  163, 174, 191
Sectoral technological level  50–54
Shipping  204, 207, 210, 213, 226
Simitis, Kostas  233
Social coalition  68, 80–83
Social rift  152
Sotiropoulos, Dimitris  22–23
Sovereignty  281–283
spontaneity  252, 255, 259–60
Squares movement  141, 165–166, 170, 172, 272
State  245–7, 249, 251, 254, 262
    bourgeois  251
    generic communism  262n59
    radical-generic  262
    welfare  253, 263
Stathakis, Giorgos  19–20
Street politics  142
Student Mouvement 2006–2007  183–184
Synaspismos  161
Syntagm Square  166, 171

SYRIZA    2, 109–110, 179, 193, 199–200, 229–
       231, 233–236, 237–242, 261, 263, 272, 274,
       276–277, 287
SYRIZA-ANEL government    151

Tax evasion    68, 80–83
Tax revenues    68, 80–83
Taxes on capital    68, 77–78
Taxes on labour    68, 77–78
Tendency of the Rate of Profit to Fall    13, 25–
       26
Terms of trade    57–59
Third International    284
Thomas, Martin    264n66
Thomas, Peter D.    230n2, 264n66
Timmermans, Frans    101, 101n47
Trade structure    50–54
Trade unionism, official    148

Transformation, of consciousness    149
Troika    1, 89, 92–95, 113, 131, 274
Tsakalotos, Euclid    20
Tsipras, Alexis    230
Turkey    206, 207, 211, 213, 221, 223, 223n
Twin Deficits Hypothesis (TDH)    18

Unemployment    125–126
United Nations Charter    114
United Front    284

Value Added Tax (VAT)    78, 81, 82
Value extraction    43–47

Wage earners    78–81

Žižek, Slavoj    245n6, 246, 248–50, 252, 255–6,
       261, 263–4